Islamic Reform and Political Change in Northern Nigeria

Islamic Reform and Political Change in Northern Nigeria

ROMAN LOIMEIER

NORTHWESTERN UNIVERSITY PRESS

EVANSTON, ILLINOIS

Northwestern University Press
www.nupress.northwestern.edu

Printed in the United States of America

1 0 9 8 7 6 5 4 3 2 1

ISBN 978-0-8101-2810-1

The Library of Congress has cataloged the original, hardcover edition as follows:

Loimeier, Roman.
Islamic reform and political change in northern Nigeria / Roman Loimeier.
p. cm. — (Islam and society in Africa)
Includes bibliographical references (p.) and index.
ISBN 0-8101-1346-5 (cloth : alk. paper)
1. Islam—Nigeria—History—20th century. 2. Nigeria—Politics and government—1984– 3. Islam and politics—Nigeria. I. Title. II. Series: Series in Islam and Society in Africa.
BR64.N6L65 1997
322'.1'0966909045—dc21 96-47274
CIP

∞ The paper used in this publication meets the minimum requirements of the American National Standard for Information Sciences—Permanence of Paper for Printed Library Materials, ANSI Z39.48-1992.

Contents

Preface

The present study was carried out in the framework of a greater research project (new tendencies in African Islam and their influence for the determination of the cultural and national identities of black African Muslims: part 1—Nigeria) under the supervision of Prof. Dr. Jamil M. Abun-Nasr at the University of Bayreuth (Bavaria, FRG). The project's aim was to examine "the new religious tendencies under Nigeria's Muslims that cause changes in their religiopolitical definition of identity" (Sonderforschungsberich 214 Report 1986–1988: 203). The working hypothesis was that these religiopolitical processes of change result from recent sociopolitical developments.

Work on this study started in October 1985 and included three visits in Northern Nigeria from 28 September 1986 to 13 March 1987, 28 August 1987 to 5 November 1987, and 26 February 1988 to 5 May 1988. During my stay in Nigeria I was living for about nine months in a quarter of the old city of Kano (Sani Mai Nagge). Several journeys to Sokoto, Maiduguri, Bauchi, Jos, Zaria, Kaduna, and Ibadan, where I worked in the respective centers of research, completed my studies in Nigeria. The historical foundations of my thesis were established by consulting the relevant sources in the libraries of the universities in Bayreuth, Kano, Zaria, Maiduguri, Sokoto, Jos, and Ibadan, as well as research carried out in the Arewa House in Kaduna and the Nigerian National Archives in Kaduna.

An essential part of my research were the discussions I had with a great number of Nigerian counterparts. The complete list of my partners in research is found at the end of this work. Discussions were generally conducted in English, some in Hausa and Arabic. Apart from some exceptions, discussions were neither electronically nor manually recorded during an interview. I usually prepared a number of key questions before I met with an interlocutor, and I usually asked permission to note numbers, names, or dates immediately. After concluding a discussion I recorded the talk in a protocol from memory. If I encountered any irregularities, had further questions, or wanted to clear up contradictions, I arranged for further discussion. Some interviews were, with the permission of my interview partners, for reasons of control recorded or noted down during the discussion. Thus I found that my interlocutors were usually more forthcoming in informal talks (without tape recorders) than in formal interviews. This was clearly connected with the nature of my research. Again and again I touched on delicate topics that my interview partners desired only very circumspectly to talk about. An informal atmosphere helped much to overcome the initial reserve or mistrust in this respect. Being a Bature (European), who would after all publish his research findings in faraway Germany, was also very helpful in this regard. Thus I was not suspected of channeling confidential information to the "other side." A great number of the elder religious scholars in Northern Nigeria mistrust indigenous scholars from Nigerian universities because of this danger much more than an "outsider" from Turai (Europe). Before any discussion I usually informed my interlocutors exhaustively about my project of research, my position, and my methods, and they were thereupon quite prepared to offer an account of their ideas and knowledge in order to counterbalance information from their opponents. In discussion with some interlocutors I had the impression that they were especially talkative in order to influence my view of their ideas on certain issues in a certain way.

On the basis of my contacts with representatives of all groups and movements I was in a position to clear up insecurities, mistakes, misinterpretations, and outright propaganda through control questions, the repeating of questions, the change of emphasis in questions asked, and the comparison of answers. In this way I was able to gain and to verify reliable information on a number of delicate issues. Asking about the personal curricula of my interview partners was especially problematic. These questions are seen in Hausa society as an infringement and violation of the inherent feelings of shame and modesty (*Kunya*). Questions concerning the biography of a certain person should therefore be put to a close relative or friend; they are then usually answered satisfactorily.

I should mention at this point my use of network analysis as a methodological concept and tool of research. The network concept was originally developed in the 1940s by British anthropologists such as Mitchell, Turner, and Epstein, who were working at the Rhodes-Livingstone Institute in what was then Northern Rhodesia. In this study I stick to the definition of the term introduced by Streck (1985: 574):

> Apart from its character of egocentrics a transactional network has the following aspects: it is situational, instrumental, open to the outside and singular. It is a living cell which has to be cultivated in order to prevent disintegration. Networks cut through institutions, classes and social strata. They are constituted by transactions and interactions, actions which follow either the principle of avoiding damage or the principle of reciprocity. Its content may be of a friendly character in the sense of services and counterservices or of a hostile character in the sense of harming and being harmed. The final aim of the set-up, the activating, the reactivating or the renewal of a network or of a part of it, may be very diverse: gain of power, *Lustgewinn* (fulfillment, attainment of desires), progress, promotion or similar things.

In the context of fieldwork the researcher is facing, the problem that a set of measures that may be utilized by a certain person who is bound and willing to act like, for instance, the building-up and utilization of a network, usually remain as hidden from the face of the researcher as the social structure of the respective society itself. The network analysis is thus forced to pay attention to events that are likely to mobilize a network or parts of it. Such events of extraordinary power of mobilization are catastrophes, scandals, affairs, conflicts, special campaigns, but also initiatives to solve everyday problems. In this context it can be assumed as a rule that a person's degree of success is closely related to his or her age and expertise in handling situations and the amount of cleverness with which he or she is able to activate and mobilize his or her network of connections (Streck 1985: 574). It should be stressed that (informal) network connections (*Beziehungsgeflechte*) are of particular importance in times and places where and when (formal) institutions are unable to fulfill their social, economic, political, or religious tasks, duties, or obligations. In the present work mechanisms of mobilization and different ways of functioning of religiopolitical networks are examined in the context of different conflicts, and their success or failure are analyzed in their respective historical, political, and social frames. The network analysis serves above all as a tool to explain the enormous efficacy of religious movements in Nigeria in their ability to mobilize popular mass support and, second, to answer the question of why struggles concerning the transformation of policy, economy, society, culture, and personal relations are carried out on the platform of religious disputes and dogmatic arguments.

In describing and analyzing the character of network connections, the term "influence" (*Einfluß*) is of great importance, whereas terms like "power" (*Macht*) or "domination" (*Herrschaft*) are either too strong or too inflexible to explain the subtle structures of a given network or they are too clearly related to the result of a process that they can no longer explain. "Influences," on the other hand, have already become manifest in terms like "power" or "domination"; the term "influence" itself offers the chance to understand "power" and "domination" in the process of their formation. In other words, whereas "power" and "domination" are already results of successful interventions, fore-forms, or the conditions of the formation of phenomena like "power" and "domination" may be better described by the term "influence." *Herrschaft* according to Max Weber is the "chance to find obedience to a command with definite content among specific persons," whereas *Macht* is defined as the "chance to enforce one's own will within a certain social relationship even against resistance to it and not regarding whereupon this chance is based" (Weber 1922: 28). In contrast to the Nigerian state or the emirs, the Nigerian religious scholars do not command direct or indirect means of power (police, army, administration, bailiffs) with which they could enforce their will against the resistance of their opponents or even their own followers. The religious scholars rather carry out their conflicts on the level of religious disputes or try to achieve their aims by mobilizing and using their wealthy and politically influential supporters. Therefore they do not dominate or rule, but work through their networks. They do not command institutions of power, but fight on the level of religious arguments or the legal prescriptions of the sharî'a. Furthermore the position of religious scholars is not defined by success in elections or the convincing brutality of weapons, but by their ability to get their spiritual claims accepted by their followers. This ability can be defined as their "spiritual power" (baraka). The degree of their influence over people is therefore dependent on a number of internal and external factors and secured neither institutionally nor formally.

The historical frame of this work spans the time from the 1930s to 1990: from the beginning of the movement of reform of the Tijâniyya and the installation of the sixteenth Sultan of Sokoto, Abubakar Siddiq III (1938), touching on the rise of Ahmadu Bello and his efforts to unite the Muslims in Northern Nigeria in the 1960s, to the conflict between the Sufi brotherhoods and their opponents, the 'Yan Izala, in the 1970s and 1980s. The study concludes with the reconciliation between the Sufi brotherhoods and the 'Yan Izala in 1988 and the takeover of power by the seventeenth Sultan of Sokoto, Ibrahim Dasuki, in November 1988. Relevant data have been taken into account until 31 December 1993. The geographical frame of the work covers the northern belt of the former Northern region, the federal states Sokoto, Kano, Kaduna, Katsina, Bauchi, and Bornu. The developments in the economic metropolis of the north, Kano, will find special attention.

In this historical and geographical context the study complements and continues the earlier works of J. Paden (1973), J. W. Chamberlin (1975), I. Tahir (1975), and P. Lubeck (1986). In addition, recent works by Nigerian collegues are taken into account, studies that have not yet been published but nevertheless added an important share to research about Islam in Northern Nigeria: the works of Y. A. Quadri (1981), M. S. Umar (1983, 1988), A. F. Ahmed (1986), U. A. Dan Asabe (1987a), and A. Anwar (1989). Whereas these works are restricted in a regional, historical, or thematic sense to specific aspects of the development of Islam in Northern Nigeria, my thesis tries to present the different religious and political developments in Northern Nigeria in the last few decades and their inherent dynamics in a meaningful context and to show thereby certain regularities and ways in which networks "work." This effort to develop a synthesis would not have been possible without the foundations laid by the earlier studies.

The present study would also never have been completed without the constant support of Prof. Dr. Jamil M. Abun-Nasr whom I would like to thank first and foremost. Furthermore I am deeply indebted to a great number of friends and colleagues whose names I would like to cite here in alphabetical order, so as to prevent the establishment of an hierarchy of affection: Shaykh Aminu d-Din Abubakar (Kano), Dr. A. E. Ahmed (University of Ibadan), Malam Auwalu Anwar (University of Maiduguri), Prof. S. O. Balogun (University of Sokoto), Renate Cedzich (University of Bayreuth), Malam A. U. Dan Asabe (Advanced Teachers' College, Kano), Prof. 'Abd ar-Rahman Doi (Center of Islamic Legal Studies, Ahmadu Bello University, Zaria), Malam Saidu A. Edamivoh (Bayero University, Kano), Shaykh Abubakar Gumi (Kaduna), Prof. John Hunwick (Northwestern University, Evanston), Shaykh Nasiru Kabara (Kano), Malam S. U. Kabara (Bayero University, Kano), Ousmane Kane (Université de Paris VII), Dr. Anke Kleiner-Bosaller (Universität Bayreuth), Dr. Murray Last (University College, London), Prof. J. Lavers (Bayero University, Kano), Dr. Tijani al-Miskin (University of Maiduguri), Dr. Gottfried Müller (Universität Bayreuth), Dr. Cornelia Panzacchi-Loimeier (Universität Bayreuth), Dr. Stephan Reichmuth (Universität Bayreuth), Dr. Khalil b. Sa'id (Bayero University, Kano), Shaykh Ibrahim Ṣâliḥ (Maiduguri), Mrs. Priscilla

Starratt (Bayero University, Kano), Malam Ibrahim Sulaiman (Center of Islamic Legal Studies, ABU, Zaria), Malam M. S. Umar (University of Jos), Malam J. H. Yola (Bayero University, Kano), and Prof. Dr. M. S. Zahradeen (Bayero University, Kano).

Special thanks go to Justin Morris (Tübingen), who has not only worked through my manuscript and corrected the mistakes and Germanisms of my original translation but who has also provided many helpful suggestions from an outsider's point of view. Remaining shortcomings are my own. Likewise I would like to thank Ellen R. Feldman and David E. Anderson of Northwestern University Press for meticulously carrying out the tedious work of revision and for applying the finishing touches.

List of Abbreviations

ABU	Ahmadu Bello University (Zaria)
AG	Action Group
BCCI	Bank of Credit and Commerce International
BUK	Bayero University Kano
BYM	Bornu Youth Movement
CAN	Christian Association of Nigeria
CCC	Concerned Citizens Committee
FOMWAN	Federation of Muslim Women's Associations of Nigeria
GPC	General Purpose Committee
GRA	Government Residential Area
ICSA	Interim Common Services Agency
IET	Islamic Education Trust
JNI	Jamâ'at Naṣr al-Islâm (Association for the Support of Islam)
KCTC	Kano Citizen Trading Company
KPP	Kano People's Party
KSM	Kano State Movement
LBA	Licensed Buying Agent
LGC	Local Government Council

MSS	Muslim Students Society
NA	Native Administration
NCNC	National Congress of Nigeria and the Cameroons
NEPU	Northern Elements Progressive Union
NITEL	Nigerian Telecommunications
NNDC	Northern Nigerian Development Corporation
NNHC	Northern Nigerian Housing Corporation
NNPMB	Northern Nigerian Produce Marketing Board
NPC	Northern People's Congress
NPN	National Party of Nigeria
NSCIA	Nigerian Supreme Council for Islamic Affairs
NSO	Nigerian Security Organization
OIC	Organization of the Islamic Conference (Munaẓẓamat al-Mu'tamar al-Islâmî)
PRP	People's Redemption Party
SAS	School of Arabic Studies
Râbiṭa	Râbiṭat al-'Alam al-Islâmî (Islamic World League)
UMBC	United Middle Belt Congress
UPN	Unity Party of Nigeria
'Yan Izala	Jamâ'at Izâlat al-Bid'a wa-Iqâmat as-Sunna (Association for the Eradication of the Innovation and the Establishment of the Sunna)

List of Arabic Terms

adab	culture, refinement: good manners; belles lettres
'âlim	knowing; expert, religious scholar (pl. *'ulamâ'*)
'amal	doing, acting; practice; act of faith (pl. *a'mâl*)
amîr (al-mu'minîn)	emir, commander (of the faithful)
anfâs	breath; technique of breathing in (*dhikr*)
'âṣî	rebel; sinning, disobedient
baraka	blessing, blessing power
bâṭin	hidden, concealed
bid'a	innovation, heresy; heretical doctrine (pl. *bida'*)
da'wa	call, summons; missionary work
dhikr	remembrance; invocation of God; in Sufism, incessant repetition of certain words or formulas in praise of God
dîn	religion
faiḍa	overflowing stream (of God's mercy)
faraj	joy; release from suffering
fâsiq	godless; offender, sinner, trespasser
fatwâ	formal legal opinion

fiqh	jurisprudence
fitna	temptation; trial; civil strife
ghauth	succor, help
ḥadîth	prophetic tradition; report, account
hadiyya	gift, offering (pl. *hadâya*)
ḥajj	pilgrimage (to Mecca)
ḥijâb	cover, veil; screen
hijra	emigration, exodus; *al-hijra:* the emigration of the Prophet from Mecca to Medina in 622
ḥisâb	arithmetic, calculation; in West Africa, also astrology
'ibâdât	worship, acts of devotion
iḥsân	beneficence, performance of good deeds
ijâza	permission, authorization
ijtihâd	effort, independent judgment in a legal or theological question
ikhtilâṭ	mixing, the process of mixing
'ilm	knowledge, learning, science
imân	faith
irshâd	guidance, instruction
isnâd	ascription (of an Islamic tradition), chain of authority
iṣṭilâḥ	agreement; *terminus technicus*
istiṭâ'a	ability, capability
jâhiliyya	state of ignorance; the pre-Islamic times; to-day often the characterization by Islamists of the condition of the modern societies in re-

	spect to their concordance with the sources of the religion
jamâ'a	group, community; association, society
jihâd	effort, fight; the holy war
jinn	demon
jumûd	rigidity, inflexibility
kâfir	unbeliever, infidel
khalîfa	successor, caliph
kufr	unbelief, infidelity
mahdî	rightly guided
majlis	assembly, meeting; praying place
ma'rifa	knowledge; realization; gnosis
masjid	mosque
maṣlaḥa	public welfare
maulid	birthday (of the Prophet or a saint)
mujaddid	renewer, reformer
muqaddam	supervisor, trustee
murshid	leader, spiritual guide
nabî	prophet
naḥw	grammar
qabḍ	holding the arms crossed (during prayer)
qâḍî	judge
quṭb	pole, axis, pivot
ramadhân	the holy month of fasting
rasûl	messenger; *rasûl Allâhi:* the messenger of God

ṣadaqa	alms, charity
sadl	arms hanging down (during prayer)
ṣaḥâba	companions (of the Prophet)
salât	ritual prayer
aṣ-ṣaum	fasting (in the month of *Ramadhân*)
sharî'a	Islamic law
shaykh	elder, chief, head (pl. *shuyûkh*)
shirk	polytheism
siḥr	secret, sorcery, magic
silsila	chain (of transmission) (pl. *salâsil*)
tafsîr	interpretation, commentary (of the Qur'ân)
taḥrîf	distortion, perversion, corruption
tajdîd	reform, renewal, rejuvenation
takfîr	charge of unbelief, expiation
ṭalâq	divorce
talfîq	invention, fabrication; looking for a solution among all four legal schools in Islamic law
tarbiya	spiritual education
ta'rîkh	history, historiography
ṭarîqa	way, method; Sufi brotherhood (pl. *ṭuruq*)
taṣawwuf	Sufism, mysticism
tawassul	plea, intercession
tawḥîd	belief in the unity of God
tayammum	ritual washing with sand
umma	nation; the community of all Muslims

walî	saint
waẓîfa	office; Sufi recitation; religious exercise
wird	Sufi litany (pl. *awrâd*)
wuṣûl	arrival (at gnosis); achievement
zakât	alms, alms tax
zâwiya	corner; Sufi center
zindîq	heretic, unbeliever
ziyâra	pilgrimage, visit (of the tomb of a saint)
zuhd	asceticism, renunciation

List of Hausa Terms

Alkali	judge (pl. *Alkalai*)
Allo	slate
Almajiri	student of a Qur'ânic school (pl. *Almajirai*)
Arewa	North (*Jama'ar Arewa:* the Community of the North)
Birni	walled city
Boko	the latin script, in extension also western education, fraud
Cin rani	"to eat the dry season" (i.e., to migrate in the dry season to a city in order to earn money)
Darika	Sufi brotherhood (pl. *Darikoki*)
Gaisuwa	present of honor
Gari	town (*Sabon Gari:* the new town)
Jangali	cattle tax
Kasuwa	market
Laada	commission, payment of provision
Mai	master, mister (pl. *Masu*)
Makaranta	school
Malam	teacher, mister (pl. *Malamai*)
Masallaci	mosque
Salla	prayer

Sarauta	the nobility (*Masu Sarauta:* title holders, aristocrats)
Sardauna	title: "chief of the bodyguard"
Sarki	king, ruler (*Sarkin Kano:* ruler of Kano)
Sha Rubutu	"to drink the written"
Shege	bastard
Shehu	name, title
Shugaba	president, chairman
Talakawa	commoners
Tsubbu	magic, divination
Unguwa	ward, quarter of a town
Waje	outside (*Wajen Birni:* outside the city)
Waziri	title: chancellor, vizier
'Yan	Sons of . . . (*'Yan Izala,* Sons of Dan)

I

Introduction

The Federation of Nigeria according to the recent census of 1992 is, with a population of about 88.5 million (*West Africa*, 5 Apr. 1992) and an extension of 923,768 square kilometers, not only Africa's most populous state, but also one of the most heterogeneous countries of the continent. Apart from the three great linguistic groups of the Hausa, the Yoruba, and the Igbo, there are numerous smaller languages to be found, a number spoken by only some hundred speakers. Others like Kanuri, Bini (Edo), Nupe, Tiv, Urhobo, Efik, Fulfulde, or Ibibio serve as a regional language of communication for millions of Nigerians (Isichei 1983: 5 ff.). On account of the linguistic and cultural heterogeneity of the federation none of the three major national languages achieved predominance as the sole national replacement for English. Important factors of unification and solidarity in respect to the lack of ethnic, cultural, and linguistic unity of the country have been the two great religions of Islam and Christianity. Because of the insufficient statistics on the Nigerian population it is not possible to give exact data concerning the numerical strength of the different religious groups. Additionally it has to be taken into account that Christians as well as Muslims tend to exaggerate their respective numbers in order to prove their supremacy over the other faiths. In 1989 the German statistical yearbook estimated the Muslims (45%) to be the most numerous religious group, whereas the Christians (34%) came second, and the adherents of the African polytheistic religions (19%) third (*Fischer Weltalmanach* 1989: 402).

During the course of the British conquest the precolonial regions and states of present-day Nigeria were united in a new system of administration. Although the precolonial regions had been connected by long-distance trade networks, they were differentiated by their specific historical traditions and experiences. In the North the Islamic Sokoto empire with its emirates dominated the political and economical development of the subregion in the nineteenth century (see map 1), whereas the Southwest was characterized in the same period by the competition and rivalry of the Yoruba city-states. In the Southeast and the center of the country the acephalous societies of the Igbo, Ibibio, Tiv, Birom, and other smaller ethnic groups had developed still other forms of political and economic organization. The three great regions of present-day Nigeria continued their autonomous development in the British colonial era almost independently from each other and could thus be regarded as three different colonies under one administration with its center in the crown colony of Lagos. The Nigerian movement of independence was dominated in its early phase by politicians from the Southwest and the Southeast of the country, whereas political parties in the North formed only in the late 1940s and early 1950s.

When Nigeria finally achieved her independence in 1960 the unifying forces in the country had thus developed only weak roots. Regional interests also dominated the politics of the first republic which failed because of the diverging regional orientations. On 15 January 1966 the Nigerian army overthrew the government of President Abubakar Tafawa Balewa, a centralistic military regime was set up, and the regions dissolved. In 1967 the crisis of the Nigerian state escalated, owing to the secession of the East (Biafra), and developed into a civil war which could be brought to a peacuful end only in 1970. Despite the war, in the late 1960s the restructuring of Nigeria began: the great regions were replaced by a number of smaller federal states (see map 2), with the support of the oil money the federal administration started serious efforts to industrialize the country, and in 1976 the return to civilian rule began. The federal elections of 1979, however, brought about the victory of the old power blocks: Thus the new ruling party, the NPN (National Party of Nigeria), represented interests similar to those of the former NPC (Northern

People's Congress) under the leadership of Ahmadu Bello in the 1950s and 1960s. When the government of President Shehu Shagari demonstrated in the early 1980s its incapacity to manage the country's economic problems, the army staged a second coup on 31 December 1983. Under General Buhari the new military regime started a thorough disciplinary exercise called War against Indiscipline (WAI) but failed to tackle the pressing economic problems, especially the rising indebtedness of the federation to external creditors, inflation, and unemployment. After an internal coup on 27 August 1985, General Babangida took power and began the task of stabilizing the Nigerian economy, a policy which has been labeled Structural Adjustment Program (SAP) by the government and Seriously Approaching Poverty by the lower income groups of the Nigerian population because of its disastrous economic effects. By late 1986 the Babangida administration began the process of transition to a democratic third republic, a process which was stopped by the cancellation of the general elections of June 1993 and yet another military coup under the leadership of General Sani Abacha in November 1993.

In his work *Power and Diplomacy in Northern Nigeria* (1971) R. A. Adeleye remarks that the striving for the unity among Muslims and the efforts of reform and revitalization (*tajdîd*) of Islam have been the two major topics in the history of Islam in the Hausa states (Adeleye 1971: 7). Whereas the Muslims in present-day Northern Nigeria until the beginning of the nineteenth century were living in a number of more or less Islamized states like Kano, Katsina, Gobir, Zamfara, Zaria, Daura, or Bornu, the *jihâd* (holy war) of Usman dan Fodio managed to unite the Muslims of these regions, with the exception of Bornu. After the establishment of the Sokoto empire the Muslims of the North were for the first time in the history of Northern Nigeria united in a state which claimed to be an Islamic community (*jamâ'a*) and which drew its legitimization from Islam. The importance and the legacy of the Sokoto empire for the development of the Muslim communities in present-day Nigeria cannot be overestimated. Until the present day, politicians of the North, the religious scholars, and the modern Muslim intellectuals claim the legacy of Usman dan Fodio for themselves in order to legitimate their political strategies and programs. Thus both the first prime minister of the Northern Region, Ahmadu Bello, and the leader of the opposition party, the Northern Elements Progressive Union (NEPU), Aminu Kano, as well as the president of Nigeria, Shehu Shagari, claimed the legacy of Usman dan Fodio. Shehu Shagari even wrote a book about the leader of the jihâd which was published in Lagos in 1978 (Williams 1982: 235–41). The great mentor of the 'Yan Izala movement, Abubakar Gumi, stressed that without the achievements of Usman dan Fodio his own efforts to revitalize Islam would have been useless (Interview Gumi, 17 Sept. 1987). Besides Gumi, the leaders of the Sufi brotherhoods also refer to the teachings of Usman dan Fodio in order to underline their bonds with this political and religious tradition. Finally, the radical speakers of the younger generation of Muslim intellectuals and the Muslim Students' Society (MSS) legitimate their radical political ideas, like their call for a second jihâd, with reference to Usman dan Fodio in order to protect their radical stance against criticism: "he who is criticizing us, attacks also the legacy of Usman dan Fodio" (Interview Sulaiman, 9 Sept. 1987). The representatives of the new Muslim intelligentsia compare the present system of government in Nigeria with the system of government in the old Hausa states before the jihâd and say that there are no great differences between the two systems. Although the governing elites would call themselves "Muslim," in reality they should be regarded as representatives of a system of *jâhiliyya* (ignorance) and therefore should be fought in a second jihâd if they do not consent to establish a truly Islamic state (Interviews Sulaiman 9 Sept. 1987, Abdullahi 5 Feb. 1987, Maikarfi 5 Feb. 1987, Kurawa 23 Feb. 1987).

The question as to why the jihâd and the legacy of Usman dan Fodio are still kept in such high esteem can be answered only with a look on Nigeria's recent history. The Sokoto empire and Bornu were conquered by the British in 1903 and united under the name Northern Nigeria with the British protectorate in the

South in 1914. But whereas in the South the British engaged themselves directly in the development of their colony, they shared their power in the North with the emirs. This system of indirect rule gave the emirs a strong position in the colonial administration. Although the British implemented a number of basic reforms in the areas of finance and taxation, the judicial system, and territorial law, they did not question the existing social system in the North but modernized it along existing lines. Thus, in comparison with the South, the North remained, as a whole, intact. Although the Nigerian independence movement was active much earlier in the South than in the North and although the South proved to be much more dynamic economically than the North, this situation created no problems for Muslims in the North as long as they had the control over the most populous part of the country. The policy of the most outstanding politician of the North in the 1950s and 1960s, Ahmadu Bello, has to be seen in this context. He was the living symbol for the motto of the North's dominant party, the Northern People's Congress (NPC): "One north, one people" (Whitaker 1970: 352–61). Bello tried to implement his policy of unification not only in collaboration with the Muslim majority in the North, but he also tried to win over the non-Muslim groups in the so-called "Middle Belt," the present federal states of Gongola, Benue, Plateau, Niger, Kaduna, and Kwara. Bello had realized that a majority for the NPC on the federal level, which was the precondition for the preservation of the power of the NPC within the federation, could not be achieved without the support of the Middle Belt (Paden 1986: 350 ff.). His decision not to go to Lagos as the candidate of the North for the office of the prime minister of the federation after the victory of the NPC in the 1959 federal elections, but instead to stay in the North and to influence federal politics from his home base in Kaduna, shows how important the leadership of the Jama'ar Arewa, the "Community of the North," was for Bello. Instead Ahmadu Bello supported Abubakar Tafawa Balewa, who had already been appointed prime minister by the British governor, Sir James Robertson, in 1957 for the transition period, to take over the office of the prime minister in 1959. After the victory of the NPC in the federal elections of 1959 Tafawa Balewa was asked to form a federal government and was thereupon elected prime minister with the votes of the NPC and the NCNC (National Congress of Nigeria and the Cameroons). The character of the relationship between Bello and Balewa is best shown by a remark of Bello at the occasion of a speech in Bauchi, the home region of Balewa, during the campaign for the 1959 elections when he described Tafawa Balewa as his "biggest lieutenant in the present-day setup in Nigeria" and compared their relationship with the connection between the Sultan of Sokoto, Muhammad Bello, and his "lieutenant," the Emir of Bauchi. In 1961 Bello repeated this characterization when he again called Balewa "his lieutenant in the South" (Whitaker 1970: 352).

Bello created the preconditions for the NPC's national position of power basically through his policy of the unification of the North under his leadership. In pursuit of this goal, in the 1950s he created a new bureaucratic elite devoted more or less exclusively to himself. As a basis for this new elite he developed Kaduna instead of Sokoto as the political center of the North, and to this end he also pursued reform of the existing administration. This system of administration was labeled the "Native Administration" and had developed out of the doctrine of "Indirect Rule" introduced into Northern Nigeria by its first governor, Lord Lugard. Because the British were unable to finance a huge apparatus of administration in Northern Nigeria they used the existing structures of government to their own ends and transformed the existing local administration into a modern colonial system. At the top of the new system, however, was still the emir. The staff of the new Native Administration, which was taken over from the old emirate's offices, could be deposed, transferred, or appointed by the emirs at will (Fika 1978: 105 ff.). It was this system of power that Bello began to transform in the 1950s with his internal reforms so as to make it conform with his political plans. In addition Bello stressed the political and religious ideas of Usman dan Fodio as an example for his own policy and tried to consolidate the political unity of the North in his efforts to unite the area on a religious basis. Through the deposition of the Emir of Kano, Muhammad Sanusi, Bello proved in 1963 that he was willing to fight against regionalistic interests and stubborn opponents of his policy within his own party and even to depose "great emirs." The claim for undisputed leadership and dominance is also shown in the ruthless way in which he and the NPC crushed the Bornu Youth Movement (BYM) in the late 1950s and the Kano People's Party (KPP) in 1963 (Osuntokun 1987: 63 ff.).

However, the military coup of 1966 together with the murder of Ahmadu Bello and the ensuing civil war distroyed the political foundations for the dominance of the North. The regions were dissolved in 1967 and replaced by a number of federal states. In the new states (21 in 1987, 30 in 1991, plus the "Federal Capital Territory" of Abuja) the regional interests soon dominated, especially as far as the allocation of the oil revenues were concerned. The political fragmentation of the old Northern region resulted in a slow erosion of the power of Muslim politicians of the North, the heirs and successors of Bello. The federal capital Lagos, where an increasing number of political, military, and economic functions were concentrated, was situated in the heterogeneous South of the federation. This led to the situation where not only the administrations led by the Christian heads of state (Gowon 1967–75 and Obasanjo 1976–79) but also the administrations of the Muslim heads of state (Shagari 1979–83, Buhari 1983–85, Babangida 1985–93) were increasingly influenced by interest groups of non-Muslim origin from the South or the Middle Belt. Thus thirteen out of the twenty-one personal assistants and personal advisors of President Shagari were Christians from the South (Williams 1982: 246 ff.) and until the cabinet reshuffle of March 1989 sixteen of the nineteen ministers in the Babangida "Armed Forces Ruling Council" (AFRC) were Christians, a situation which led to complaints in some quarters that the ruling body was dominated by "Johns, Peters, Joshuas, and Pauls" (*Newswatch*, 27 Feb. 1989).

The breakup of the Northern region made the political, cultural, and economic emancipation of the new Middle Belt states possible. Although they had predominantly been part of the old North and the Sokoto empire, they were much less Islamized than the states of the far North (Sokoto, Katsina, Kano, Bauchi, Bornu). Nevertheless the Middle Belt in Ahmadu Bello's times was claimed as the domain of the North, as was shown by the integration in 1961 of the former mandate territory of the British Northern Cameroons into the Northern region as "Sardauna Province," *Sardauna* being the title of honor of Ahmadu Bello. After 1966, however, the federal states of the Middle Belt oriented themselves more and more toward Southern Nigeria. The South was not only stronger in economic terms than the North but also had a number of cultural affinities with the Middle Belt. The reorientation of the Middle Belt is reflected, for instance, in a geographical atlas for teaching in Northern Nigeria, where the federal states of Kwara and Benue, both south of the Niger and Benue rivers, are not shown as part of the North anymore, but as part of the South (Taswirar Jihohin Arewa 1983: 9–12). The restructuring of the North had the effect that the Northern Muslims felt themselves increasingly pushed into a politically problematic position as far as their chances to keep their share of power in the federation was concerned. Nevertheless the Muslims were able to fill the presidency after the elections of 1979 with a candidate of their own (Shehu Shagari) and to recover lost positions in the government, army, and administration. Shagari, however, was ousted by another military coup in 1983, and according to the taste of some radical Muslim intellectuals, the Babangida administration had far too little regard for the interests of the Muslims in Northern Nigeria. When, in addition, Christian candidates in 1987 won large parts of the Middle Belt during the first local government council elections after the Buhari coup in 1983, many politically sensitive Muslims for the first time saw the possibility of a political dominance by the Christians in the whole federation as a result of free elections.

The development of a religiously neutral, indifferent, or even secular state, a state since 1967 increasingly controlled by non-Muslim and Southern-orientated power groups, was not only regarded by many Muslims in the North as a surrender of the achievements of the jihâd and of the results of the policy of Ahmadu Bello but also signified to them that the chances to realize their political and religious programs and aims, for instance, the establishment of a federal Sharî'a court of appeal, became increasingly smaller under these frame conditions. In the face of this development the Muslim politicians and intellectuals as well as the Muslim religious scholars in the North stressed more and more the ever growing need for political and religious unity of all Muslims as a prerequisite to maintain their dominant position in the federation or to reassert it. The efforts of the Muslim intellectuals who since 1986 have been organized in the Council of 'Ulama' must be seen in this context. These efforts were namely to unite the Muslims in the North regardless of both their religious affiliations and the ongoing conflict between the Sufi brotherhoods and the 'Yan Izala movement.

The fragmentation of the North and the dissolution of the Muslims' political unity in the Northern region after Bello's death have led to the situation in which, since the 1970s, the Muslims have carried out a bitter struggle for every cultural symbol of Islam. As long as the North was united and as long as the activities of the Christian missions remained restricted to some small and peripheral areas of the North, it was not necessary for the Muslims to emphasize the importance of certain symbols of their religion. Until 1966 Northern Nigeria could be regarded as the political basis for Islam in the whole federation. Since the breakup of the North, the Muslim religious and political leaders have stressed at every opportunity how important it was to acknowledge the *sharî'a* on all levels of the judiciary system and in all spheres of law, and to embody the sharî'a in the constitution of Nigeria. They underlined the importance of "correct Islamic dressing" for the Muslim children and the acknowledgment of the Islamic holy days as national holidays, and they were at least partially prepared to fight for these symbols of an Islamic society in a militant way. Quite a number of religious conflicts in the last few years have resulted from seemingly minor causes. Muslims' insistence in acknowledging the cultural symbols of Islam and the brutality of the clashes of the 1970s and the 1980s were a sign that the Muslims in Northern Nigeria reacted with increasing awareness to the changes in the social, political, and economic structure of the federation.

Apart from the unity of the Muslims, the other dominating question in the history of Northern Nigeria has been the problem of the revitalization (*tajdîd*) of the religion. The quest for tajdîd influenced the development of Islamic society in Hausaland since Islam reached this region. The coming of Islam is often connected with the arrival of the Wangarawa, traders and scholars from Mali. Nevertheless there are hints in the Kano chronicle, for instance, that Muslims were living in Kano even before the first Wangarawa came to Kano (Palmer 1967 III: 102–4). The Wangarawa were led to Kano by 'Abd ar-Raḥmân Zagaiti, presumably at the end of the fourteenth century. Under the reign of Sarkin Kano Yagi (1349–85) they came to occupy important posts at the court (Philips 1985: 40; A. Smith 1983: 35). Thus Islam was established in Kano, as in the other Sudano-Sahelian states, as the religion of the court and of the scholar-traders. The pre-Islamic cults continued to exist, however. In this historical context a Maghribinian scholar, Muḥammad b. 'Abd al-Karîm al-Maghîlî (1425–1504), who visited Kano under the reign of Sarkin Kano Muhammad Rumfa (1463–99), wrote a treatise on the art of government which is known under the title *Tâj ad-dîn fî mâ yajib 'alâ l-mulûk* (The Crown of the Religion concerning the Rulers' Obligations). In this work he described the guiding principles of government according to the laws of Islam. His work was later used by the leaders of the jihâd as a theoretical basis for their attacks on the government of the Hausa states. Since the jihâd, al-Maghîlî came to be regarded as the first reformer (*mujaddid*) of Islam in Hausaland. Al-Maghîlî was, however, not the only Islamic scholar who visited Hausaland at that time. In 1487 Aḥmad b. 'Umar b. Muḥammad al-'Aqît from Timbuktu had been in Kano, followed in about 1500 by the Maghribinian scholar 'Abd ar-Raḥmân b. 'Alî al-Qaṣrî. Between 1504 to 1509 the Moroccan scholar 'Abd ar-

Raḥmân as-Suqqain had been living in Kano, and after him Makhlûf b. 'Alî al-Balbalî, who also visited Katsina and died in Timbuktu in 1534 (Chamberlin 1975: 66 ff.). Thus it has to be assumed that many of the deeds attributed to al-Maghîlî's stay in Kano, for instance, the introduction into Hausaland of the Maliki school of law or of Sufism, cannot be ascribed to the efforts of one "cultural hero" alone, but rather to have been spread through Hausaland during the course of a much longer process, namely, the dispersion of Islam by a multitude of scholars.

Islam was accepted during this process of dispersion by an increasing proportion of the population, the commoners (*talakawa*), whereby a mixing of Islam with elements of the pre-Islamic cults occurred. This amounted, however, not to a rejection of Islam as such but should be seen as a sign of only partial understanding and of selective acceptance of the new religion; as Philips says, "Islam was accepted by all, even by those who never practiced it, in the sense that they believed in its power and sought its blessing in such forms as amulets and charms" (Philips 1985: 44). At the end of the eighteenth century, however, a protest movement formed against this mixing of the pure faith and against a number of social and political grievances. This movement called for a purification of the religion and for a general social and political reform. The leader of the reform movement was Usman dan Fodio, descendent of a family of scholars who came originally from the Futa Toro region in present-day Senegal. He made his views on reform clear in the title of one of his major works, *Iḥyâ' as-sunna wa-ikhmâd al-bid'a* (The Revitalization of the Sunna and the Elimination of the Innovation), written about 1793. The irreconcilable positions of the party of the reformers and of the political establishment finally led to the outbreak of the jihâd in Hausaland in 1804. According to Murray Last, "The jihâd of 1804 was primarily a reform movement, reforming lax Muslims, not converting pagans. It was ideologically probably less concerned with the kufr of pagans than with the kufr of those Muslims who opposed the jihâd" (Last 1979: 273).

The success of the jihâd led not only to the establishment of the Sokoto empire; the leaders of the jihâd and their successors also propagated a new conscience of community among the Muslims. They legitimized their religious and political reform efforts by arguing that it was necessary to purify the religion. After the victorious end of the jihâd, Usman dan Fodio as well as his brother Abdullahi dan Fodio devoted themselves to work on the theoretical foundations of the new state, and they tried to stabilize the achievements of the jihâd on a dogmatic level. Through the jihâd the Sufi brotherhood of the Qâdiriyya was established as the quasi-official *ṭarîqa* (Sufi brotherhood) of the Sokoto empire (Brenner 1988: 47). In spite of the efforts of the leaders of the jihâd to establish an Islamic system, it became clear soon after the death of Usman dan Fodio in 1817 that their idealistic concepts could not be implemented on account of the social, political, and economic realities of Hausaland. Thus, the second Emir of Kano, Dabo, reinstituted the former offices of the nobility and the old etiquette of the court. In addition, the cattle tax (*jangali*), which had been hotly contested during the jihâd, was reintroduced under the label of *zakât* (alms tax) in order to give it a legitimate Islamic color (Sa'id 1978: 55). Dabo's successor, Usman, even began to tax some of the religious scholars, although they had been exempted from all taxation since the time of Muhammad Rumfa.

The growing discontent over the developments in the Sokoto empire led to resistance and rebellion. The discontented withdrew to distant regions and erected a number of small rebel enclaves far away from the immediate control of the center in Sokoto. One of these rebel organizations was Ningi, north of Bauchi, founded by Malam Hamza Tsakuwa from Kano in the mid-nineteenth century (Patton 1987: 195 ff.). Other dissidents emigrated under the pretext of the *ḥajj* to the East. To the group of the latter belonged Malam Hayatu b. Sa'id, who at the end of the nineteenth century became the leader of a Mahdist movement which threatened the stability of the Sokoto empire and the security of its eastern boundaries (Al-Hajj 1973: 80 ff.). Some of the discontented also reoriented themselves toward the new ṭarîqa of the Tijâniyya which had won a growing number of disciples in the Sokoto empire under the influence of al-Ḥâjj 'Umar Tal al-Fûtî since the 1830s. The political establishment of the Sokoto empire reacted in an increasingly irritated way to the propaganda of the Tijâniyya. Thus in 1854 the Emir of Zaria was deposed because he had made his affiliation with the Tijâniyya public. The political elite of the Sokoto empire reacted extremely nervously when the Tijânis started to claim by the late 1840s that Muhammad Bello, the first sultan of the empire and son of Usman dan Fodio, had become one of their own shortly before he died (Minna 1982: 363 ff.). Through their affiliation with the Tijâniyya the religious scholars and the emirs who carried out this decisive step not only expressed their discontent with the existing system, but also put the monopoly of power of the leading elite in Sokoto into question. Affiliation with the new ṭarîqa could therefore be regarded as an effort to dissociate oneself from the central religious and political authority in Sokoto. These endeavors for autonomy could not be accepted by the central power and affiliation with the Tijâniyya was thus punished with deposition by Sokoto. After the British conquest of Sokoto in 1903 the sympathizers and followers of the Tijâniyya no longer had to fear sanctions from Sokoto. This led to a widespread process of reaffiliation with the Tijâniyya in the first decades of the twentieth century. Not only did the emirs of Kano, Zaria, and Katsina affiliate themselves publicly with the Tijâniyya, but a growing number of religious scholars did as well. The extent of the movement of reaffiliation, described as "realignment" by Paden (1973: 82 ff.), was so great that the British administration soon viewed the activities of the Tijâniyya with great mistrust (Quadri 1981: 83). This attitude of the colonial administration caused many religious scholars in the 1920s and 1930s to consider the affiliation with the Tijâniyya not only as a form of their emancipation from the claim of spiritual hegemony represented by Sokoto, but also as a symbol of their resistance to the "new habits" (Tahir 1975: 350–51) introduced by the British colonialists.

The affiliation with the Tijâniyya reached a new dimension in the 1940s when the so-called movement of *tarbiya* (education), which had been founded by the Senegalese Shaykh Ibrahim Niass, spread from Senegal to Nigeria. By 1930 Ibrahim Niass had already claimed to be the *ghauth az-zamân* (the succor of the time), that is, the highest among the Sufi saints (Hiskett 1980: 102 ff.). As part of religious and political considerations a movement of reaffiliation among Tijâniyya scholars began in Kano in the 1940s and thereafter in the whole of Nigeria under the leadership of Ibrahim Niass. The process of revitalization led in the 1950s to the transformation of the Tijâniyya into a religious mass movement. The Tijâniyya's success triggered a similar movement for tajdîd within the Qâdiriyya, a movement initiated and led by the Kano-based scholar Nasiru Kabara. The aim of his endeavor for revitalization was to activate the Qâdiriyya and also to transform it into a mass movement, in order to prevent the further expansion of the Tijâniyya to the detriment of the Qâdiriyya.

It would be misleading, however, to regard these tajdîd movements within the two Sufi brotherhoods in Paden's sense as "modernizing" (Paden 1973: 70–71). This characterization implies that these movements introduced new things into the religion of Islam. Such an idea would be rejected outright by followers of both the Qâdiriyya and the Tijâniyya. Both Nasiru Kabara and the leaders of the Tijâniyya interpret their efforts of tajdîd as the purification and revitalization of a corrupted faith. Their aim was not to give a "modern" interpretation of the religion of Islam, but to educate the ignorant masses. Hiskett, in my opinion, has made a much more valid point by stressing the aspect of popularization in describing these tajdîd movements (Hiskett 1980: 102). Last but not least, it has to be taken into account that the term "reform/reformed" was already used in 1928 in a clearly political way when the British colonial officer Hoskys Abraham denounced a "group of Sufi militants" in Kano as "reformed" Muslims (Tahir 1975: 20).

Another misleading aspect of Paden's terminology is the way he uses the terms "reformed" and "traditional" to describe different groups within the Qâdiriyya and the Tijâniyya and the way he uses them as criteria to deliminitate certain groups within the Sufi brotherhoods against each other. Neither the "reformed" nor the "traditional" Tijâniyya (and the same is valid for the Qâdiriyya) can be delimited as a clear, quasi-monolithic group. The point is rather that both Sufi brotherhoods are split up in a multitude of different networks coexisting and competing with each other, each grouped around a number of spiritually, politically, and economically influential religious scholars (Interview Miskin, 18 Mar. 1988). Relationships of concurrence and competition exist between the different Sufi brotherhoods as well as within Tijâniyya and Qâdiriyya themselves. Both the Tijâniyya-Ibrâhîmiyya (Paden's "reformed Tijâniyya") and the Qâdiriyya-Nâsiriyya (Paden's "reformed Qâdiriyya") differ in comparison with other networks within the Tijâniyya or the Qâdiriyya. But this difference is based to a large extent on the success of both networks, derived from their early acceptance of modern technical means to propagate their spiritual and political concepts, and drawn from their emphasis on certain aspects of their teachings and religious practice. An important point of departure for the success of the leading representatives of these networks, like Ibrahim Niass or Nasiru Kabara, was their strategy and ability to establish shorter and more direct links to the centers of the origin and spiritual power of their specific Sufi brotherhoods. In this way they could claim to be closer to the *baraka* (blessing) of Aḥmad at-Tijânî or 'Abd al-Qâdir al-Jîlânî than other *shuyûkh* (elders) of their own ṭarîqa. The strategy to establish as many direct contacts with as many centers of the ṭarîqa as possible was again successful because it is desirable for the adherents of a Sufi brotherhood to be connected with chains of authority (*silsila*, pl. *salâsil*), with as many saints of their ṭarîqa as possible in order to enhance their own baraka. Thus Nasiru Kabara commands more than seven different salâsil of the Qâdiriyya, whereas Ibrahim Ṣâliḥ, one of the leaders of the Tijâniyya in Maiduguri (Bornu), has five different salâsil of the Tijâniyya. A more direct silsila, like the silsila to Aḥmad at-Tijânî through Ibrahim Niass, nevertheless does not neutralize the validity of longer chains of authority, like the connection with Aḥmad at-Tijânî through al-Ḥâjj 'Umar, but rather represents another step of an ongoing process of the personal tajdîd of one's spiritual affiliations. Both Sufi brotherhoods therefore cannot be regarded as homogenous blocks of power but ought to be seen as systems of networks and links, subject to a constant dynamic of change due to the permanent process of spiritual renewal as well as the economic and political influences they are exposed to.

Thus the disputes described by Paden are not a manifestation of a single conflict between two great Sufi brotherhoods but rather a multitude of controversies, quarrels, and jealousies among a whole series of networks. These networks compete among and against each other for influence, followers, supporters, and economic resources, and some of them, like the Tijâniyya-Ibrâhîmiyya and the Qâdiriyya-Nâṣiriyya, were disproportionally successful in this struggle. The success of a network is not necessarily permanent. It might change under the dynamics of economic, political, or religious developments and be transformed into a crisis, as the disintegration of the Tijâniyya-Ibrâhîmiyya after 1963 has shown. In this work the individual networks are thus not labeled as "reformed" or "traditional" but described as the systems of influence of their respective leaders. In this respect the Qâdiriyya-Nâṣiriyya or the Tijâniyya-Ibrâhîmiyya do not constitute new branches of a Sufi brotherhood but rather are networks of one ṭarîqa affiliated to an especially successful *shaykh* (elder) of the ṭarîqa.

The process of tajdîd and reorientation of the Muslims in Northern Nigeria did not end, however, with the efforts of Nasiru Kabara or Ibrahim Niass in the 1940s, 1950s, and 1960s. In the 1970s a new movement of tajdîd started, aimed like its predecessors at the purification of the religion and the eradication of all *bid'a* (heresy). Its adherents regarded Abubakar Gumi (1922–92), the former Grand Kadi of the Northern region and religious advisor of Ahmadu Bello, as the mujaddid of the present era (Shanono 1976: 1). Like Nasiru Kabara and Ibrahim Niass, Gumi stressed the importance of education for the Muslim masses in order to cleanse the religion of all bid'a. He tried to achieve his aims with the support of an organization, founded and inspired by him, the Jamâ'at Izâlat al-Bid'a wa-Iqâmat as-Sunna (the Association for the Eradication of the Innovation and the Establishment of the Sunna; Hausa: 'Yan Izala). However, for the first time in the history of Islam in Nigeria a religious leader has turned explicitly against Sufism and the ṭuruq. Abubakar Gumi described the Sufi brotherhoods as the actual bearers and propagandists of the bid'a. This attitude led to a bitter struggle with the Sufi brotherhoods beginning in the late 1960s. The attacks of the 'Yan Izala have on the other hand prompted the ṭuruq to shelve their internal quarrels in order to concentrate their energies on the fight against Gumi. The conflict betwen Gumi and the Sufi brotherhoods has had a number of positive aspects in addition to its destructive effects on the unity of the Muslims in Northern Nigeria: The push for better Islamic education has increased considerably, and since the 1970s the Muslim women have been gradually integrated into the social and political life of the country. Abubakar Gumi and the 'Yan Izala also stressed the importance of better education for the Muslim women. In this way the ṭuruq were forced to follow suit. At the same time Gumi supported the stronger participation of Muslim women in the political process, at least since 1982, even if this strategy in the beginning grew primarily out of tactical considerations in regard to the 1983 federal elections for which the Muslim women had to be mobilized as voters.

Through their open disputes Abubakar Gumi and his opponents did not only achieve a greater sensibilization of the Muslims concerning religious issues. They also—willingly or unwillingly—contributed to a stronger politicization of Islam in Nigeria. Symptomatic of this recent development of Islam in Nigeria was a statement of Gumi, when he appealed in 1982 to the Muslims to allow their wives' registration for the next federal elections arguing that "politics are more important than prayer" (Siyasa tafi muhimmanci da salla) (Christelow 1987: 233). Gumi legitimized this statement by saying that the Muslims could expect to keep their positions of power in Nigeria only if they would use the voting power of Muslim women. The question of Gumi's real intentions thus has to be raised: Was it the propagation of Islam and the education of the Muslim masses or the conservation of the political power for the Muslims in the federation of Nigeria? Or, put in other words: Was the constant stress on the necessity of tajdîd only used by Gumi as a form of religious legitimization for his political struggle?

From their ideological orientation Abubakar Gumi and the 'Yan Izala appear as a Nigerian manifestation of the radical Islamist movements in the Islamic world: They believe that they can overcome the crisis of their respective societies by a return to the original sources of religion and by the reviviscence of Islam, and they think that they can supply an answer to the growing Westernization and secularization of their societies. As Gumi and the 'Yan Izala followed political strategies as well as religious ones in their struggle with their opponents in Nigeria, one may well speak of a repoliticization of Islam in Nigeria.

2

The Development of the Sufi Brotherhoods in Nigeria

The Qâdiriyya and the Tijâniyya are, apart from a few followers of the Mahdiyya in Kano (Paden 1973: 169 ff.), the only Sufi brotherhoods of importance in Nigeria. Their development and their struggles against each other had a decisive influence on the formation of Islam in Nigeria. Whereas the Qâdiriyya had been present in Hausaland for several centuries and had played an important role in the jihâd of 1804–8, the Tijâniyya was introduced only in the nineteenth century. Nevertheless the Tijâniyya became the second most important religious force in the Sokoto empire. A number of emirs and scholars, discontented with the status quo, joined the Tijâniyya. In the twentieth century indigenous scholars of the Tijâniyya initiated a movement of renewal which, beginning in the 1940s, tried successfully to extend the influence of the ṭarîqa on the mass level under the leadership of Ibrahim Niass. The rapid expansion of the Tijâniyya induced some scholars of the Qâdiriyya under the leadership of Nasiru Kabara to instigate a similar movement of tajdîd within the Qâdiriyya. The rivalry between the two Sufi brotherhoods led to serious conflicts between them in the 1950s and 1960s and ended only in the late 1970s following the attacks by the 'Yan Izala. As the efforts of revitalization of the Tijâniyya began earlier than those of the Qâdiriyya and as the strategies adopted by Nasiru Kabara to a great extent resembled the example set by the Tijâniyya, I shall discuss the movement of Ibrahim Niass before covering that of the Qâdiriyya-Nâṣiriyya. In my analysis of the two Sufi movements of tajdîd as well as in my final presentation of the religious and economic connections between the networks of traders and those of the religious scholars, I refer to developments in Kano: A great many distinguished religious scholars of both Sufi brotherhoods in Northern Nigeria were and are living in this city, and it was in Kano where the movements of tajdîd within both Sufi brotherhoods began. Furthermore, the ṭuruq in Kano were able to mobilize the majority of the Muslim population for their objectives and were capable of establishing a number of important networks incorporating numerous wealthy traders and entrepreneurs.

2.1. The Qâdiriyya and the Tijâniyya after the Jihâd

The historical context for the development of the Qâdiriyya was very favorable in the nineteenth century. The Qâdiriyya was the only Sufi brotherhood in the region and could claim a long tradition of scholars and teaching. Its first salâsil were introduced into Hausaland presumably in the fifteenth century (Norris 1975: 42 ff.; Ahmed 1986: 94 ff.). Through the jihâd the Qâdiriyya was established as the dominant ṭarîqa of the Sokoto empire. All leaders of the jihâd were followers of the Qâdiriyya, 'Abd al-Qâdir al-Jîlânî was their "patron saint" (Brenner 1988: 47), and close links to other important centers of the ṭarîqa in West Africa existed, especially to the Kunta in Timbuktu (ibid.: 36 ff.). After the victory of Usman dan Fodio the Qâdiriyya was confirmed as the "established" (ibid.: 47) ṭarîqa of the empire. The affiliation with the Qâdiriyya and the study of Sufism remained, however, an affair of scholars. The familiarity with Sufism is shown by a number of the works of Usman dan Fodio such as *Wa lammâ ballaghtu* (And When I Handed over the Message), in which he describes his dreams containing visions of 'Abd al-Qâdir al-Jîlânî. In his major work *Iḥyâ' as-sunna* Usman dan Fodio took pains to distinguish Sufism from the bid'a (evil innovations). However, in the course of the jihâd the Qâdiriyya did not assume the function of official ideology for the empire (Brenner 1988: 44), and because of the introduction of the Tijâniyya in the Sokoto empire during the stay of al-Ḥâjj 'Umar Tal, the Qâdiriyya also lost its spiritual monopoly. Thus, the Qâdirî elite of the empire began to increasingly stress its "corporate identity" (ibid.: 49). The outstanding leaders of these attempts were the Wazirin Sokoto, Gidado dan Laima, and a daughter of Usman dan Fodio, Nana Asma'u. They compiled numerous poems and treatises to honor the memory of Usman dan Fodio (ibid.: 50). Last mentions that in an anonymous manuscript (Sok.prov. 22:39) it was even claimed that the whole empire from Adamawa in the east to Gonja in the west was "Qâdirî." In a reference note in the work of the Wazirin Sokoto Gidado dan Laima *Kashf al-ḥijâb wa-raf' an-niqâb* (The Lifting and Raising of the Veil) it was argued that all communities which had followed Usman dan Fodio were by implication Qâdirî, as Usman dan Fodio himself had been Qâdirî (Last 1967: 216). Gidado wrote, "As far as Adamawa, Kano, Katsina, Zekzek, and Nupe are concerned: it is not permitted to them to leave Qâdiriyya because our shaykh has obliged them with the following words: I belong to the Qâdiriyya and everybody who follows me belongs to it, be he man or jinn" (Ahmed 1986: 199).

The dispute between the Qâdiriyya and the Tijâniyya in the nineteenth century was, however, fought out within the circles of the ruling elite and among the religious scholars. Emirs like Abdulkadir of Zaria (Zekzek), who attached themselves to the Tijâniyya, were deposed as their change of affiliation could be interpreted not only as a sign of a movement toward greater autonomy but also as an indirect attack on the legitimacy of the ruling elite who stressed the legacy of Usman dan Fodio and their adherence to the Qâdiriyya. Only after the conquest of the Sokoto empire by the British was the central authority of the sultan weakened to a degree that political and spiritual movements toward autonomy from Sokoto could no longer be repressed and individuals penalized. The weakening of the central authority led, however, not only to a further expansion of the Tijâniyya but also to a reorientation within the Qâdiriyya itself. This reorientation was implemented by the establishment of new links to new sources of authority independent of the traditional allegiances with Sokoto. Kano, the center of trade and commerce in the North, was the focus of the reorientation of Qâdirî scholars as numerous traders from North Africa had settled there and were, due to their expanded trade networks, in a position to offer new salâsil.

A great number of the North African traders based in Kano originally came from the oasis settlements of Ghat and Ghadâmis and were connected with the branches of the Qâdiriyya-Salâmiyya and the Qâdiriyya-'Arûsiyya, whose centers were located in Tunisia, Tripolitania, and the Fazzan. One of these traders was the Ghadâmis-born scholar Muḥammad Sagâya al-Ghadâmisi. He settled in Kano at the end of the nineteenth century in the old traders' quarter of Alfindiki, where he began practicing the dhikr (Sufi ceremonies, lit. invocation) of the Qâdiriyya-Salâmiyya in a little mosque (Adamu 1968: 47). Muḥammad Sagâya was a *muqaddam* (authorized representative) of this branch of the Qâdiriyya founded in the sixteenth century by Shaykh Aḥmad b. 'Abdallah and at the end of the nineteenth century led by Shaykh Siyâla of Tripoli (Paden 1973: 150). In regard to the use of the so-called bandiri drums, the dhikr of the Qâdiriyya-Salâmiyya was different from the dhikr of the Qâdiriyya-Kuntiyya, until then the only one known in Kano (Interview S. U. Kabara, 9 Mar. 1987). Bandiri drums are of a diameter of about fifty centimeters, covered with a hide on only one side of the drum's body. The drums are beaten to the rhythm of the specific *awrâd* (litanies, sg. *wird*) of the dhikr and in this way support the effect of the singing and breathing exercises of the dhikr.

After the death of Muḥammad Sagâya a quarrel broke out over the question of succession between Muḥammad Sagâya's son 'Abd al-Qâdir and another Ghadâmis-born trader named Sa'd b. Aḥmad (1860–1933). This dispute was taken to Shaykh Siyâla in Tripoli who decided in favor of the succession of Sa'd b. Aḥmad, who thus became the *khalîfa* (successor) of Muḥammad Sagâya as leader of the Qâdiriyya-Salâmiyya in Kano (Adamu 1968: 48). At the beginning of the 1920s under the reign of Emir Usman (1919–26) Shaykh Sa'd b. Aḥmad constructed a new mosque and zâwiya (center) of the Qâdiriyya-Salâmiyya in the Alfindiki quarter

(Hausa: Unguwar Alfindiki). This mosque became the center of the Qâdiriyya-Salâmiyya and has since then been known by the name Masjid Halla Halla. As these meetings were public in contrast to the dhikr meetings of the elitist Qâdiriyya-Kuntiyya, they rapidly attracted a growing number of indigenous Muslims. The new adherents received a *silsila* from Shaykh Sa'd b. Aḥmad and took part in the the activities of the Qâdiriyya-Salâmiya (ibid.). However, the real naturalization of the Qâdiriyya-Salâmiyya began only when Shaykh Sa'd b. Aḥmad appointed his disciple Adamu Na Ma'aji muqaddam of the Qâdiriyya-Salâmiyya. Only then did Adamu Na Ma'aji have the permission to initiate other local followers of the Qâdiriyya into the branch of the Qâdiriyya-Salâmiyya and, in addition, to appoint muqaddamûn among them (S. U. Kabara 1981: 87). The khalîfa of Shaykh Sa'd b. Aḥmad after his death in 1933 was not Adamu Na Ma'aji, but another son of Shaykh Sa'd b. Aḥmad, Muḥammad as-Sayyid Sa'd, who was to do little to spread the Qâdiriyya-Salâmiyya, incurring a period of stagnation in its development in Kano after 1933 (ibid.: 88).

At the turn of the century another silsila was introduced into Kano, namely, the Qâdiriyya-'Arûsiyya with its center in the Fazzan. The Qâdiriyya-'Arûsiyya came to Kano through the mediation of Shaykh 'Abd as-Salâm al-Asmar (Ahmed 1986: 207). Like the Qâdiriyya-Salâmiyya, the Qâdiriyya-'Arûsiyya practiced a public bandiri-dhikr, but in contrast to the Qâdiriyya-Salâmiyya or the other North African branch of the Qâdiriyya, which was introduced into Kano during this period, the Qâdiriyya-Shâdhiliyya, it was not as dynamic in its activities.

The Qâdiriyya-Shâdhiliyya was introduced into Kano under the reign of Emir Usman by the Tunis-born trader Shaykh 'Alî Mûsa, who settled in Unguwar Dandalin Turawa (Ahmed 1986: 206). After his death he was succeeded as khalîfa of this branch of the Qâdiriyya by Shaykh Sîdî Muḥammad. Only under his leadership was the naturalization of the Qâdiriyya-Shâdhiliyya to begin in earnest. In 1940 Shaykh Sîdî Muḥammad appointed two of his local disciples, Malam Ahmad b. 'Alî (c. 1915–1970) and Malam Baba 'Alî muqaddamûn (Ahmed 1986: 207). Already having assumed leadership of the stagnating Qâdiriyya-'Arûsiyya, Malam Aḥmad b. 'Alî became khalîfa to Shaykh Sidi Muḥammad after the latter's death (Ahmed 1986: 207). The unification of all branches of the Qâdiriyya in Kano was realized, however, only by Nasiru Kabara in the 1940s and 1950s.

The establishment of the Tijâniyya in present-day Northern Nigeria goes back to al-Ḥâjj 'Umar Tal al-Fûtî who on his way back from the hajj stayed in Bornu and in Sokoto from 1831/32 to 1838. He was initiated into the Tijaniyya in the late 1820s by 'Abd al-Karîm b. Aḥmad an-Nâqil whose own silsila led back to Aḥmad at-Tijânî through Shaykh Maulûd Faal al-Ya'qûbî and Muḥammad Ḥâfiẓ wuld al-Mukhtâr b. Ḥabîb al-Baddî. During his stay in the Hijâz al-Ḥâjj 'Umar received a new silsila from a companion of Aḥmad at-Tijânî, Shaykh Muḥammad al-Ghâlî. The silsila connected him directly with the founder of the Sufi brotherhood. This intensification of his spiritual connections made it possible for al-Ḥâjj 'Umar to present himself in West Africa as the khalîfa of the ṭarîqa (Robinson 1985: 97–98). After a short stay in Bornu where he initiated his host Muhammad Na Kumami, as well as the future Shehu of Bornu, 'Umar (1837–53), and Shaykh al-Miskin into the Tijâniyya (Interview Ṣâliḥ, 27 Mar. 1988), he continued his journey to Sokoto, where he was given a cool reception due to the war between Sokoto and Bornu some few years before. Al-Ḥâjj 'Umar succeeded, however, in gaining the trust of Sultan Muhammad Bello; he became one of his councillors and even married one of his daughters. In the course of his six-year stay in Sokoto al-Ḥâjj 'Umar initiated a number of religious scholars into the Tijâniyya, for instance, the *Babban Malami Madabo* (the great scholar of the Madabo quarters) Shehu Umar, in Kano, the Mallawa clan in Zaria, which had led the jihâd in Zaria under Malam Musa (M. Smith 1960: 74), as well as 'Umar al-Wali from Zaria (Paden 1973: 75–76). Al-Ḥâjj 'Umar was less successful in Sokoto itself. Only in 1845, eight years after he had left Sokoto, did the highest Alkali of the Emir of Gwandu, Muhammad b. Raji b. 'Ali, make his secret affiliation with the Tijâniyya public. In 1852 he left Gwandu and Sokoto and went eastward with the intention of undertaking the ḥajj. However, he was to settle in Adamawa where he died in 1862 (Last 1967: 218). In a letter to the Emir of Gwandu, Khalil, which he wrote in about 1845, Muhammad b. Raji claimed that al-Ḥâjj 'Umar had been able to win the Sultan Muhammad Bello for the Tijâniyya (ibid.), a claim raised in the same year by al-Ḥâjj 'Umar himself in his major work *Rimâḥ ḥizb ar-raḥîm 'ala nuḥûr ḥizb ar-rajîm* (The Spears of the Party of the Graceful against the Throats of the Party of the Damned). This allegation seems to have had a political motive, namely, to support the efforts of the Tijâniyya in strengthening its claim of superiority over the Qâdiriyya: "Bello's alleged initiation into the Tijâniyya . . . implied a rejection of both Shaykh 'Uthman and 'Abd al-Qadir al-Jilani" (Brenner 1988: 49). There exists, however, no written evidence of a real change of affiliation of Muhammad Bello, as Minna has shown extensively in his thesis (Minna 1982).

The Tijânîs' claim that Muhammad Bello had joined the Tijâniyya resulted from 1845 on in an increasing politicization of the question of adherence to one of the two great Sufi brotherhoods as the Tijâniyya threatened the spiritual hegemony of the Qâdiriyya in the Sokoto empire. The deposition in 1854/55 of the Emir of Zaria, Abdulkadir, has to be seen in this context. He was a member of the Mallawa clan and had been enthroned only in 1853; according to al-Ḥâjj Sa'id (*Ta'rîkh Sokoto*) the official reasons for his deposition were "oppression, illegal killings, dissipation of official funds and voluptuous living with strange women" (Adeleye 1971: 80). In spite of the repressive policy of Sokoto the Tijâniyya in the second half of the nineteenth century spread over the whole territory of the empire and developed strongholds in the emirates of Zaria, Bauchi, and Adamawa. At the same time the Tijâniyya advanced in Bornu and was disseminated by learned traders from there into the regions of the South.

The first silsila of the Tijâniyya introduced by al-Ḥâjj 'Umar was supplemented in the nineteenth century by other salâsil of the ṭarîqa. Among them was a silsila going back to Shaykh 'Alî b. 'Isa at-Tammâsinî (d. 1844), a disciple of Aḥmad at-Tijânî and his khalîfa in North Africa. Some of his followers brought his silsila to Nigeria, especially into the region of Lokoja in the Niger-Benue confluence area (Interview Sâlih, 27 Mar. 1988). The most important support for the Tijâniyya in the Sokoto empire came, however, in the form of some ten thousand refugees from the Tukulóór empire of Segu, which had been distroyed by the French in the early 1890s. The refugees reached Sokoto under the leadership of Ahmadu, one of the sons of al-Ḥâjj 'Umar and his successor as ruler of the Tukulóór empire. Among them were numerous members of the ruling elite of the Tukulóór empire as well as a number of religious scholars of the Tijâniyya. At the time of the British attack on Sokoto in 1902/3 the Tukulóór refugees supported the Sultan of Sokoto, Attahiru, in his struggle and were defeated together with him in the last battle against the British in Burmi (Quadri 1981: 81). A part of the surviving Tukulóór thereafter settled with the consent of the British near Hadejiya, northeast of Kano. They were led by Ahmadu Madani, a nephew of al-Ḥâjj 'Umar (Paden 1973: 82). In 1903 another group of the Tukulóór joined the *hijra* (emigration) of the Mai Wurno, Muhammad Bello, who emigrated after the defeat of Burmi to the east. The emigrants, numbering about twenty-five thousand, seeing no end to British territorial control, finally settled in the Jazîra region of British Sudan. Some of the refugees continued their flight and finally reached the Hijâz. Another nephew of al-Ḥâjj 'Umar, the supreme Alkali of Ahmadu b. 'Umar, Alfa Hâshim (1866/67–1931), was the head of this small community of Tukulóór emigrants in the Hijâz. Alfa Hâshim had fought against the British in Burmi, and after taking up his residence in Madina he soon became one of the most popular scholars of the Tijâniyya in the Hijâz and a focus of attraction for many pilgrims from West Africa. A considerable number of them renewed their salâsil through Alfa Hâshim and were appointed muqaddamûn of the

Tijâniyya by him. On their way back to their regions of origin these pilgrims spread the silsila of Alfa Hâshim throughout West Africa. In this way Alfa Hâshim became one of the most important links between the Nigerian Tijâniyya and the Tijâniyya in the Hijâz. The spiritual successor of Alfa Hâshim, after his death in 1931, was Ibrâhîm al-Khalîl who was followed by Aḥmad b. 'Abd ar-Raḥmân, a son of the Emir of Katagum, Ibrahim Zaki (Paden 1973: 85–86).

The British in Nigeria originally mistrusted the Tijânîs on account of their collaboration with the Sultan of Sokoto. Because of their recent bad experiences with the Mahdi in the Sudan the British in the early twentieth century suspected, as the work of Garba (1983) shows, "mahdist" machinations behind almost every religious movement which resisted them or which did not collaborate with them openly. Rufa'i mentions that among twelve emirs from the former Sokoto empire imprisoned after 1903 in Lokoja, six were affiliated with the Tijâniyya, only one with the Qâdiriyya, another with the Mahdiyya, whereas four were not affiliated with any Sufi brotherhood (Rufa'i 1986: 155). The British were extremely suspicious about the international connections of the Tijâniyya, particularly traders and traveling scholars from the French colonial territories in West and North Africa. One of the first of these scholars who came to Northern Nigeria after the British conquest was the Mauretanian Shaykh 'Abd al-Wahhâb Ujdûd, also known in Nigeria as "Sharîf Ujdûd." He came to Kano for the first time in 1909 and visited the town several times until 1918. Under his influence a number of traders and malamai in Kano who were already affiliated with the 'Umarian branch of the Tijâniyya renewed their affiliations and got a new silsila through him, a process they described as a *tajdîd* (renewal) of their personal spiritual allegiances. Among these traders and scholars were the malamai of the Madabo clan, led by the *Babban Malami Madabo,* as well as the Adhama clan, led by the trader-scholar Muhammad Salga (Tahir 1975: 341).

The example of Muhammad Salga (1871–1938) clearly shows the intensity of the efforts of the followers of the Tijâniyya to collect as many salâsil from as many different centers of authority as possible, in order to strenghten their personal *baraka*. Muhammad Salga originally studied in Katsina and later came to Kano, where he was a student of the *Babban Malami Madabo*, traditionally known and respected in Kano as an expert on the Islamic law (Anwar 1989: 43). Salga was initiated into the Tijâniyya by a scholar from Fez (Morocco), Sharîf Muḥammad b. Shaykh, who had come to Kano in the early years of the reign of Emir Abbas (1903–19) and who had been living in Unguwar Dandalin Turawa. Muḥammad b. Shaykh had received his *ijâza* (authorization to spread a certain silsila or tradition) from his father who had in turn received his own silsila directly from Aḥmad at-Tijânî. With this new silsila Muhammad Salga had acquired a more direct link to Aḥmad at-Tijânî than all other followers of the ṭarîqa in Kano, including the *Babban Malami Madabo*, who were as yet still connected with Aḥmad at-Tijânî through al-Ḥâjj 'Umar. After the initiation through Muḥammad b. Shaykh, Muhammad Salga received a second silsila from another scholar of the Maghrib, Maula 'Abd ar-Raḥmân, who also visited Kano in the early years of the reign of Emir Abbas. Only by about 1910 did he receive his third silsila from Sharîf Ujdûd. His acquisition of salâsil was, however, not yet completed. In 1923 he received a silsila from Shaykh 'Alamî and, finally, the silsila from Alfa Hâshim (Paden 1973: 87). Muhammad Salga passed his salâsil on to his followers and other members of the Kano traders' community. Thus he was able to gradually build up his spiritual leadership among the Hausa traders in Kano. This movement of reorientation and realignment within the Kano trading community was so successful that the Emir of Kano, Abbas, affiliated himself with the Tijâniyya in about 1914.

The emir's change of affiliation can be interpreted as a sign of growing self-consciousness within the ruling elite in Kano insofar as the claims of spiritual and political superiority of Sokoto were concerned. In contrast to the nineteenth century, the Sultan of Sokoto had now lost the power to discipline disloyal emirs like Abbas of Kano or later the emirs of Katsina, Muhamman Dikko, and Zaria, Aliyu dan Sidi. The association with the Tijâniyya could therefore be a way for the emirs to openly show their independence from Sokoto. On the other hand, the affiliation of Emir Abbas with the Tijâniyya can also be understood in the context of the internal development of Kano during this period. Many religious scholars (*malamai*) condemned the "new habits" which had been introduced after the British conquest, for instance, new hair-cutting fashions, the increasing consumption of alcohol, the use of torches and walking sticks, or the English language as a means of communication. All these innovations were regarded by the conservatives as signs of an increasing "Westernization" (Tahir: nasarasation) of the young, not to mention the new institutions of education and administration where a new generation of malaman gwamnati (government teachers), clerks, and administrators were being raised (Anwar 1989: 29). The following poem, written by an anonymous author c. 1930 and published by Hiskett (1973: 164), indicates the manner in which the protest against Westernization was expressed:

> Today unbelief is established, and also innovation,
> well, as for us, we have no use for this in our time,
> this that I am about to say, there is no jesting in it,
> now I am going to warn you, O people,
> whoever heeds it, he will be happy,
> whatever article of their clothing, if you wear it,
> I tell you that you may understand,
> *if you pray a thousand times you will not be vindicated,*
> and the same applies to the maker of hurricane lamp globes,
> your short trousers together with your tight fitting trousers,
> whoever puts them on, his unbelief is wide,
> whoever wear suits with buttons, he has apostatized,
> he has no religion at all, only pride,
> his state is the state of the makers of silver dollars,
> they are beyond our power to imitate,
> one should not wear shirts with collars,
> whoever wears them, his unbelief is wide,
> Khaki and pyjamas, whoever it is,
> who wears them and prays in them, he has committed a crime,

here they are, three things, do not use them,
all of them, avoid them, without arguing,
for to use them is not right, you have seen them,
towel and washing-blue, and powder, whoever uses them,
certainly on the Last Day the fire is his dwelling.

After the connection of Kano with the national railway network in 1911 and the foundation of the "new town" (Sabon Gari) to the east of the old city of Kano in 1912, the opportunities of contact with the Christian South had increased considerably. Implicit in the malamai's protest against the "new habits" was the protest against the collaboration of the emir with the British colonial power. The acknowledged leader of this internal opposition was Muhammad Salga. He was accepted in the early 1920s as leader by the majority of the Hausa traders in the northern part of the old city (Tahir 1975: 350–51). The association of Emir Abbas with the Tijâniyya can therefore be seen as an effort to take the wind out of the sails of this protest movement at a time when growing parts of the population of Kano began to identify the emir with the colonial administration. Under the influence of Emir Abbas, Wali Sulaiman, his most influential advisor, was to join the movement of tajdîd as well, and he received a silsila from Sharîf Ujdûd (ibid.: 342). Wali Sulaiman was of central importance for the later development of the Tijâniyya in Kano not only because he was to become the teacher and councillor of Emir Abdullahi Bayero (1926–54) but also because, being a member of the Fulani aristocracy of Kano, he could make the Tijâniyya respectable at the court and among the title-bearers, the Masu Sarauta (Quadri 1981: 92).

After the last visit of Sharîf Ujdûd to Kano in 1918, the movement of reorientation and of tajdîd within the Tijâniyya was strengthened by another visitor from the Maghrib, Shaykh Muḥammad 'Alamî (d. 1969 in Casablanca), who came to Kano in 1923. He had an ijâza from Shaykh Aḥmad Sukairij (1878–1944), one of the most important leaders of the Tijâniyya in the Maghrib at that time, and was thus in a position to introduce still another silsila into Kano (Paden 1973: 89). Shaykh 'Alamî not only spread his silsila in Kano, he also established a new zâwiya of the Tijâniyya in Unguwar Koki. After his departure, this center of the ṭarîqa was taken over by Muhammad Salga and expanded by him into one of the most important centers of the Tijâniyya in Kano (Quadri 1981: 93). In the 1920s and 1930s Muhammad Salga succeeded in uniting a large section of the trading community in Kano under his leadership. Apart from Muhammad Salga himself, his son Abdullahi Salga (d. 1962) as well as the respected scholar-trader Abubakar Mijinyawa from Unguwar Bakin Ruwa belonged to this economically very influential group of "Salgawa." Abubakar Mijinyawa took over the leadership of the group for a short period of time after the death of Muhammad Salga in 1938, before Abdullahi Salga assumed the leading role. After his death in 1962, his younger brother Mudi Salga (b. 1938) followed him in leading the Salgawa network. In the center of the network were also a number of other young scholar-traders who were not part of the Salgawa family and who later played important roles in Kano's religiously based network politics like Tijani Usman from Unguwar Zangon Barebare, Abubakar Atiku from Unguwar Sanka, the Kafanga brothers Hassan and Muhammad Sani from Tudun Wada, Umaru Falke from Unguwar Zangon Barebare, Shehu Usman Mai Hula from Unguwar Ciromawa, and Muhammad Dan Gwaggo "Dan Agogo" from Unguwar Alfindiki (Paden 1973: 86).

The second important network of Tijânî scholars in the 1920s and 1930s comprised members of the Fulani aristocracy under the leadership of Wali Sulaiman together with members of the influential Madabo clan led by the *Babban Malami Madabo,* Shaykh Adamu Abdurrahman Suyudi, popularly named "Malam Cindo" (Anwar 1989: 47). Both networks had started to diversify their salâsil connections at about the same time, but they represented different social strata of the Kano population: the Salgawa network stood for the group of rising, rich, and economically dynamic Hausa traders who wanted to put an end to the tutelage of the palace and despised the aristocracy. They protested against the westernization of the young and against the collaboration of the emir with the British colonialists. In their reorientation within the Tijâniyya they saw a way to renew the religion and to stop the moral decay. The network around Wali Sulaiman and the Madabo clan represented the traditional establishment of the scholars and the palace. They supported the policy of modernization initiated by the British, and they defended the position of the emir. In their reorientation within the Tijâniyya they saw a way to weaken the criticism directed against their policy by the Salgawa and other dissidents (Tahir 1975: 350–51).

The rise of the economically dynamic network of the Salgawa threatened the leading role of the Madabawa scholar-traders and in the 1920s finally led to the break between the Salgawa and the Madabawa, when Muhammad Salga established his image as an independent scholar with his own international salâsil connections. The ultimate parting of the ways came when Muhammad Salga started to reject the teachings of the *Babban Malami Madabo* as a sign of spiritual independence from his former Madabawa teachers (Anwar 1989: 44). In the 1920s, as an symbol of their independence, the Salgawa adopted the position of *qabḍ* (arms folded) during prayer, whereas the Madabawa were to remain with the position of *sadl* (arms outstretched). On doctrinal matters Muhammad Salga attacked a number of rituals practiced by the Madabawa like the collecting of alms (Sadakokin Mutuwa) for the poor during the ceremony of the burial of the dead (ibid.: 26–27). He argued that this custom was not in concordance with the sharî'a and even wrote a treatise concerning this question, *Risâlat as-su'âl* (The Book of Questions). The *Babban Malami Madabo* answered his former disciple in another booklet, *Hujâj al-'ulamâ' al-madabawiyîn* (The Arguments of the Madabawa Scholars), and defended the position of the Madabawa (ibid.: 45 ff.). As a result of these quarrels, the Tijâniyya, like the Qâdiriyya, were split up in the late 1930s into a number of competing networks not willing to submit themselves to a single authority. The task of uniting these networks fell to Ibrahim Niass for the Tijâniyya and to Nasiru Kabara for the Qâdiriyya.

2.2. *The Development of the Tijâniyya-Ibrâhîmiyya*

The development of the Tijâniyya in Kano and Northern Nigeria in the 1940s, 1950s, and 1960s was dominated by the efforts of the tajdîd of Ibrahim Niass. He succeeded in uniting the different competing networks of the Tijâniyya in Kano under his own authority and in establishing the Tijâniyya-Ibrâhîmiyya as a mass movement in Northern Nigeria. In the course of this development a number of religious scholars could build up a reputation of their own after having been nominated muqaddamûn by Ibrahim Niass, and they consequently set up their own networks of followers and disciples. After the withdrawal of Ibrahim Niass from Nigerian politics in 1963 the quarrels between these networks broke out again, thereby openly incurring a permanent weakening of the Tijâniyya in Northern Nigeria. As mentioned above, the Tijâniyya in Kano had split up into two great networks during the 1920s. Both sides tried to strengthen their respective positions spiritually by collecting as many salâsil as possible from different centers of authority of the ṭarîqa. In this process the elder chain of affiliation through al-Ḥâjj 'Umar lost its former importance, whereas more recent and direct links with North Africa became dominant. The differences between both networks were exploited by the emirs, especially by Abdullahi Bayero, so as to maintain their own claims of political and spiritual leadership. They wanted to be acknowledged as the spiritual leaders of all Muslims in Kano. If this should not be possible they wanted to at least prevent one network from becoming too strong. By way of these considerations Emir Abdullahi Bayero, who had become the successor of the Qâdiriyya-affiliated Emir Usman in 1926, supported the economically and numerically weaker group around Wali Sulaiman and the Madabawa (Tahir 1975: 358). He forced Muhammad Salga to give up the major zâwiya of the Tijâniyya in Unguwar Koki and to resettle in Gidan Salga (Unguwar Salga). Thus he removed the control of the most important zâwiya from the Salgawa (ibid.: 352). In addition, he was to make an unsucessful attempt to "buy over" fractions of the Salgawa network with the help of Wali Sulaiman (ibid.: 358).

In the face of this situation, in the 1930s the Salgawa again tried to draw support from the outside by using their extended networks of trade. In the early 1930s trade contacts had been established with Senegal, where the rise of Ibrahim Niass was already under way. The Salgawa established contacts with Niass and furthermore were to support in Kano the most important aristocratic opponent of Emir Abdullahi Bayero, Turaki Muhammad, who in 1926 failed to become the successor of Emir Usman. In order to thwart the strategy of the Salgawa, Wali Sulaiman proposed to Abdullahi Bayero that he should, as first emir of Kano, make the pilgrimage to Mecca in that year (1937) to meet Ibrahim Niass. In 1936 the latter had already begun his own first ḥajj via Morocco. The purpose of the meeting between Bayero and Niass should be "to outflank the Salgawa revivalists and to smother Turaki Muhamman's intrigues" (Tahir 1975: 361–62).

Ibrahim Niass was born in 1902 (according to some sources in 1900) in Taiba-Niassène in Senegal (for his biography see Hiskett 1980 and Maigari 1981). His father Abdullahi Niass had been initiated into the Tijâniyya by Muhammad Jallo and was connected through the latter with Ceerno Ahmadu and al-Ḥâjj 'Umar. He was also in possession of a second silsila, which he had obtained from Aḥmad Sukairij in Morocco on his way to Mecca. Ibrahim Niass had laid the foundations for his rise within the Tijâniyya in Senegal prior to meeting Abdullahi Bayero. After the death of his father in 1922 he refused to accept the succession of his elder brother Muhammad as khalîfa of the Niass branch of the Tijâniyya. In 1930 he left the seat of his brother in Taiba and started to construct a new settlement in the immediate neighborhood of Kaolack, the capital of the groundnut region of Siin-Saalum. The new settlement was called al-Madîna al-jadîda (the new town, the new Medina). Being a notably more dynamic and charismatic personality than his brother Muhammad, Ibrahim Niass rapidly succeeded in winning over a large part of the Niass clan and its followers. He underscored his claim to the leadership of the

Niassènes in 1930 when he gave up the practice of sadl. Sadl was accepted by the Maliki school of Islamic law as the correct position of arms during prayer. As with the Salgawa in Kano, Niass was to switch over to qabḍ, which was accepted by the other three schools of Islamic law (Interview Kane, 18 Jan. 1989). This move was to symbolize the break with the other branches of the Tijâniyya in Senegal, a clear and emphatic demonstration of his adherence to a greater Islamic world, where qabḍ and not sadl was the dominant practice. In the following year Niass established his reputation as a scholar of the Tijâniyya by publishing his major programmatic work entitled *Kâshif al-ilbâs 'an faiḍat al-khatam abî al-'abbâs* (The Exposer of the Veils of Overflowing Grace of the Seal of Abî al-'Abbâs), a book analyzed by Hiskett (1980) as well as Maigari (1981). In *Kâshif al-ilbâs* Ibrahim Niass explains above all his concept of spiritual education: *at-tarbiya al-ibrâhîmiya at-tijâniyya.*

The concept of *tarbiya* (education) is very ambiguous. Maigari (1981: 128) defined the purpose of tarbiya as *al-wuṣûl ilâ 'ilm al-ḥaqîqa bi-Allâhi* (The attainment of the knowledge of the truth of God). Tahir described tarbiya as a secret process of initiation with the purpose of wuṣûl (arrival at gnosis) (Tahir 1975: 126). The most exhaustive analysis of tarbiya in English is found in Hiskett's presentation (1980: 120 f.) of tarbiya. According to him, tarbiya is a process of initiation in five stages. In the first stage of this process the adept is shown by his Shaykh murabbî (Master of tarbiya) the unity of God (*tawḥîd*) and the creation of man through God. In a second step the disciple learns that the Prophet Muhammad was God's first creation. In the following stages, the chain of argument is continued by presenting Aḥmad at-Tijânî as a creation of the Prophet and Ibrahim Niass as a creation of Aḥmad at-Tijânî. Finally, the adept learns that Niass embodies the present earthly manifestation of the wholeness of creation (Hiskett 1980: 120–21). According to Umar (1988: 117–19) Niass's concept of tarbiya is derived from Aḥmad at-Tijânî's theory of the "seven strata of cosmic existence," an idea laid down in *Jawâhir al-ma'ânî* (The Diamonds of Meaning), the most important book of the Tijânîs. The theory of the "seven strata of cosmic existence" argues that all cosmic existence is arranged in seven circles or steps: From an exterior circle, called *al-ḥaqîqa al-aḥmadiyya* and known only to God himself, grace (*al-faiḍa*) flows down to the next circle, called *al-ḥaqîqa al-muḥammadiyya*. On this level the Prophet Muḥammad is to be found. From his circle al-faiḍa flows over to the third stratum, where all other prophets as well as Aḥmad at-Tijânî are placed. Aḥmad at-Tijânî, the Khâtim al-wilâya (the seal of the saints), has direct access to the Prophet. On the fourth circle the other saints are placed. On the fifth layer the adherents of the Tijâniyya are situated and on the sixth stratum the disciples of the other Sufi brotherhoods, whereas the seventh and last stratum seems to be reserved for the rest of the faithful.

This concept of tarbiya in the teaching of Ibrahim Niass, originally kept secret, was to repeatedly excite the criticism of other religious scholars. Thus in 1964 Abubakar Gumi asked Niass to explain his concept of tarbiya publicly. Niass answered with a treatise entitled *Ijâbât al-fatwâ* (The Answers to the Legal Opinion) stating that his concept of tarbiya was not a form of bid'a but had always been practiced, even in the times of the Prophet Muhammad. Apart from this only God alone is in the position to decide on questions of right or wrong. Accordingly tarbiya cannot be explained in ordinary language but is to be experienced (Paden 1973: 131). The process of tarbiya as prescribed by Ibrahim Niass has to be practiced under the supervision of a Shaykh murabbî. It should lead the adept to the realization that unlike the teachings of the other ṭuruq a long silsila is not needed in order to be spiritually connected with the Prophet and his flow of grace, but that the affiliation with Ibrahim Niass and the learning of tarbiya are sufficient to this end: The shortest way to the Prophet leads through Niass. In addition, Ibrahim Niass stressed that the process of tarbiya was in principle open to every Muslim who wanted to reach the ultimate perception of the truth of God. This perception was, however, closed (*maḥjûb*) to an uninitiated Muslim.

The distinctive character of the movement led by Ibrahim Niass, the Jamâʿat al-faiḍa (The community of grace), is therefore based on the stress he laid on the general openness and possibility of the experience of tarbiya for every Muslim. Paden emphasizes that this aspect was regarded by the followers of Niass in Kano as essential: "An important function of the Kano muqaddamûn has been to emphasize that any disciple can be trained in tarbiya, not only those who are saints or ascetics" (Paden 1973: 131). In this way Niass was able to reform the character of the Tijâniyya as a "scholars' affair," and make access to the Jamâʿat al-faiḍa possible for the less educated Muslims. All of them, and not only some chosen few Sufi-shuyûkh, now had the possibility of obtaining the grace of God through the process of tarbiya. Apart from this it was believed that grace through adherence to the Jamaʿat al-faiḍa was effective not only in a spiritual way, but also relevant in a healing and protective sense in all aspects of life (Umar 1988: 139). The traders and the businessmen of Kano and Northern Nigeria in particular believed that their affiliation with the Jamâʿat al-faiḍa had positive effects on their economic success. Thus Ibrahim Niass succeeded in popularizing his teachings and created thereby an important precondition for the expansion of the Tijâniyya as a mass movement.

Ibrahim Niass had to strive, however, to win public support for his teachings as well as for his claim to be the Ghauth az-zaman (the benefactor of the time, the highest rank of Sufi saints), a claim he had already made in the early 1930s. He thus traveled to Morocco in 1936 in order to meet some of the North African leaders of the Tijâniyya. The salâsil which he could claim as his own were until then exclusively derived from local Senegalese sources of authority. Therefore he was intent on creating new and more direct links to the original centers of the ṭarîqa. In Morocco Ibrahim Niass met Shaykh Aḥmad Sukairij, who until then had not been known in West Africa and who proffered him a new silsila. Aḥmad Sukairij furthermore acknowledged Niass's astounding knowledge and learning. This was used by Niass in a later booklet entitled *Rihla ḥijâziyya* (A Journey to the Hijâz) in order to claim that Aḥmad Sukairij had acknowledged him as the khalîfa of the Tijâniyya (Hiskett 1980: 103–4). As Sukairij had in fact adressed Niass as khalîfa in a number of letters of 1937, 1942, and 1943 (ibid.), it was still easier for Niass to spread his claim to be the leader of the Tijâniyya. Hiskett judges the authencity of this claim as follows:

> Of course this evidence does not prove that Shaykh Sukairij appointed Shaykh Ibrahim Niass as his sole khalîfa. He may have envisaged more than one incumbent to succeed him. Or possibly this form of address was dictated by courtesy. . . . But such considerations are of secondary importance. What matters is that it became widely accepted throughout West Africa that Aḥmad Sukairij really had appointed Shaykh Ibrahim Niass to the exclusive rank of khalîfa of the Tijâniyya. Shaykh Ibrahim Niass was therefore able to establish his claim beyond fear of serious rivalry. (Hiskett 1980: 104)

After his visit to Morocco Ibrahim Niass continued his pilgrimage to Mecca. There he could register two decisive successes in his effort to attain acknowledgment for his claim to leadership. First, the successor of Alfa Hâshim, Aḥmad b. 'Abd ar-Raḥmân, submitted to Niass's spiritual authority (Paden 1973: 86). Second, he met the Emir of Kano, Abdullahi Bayero, and his advisor, Wali Sulaiman. Both received a new silsila from him and acknowledged the authority and Niass's claim for leadership within the Tijâniyya (Maigari 1981: 111; Paden 1973: 98–99). Hiskett even argues that Abdullahi Bayero acknowledged Niass's claim to be the Ghauth az-zamân (Hiskett 1980: 103). Bayero furthermore invited Ibrahim Niass to visit him in Kano. For the moment the recognition of his leading role as khalîfa of the Tijâniyya by Aḥmad b. 'Abd ar-Raḥman was more important than his invitation to Kano, as numerous scholars of the Tijâniyya in West Africa had obtained their silsila from this source of authority. The acknowledgment of Niass as khalîfa by the successor of Alfa Hâshim made it easier for many scholars of the Tijâniyya to accept his spiritual leadership in later years.

During his return to Senegal Ibrahim Niass visited Morocco once again and met Aḥmad Sukairij a second time (Maigari 1981:

113; Hiskett 1980: 103). After his final return to Senegal Niass began to send his muqaddamûn into other West African countries to spread the influence of his movement more effectively. His most important emissaries were his relatives Aliyu Cissé and Ahmad Tijani, as well as his Mauritanian muqaddam Shaykh Muḥammad al-Hâdî b. Maulûd Faal. Muḥammad al-Hâdî was a grandson of Maulûd Faal from Shinqîṭ who had introduced the Tijâniyya into Senegal at the beginning of the nineteenth century (Paden 1973: 106). The centers of expansion of the Jamâ'at al-faiḍa were the British colonial territories in West Africa: Gambia, Sierra Leone, Gold Coast, and Nigeria (Hiskett 1980: 104). The first official visit of Niass to Nigeria took place in 1944, but was kept secret from the mass of followers of the Tijâniyya. Only the emir and Wali Sulaiman were informed. Nevertheless, Niass used the opportunity to distribute some copies of his work *Kâshif al-ilbâs* (Maigari 1981: 121–22). Paden argues that Niass's first visit to Kano already took place in 1937, shortly after meeting the Emir of Kano in Mecca (Paden 1973: 98). Hiskett and Maigari claim, however, that nowhere in his book concerning his first pilgrimage, published in 1960, does Niass refer to a visit to Kano. Furthermore, even if the visit by Ibrahim Niass was kept secret from the public, the British colonial administration would have been informed about it. However, the first British information about a secret visit by Niass to Kano refers to the visit in 1944 (Paden 1973: 106), precisely because this journey was not "official" and because the resulting difficulties of entry into Nigeria could be overcome only by the intervention of the Emir of Kano. The second, public, visit of Niass to Kano took place the following year (1945). This time he met not only the emir but also a number of selected malamai of the Tijâniyya and explained some aspects of his teachings to them. He gave new salâsil to some religious scholars and was acknowledged by them as the al-Quṭb al-ghauth az-zamân (the supreme succor of the time) (Maigari 1981: 123).

The first visit by Ibrahim Niass to Kano to be connected with a public appearance took place in 1951 and was part of a journey through the British colonies, financed by the British themselves. Thousands of followers of the Tijâniyya from all over Northern Nigeria had come to Kano to meet him and, with the assistance of the faithful in Kano, collected a sum of 13,000 pounds sterling for his support. The French authorities later relieved him of 11,000 pounds of this sum as settlement of his debts with them (NAK ZPF C.68: Appendix). The purpose of the 1951 journey was to establish the Tijâniyya as a counterforce to the radical independence movements in the British colonies (Tahir 1975: 362; Paden 1973: 109–10). Tahir even argues that the first meeting between Niass and Abdullahi Bayero in Mecca and Niass's invitation to Kano by Bayero was prearranged by the British with the aim of convincing the Tijâniyya of British colonial policies (Tahir 1975: 362). There exists no evidence of any kind for these latter considerations, however.

The British interests in supporting the Tijâniyya became still clearer in connection with the tour by another leader of the Tijâniyya, Sîdî b. 'Umar, which they also organized. Sîdî b. 'Umar was a direct descendant of Aḥmad at-Tijânî and since the early 1940s the khalîfa of the original center of the brotherhood in 'Ain Mâḍî (Algeria). His journey through Gambia, Sierra Leone, Gold Coast, Nigeria, and the Sudan took place in 1949 and 1950. In 1949 he spent twenty-three days in Kano, Kaduna, Zaria, Katsina, Gusau, and Adamaua, and in 1950 he again stayed for some days in Nigeria on his way back from the Sudan (Paden 1973: 108–9). In Nigeria Sîdî b. 'Umar succeeded in convincing a number of malamai of the Madabawa network who had not yet accepted Ibrahim Niass to submit to his authority (Quadri 1981: 210). This success was not only connected with the fact that Sîdî b. 'Umar had been authorized explicitly by Niass to undertake this tour (Paden 1973: 108) but also because he was representing as the khalîfa of 'Ain Mâḍî, another prestigious branch of the Tijâniyya in North Africa. Thus he could offer a new silsila and a smoother transition for the last opponents in Kano to join Niass through his mediation. It is not yet clear, however, why the British invited Sîdî b. 'Umar and not somebody else to visit their colonies. The tour of Sîdî b. 'Umar was perhaps connected with an effort of the Tijâniyya of 'Ain Mâḍî to push back the influence of the dominating Tijânî-center of Fez on the West African branches of the brotherhood. In this context 'Ain Mâḍî would have been prepared to collaborate with Niass, who in Senegal represented only a minority of the Tijâniyya and who therefore was intent on further outside support.

The purpose of Sîdî b. 'Umar's tour was primarily to set up committees in the British colonies which would induce a pro-British atmosphere among the followers of the Tijâniyya and oppose the independence movements (Interview Karsani, 29 Mar. 1989). This aim was achieved only partially, however. Whereas Sîdî b. 'Umar failed in the Sudan owing to counterpropaganda disseminated by Muḥammad al-Ḥâfiẓ al-Miṣrî, leader of the Egyptian Tijâniyya (Karsani 1985: 353 ff.), he failed in Nigeria according to the British colonial officer D. Hawkesworth because "he created something of a stir in the Northern province. He was foolish enough to offend the Sultan of Sokoto who is looked upon as the senior Muslim Emir of the Northern province" (ibid.: 354).

Even before the journeys of Muḥammad al-Hâdî b. Maulûd Faal (1949), Sîdî b. 'Umar (1949/50), and Ibrahim Niass (1951), the acknowledgment of Ibrahim Niass as leader of the Tijâniyya in Nigeria was prepared by some Nigerian trader-scholars. The first Nigerians who visited Niass in Kaolack were the Salgawa Umaru Falke, Tijani Usman, and Muhammad Sani Kafanga. Umaru Falke (1893–1962) had established an extended network of trade which reached to Southern Nigeria and Ghana. On his journeys he spread the silsila of Niass to Southern Nigeria. He had been initiated into the Tijâniyya as early as 1922 by Abû 'Abdallâh Muḥammad b. 'Alî b. Sirâj ad-Dîn and was appointed muqaddam of the brotherhood in 1925. He acquired the image of an outstanding scholar and collected a large library which was transferred after his death by John Paden to Northwestern University in Evanston, Illinois (Paden 1973: 265–66). Tijani Usman (1916–70) grew up together with Muhammad Salga in Kano. After the death of 'Abdullahi Salga in 1962 he was one of the outstanding leaders of the Tijâniyya in Kano. Like Umaru Falke he was also a trader and one of the cofounders of the Kano Citizen Trading Company (KCTC) (Paden 1973: 99).

Muhammad Sani Kafanga (1909–89) was another famous leader of the Tijâniyya in Kano. He originally studied under the supervision of his father, a Kanuri *malam* from Kibiya (Rano). After completing his studies with Malam Na'iya in Zaria, Malam Kwasau in Birnin Kebbi, and Malam Muhammad Salga and Malam Mijinyawa in Kano, he started a small trade in bicycles in Fagge. Later he concentrated on the trade in gems and mirrors on the Kurmi market in the old city of Kano. Aside from his economic activities he acquired an image as a scholar and wrote about fifty small booklets. His center of teaching was the Sanka mosque in Unguwar Sanka which had been the zâwiya of the Salgawa after their expulsion from Koki. Like Tijani Usman and Umaru Falke he was a follower of the NPC and later opposed Emir Muhammad Sanusi's claim of overall spiritual leadership within the Tijâniyya in Nigeria (Interview Kane, 18 Jan. 1989). Until his death on 29 May 1989 he was one of the most renowned religious scholars of the Tijâniyya in Kano. He was a close friend of Nasiru Kabara, the leader of the Qâdiriyya, and had as one of his disciples Aminu Dantata of the great trading house of the Dantata family, who in turn was one of the most important financiers of the Qâdiriyya in Kano. In 1972 he wrote in the name of the Tijâniyya the reply to Abubakar Gumi's attack on the Sufi brotherhoods, *al-'Aqida aṣ-ṣaḥiḥa* (The Right Belief) (*The Pen,* 1989 no. 1: 11).

These three young Tijani scholars from Kano came to Kaolack in 1946 and with their visit triggered off a constant stream of further visitors from Nigeria to Kaolack. In the course of their visits Ibrahim Niass appointed them as shuyûkh murabbi whereby they became the first scholars of the Tijâniyya in Kano authorized to guide the process of tarbiya. As Niass was at that point of time already acknowledged as khalîfa of the Tijâniyya by the Emir of Kano and Wali Sulaiman, the appointment of three leading representatives of the Salgawa network meant that he was also able also win over this group within the Tijâniyya. In this way Niass succeeded in being recognized as leader of both of the important networks of the brotherhood in Kano by the late 1940s.

The acknowledgment of Ibrahim Niass by the majority of the malamai of the Tijâniyya initially in Kano, later in Nigeria as a whole, was, however, not the result of an almost revolutionary "realignment" (Paden 1973: 265–66) in a relatively short period of time (1949–51). Rather, it is to be explained as the result of the combination and interaction of a multitude of factors over a period of about fourteen years (1937–51). The specific causes for the success of Niass among the traders and scholars in Kano were the following:

1. The situation of competition between the two great networks of the Tijâniyya in Kano itself. Niass was not affiliated with one of these groups and could therefore act as an intermediary between them.
2. Both networks tried to use Niass's prestige and salâsil for their own aims. They needed him and could therefore be subtly manipulated and played off against each other by Niass.
3. Niass, through his visits to Morocco and the Hijâz and on the basis of his being acknowledgment by Aḥmad Sukairij as khalîfa of the Tijâniyya, was in possession of the necessary direct links to some external centers of authority of the Tijâniyya.
4. The alliance with Niass proved beneficial to the religious and political ambitions of the Emir of Kano. He could stress his independence from Sokoto by establishing Kano as a spirtual center of the Tijâniyya and as a counterweight to Sokoto.
5. After an initial policy of mistrust during the 1940s, the British attempted to gain the support of the Tijâniyya as part of their colonial policy. On account of this strategy they did not block the activities of selected representatives of the Tijâniyya.

6. Niass's teachings proved highly attractive to less sophisticated Muslims as a result of his specific interpretation of tarbiya. Initially his teachings were accepted by the traders not only because they could acquire through the process of tarbiya a direct connection with the Prophet but also because they believed they could obtain a relatively easy access to higher spiritual knowledge and, in addition, effective spiritual protection for their trading enterprises. This easy access to higher Sufi revelations was denied to them in the Qâdiriyya or in the 'Umarian branch of the Tijâniyya.
7. Another very significant point was that Niass stressed from an early period in his career the importance of modern Islamic education, a demand which found special appeal among the young Muslim generation in Nigeria. In his efforts to boost a modern concept of Islamic education he was the first religious scholar in Nigeria to utilize the methods of modern mass media, especially the radio, to disseminate his views. This led to a conflict with the Emir of Zaria, Ja'afar, who was still affiliated with the 'Umarian branch of the Tijâniyya. Ja'afar protested against the use of the radio for the recitation of the Qur'ân, arguing that this constituted a bid'a. Niass retorted that a distinction had to be made between "evil" and "recommended" bida'. The use of the radio for the propagation of Islam should in this context be regarded as a recommendable innovation like the use of the airplane for the transport of the pilgrims to the holy places as it was useful for the dissemination and strengthening of Islam. Niass was supported in this debate by his opponents Nasiru Kabara and Abubakar Gumi, and in view of this unanimous front of opposition to his outmoded views, the Emir of Zaria was compelled to accept defeat (Quadri 1981: 234).
8. Niass and his Jamâ'at al-faiḍa (the community of grace) distinguished themselves by emphasizing the practice of qabḍ. Although Niass had not been the first in Nigeria to practice qabḍ, according to Anwar, "his association with it has given

the practice an undue significance" (Anwar 1989: 62). Another distinguishing feature of the Jamâ'at al-faiḍa was the celebration of the Prophet's birthday (Maulid an-nabî). On the occasion of the Maulid an-nabî the Tijâniyya-Ibrâhîmiyya organized throughout Nigeria Tafsîr meetings, recitations of the Qur'ân, and recitations of poems in praise of the Prophet (Madh an-nabî). These celebrations became a symbol of affiliation with the Jamâ'at al-faiḍa and in addition attracted a large and growing number of nonaffiliated Muslims. In this way the celebrations of the Maulid an-nabî, the practice of qabḍ, and the public dhikr (*waẓîfa*) of the Tijâniyya-Ibrâhîmiyya were to evolve into further stimuli for the mobilization of Muslims for the Tijâniyya-Ibrâhîmiyya (Quadri 1981: 234).

9. Finally, the extensive religious network of the Tijâniyya-Ibrâhîmiyya offered the traders in Kano new possibilities and a basis for their commercial activities outside Nigeria in many other West African countries. This opportunity afforded them the security to expand their economic activities under the umbrella of the Tijânî network (Tahir 1975: 366). The affiliation of successful traders with the Jamâ'at al-faiḍa endorsed the image of the movement as a ṭarîqa of the "sucessful." The combination of spiritual and economic factors was important in particular as far as the support of the Jamâ'at al-faiḍa from the traders was concerned. Lovejoy mentions that in a census among traders in Kano in 1970, 137 (70%) out of 196 were affiliated with the Tijânîyya and only 33 (17%) with the Qâdiriyya (Lovejoy 1980: 100).

The economic efficiency of many members of the Tijâniyya-Ibrâhîmiyya was used, however, as a pretext by the opponents of the ṭarîqa, namely, members of the Qâdiriyya, to criticize the spiritual claims of the Tijâniyya. Thus in the 1950s the Wazirin Sokoto Junaidu criticized "Ibrahim Niass's love of money," whereas other scholars of the Qâdiriyya reproached him by referring to him degradingly as merely a successful farmer mixed up in commerce. Therefore his claim to be the Ghauth az-zamân would be questionable (Tahir 1975: 515). The Kano-based scholar Abubakar Atiku answered these attacks in the name of the Tijâniyya by arguing that the Ghauth az-zamân usually assumes the "character of his time." Therefore it would not be possible to define him by any specific forms of external behavior or appearance, or by the character of his occupation. Ascetism (*zuhd*) could thus not be seen as a precondition to holiness; rather, the strength of the baraka of a saint was demonstrated by the extent of his economic success: the greater his wealth, the greater his baraka (ibid.).

The combination of factors mentioned above made possible the transformation of the Tijâniyya in Kano from a scholars' ṭarîqa to a religious mass movement. After winning over the influential trader-scholar networks of Kano in the 1940s, the dissemination of the Tijâniyya among the Muslims was to begin in the early 1950s with the tours of Ibrahim Niass, Sîdî b. 'Umar, and Muḥammad al-Hâdî. The last named alone was able to register more than one thousand new disciples in the course of his journey through Northern Nigeria in 1949 (Maigari 1981: 131–32). The following of the Tijâniyya-Ibrâhîmiyya not only grew in the urban centers of the North like Kano but was also propagated by the trader-scholars in the trading outposts of the Hausa in the cities of the South (see Cohen 1969). Finally they pushed further along the new roads and railway tracks into the rural regions and established bases in rural centers like Gusau, Argungu, Kaura-Namoda, Funtua, Malumfashi, and Ringim. In the process of their expansion into the rural regions the trader-scholar networks like that of Uba Abdurrahman Ringim in Ringim (Kano State) were of foremost importance. They drew their clients and followers into the Tijâniyya and thereby established cells for the further spread of the ṭarîqa in the hinterland of the great cities and the smaller rural market towns. When in 1954 Muhammad Sanusi, a close friend of Niass, followed Abdullahi Bayero as Emir of Kano, the Tijâniyya-Ibrâhîmiyya in Northern Nigeria experienced a climax in its development. The new emir did his utmost in the next nine years of his reign to promote the Tijâniyya-Ibrâhîmiyya in Kano as the dominating religous force and to present himself as its leader by the grace of Niass.

Another factor which influenced the development of the Tijâniyya-Ibrâhîmiyya in the 1950s was the connection with the populist opposition movement, the Northern Elements Progressive Union (NEPU) under the leadership of Aminu Kano and Sa'd Zungur, whose center of activities was Kano. In the course of increasing politicization of public life since the late 1940s, more and more young followers of the Tijâniyya felt themselves drawn to this party. The political idol of Aminu Kano was the Egyptian President Jamâl 'Abd an-Nâṣir who at the same time had established contacts with Niass (Paden 1973: 145). It has to be noted in this context that Niass had won a reputation in the 1950s not only as the leader of the most powerful religious mass movement in West Africa but also as a leading representative of an Islamic policy of tajdîd in Senegal. Since 1953 he had been connected with the Union Culturelle Musulmane (UCM), a modern Islamic organization strongly influenced by Salafi ideas. Niass, like the UCM, was to propagate the importance of the Arabic language and of a modern Islamic education in Senegal. On the basis of this connection and on account of his position as leader of the strongest religous movement in West Africa, Niass was accepted as founding member of the "fundamentalist" pro-Saudi Râbiṭat al-'Alam al-Islâmî (Islamic World League) which had been created in Mecca in 1962. Niass was a member of this organization despite his Sufi orientation until his death in 1975 (Interview Kane, 18 Jan. 1989). The increasing radicalization of many young Tijânîs, however, was seen by the leader of the ruling party in Northern Nigeria, Ahmadu Bello, as well as by a number of conservative malamai of the Qâdiriyya and the Tijâniyya as a threat for the further development of their own policies in the North. When on the occasion of a public *tafsîr* (interpretation and exegesis of the Qur'ân) in 1956 Nasiru Kabara forbade his followers to join the NEPU, some malamai of the Tijânîyya like Tijani Usman, Muhammad Sani Kafanga, and Uba Ringim, all members of the Salgawa network, followed suit (Interview Kane, 18 Jan. 1989). Ahmadu Bello supported this group within the Tijâniyya by in 1956 temporarily suspending the ban on the public performance of the waẓîfa by the Tijâniyya (Quadri 1981: 355). Nevertheless, many young Tijânis prefered to keep their links with the NEPU and to end their affiliation with the above mentioned malamai of the Tijâniyya (Tahir 1975: 438). An official political alliance between the NEPU and the Tijâniyya-Ibrâhîmiyya was nevertheless realized only after the deposition of Muhammad Sanusi in 1963. Sanusi had until then been one of the leading politicians of the NPC in the North. In protest his followers founded in 1963 a regional party named the Kano People's Party (KPP) which recruited its followers chiefly among the Tijani supporters of Sanusi.

The dynamism of the Tijâniyya-Ibrâhîmiyya was reflected in its development as an organization. Ibrahim Niass had originally founded the Jamâ'at al-faida in Senegal in 1930. In the course of its expansion throughout West Africa after 1946 the movement was renamed Jamâ'at Anṣâr ad-Dîn (the Community of the Supporters of the Religion). Under the umbrella of this organization a number of smaller local or regional groups came into existence. Among them was the Jamâ'at Anwâr al-Faiḍat (the Community of the Rays of Grace) founded in 1958 in Kaduna by al-Ḥâjj Shittu Daniyal. It was, however, an organization that was to remain restricted to that town. Significantly more powerful was another organization named Fityân al-Islâm (the Heroes of Islam; Hausa: Jam'iyyar Samarin Musulmi na Nijeriya). The Fityân al-Islâm were founded by the leader of the Salgawa network in Kano, Mudi Salga, on 11 November 1963. It originated as a reaction to the establishment of the dissident Aḥmadiyya movement in Kano in 1962 and as a forum of the conservative Kano malamai against the modernizing efforts of Ahmadu Bello and his new Islamic organizations like the Kaduna-Sokoto-dominated Jamâ'at Naṣr al-Islâm (JNI, the Association for the Support of Islam) (Anwar 1989: 152). The Kano malamai, and among them especially those from the Salgawa network, regarded the JNI as an attempt by Bello "to convert them into salaried staff of the NPC government" (ibid.: 156) in order to control and neutralize them. Mudi Salga was elected first national president of the Fityân al-islâm and was consequently accused of "enmity towards the NPC and connections with the NEPU" (ibid.: 160), an accusation which led to a reorganization of the movement: Abubakar Atiku took over as national president with Shehu Maihula as his deputy, whereas Tijani Usman was elected secretary general with Mudi Salga as deputy. Muhammad Sani Kafanga took over the office of treasurer, Faruq Salga was nominated auditor general, and Ado Sanusi, Muhammad Sanusi's son, became liaison officer (ibid.). After Bello's death in 1966 Mudi Salga was reelected national president with the Qâdiri Malam Zubairu Kassim as his deputy (ibid.: 161).

Although the Fityân al-Islâm were accused from the very beginning of supporting the deposed Emir of Kano, Muhammad Sanusi, and although they constantly refused to join the JNI, Ahmadu Bello was finally convinced by the secretary general of the JNI itself, Abubakar an-Nafaty, that the Fityân al-Islâm would not work as a force of opposition to the JNI and that it would be more useful to win over the young generation. As a result Bello registered the organization in 1963 (Anwar 1989: 165). In the 1960s the Fityân al-Islâm rapidly became the most dynamic Islamic organization in Northern Nigeria and was soon able to set up regional headquarters in all the Northern provinces, especially Sokoto, Niger, Kaduna, Plateau, Bauchi, Gongola, and Bornu, whereas Kano remained the national headquarters (Quadri 1981: 362–63, 408). In 1989 the Fityân al-Islâm had branches in fourteen out of twenty-one federal states. The movement was financed by membership fees, contributions, and donations. In 1972 the first modern Islamiyya school of the Fityân al-Islâm was ready to be opened, and by 1983 the organization controlled 138 schools with 985 classes and 11,835 students in Kano state alone. In 1983 the Fityân al-Islâm were in control of 894 mosques in the whole of Northern Nigeria (Anwar 1989: 170), a factor which strenghtened its position as the major counterforce of the two Sufi brotherhoods in the struggle against their opponents, the 'Yan Izala. The Fityân al-Islâm also maintained a team of preachers in order to fight the anti-Sufi propaganda of the 'Yan Izala. The leader of this team of counterpropagandists was Shaykh Dahiru Bauchi (Quadri 1981: 408).

The deposition of Muhammad Sanusi that led to the cancellation of further visits to Nigeria by Ibrahim Niass triggered off a crisis in the further development of the Tijâniyya-Ibrâhîmiyya that has endured. Although Niass had nominated his friend and ally Muhammad Sanusi as his successor as leader of the Tijâniyya-Ibrâhîmiyya in Nigeria, the deposed Emir of Kano was not able to enforce acceptance of his leading authority within the brotherhood. The reasons were that Sanusi was regarded not as a religious scholar but as a politician and that considerable aversion against him existed especially within the Salgawa network in Kano. Thus instead of Sanusi, the official successor to Niass, a collective leadership took over in Kano in the 1960s. The group consisted of the Salgawa malamai Tijani Usman, Abubakar Atiku, Muhammad Sani Kafanga, Shehu Mai Hula, and Mudi Salga. This Kano-based network could not, however, prevent the development of new and independent branches of the Tijâniyya-Ibrâhîmiyya in other regions of the North. These new regional networks did not recognize Kano's claim for overall leadership and instead set up their own, autonomous networks and established their own, independent links to Kaolack, Fez, and Cairo. In addition, it ought not be overlooked that the Kano leadership was already quite old. In 1962 Abdullahi Salga and Umaru Falke had died, and in 1970 Tijani Usman and in 1974 Abubakar Atiku were to follow. This led to a change of generation in the leading circles of the Tijâniyya in Kano. With the exception of Muhammad Sani Kafanga, Mudi Salga, and Khalifa Isma'il Ibrahim, the emerging young leaders were too young to be accepted by the other ambitious networks in Northern Nigeria as the principal leaders of the Tijâniyya-Ibrâhîmiyya. In addition to this even within Kano old rivalries and quarrels broke out again and developed into bitter feuds like that between Muhammad Sani Kafanga and Khalifa Isma'il Ibrahim, who in 1970 had become the successor of Tijani Usman as leader of his network (Interview Kane, 18 Jan. 1989).

As a consequence, a multitude of locally competing networks developed within the Tijâniyya in the 1970s. No scholar within the brotherhood since the withdrawal of Ibrahim Niass in 1963 has been in a position to achieve a similarly uncontested authority as leader of the whole ṭarîqa in Nigeria. By the mid-1980s the Tijâniyya presented the picture of an accumulation of numerous quarreling networks, and only some of them have gained regional importance. Apart from the above mentioned Kano networks, these centers of power within the Tijâniyya are grouped essentially around the following malamai: in Kano the scholar-traders Uba Abdurrahman Ringim, who also supports Shaykh Dahiru Bauchi, Uba Waru, who supports Khalifa Isma'il Ibrahim, as well as the entrepreneurs Isiaku Rabi'u, Aminu Dantata, Uba Lida, and Aru Dandawaki. Another Kano-born trader and businessman, Garba Hamza (Hamza Holding Ltd.), is a major supporter of the Tijâniyya in Lagos (Interview Kane, 18 Jan. 1989). Outside of Kano there exist strong Tijânî networks in Maiduguri (Bornu) under the leadership of Ibrâhîm Ṣâliḥ, Shaykh Abû l-Fâtiḥ, and Shaykh al-Miskin, in Bauchi (Shaykh Dahiru Bauchi), Kaduna (Shaykh Umar Sanda, Shaykh Siraj, and Malam Audu Bida), and Jos (al-Ḥâjj Ṣâliḥ Nakande, who died in 1985/86) (Quadri 1981: 288–93). The breakup of the Tijâniyya-Ibrâhîmiyya since the late 1960s into numerous networks has thrown the ṭarîqa into a serious crisis (Kane 1989a: 30 ff.). This crisis had disastrous effects especially after the foundation of the 'Yan Izala-movement, which concentrated its attacks on the Sufi ("La contrérie . . .") brotherhoods after 1978 almost exclusively on the Tijâniyya. In light of the obvious weakness of the ṭarîqa, the 'Yan Izala were for a long time very successful in their efforts to fight and destroy the Tijâniyya.

2.3. The Development of the Qâdiriyya-Nâṣiriyya

The movement of tajdîd within the Qâdiriyya in Kano and Northern Nigeria which was initiated and led by Nasiru Kabara can be understood properly only in the context of its struggle with the competing networks of the Tijâniyya-Ibrâhîmiyya. Since its inception the Qâdiriyya-Nâṣiriyya was under pressure from the dynamic expansion of the Tijâniyya-Ibrâhîmiyya. In his efforts to revitalize the Qâdiriyya Nasiru Kabara used strategies which strikingly resembled those of the Tijânîyya-Ibrâhîmiyya. By using them Kabara succeeded in curing the paralysis of the Qâdiriyya and transforming the ṭarîqa into a religious mass movement along the lines of the Tijâniyya-Ibrâhîmiyya.

Nasiru Kabara was born on 18 April 1925 in Guringawa near Kano. His great-grandfather, Malam Muhammad Na Kabara (c. 1760–1844), had been a student at the Sankoré mosque in Timbuktu. At the end of the eighteenth century he had emigrated from his hometown, Kabara, the river harbor of Timbuktu on the Niger, to Hausaland. Living in Hausaland as a migrant scholar like Usman dan Fodio, he finally settled in Kano, where in 1787 he was to found a Qur'ânic school (Ahmed 1986: 171). Although he refused active participation in the jihâd, afterwards he received a piece of land close to a loam pit opposite the emir's palace. There he established a house and a little mosque. He also founded an 'ilm school in his mosque and thereby established the teaching tradition of the Kabara family in Kano (Yusuf 1983: 32). Kabara's father died a few years after his son's birth in 1927. His education was according to tradition taken over by his uncle Ibrahim Ahmad al-Kanawi Natsuguni, a religious scholar of great fame in Kano. Ibrahim Natsuguni served under four emirs of Kano (Aliyu Baba, 'Abbas, Usman, and Abdullahi Bayero) as councillor in the emir's council. His house was in Unguwar Madabo, and the emphasis of his teaching was on *fiqh* (jurisprudence), *tauḥîd* (theology), *taṣawwuf* (Sufism), and *'ilm al-falak* (astrology). Paden describes him as "the dominant figure that linked the 19th and 20th century Qâdiriyya in Kano" (Paden 1973: 156).

Ibrahim Natsuguni was not only the most important teacher of Nasiru Kabara before 1937, but he remained influential for his further development until his death in 1949. Kabara was not, however, to receive his basic religious instruction through Natsuguni alone, but also through Malam Muhammad Soron Dinki with whom he was to learn the Qur'ân until 1933. After completing his education at the the Qur'ânic school, he attended a number of 'ilm schools of other malamai like Shaykh Ibrahim b. al-Ustadh, al-Ḥâjj Mustafa Biçi, Shaykh 'Abd al-Karim al-Yunis, and Shaykh Maula 'Abd ar-Rahman (S. Kabara 1981: 49 ff.). When the Emir of Kano and Wali Sulaiman went on their hajj to Mecca in 1937, Kabara used the opportunity to give Wali Sulaiman a letter for the khalîfa of the Qâdiriyya-Sammâniyya in Mecca, Shaykh Abû l-Ḥasan as-Sammânî. In this letter he asked the leader of this branch of the Qâdiriyya to initiate him into the Qâdiriyya-Sammâniyya and to receive an *ijâza* (authorization) as his muqaddam. Shaykh Abû l-Ḥasan was evidently astonished by the degree of learning that the twelve-year-old boy demonstrated in this letter and thus granted his request by appointing him, again by letter, his muqaddam and leader of the Qâdiriyya-Sammâniyya in Kano (Adamu 1968: 48). As the Qâdiriyya-Sammâniyya was not present at all in Northern Nigeria at this time, Shaykh Abû l-Ḥasan had nothing to lose in appointing Kabara his muqaddam, but everything to win. In this way Kabara was able to introduce a fifth silsila of the Qâdiriyya to Kano. At the same time he had accomplished an initial step toward the unification of the Qâdiriyya in Kano under his leadership. His nomination as muqaddam of the Qâdiriyya-Sammâniyya was not only to gain for Kabara the prestige of being the local leader of this new branch of the ṭarîqa but was also to represent his first direct connection to an external source of authority within the brotherhood. Accordingly Kabara began his personal endeavor to renew and diversify his salâsil: He established direct contacts to the centers of origin of the different branches of the Qâdiriyya, and once in possession of the new salâsil he became the focus of attention for other followers and malamai of the Qâdiriyya in Kano and Nigeria who wanted to renew their own salâsil through him and who therefore had to recognize his superiority. Thus between 1937 and the late 1950s Kabara's bid for leadership within the Qâdiriyya in Kano and Nigeria was essentially successful.

After his nomination as muqaddam of the Qâdiriyya-Sammâniya Nasiru Kabara consolidated his connections with this branch of the Qâdiriyya by establishing during the course of his own first ḥajj in 1949 direct personal contacts with the leader of the Qâdiriyya-Sammâniyya in the Sudan, Shaykh Muḥammad al-Fâtiḥ b. Qarîb Allâh (Adamu 1968: 49). As early as 1941 he had received the silsila of the Qâdiriyya-Salâmiyya, which at that time continued to be led by Muḥammad as-Sayyid Sa'd (Paden 1973: 157). Adamu Na Ma'aji, a muqaddam of this branch of the Qâdiriyya and one of the teachers of Kabara, supported him in his efforts to unite the Qâdiriyya in Kano. Muḥammad as-Sayyid Sa'd was, however, not yet prepared to accept the claim for leadership by Kabara and to give up his control over the Halla-Halla mosque and zâwiya. Thus for the time being Kabara had to postpone his attempt to achieve acknowledgment of his authority within the Qâdiriyya-Salâmiyya. The situation was different in the case of the Qâdiriyya-Shâdhiliyya and the Qâdiriyya-'Arûsiyya. One of the muqaddamûn of Shaykh Sîdî Muḥammad, the leader of the Qâdiriyya-Shâdhiliyya, Aḥmad b. 'Ali from Unguwar Cediyar Hudu, proved to be a particularly dynamic personality. He had an influential position within the Qâdiriyya-Shâdhiliyya and took over the leadership of the Qâdiriyya-'Arûsiyya which had stagnated until then (Ahmed 1986: 207). Aḥmad b. 'Ali did not only become one of the most important disciples and followers of Nasiru Kabara, he also represented like Kabara a younger generation of scholars of the Qâdiriyya in Kano who supported the revitalization and tajdîd of the ṭarîqa and who were willing to overcome the existing network rivalries. Aḥmad b. 'Ali's center was the new mosque of the Qâdiriyya-Shâdhiliyya which had been established by Shaykh 'Alî Mûsa in Unguwar Shatshari (Paden 1973: 152).

In this historical context, which was characterized in the late 1940s and early 1950s by the existence of a number of competing networks within the Qâdiriyya in Kano, Nasiru Kabara recognized the need to establish a direct link to the original center of the ṭarîqa in Baghdad. In 1953 he therefore traveled there together with his trader-disciple Sanusi Dantata and met the supreme leader of the brotherhood, Shaykh Sharîf Ibrâhîm Saif ad-Dîn al-Jîlânî (S. Kabara 1981: 113). The khalîfa of the Qâdiriyya in Baghdad appointed Kabara in the course of his visit supreme leader of all branches of the Qâdiriyya in West Africa, a gesture signifying acknowledgment of Kabara's efforts. As with Ibrahim Niass's alleged nomination as khalîfa of the Tijâniyya for West Africa by Aḥmad Sukairij in 1936, this decisive event in the biography of Nasiru Kabara likewise requires cautious interpretation. It is first of all questionable whether the khalîfa of the Qâdiriyya in Baghdad, as is claimed by Kabara and his followers, actually bestowed such a prestigious title and honor on a scholar who not only was absolutely unknown to him, but also relatively young (twenty-eight years old). This problem is not, however, really that relevant for the further development of the ṭarîqa. Rather more important is the fact that Kabara actually met the khalîfa of the Qâdiriyya and that he did in fact receive from him a new silsila. The directness and brevity of this silsila alone had enough weight to enormously increase Nasiru Kabara's prestige and baraka in Kano and Nigeria. Likewise, Shaykh Saif ad-Dîn had nothing to lose and everything to gain: The zâwiya of the Qâdiriyya in Baghdad had long since lost its influence on the development of the other branches of the Qâdiriyya, and the visit of a scholar from Nigeria could therefore be regarded as a revalorization of Baghdad. How important Kabara has become for Baghdad in the last few decades is indicated by the fact that Shaykh Saif ad-Dîn has visited Kabara twice already in Kano on the occasion of the Maulid 'Abd al-Qâdir. Usually, it is the disciple who visits his shaykh and not vice versa. Aside from the question as to whether Shaykh Saif ad-Dîn actually had the authority and the power to appoint Kabara as the khalîfa of all branches of the Qâdiriyya in

West Africa, the latter had obtained through his visit in Baghdad a tremendous boost to his personal standing: He had de facto become the first scholar of the Qâdiriyya in Nigeria and the whole of West Africa to have established a direct personal link to the spiritual center and the supreme leader of the brotherhood. Thus he had created the formal preconditions for the further acceptance of his authority by the other branches of the ṭarîqa.

Nasiru Kabara's disciple and follower Aḥmad b. 'Ali, the leader of the Qâdiriyya-Shâdhiliyya and the Qâdiriyya-'Arûsiyya, was the first to acknowledge Kabara's claim for overall leadership within the Qâdiriyya. The leader of the Qâdiriyya-Salâmiyya, Muḥammad as-Sayyid Sa'd, continued, however, to refuse to submit to Kabara's authority. The latter reacted by imposing a boycott on the Halla-Halla mosque after his return from Baghdad and by establishing a new mosque in his house in Unguwar Kabara, which rapidly became the center for the Qâdiriyya-Nâṣiriyya in Kano. In 1956 Muḥammad as-Sayyid Sa'd could no longer resist the pressure of Kabara and his growing following and finally accepted his claim to leadership (Paden 1973: 157). Thereby Kabara achieved the unification of all branches of the Qâdiriyya in Kano under his authority by 1956. Nevertheless he intended to strengthen his authority further in the following years to consolidate his spiritual influence. He therefore tried to establish personal links to other important centers of the Qâdiriyya outside Nigeria. In the course of these efforts he extended his connections to the Qâdiriyya-Kuntiyya, to which he was already linked through a silsila of the Qâdiriyya-Ahl al-Bait (Usman dan Fodio's silsila), which he had received from his uncle Ibrahim Natsuguni (ibid.: 156), and established another contact to the old Shinqîṭ center of learning in Mauretania by establishing links with Shaykh Muḥammad al-Mujtabî ash-Shinqîṭî (S. Kabara 1981: 114). He also expanded his links to the Qâdiriyya-'Arûsiyya by visiting the leader of this branch of the ṭarîqa, Shaykh Sayyid al-Hâdî as-Sûr, in the Fezzan and by forging links with the Qâdiriyya-Manzaliyya, whose leader Shaykh Muḥammad aṣ-Ṣâdiq al-Imâm al-Manzalî al-Qâdirî he visited in 1969 (ibid.: 116). While Nasiru Kabara was thus able to pursue his claim for leadership within the Qâdiriyya in Kano and great parts of Northern Nigeria until the late 1950s, the old center of the Qâdiriyya in Sokoto continued to resist his efforts. Ahmed characterizes the situation in the 1960s as follows: "Since about 1958 he had been considered the leader of the Qâdiriyya in West Africa although some Sokoto oriented and other traditional Qâdiriyya leaders seem not to accord recognition to this claim with enthusiasm" (Ahmed 1986: 212).

Acknowledgment by Sokoto of the leading role taken by Nasiru Kabara came as late as the 1970s under growing pressure from Abubakar Gumi and the 'Yan Izala. The breakthrough occurred in 1978: During the course of one of his regular visits to the tomb of Usman dan Fodio, the Sultan of Sokoto handed Kabara the "sword of the army of Usman dan Fodio" with the mission to lead the Qâdiriyya in Nigeria in its struggle against the 'Yan Izala (Interview S. U. Kabara, 9 Mar. 1988). This internal success was complemented in 1987 by a further external success, when the supreme khalîfa of the Qâdiriyya, Shaykh Saif ad-Dîn, appointed Kabara, during his visit in Kano on the occasion of the Maulid 'Abd al-Qâdir, "supreme leader" of the Qâdiriyya for the whole of Africa (*The Pen* 1987, no. 1). With this promotion Nasiru Kabara attained a degree of national and international authority and recognition in the West African context comparable only to the position Ibrahim Niass had at the climax of his career in the early 1960s.

The success of Nasiru Kabara can, however, only partially be explained by his erudition and his efforts to establish direct links to different centers of the brotherhood. The faith in Kabara's baraka is also supported by the fact that since the 1950s a growing number of disciples and influential followers have gathered around him. This following regards Kabara not only as their spiritual leader, but also as their advisor in earthly affairs. They support Kabara financially "in exchange" for his spiritual protection of their commercial enterprises. The combination of these spiritual and economic factors has again strengthened Kabara's political importance. The number and the socio-economic weight of his following are therefore in addition to the strenght of his baraka the determining factors of his "bargaining power" with other religious and social power groups in Nigeria.

The establishment of Nasiru Kabara's power base began in Kano itself. After his return from Baghdad he founded a new zâwiya in his house in Unguwar Kabara which was to become the center of his activities and his teaching. He began by appointing a number of his disciples as muqaddamûn, whereby he not only stressed the necessity that they already possess a certain degree of erudition, but also as a further precondition that they also taught in their new mosques. Among these early Kabara muqaddamûn was Malam Yusufu Abdullahi Makwarari. Through him the influential and wealthy network of the Makwarari clan was integrated into Kabara's own network (see the overview of Nasiru Kabara's network in Appendix 1) (Ahmed 1986: 211). The focal points of the expansion of the Qâdiriyya-Nâṣiriyya in Kano were the Unguwoyi Makwarari, Alfindiki, Koki, Bakin Zuwo, Limanci, Fagge, and Tudun Nufawa. At the same time he also began to gather followers in the region of Kano and to appoint some of them as muqaddamûn. Muslims from the Kano area still visit Kabara today to ask him to act as patron of a new mosque, as I was able to witness personally on 21 February 1987. Kabara was especially successful in winning supporters in Bichi (Bici), Dambatta (Danbatta), Ringim, Rano, Dutse, Sumaila, Gaya, Kunya, Nguru, Gezo, Rugu, Wudil, Daura, and Jamaare. After the spread of his movement into Kano province the expansion into other regions of Nigeria followed in the 1950s and especially in the 1960s. Centers of expansion were Sokoto, where Kabara was able to win support in Kaura-Namoda, Gummi, and Gusau, as well as Kaduna, Zaria, Bauchi, Plateau, and Bornu. In the South he won followers in Lagos, Abeokuta, and Ibadan, a development Ahmed has documented in his thesis (1986). After the establishment of a network of muqaddamûn in Nigeria in the 1960s, Nasiru Kabara endeavored to expand his influence abroad, usually in the course of his own journeys. The countries he visited most often and regularly were Iraq, Saudi Arabia, and Libya. He also visited Togo, Benin, Niger, Mali, Ghana, Egypt, Lebanon, Kuwait, Algeria, Turkey, Pakistan, Malaysia, Indonesia, Great Britain, Italy, and even the Soviet Union (S. Kabara 1981: 92).

Nasiru Kabara was not only a well-traveled man, but also an erudite scholar. His private library in Kano was one of the biggest in the city and contained about two thousand titles. He was a busy writer and has written treatises and books on numerous subjects and topics of the Islamic sciences. There are, however, divergent estimates about the exact number of his works. Ahmed (1986: 212) estimates their number at about two hundred titles, whereas Kabara's nephew Shehu Usman Kabara (N. Kabara 1972: Introduction) counts about 150, as does Sa'id (1983a). Tahir (1975: 153) counts seventy-seven, and my own work of collecting titles resulted in a list of 116 works (Loimeier 1991: 165 ff.). The greatest part of the published works of Nasiru Kabara deals with his description of the Qâdiriyya and Sufism in general. His "magnum opus" is his translation of the Qur'ân into Hausa, which was supposed to have been published in Libya, where an edition of his collected works was also in preparation (Interview S. U. Kabara, 9 Mar. 1987). This work is seen as an answer to the translation of the Qur'ân into Hausa by Abubakar Gumi, the correctness of which Kabara rejected. According to Ibrahim Isa Abdullahi, Kabara's advisor on business affairs, Gumi sent him his translation of the Qur'ân for revision. The latter found about two hundred faulty entries, but as Gumi refused to accept Kabara's proposals, Kabara refused to recognize Gumi's translation of the Qur'ân (Interview I. I. Abdullahi, 14 Jan. 1987). The most important topic of Nasiru Kabara's works about the history and development of the Qâdiriyya was the description and defence of the rites of the Qâdiriyya-Nâṣiriyya as they were practiced in Kano against attacks from the Tijâniyya as well as later from the 'Yan Izala. Central to their criticism was the communal bandiri-dhikr and the annual celebrations of the Maulid 'Abd al-Qâdir with its great procession through the streets of the old city of Kano.

Whereas the bandiri-dhikr was not introduced into Kano by Nasiru Kabara himself, but by the Qâdiriyya-Salâmiyya and the Qâdiriyya-'Arûsiyya, the practice of a number of other rituals went back to the initiatives of Nasiru Kabara. Among these were a series of new *awrâd* (litanies), which are recited during the dhikr. An important element of the dhikr was a new technique of breathing (*anfâs*), which was practiced in Baghdad and brought to Kano by Nasiru Kabara. The technique of anfâs is based on the constant repetition of a certain word or short sentence like *Allah, Allah,* whereby the participants breathe in or against the rhythm of their chanting. This practice of anfâs demands high concentration and has to be supervised by experienced members of the ṭarîqa, so that the rhythm is not broken. This kind of dhikr leads to trancelike conditions in a relatively short period of time. Many participants, children and wealthy traders alike, become ecstatic and have to be restrained and cared for by special guards. Since 1953 the bandiri-dhikr has been propagated by Kabara as an important symbol of his movement and has thus become an excellent means of mobilizing his followers. Especially for the young members of the Qâdiriyya, the bandiri-dhikr is an important social event. Many of Kabara's young followers are organized in bandiri groups and move from mosque to mosque every evening in order to participate in the bandiri-dhikr. The beating of the bandiri drum is a prestigious and sought-after occupation. It demands great concentration on the part of the drummer because he not only has to know and to command the correct rhythm of drumming, which speeds up during the chanting of the awrâd, but also has to know by heart the different awrâd themselves, which are recited and given by the respective leader of the bandiri-dhikr and vary from mosque to mosque. As the bandiri-dhikr takes place every evening in a number of different mosques of the Qâdiriyya in Kano, the presence of the ṭarîqa in the city is underlined not only visually but also acoustically from day to day and from night to night. The attraction of the bandiri-dhikr for the young is emphasized by the fact that after the dhikr usually small gifts like sweets, money, or food are distributed to the participants of the dhikr by wealthy sympathizers or members of the Qâdiriyya. Rich followers of Kabara occasionally organize bandiri-dhikrs at their own houses and then distribute gifts to the participants (Yusuf 1983: 58).

While analyzing the social origin of the participants of the dhikr, it ought to be stressed that in the case of the Qâdiriyya most participants come from rather poor strata of the society in Kano. Many Qâdirîs who take part in the great communal dhikr every Friday in the Dâr al-Qâdiriyya mosque of Nasiru Kabara walk in from the neighboring wards. Many bicycles and some motorcycles are to be found parked in front of the main entrance to the yard of Kabara's house and mosque, whereas cars are usually few. In fact, my own Volkswagen beetle was often the only car in the parking area. The great communal waẓîfa of the Tijâniyya-Ibrâhîmiyya, which takes place in one of the most important zawâya of the ṭarîqa in Kano, the mosque of Uba Ringim in Kofar Sabuwa Road in the aristocratic south of the old city, is characterized on the other hand by the fact that the whole street is parked with big cars (Mercedes, Peugeots), which surely is a sign of a correspondingly wealthy community of participants. For many young adherents of the Qâdiriyya, especially if they come from poor families, the participation in the bandiri-dhikr signifies a welcome supplement to the dire conditions of their everyday life. Therefore they belong to the most engaged and stubborn defenders of this practice of the Qâdiriyya-Nâṣiriyya. Regardless of the socioeconomic and religious aspects, the bandiri-dhikr also exerts a strong musical attraction on many young Qâdirîs. Thus I personally met during the course of a visit to three different bandiri-dhikr meetings, which took place in one evening in three different mosques in Unguwar Alfindiki, a group of about ten youths who drifted from mosque to mosque to get a chance to beat the drums in each and to collect the prospective gifts.

The bandiri-dhikr can thus be regarded as an important element of the youth subculture in Kano. The attacks of the 'Yan Izala on the bandiri-dhikr, in the case of the Qâdiriyya, therefore did not lead to questioning of the religious correctness of the practice but rather to a further entrenchment of the ṭarîqa and solidarization of the Qâdiris with Nasiru Kabara. A similar phenomenon is not noticeable in connection with the Tijâniyya. The critics of the Qâdiriyya, especially Abubakar Gumi, condemned the practice of the bandiri-dhikr as a *bid'a makrûha* (a damnable innovation), arguing that the use of musical instruments in mosques made the religion look ridiculous (Gumi 1976: 40–43). In order to confront these criticisms, Kabara wrote a number of treatises like *Tanfîs al-jullâs fî dh-dhikr bi-l-bandîr wa l-anfâs* (The Refreshing of the Participants of the Bandiri- and Anfâs-dhikr) or *Khulâṣat at-takhrîr fî dh-dhikr bi-l-anfâs wa l-bandîr* (The Quintessence of Liberation through the Anfâs- and Bandiri-dhikr). His major argument is that Muhammad Bello as well as Usman dan Fodio had already approved of the practice of the communal dhikr and that the practice could not be regarded as a bid'a, as it had long been known in other Islamic countries (Sa'id 1983a: 7).

The celebration of the Maulid 'Abd al-Qâdir has been as similarly controversial as the bandiri-dhikr. This festival was introduced by Nasiru Kabara after his return from Baghdad in 1953, and the ritual corresponds to the celebration of the Maulid an-Nabî by the Tijâniyya-Ibrâhîmiyya. The Maulid 'Abd al-Qâdir takes place annually on 20 Rabi' ath-thânî and consists not only of a solemn dhikr, but also of a great procession by the Qâdirîs from the Kabara's house through the old city of Kano to the great cemetery of the Qâdiriyya at the northeastern periphery of the old city. In front of the cemetery, where the tombs of the local saints of the Qâdiriyya are buried, prayers are spoken for the dead, and Kabara and a number of other dignitaries hold speeches about 'Abd al-Qâdir al-Jîlânî and the history and achievements of the Qâdiriyya. Not only the local communities of the Qâdiriyya in Kano, each carrying a banner, and a great number of bandiri groups take part in the procession, but also numerous delegations of the Qâdiriyya from the surrounding Kano region, from other parts of Nigeria, and from abroad. In 1986, for instance, the supreme khalîfa of the Qâdiriyya, Shaykh

Saif ad-Dîn from Baghdad, was present for the second time together with a delegation of the Iraqi Ministry of Foreign Affairs. In addition there were delegations of the Qâdiriyya-Sammâniyya from the Sudan, numerous leaders of the Qâdiriyya from Southern Nigeria, as well as guests of honor from the Tijâniyya like Khalîfa Isma'il Ibrahim, and representatives from the Kano state government and from the Nigerian federal government. The Maulid 'Abd al-Qâdir is thus an excellent opportunity to demonstrate to the public and to the enemies of the ṭarîqa the strength and unity of the Qâdiriyya-Nâṣiriyya.

Over time the number of the participants in the Maulid celebrations in Kano has grown: While "only" 30,000 people were taking part in 1963, in 1986 the number of participants had increased to about 150,000 and the traffic in the old city was almost totally blocked for one day, as I could observe myself (13 December 1986). Efforts by the administration, especially during the authoritarian Buhari regime in 1984, to limit the extent of the celebrations or to prohibit the procession at all have always failed on account of the stubborn resistance of the Qâdiriyya. In 1984 the young followers of the ṭarîqa in Kano were, according to the chairman of the committee for the organization of the Maulid, al-Ḥâjj Ibrahim Isa Abdullahi, even prepared to enforce the Maulid celebrations, although Nasiru Kabara himself had shown himself willing to compromise. The defenders of the Maulid 'Abd al-Qâdir argue that the celebration is a central symbol of their adherance to the Qâdiriyya which could not simply be given up (Interview I. I. Abdullahi, 3 Mar. 1987). The major criticism from the side of the opponents of the Qâdiriyya in connection with the Maulid is that during the Maulid the prayers at the tombs of the deceased are not spoken for the dead, but the dead are rather asked for *tawassul* (intercession) by the saints. The practice of tawassul, however, according to the critics signifies that the saints are regarded as intermediaries between man and God, which is a flagrant violation of the principle of *tauḥîd* (uniqueness of God).

Nasiru Kabara answered these criticisms with a number of treatises like *Fatḥ ar-raḥmân fî t-tawassul ilâ Allâh* (The Introduction to the Merciful in the Intercession to Allah) or *Maukib al-qâdiriyya fî sh-shaurâ' al-kanawiyya* (The Procession of the Qâdiriyya in the Kano Streets), where he accepts in essence the correctness of the reproaches of his critics. He adds, however, that the practice of tawassul was not confined to the celebrations of the Maulid 'Abd al-Qâdir alone. In order to eliminate tawassul, Nasiru Kabara threatened during a Maulid in the early 1980s even to break off the procession when he learned that "some women" were practicing tawassul at the tombs (Interviews Shea, 27 Nov. 1986, and S. U. Kabara, 15 Feb. 1987). This threat was of serious concern to his followers, as the breaking off of the procession would have meant that the blessing effect of the participation in the celebrations was no longer guaranteed. Kabara's strategy has to be seen in the context of the heavy attacks of the 'Yan Izala on the Sufi brotherhoods. He did not want to give the critics of the Qâdiriyya an easy target for their propaganda. In spite of the criticism of the Maulid 'Abd al-Qâdir as well as of the bandiri-dhikr, Kabara and his followers stick to these practices because they are an excellent way to mobilize the followers of the Qâdiriyya and at the same time are also symbols of solidarity and distinctness compared with other religious movements.

Apart from the practice and defence of these rituals Nasiru Kabara has done much for the development of modern Islamic education in Kano, thereby contributing to the present-day identification of Kano with the educational efforts of the ṭuruq. Thus no vacuum existed in this respect in Kano into which the 'Yan Izala could have penetrated and established a foothold. Although the first modern Islamiyya school, which combined elements of an Islamic curriculum with the official curricula of the state schools, was already founded in Kano in Unguwar Yolawa in the 1940s by traders affiliated with the Tijâniyya, the idea of Islamiyya schools was propagated on the regional level by the NEPU since the late 1940s. Nasiru Kabara was originally opposed to the idea of Islamiyya schools and had characterized this concept of education as "Christian" (Chamberlin Fieldnotes: Kano 1971). But when it became clear that the attraction of this type of schools was considerable, he founded an Islamiyya primary school of his own in Unguwar Gwale. This school was opened in 1960 under the name Ma'had Shaykh Nasiru Kabara by al-Ḥajj Muhammad Inuwa 'Abbas with a staff of two teachers and thirty-eight pupils. By 1987 the number of students and teachers had exploded: Under the lead of two principals, Shaykh Gariballa Nasiru and Malam Dahiru Khalid, thirty teachers were teaching 1,582 students (671 boys and 911 girls). The students are divided into thirty-four classes and attend the school for six years. The number of subjects has multiplied, too: Qur'ân, fiqh, sîrat annabî, tauḥîd, tafsîr, ḥadîth, naḥw, al-imlâ', al-inshâ', English, Hausa, sports, mathematics, geography, history, Arabic, social studies, and hygienics (Visit on 21 February 1987).

In 1988 an Islamiyya secondary school opened in Unguwar Goron Dutse. This school will receive the graduates of the Gwale primary school. After completion of the final exams at the secondary school the students have the opportunity to start their studies either at the School of Arabic Studies (SAS) or at the Bayero University Kano (BUK). The setting of the foundation stone of the Goron Dutse Islamiyya secondary school was performed in 1986 in the presence of the Shaykh al-Azhar from Cairo, Shaykh Jadd al-Ḥaqq (Interview I. M. Kabara, 21 Feb. 1987), thus underlining the importance modern Islamic education is given in present-day Kano. Apart from his support for the Islamiyya schools, Nasiru Kabara is planning the establishment of an Islamic university in Kano along the lines of the Islamic university of 'Umdurman in Sudan (Interview S. U. Kabara, 10 Jan. 1987). Following Kabara's example a number of wealthy members of the Qâdiriyya have founded other Islamiyya schools in Kano. These are situated mainly in the Unguwoyi Makwarari, Dala, Masukwani, Mandawari, Koki, Fagge, Ayagi, Soron Dinki, and Tudun Wada (Interview Atamma, 2 Mar. 1987). In Koki the Ma'had 'ulûm ad-dîn exists, which was built in 1955 by Sanusi Dantata; in Fagge Malam Atamma has established a school with fifteen teachers and more than six hundred students, and in Ayagi the school of al-Ḥâjj Sharu Bala attracts more than one thousand students (Visit, 28 Feb. 1987). Nasiru Kabara himself teaches in his Dâr al-Qâdiriyya mosque. His teaching of tafsîr and ḥadîth takes place on Saturday and Sunday and is oriented to the instruction of advanced scholars. On the other days of the week, except Thursday and Friday, other scholars of the Qâdiriyya, like Kabara's nephew, Shehu Usman Kabara, teach in the Dâr al-Qâdiriyya mosque (Interview S. U. Kabara, 10 Jan. 1987).

The importance of Nasiru Kabara as a religious scholar is underlined by the fact that he conducts the solemn tafsîr in the palace of the emir in the month of Ramadhân. Kabara's tafsîr is based upon the Tafsîr al-jalâlain by as-Suyuṭî and al-Maḥallî (Sa'id 1983a: 9). In 1958 Kabara was also appointed principal of the Shahuci School of Law (ibid.: 10), and after the death of his teacher Ibrahim Natsuguni in 1949 he advanced to the latter's chair in the influential emir's council. In 1963 he joined the Kaduna Council of Malamai, which was inspired by Ahmadu Bello as an assembly of the most important religious scholars of Northern Nigeria. Today Kabara is also a member of some other organizations like the Jamâ'at Naṣr al-Islâm (JNI), the Nigerian Supreme Council for Islamic Affairs (NSCIA), and the Council of 'Ulama'. His membership in the emir's council and his appointment as principal of the Shahuci School of Law show that Kabara was already recognized by the state in the 1950s as an important scholar. In this respect Kabara's position resembles that of his later opponent Abubakar Gumi in the 1950s and 1960s.

Although the support of Nasiru Kabara by wealthy Kano traders was not as important as it was in the case of the scholars of the Tijâniyya, their assistance was still considerable. To the group of financial supporters of the Qâdiriyya in Kano belong primarily Sanusi Dantata, al-Ḥâjj Sabo Danbatta, Aminu and Sani Ahmad, al-Ḥâjj Musa "U.A.C.," al-Ḥâjj Sharu Bala, and the Makwarari family; Ibrahim Isa Abdullahi Makwarari is the personal advisor of Kabara in all organizational and financial matters (Interview I. I. Abdullahi, 3 Jan. 1987). Nevertheless, Kabara is not dependent on the the financial contributions of his rich followers.

Their monies are rather invested in the construction of mosques and schools. Kabara owns considerable property of his own, comprising among other things a farm in Rantan (Kiru Local Government Area) and an estate in Unguwar Hausawa (Kano) as well as his house in Unguwar Kabara. He is the owner of a number of houses in his ward and leases the shops in front of his estate opposite the Kano central mosque to the shopkeepers (Interview I. I. Abdullahi, 3 Jan. 1987). Kabara is also shareholder in the Bayajidda Amenity Trading Company, which is a large commercial enterprise led by the Makwarari family, and he draws income from the sale of his publications. Finally, a significant part of his expenditures is taken care of by his wealthy disciples, be it the acquisition of a new car or a journey abroad (Interview I. I. Abdullahi, 3 Jan. 1987). The combination of spiritual and economic factors has strengthened his position in such a way that since the 1970s he has to be regarded as one of the most influential religious scholars in Kano. As Tahir has mentioned (1975: 151), social changes in Kano are today no longer possible without the consent and support of the 'ulama'. The palace as well as the traders have to take them into account. They are connected with the scholars in a network of of services and counterservices. Only one wealthy trader has ever tried to protest against the authority of Nasiru Kabara. This was the rebellion of Sanusi Dantata in 1972, which was supported by an influential scholar of the Qâdiriyya, Shaykh 'Ali Kumasi (1915–86).

'Ali Kumasi was one of the most outstanding scholars of the Qâdiriyya in Kano. At the age of two he moved with his father from Maiduguri to Kano. His father, Muhammad Balbali Kumasi, was active in the kolanut trade with Gonja and Kumasi in the Gold Coast. In Kumasi he met the Kano trader al-Hassan Dantata, who became his student; thereby the close connection between the two families was established. 'Ali Kumasi himself was initially a student of his sister, a reknowned Qur'ânic scholar. In Kano 'Ali Kumasi studied like Nasiru Kabara with Adamu Na Ma'agi, who taught him tafsîr, taṣawwuf, and 'ilm al-falak. He was also in contact with the Tijânî scholars Isiaku Rabi'u and

Muhammad Salga. After completing his studies he started to set up a trading network of his own, which extended into Sudan and to Egypt. In Sudan 'Ali Kumasi completed his education under the tutelage of the leaders of the Qâdiriyya-Sammâniyya, Shaykh Qarîb Allâh and his son Muḥammad al-Fâtiḥ. In the course of his studies he collected a number of salâsil from different branches of the Qâdiriyya. Like Nasiru Kabara he was a prolific writer, and his knowledge was compared with that of Kabara (Interview 'Abd ar-Rahman b. 'Ali Kumasi, 10 Mar. 1987). He settled in Kano in Unguwar Tudun Nufawa in the late 1960s, by which time Kabara had already consolidated his authority within the Qâdiriyya for many years. In Kano 'Ali Kumasi affiliated himself to al-Hassan Dantata's son, Sanusi Dantata. With the latter's support he moved to the Dantata quarter of Koki and became the imam of the Sanusi Dantata mosque. Shortly after his move to Kano 'Ali Kumasi established his reputation as a scholar here in many branches of the Islamic sciences. Because of his own spiritually and economically autonomous position he was not willing to accept Kabara's authority who was furthermore about ten years younger. In this attitude of opposition 'Ali Kumasi was supported by Sanusi Dantata, who obviously wanted to loosen the close ties to Kabara. Thus 'Ali Kumasi became Sanusi Dantata's personal malam.

In 1972 the decisive struggle between 'Ali Kumasi and Nasiru Kabara over the supreme authority within the Qâdiriyya in Kano began. The incident that triggered off their conflict was 'Ali Kumasi's and Sanusi Dantata's refusal to take part in the annual Maulid 'Abd al-Qâdir celebrations. They argued that in the course of the celebrations the mixing of men and women (*ikhtilâṭ*) occurred and that this mixing violated the prescriptions of the religion (Interview Kumasi, 10 Mar. 1987). As Kabara seemed to accept the mixing of men and women, they were left with no choice but to break off relations with him and boycott the celebrations. Kabara refuted this criticism in a special treatise entitled *Maukib al-qâdiriyya fî sh-shauâri' al-kanawiyya* (The Procession of the Qâdiriyya in the Streets of Kano). He argued that ikhtilâṭ also occurred during the ḥajj in Mecca without being regarded as un-Islamic. As long as men and women were dressed properly according to the prescriptions of the law there could be no objection against the mixing of men and women during such occasions, an argument which was also used by Abubakar Gumi in a different context in 1982. With his arguments Kabara was able to convince the majority of the malamai of the Qâdiriyya in Kano and thus stifle Kumasi and Dantata's rebellion. As Kumasi did not have any power base of his own in Kano and as the support of Danata was not sufficient enough to push his claim for supreme leadership within the Qâdiriyya in Kano, both Kumasi and Dantata finally came around and ended their quarrel. With the capitulation of Kumasi, Kabara had asserted his claim to the supreme leadership of the Qâdiriyya in Kano and had also defeated his most important internal opponent. In 1972, at his own expense and as a sort of spiritual compensation, Kumasi published Kabara's major work against the attacks of Gumi, *an-Naṣîḥa aṣ-ṣarîḥa fi l-radd 'alâ l-'aqîda aṣ-ṣaḥîḥa* (The Frank Advice as the Answer to *al-'Aqîda aṣ-ṣaḥîḥa*). Sanusi Dantata for his part donated 8,000 naira ($8,000) for the extension of the Dâr al-Qâdiriyya mosque in Kabara's house, thus also making his reconciliation public (Tahir 1975: 150).

The conflict between Nasiru Kabara and 'Ali Kumasi shows how important a sound religious learning was in such quarrels. If Kabara would not have been able to counter Kumasi's arguments, his image as a religious scholar would have been damaged to a great extent, and his claim for supremacy within the Qâdiriyya would have been put into question. The conflict between Kabara and Kumasi in reality was thus not only a dogmatic conflict but also a struggle among religious concurrents over the spiritual and by implication also the economic and political leadership within the Qâdiriyya in Kano. That this conflict was nevertheless fought out on the basis of a religious argument shows that religious learning and dogmatic arguments in the early 1970s were still a valid platform for all kinds of disputes between religious scholars and their networks. This assessment is not only valid for the struggle between Kumasi and Kabara, but also for the conflicts between the ṭuruq themselves, as well as for their common struggle against the 'Yan Izala movement.

However, Nasiru Kabara not only succeeded in defeating 'Ali Kumasi's rebellion and putting Sanusi Dantata in his place, but he also showed that he could even stand up against the authority of the emir. Tahir remarks that Kabara refused on two occasions to accept the testimony of other scholars in regard to the sighting of the new moon, which is essential for the exact timing of the beginning and the end of the Ramadhân (Tahir 1975: 151). The sighting of the moon is an excellent opportunity to make public conflicts of interpretation and authority within the Muslim community. In 1971 and 1972 Kabara advised his followers to ignore the decision of the JNI in regard to the fixing of the dates of the month of Ramadhân and to start and to stop fasting only on the next day (ibid.). His followers obeyed and put themselves with their refusal in a conscious opposition to the Emir of Kano, who, as the Amîr al-Mu'minîn (the leader of the Faithful) and local chairman of the JNI, should be obeyed at least in a symbolic way. Nevertheless, this blatant contravention against a majority decision was not punished, which shows how influential Kabara already was at that time.

If one compares the development of the Qâdiriyya-Nâṣiriyya in the last five decades with the development of the Tijâniyya-Ibrâhîmiyya the following picture emerges: Nasiru Kabara was and is without any doubt the undisputed leader of the Qâdiriyya in Northern Nigeria. Changes in the appearance of the ṭarîqa were brought about only through the natural death of some elder muqaddamûn and supporters of Nasiru Kabara and by their replacement through younger malamai with the expressive consent of Kabara himself. In contrast to the Tijâniyya-Ibrâhîmiyya the Qâdiriyya-Nâsiriyya has not experienced a splitting-up into numerous local and regional networks, competing against each other. The Qâdiriyya-Nâsiriyya therefore could look forward to the conflict with the 'Yan Izala movement without unnecessary worry.

2.4. *The Conflict between the Qâdiriyya and the Tijâniyya in Northern Nigeria*

Although the disputes and quarrels between the Qâdiriyya and the Tijâniyya had already begun in the mid–nineteenth century, until the early twentieth century they were restricted to a small circle of religious scholars and the political establishment. The affiliation with the Tijâniyya was a sign of a political and religious protest against the claim to supremacy of Sokoto. With the arrival of the Ibrahim Niass, however, the character of the conflict between the two Sufi brotherhoods changed. The quarrels of the religious and political elite developed into an all-embracing confrontation in the 1940s, influencing the political life in Northern Nigeria up to the 1960s in a decisive way.

In the late 1940s Ibrahim Niass and his Nigerian followers, especially Muhammad Sanusi and the Salgawa network, started to transform the Tijâniyya-Ibrâhîmiyya into a religious mass movement. The trader-scholars of the ṭarîqa established new centers of the Tijâniyya in all cities of the North as well as along the new roads and railway lines in the rural regions. The success of the Tijâniyya was greatest among the traders themselves, who saw many advantages in becoming members of an extended religious and economic network. On the other hand, the Tijâniyya was also successful among the farmers in the groundnut-cultivating areas and among the artisans of the North, who were dependent economically on the Tijânî trader-scholars and their middlemen. Although these new followers of the Tijâniyya had not customarily been affiliated with the Qâdiriyya, they were nevertheless regarded by many malamai of the Qâdiriyya as their own natural clientele. As long as the the spread of the Tijâniyya was restricted in the nineteenth and early twentieth centuries to the circles of the scholars and the political elite, the leaders of the Qâdiriyya could interprete this expansion of a rival Sufi brotherhood as a primarily dogmatic problem and fight the Tijâniyya on the political level, as in the case of the deposition of the Emir of Zaria, Abdulkadir, in 1854/55. Through the transformation of the Tijâniyya into a mass movement, however, the very economic and social basis of the Qâdiriyya was threatened. The Tijâniyya was about to literally remove the ground from under the feet of the Qâdiriyya. Furthermore, with the British colonization a gradual opening of the fairly closed world of the North had started, and slowly the consciousness of living in a greater Islamic world had grown among at least the urban population in Northern Nigeria. New books, ideas, and ideologies streamed into the country, and the establishment of Western schools like the Katsina College had favored the rise of a small but growing modern, Western-educated elite. In the course of the growth of the Nigerian movement for independence, political parties and groups had been founded in the North, and the politicization of public life had begun by the late 1940s. The establishment of political parties in Northern Nigeria since the late 1940s made the control of their bases, the urban and rural *talakawa* (commoners), more and more important for the politicians. If they wanted to succeed in the long run, they could do so only by cultivating as many voters as possible.

The first electoral victories of the populist NEPU in Kano in the primaries of 1951 had shocked the conservative establishment of the North. Under the charismatic leadership of Aminu Kano the NEPU was the first party to mobilize the talakawa, and the NPC had no other choice than to follow the NEPU in this strategy. As both parties were still in the process of building up their organization and commanded only a very restricted party apparatus, they were forced, if they wanted to conduct an extensive campaign, to look for allies. Besides the administrative network of the "Native administration," the Sufi brotherhoods and their networks were the only other potential partners who could offer extended connections throughout the North, which could be used for political mobilization. Anwar characterizes the atmosphere of the time by saying that "political leaders smuggled their ways through to capture religious leaders so as to get the sympathy and support of their followers" (Anwar 1989: 31). The ṭuruq commanded the necessary infrastructure, the middlemen, with whose help political ideas could be propagated at the mass level.

The success of the NPC under Ahmadu Bello in the 1950s and 1960s can be explained to a large extent by the fact that the NPC succeeded, in contrast to the NEPU, not only to get the support of the "Native administration" but also to acquire support of a great number of the trader-scholar networks of the Tijâniyya and the Qâdiriyya. Through the competition between the political parties for control of these religious networks the political weight of the networks grew accordingly. Because the possibilities of gaining influence for a religious scholar was dependent on the number of his followers and supporters, a bitter struggle between the numerous networks of the Tijâniyya and the Qâdiriyya broke out in the late 1940s to acquire as many followers as possible in order to increase the "bargaining power" of the different shuyûkh. The role of the religious scholars was therefore extended by a new facet: not only were they now the spiritual leaders of their networks, but they also took over the political task of mobilizing their followers. This politicization of Islam on a mass level began in the late 1940s in Northern Nigeria. Although the conflicts between the religious scholars continued to be fought on a dogmatic level, the character of the arguments showed that Islamic religious language and dogma were increasingly instrumentalized in a changing political context for the political debate (Interview Sa'id, 3 Mar. 1987).

After the mission tours of Ibrahim Niass, Sîdî b. 'Umar, and Muḥammad al-Hâdî in the late 1940s and early 1950s, the networks of the Tijâniyya-Ibrâhîmiyya had gained a clear advantage in comparison with the Qâdiriyya as far as the mobilization of the talakawa was concerned. At the same time these journeys, especially that of 'Umar, led to the outbreak of the animosities between both Sufi brotherhoods. 'Umar's visit to Sokoto province, where he could win a number of new disciples for the Tijâniyya, in particular incited the indignation of the Sultan of Sokoto. The Tijâniyya established new mosques in Kaura-Namoda, Argungu, Gusau, and other smaller urban centers in Sokoto and thereby infiltrated the Qâdiriyya's own territory. This competition was enhanced by the fact that besides 'Umar, who remained in Sokoto only for a short period of time, a number of other networks of the Tijâniyya became active. The most important among them was the circle around the trader-scholar Shaykh Atiku Sanka, one of the most influential and wealthy members of the Salgawa clan in Kano. He had business contacts with the Cameroons, Saudi Arabia, Kuwait, Egypt, Sudan, and Niger. A number of his muqaddamûn had, through their business contacts, also established direct connections with Niass in Senegal (Tahir 1975: 425). At the end of the 1940s the network of Shaykh Atiku Sanka had been extended to Sokoto and while developing there had become a special danger for the political establishment, as the recently established muqaddamûn of the Tijâniyya claimed the *zakât* payments and *ṣadaqa* (alms, charity) contributions of the faithful for the construction of their own new mosques. These monies had until then, however, been claimed by the sultan himself, who had publicly refused to accept a salary from the British colonial administration and who was therefore dependent on the zakât and ṣadaqa. On account of this, the Sultan of Sokoto could not but see the expansion of the Sanka network and other Tijânî groups in Sokoto as a direct attack on his sources of finance. Additionally some malamai of the Sanka network characterized the sultan as "a block on the way to the redemption of the muslims" (ibid.: 427–28). Thus Atiku Sanka in 1949 published a poem in which he strongly attacked the sultan:

> I call upon You Allah, the Allmighty One.
> I pray to You to destroy the chief of Sokoto
> to shake off his affairs, to demolish his conscience
> to ruin his house, to overthrow his rule
> to put him to shame and to send a thunderbolt to him
> and to destroy him utterly. (Tahir 1975: 428)

The aggressive presence of the Tijâniyya in Sokoto induced the Sultan of Sokoto in 1949 to order the demolition of all recently built Tijâniyya mosques in Sokoto. He argued that their construction constituted a bid'a as there had been no real need for new mosques. The British report of enquiry about the first massive hostilities between the Qâdiriyya and the Tijâniyya described the escalation of the events in 1952 with the following account:

> His [Sidi b. 'Umar's] ill-judged arrogance in dealing with the Sultan of Sokoto and the Emir of Bauchi . . . brought to a head the struggle between the Tijaniyya and the Kadiriyya tarikas which had been more or less silently developing for the last thirty years. . . . But it can be said that it [the Qâdiriyya] is losing ground yearly to the Tijaniyya. It may be said that it was the realization of this fact that led the Sultan of Sokoto, no doubt exasperated by the excesses of Sidi ben Omar, to order the demolition in 1949 of certain Tijani mosques within his territory. (quoted in Paden 1973: 213).

The politicization of the Tijâniyya is documented by the fact that already in 1950 some malamai of the Salgawa network handed a petition to the British administration for the allowance to found a Jam'iyyar Tijaniyya (Congress of the Tijâniyya) on the model of the Jam'iyyar Mutanen Arewa, the Northern People's Congress (Tahir 1975: 428). This is a clear indication that at least some religious scholars already regarded their networks in the early 1950s as instruments of political mobilization and wanted to use them accordingly (ibid.: 435). The virtual establishment of a "party" of the Tijâniyya was realized, however, only after the deposition of Emir Muhammad Sanusi of Kano in 1963.

Whereas in Sokoto the conflict between the ṭuruq had assumed a very violent character and was marked by a number of heavy clashes like that in 1956 in the districts of Isa and Zurmi when four people were killed (Paden 1986: 306), in Kano the antagonisms between the Tijâniyya and the Qâdiriyya developed on a more peaceful level and were essentially a competition of the religious scholars on dogmatic points of dissonance. This phenomenon may be linked to the fact that the Sultan of Sokoto was himself a member of the Qâdiriyya, whereas in Kano Emir Abdullahi Bayero (d. 1953), as well as his successor, Muhammad Sanusi (1954–63), were followers of Ibrahim Niass. Their sympathies toward the Tijâniyya can be interpreted as a symbol of their efforts to achieve greater political and spiritual independence from Sokoto. As the Qâdiriyya in Kano also dissociated itself from

Sokoto under the lead of Nasiru Kabara, at least in the political arena no conflict developed between the emir and a Sufi brotherhood, because both brotherhoods stressed their independence from Sokoto. Furthermore the situation in Kano was charcterized not by a clear-cut confrontation between the Qâdiriyya and the Tijâniyya as such but rather by the competition between several of the networks of the ṭarîqas with changing alliances between these networks, sometimes even cutting across ṭarîqa lines. Thus Tahir writes in regard to the the development of the Tijâniyya in Kano: "They themselves present a fairly united front but among themselves they are divided by the usual quarrels and jealousies" (Tahir 1975: 425).

Competition in Kano was also to become increasingly sharp with the accession of Muhammad Sanusi to the throne in 1954. Sanusi was connected with Ibrahim Niass closer than Abdullahi Bayero had ever been. Immediately after his accession to the throne he began to change the existing balance of power between the different groups in the palace as well as between the trader-scholar networks in Kano itself by directly supporting a certain faction of the Tijâniyya-Ibrâhîmiyya. This group was the circle of malamai within the ruling Fulani aristocracy, which had been traditionally connected with the palace and which was led in the 1920s and 1930s by Wali Sulaiman. In 1954 Sanusi dismissed all scholars who did not belong to this network of palace-oriented malamai from the influential Council of Malamai, the function of which was to give the emir advice on all questions concerning Islamic law. Among the dismissed were Nasiru Kabara (Qâdiriyya), Muhammad Dan Amu (Tijâniyya-'Umariyya), and Abubakar Mai Sajen Jamus (Tijâniyya-Ibrâhîmiyya, Salgawa network). The imams of Yola and Galadanci remained and were joined by the Alkali Inuwa Wudilawa and the Imam of the Friday mosque, Shehu Waziri. Thus the new council was set up entirely by representatives of the palace-oriented network of the Tijâniyya-Ibrâhîmiyya or by confidants of Sanusi (Paden 1973: 228). Because of this one-sided policy of the allocation of political functions Sanusi attracted not only the hostility of the Qâdiriyya and the Tijâniyya-'Umariyya networks, but also that of the Salgawa network within the Tijâniyya-Ibrâhîmiyya.

In addition, Muhammad Sanusi's policy led to a conflict with the prime minister of the Northern region. Although Sanusi was an influential member of the NPC in Kano and a minister "without portfolio" in Ahmadu Bello's cabinet, his active support of the Tijâniyya-Ibrâhîmiyya contradicted the strategy of Bello, which was to unite the North politically and religiously under his own leadership. When in 1962 Sanusi was to oppose an all-embracing reform of the "Native administration," Bello began the process of removing him from office. In this effort Bello was supported by the Salgawa network, especially by Muhammad Sani Kafanga, Tijani Usman, and Uba Ringim. In this way they were to avenge the one-sided allocation of influential posts by the emir and were able to thwart Sanusi's far-reaching political and religious ambitions (Interview Kane, 18 Jan. 1989). Facing the increasing pressure of his opponents, Sanusi finally resigned in 1963. After a short interim government headed by Emir Muhammad Inuwa in 1963, Ado Bayero ascended to the throne of Kano in the same year. He was the first Emir of Kano since the jihâd who was not affiliated with any ṭarîqa and therefore in a position to act as an intermediary between the feuding parties. One of his first acts was the restructuring of the Council of Malamai. Malam Dan Amu and Nasiru Kabara were reinstated and once more integrated, the Babban Malami Madabo, Ibrahim, and the new Imam of the Central mosque, Malam Dalhatu, were co-opted as new members, Shehu Waziri, Limamin Galadanci, and Inuwa Wudilawa kept their positions, and the Limamin Yola was dismissed (Paden 1973: 228).

The intensive disputes on the religious level enhanced among other things the development of a lively literary production in Kano from the late 1940s among religious scholars and thus reinforced the importance of a sound Islamic education. The religious scholars were to cultivate for reasons of profilation branches of the Islamic sciences, which, until this time, as with *ta'rîkh* (history), had been rather neglected (Interview Sa'id, 3 Mar. 1987).

The real religious dispute was to erupt by 1950 when Nasiru Kabara published a treatise entitled *Sulâlat al-miftâḥ min minâḥ al-fattâḥ* (The Descendants of the Key of the Donations of the Opener), in which he claimed to be the Ghauth, the supreme Sufi saint of the time (Paden 1973: 136 f.). This title had already been claimed by Ibrahim Niass in the early 1930s, and as the position of the Ghauth could be occupied by only one saint, the question was thus to arise as to whose claim was credible. This problem could be solved only in the context of the ongoing socioreligious confrontation. An important sign for the strength of the baraka of both opponents was the actual number of their respective followers and their economic power. After the publication of his first treatise against the spiritual claims of the Tijânîs, Kabara was therefore intent on emphasizing his claim for leadership within the Qâdiriyya and began to increase his mass following. At the same time he also put himself forward as a legitimate heir of the leaders of the jihâd. In 1955 he published another work with the title *Naf' al-'ibâd bi-ḥaqîqat al-mi'âd fî madînat baghdâd* (The Well-being of Mankind through the Truth concerning the Visit in the City of Baghdad), where he emphasized his spiritual links with Usman dan Fodio and Muhammad Bello.

This strategy was also supported by his followers. Thus Yusufu Abdullahi Makwarari wrote a poem in Hausa titled *Begen Shehu Abdulkadir* (The Longing for Shaykh 'Abd al-Qâdir), in which he underlined the connection between Nasiru Kabara and the leaders of the jihâd (Paden 1973: 167). In view of the increasing threat of the expansion of the Tijâniyya-Ibrâhîmiyya developing into a mass movement in the 1950s, Kabara in 1958 was to respond with yet another treatise entitled *an-Nafaḥât as-nâṣiriyya fî ṭ-ṭarîqa al-qâdiriyya* (The Naṣirine Fragrances within the Qâdiriyya Sufi Brotherhood). In this work he argued that all ṭuruq were essentially the same and differed only in respect to strategy. He discussed the different branches of Sufism and concluded that the Qâdiriyya was the most beneficial ṭarîqa because it was closest to God. From this premise Kabara was to deduce his claim to supremacy of the Qâdiriyya over all other ṭuruq. In addition he stated that the saintliness of 'Abd al-Qâdir al-Jîlânî was superior to that of all other saints. Emanating from him, grace would overflow to all other saints until the day of judgment (Kabara 1958: 15). Kabara argued further that it was not permitted for the adherents of the Qâdiriyya to leave the Qâdiriyya, as this signified an act of disrespect in regard to the saints and an insult to the prophet (ibid.: 20–21). Thus Kabara not only adopted the concept of the "overflowing grace" (*al-faida*) of the Tijâniyya, but he also turned the Tijânî claim of supremacy on its head by claiming supremacy for the Qâdiriyya itself. To this attack the renowned Kano scholar of the Tijâniyya, Abubakar Atiku, replied in the same year. In his reply, entitled *Risâla fî taḥdhîr al-'iṣâba* (Treatise of Caution in Respect of Factionalism), he accused Kabara of hypocrisy, arguing that, while criticizing the Tijâniyya in lieu of the ban it imposed on her members to join another ṭarîqa, he was quite willing to insist on the same prohibition for his own movement. Thus, concluded Atiku, he was merely "deluded by his own envy" (Paden 1973: 147).

The most important topic of dogmatic dispute in the 1950s and 1960s was the question of the correct position of the arms during prayer. Since 1930 Ibrahim Niass had practiced the position of qabḍ (arms folded), and this position became the most important public symbol of his followers. When Niass made his first public appearance in public in Nigeria in 1951 he thus practiced qabḍ. Nasiru Kabara, who had until then been one of the few scholars in Kano who was identified with the practice of qabḍ prior to Niass (Anwar 1989: 62), responded by reverting to the practice of sadl (arms outstretched) in order to dissociate himself from the Tijâniyya-Ibrâhîmiyya (Interview Sâlih, 27 Mar. 1987; Anwar, 28 Mar. 1987). Thus the question of the correct position of the arms during prayer became impregnated with a significant symbolic meaning. The conflict surrounding the problem of qabḍ and sadl was intensified by the fact that the followers of each ṭarîqa refused to pray behind an imam who practiced a position of arms different from their own.

In order to strenghten his position, Ibrahim Niass published a treatise in which he condemned the practice of sadl and promised to donate his library to anybody who could quote a ḥadîth showing the practice of sadl by the Prophet (Quadri 1981: 223). Nasiru Kabara took up the challenge in 1958 by publishing a work with the title *Qam' al-fasâd fî tafḍîl as-sadl 'alâ l-qabḍ fî hâdhihi al-bilâd* (The Avoidence of Error by Preferring Sadl Rather than Qabḍ in This Country). In this treatise Kabara argued that the Prophet had practiced both qabḍ and sadl but that the number of ḥadîth supporting sadl was greater than those supporting qabḍ. He further argued that sadl was a traditional practice in Hausaland for centuries, whereas qabḍ was a recent innovation. Niass's stress on qabḍ had brought disunity and strife among the Muslims, though being an adherent of the Maliki school of law he would have been obliged to follow the practice of sadl (Anwar 1989: 63). For the defense of the Tijânîs, Muhammad Sani Kafanga wrote a pamphlet entitled *Sabîl ar-rashâd* (The Path of the Correct Guidance), in which he argued that the hadîth quoted by Kabara in support of sadl were not reliable and, further, that neither sadl nor qabḍ had been mentioned in describing the manner of praying of the Prophet (ibid.: 67). Last but not least, a custom would not become correct in regard to the Sunna of the Prophet on account of its long practice alone. The practice of sadl should therefore be rejected as a bid'a (Quadri 1981: 224). The dispute was continued by a number of other scholars like 'Ali Kumasi in his treatise *Fatḥ al-ḥakam al-'adl* (The Revelation of the Just Judge) and finally taken up by Abubakar Gumi who stated on 4 October 1971 in the newspaper *Gaskiya Ta Fi Kwabo* in the name of the Jama'at Naṣr al-Islam that both sadl and qabḍ were correct and in accordance with the Sunna of the Prophet. He continued, however, that those like Niass and the Aḥmadiyya movement, who had introduced qabḍ into Nigeria where the Maliki school of law was predominant, had created confusion among Muslims (ibid.: 228; Anwar 1989: 80).

The problem of the correct position of the arms was finally used in the 1960s in the political confrontation between Ahmadu

Bello on the one side and the NEPU, Muhammad Sanusi, and the Tijâniyya-Ibrâhîmiyya on the other to condemn the practice of prayer of the Tijaniyya-Ibrahimiyya on the level of dogmatic arguments. The occasion for the condemnation of the Tijaniyya-Ibrahimiyya's way of praying was the so-called Argungu riots of 1965 (Paden 1986: 306–7) which had been preceded by a number of violent clashes between the followers of the Tijâniyya and the Qâdiriyya in the 1950s (Paden 1973: 198). In 1965 the public health authorities of Sokoto province conducted a vaccination campaign in the Yeldu district (Argungu) against which the inhabitants of some villages protested because they had not been consulted and informed about the meaning and importance of the campaign. They vehemently resisted the security forces whose task it was to guarantee the safe conduct of the campaign, and in the course of fighting a number of people were killed. The days that followed the conflict in Argungu were to witness extensive reports from the mass media, especially Radio Kaduna. The riots in Argungu were not, however, presented in their real context, but described as a bloody confrontation between supporters of the Tijâniyya and the Qâdiriyya (Paden 1973: 185; Interview Ṣâliḥ, 27 Mar. 1987). Thus the Sultan of Sokoto denounced the protesters in Yeldu afterwards as 'Yan Waẓifa, thereby laying the blame for the riots at the feet of the Tijâniyya-Ibrâhîmiyya (Paden 1973: 199). In the heated atmosphere of the time the riots could thus be instrumentalized by Ahmadu Bello and his supporters for their political and religious aims.

As early as 1963 a commission on the problem of the correct position of the arms during prayer had been set up within the Kaduna Council of Malamai, an organization of religious scholars initiated by Ahmadu Bello. The members of this commission of inquiry were Nasiru Kabara (Qâdiriyya), Tijani Usman (Tijâniyya-Ibrâhîmiyya, but Salgawa network), Husaini Adamu, and Abubakar an-Nafaty (both members of the JNI and followers of Bello). The commission existed for about two years but failed to reach any conclusions. In the intense atmosphere after the Argungu riots Abubakar Gumi, Bello's religous advisor, proposed that the latter bring the different groups within the Council of Malamai together in order to solve the qabḍ-sadl problem (Adekilekun 1989: 115). Under Bello's pressure the commission was prepared to submit a proposition concerning the qabḍ-sadl issue to the Council of Malamai, and this proposition was to gain acceptance during the third meeting of the Kaduna Council of Malamai on 18 June 1965. The decision of the council was that in the future all imams were prohibited from practicing qabḍ if the majority of the faithful in a mosque were adherents of the Maliki school of law, which prescribes sadl (Paden 1986: 550). As the Maliki school was virtually the only school of law existing in Nigeria, the decision of the Kaduna Council of Malamai meant a public ban of the practice of prayer of the Tijâniyya-Ibrâhîmiyya throughout Nigeria. Nevertheless, the qabḍ resolution of 1965 was not to be realized. Only six months later, 15 January 1966, Ahmadu Bello was killed in the course of the coup by young officers. In the ensuing disorder and civil war that was to last until 1970 the qabḍ-sadl resolution was forgotten as other problems took precedence. In the 1970s the struggle against the critics of the ṭuruq began, and in the context of this new conflict between the ṭuruq and the 'Yan Izala, who ironically enough also practiced qabḍ, other ritual practices were taken up in the religious discussion and declared symbols of deviation.

The conflict surrounding qabḍ and sadl shows how a common religious ritual, in a certain political and social context, can become a symbol in the struggle for power among religiopolitical networks. The qabḍ-sadl dispute also documents that not only religion and dogma but also the system of religious symbols have kept their validity as an important level of argument. The correct ritual was and is in Islam of paramount importance for the practice of the religion. Deviations from the Sunna are seen in this respect as highly problematic. It would therefore be misleading to think that the qabḍ-sadl discussion was only manipulated for political means. Rather, the conflict around qabḍ and sadl was the public expression of the underlying conflict between the Qâdiriyya and the Tijâniyya and their networks. This was a conflict in which not only social and political influence but also spiritual power and personal spheres of influence were at stake and in which the demonstration of religious learning was of importance. The development of the qabḍ-sadl dispute also signified the corresponding development of religous consciousness in Muslim Northern Nigeria. In the course of the pilgrimage more and more Muslims had observed that the position of arms in prayer practiced by the majority of the pilgrims in Mecca was not the sadl of the Maliki school of law, but the qabḍ of the other three schools of law. The rejection of sadl and the acceptance of qabḍ was thus an indication for the increasing integration of the Nigerian Muslims into a greater Islamic community. Last but not least, the qabḍ-sadl debate was a sign of the growing political importance of the religious scholars, an importance recognized and enhanced by Ahmadu Bello through the foundation of the Kaduna Council of Malamai.

2.5. Holy Men and Wealthy Men

A number of scholars have in the last decades recorded a significant increase in the social, political, and economic influence of the religious scholars in Northern Nigeria (Paden 1973; Tahir 1975; Anwar 1989). Tahir wrote in 1975 that in Kano important social changes can no longer be enforced without the consent of the religious scholars (Tahir 1975: 150). He explains the increasing influence of the religious scholars since the early twentieth century by pointing to the economic and spiritual accordance of interests that have developed between the religious scholars and the traders of Kano. The social and political influence of the trader-scholar networks in the mid-1970s concluded the revolution of the political structures in Kano, a process of change which has led to the increasing deprivation of power of the traditional aristocracy. Today, social and political influence is no longer a prerogative of the aristocracy, but is also exercised by an oligarchy of religious scholars, traders, and aristocrats (Tahir 1975: 150).

The social ascent of the malamai in Kano was grounded not only on the belief in their baraka but also on their ability to support their spiritual influence economically and politically. The claim of Nasiru Kabara or Ibrahim Niass for the leadership of the Qâdiriyya or the Tijâniyya or certain spiritual positions could be pushed through only if their claims were bolstered economically and politically. The more disciples and clients a shaykh had, the more credible was his claim to the position of the *qutb* or *ghauth*. Disciples and followers are connected with a shaykh permanently only if he is able to support his baraka by economic means. A shaykh must not only be a wealthy man, but is expected to redistribute at least part of the donations of his wealthy followers among his needy supporters and disciples. Only the combination of these two factors—the belief in his baraka and his economic resources—enables the building up of a following, makes the recognition of certain spiritual claims possible, and renders the transformation of spiritual into political influence easier. The more followers a shaykh has and the greater his network, the stronger his political weight becomes in elections, and consequently his bargaining power grows. The position of a shaykh in the political system also has repercussions on the influence he can exert on his following. The greater political influence he has, the more favorable are the frame conditions under which he and his followers are able to operate. These favorable conditions can take the form of politico-judicial protection by the state or access to external financial ressources. Such network connections exist not only in Northern Nigeria and Senegal (see Cruise O'Brien 1971 for the latter) but also in other parts of West Africa and were historically substantiated for the Kunta in the region of Timbuktu in the late eighteenth century (Saad 1983) and for the Awlad Ibírri of Shaykh Sidiyya in Southern Mauretania in the nineteenth century (Stewart 1973). The Kano networks of religious scholars distinguish themselves in comparison to other such structures in the sense that they have formed a particularly close symbiosis between themselves and the traders, between holy men and wealthy men. The expansion of religious networks has not only been confined to the development of the Sufi brotherhoods, but is also to be observed in the development of the 'Yan Izala movement since the 1970s. The following analysis of the networks of traders and scholars refers exclusively to the case of Kano.

After Kano had experienced a significant economic decline in the seventeenth and eighteenth centuries, it was to recover again in the course of the nineteenth century as an emirate of the Sokoto empire. At the time of the visit by Heinrich Barth in 1851 Kano had a population of about thirty thousand (seasonally up to sixty thousand) (Barth 1857: 141) and found herself on the threshold of an economic boom which gave Kano not only predominance over competing commercial centers like Katsina, but enabled it to develop into the most important economic and commercial center of the Sokoto empire. Thus under the government of Emir Muhammad Bello (1883–92) Kano already contributed the greatest financial and economic share of all emirates to the central government in Sokoto (Ubah 1979: 314). The destruction of the Sokoto empire, the conquest of Kano in 1903, and the succeeding integration of the North into the British colonial empire failed to block the economic development of the city. Rather, Kano's market outlet expanded to the South, using the existing kolanut-trade networks which already extended to Lagos, Kumasi, and Accra. Especially important for the further development of the town was the connection with the national railway system in 1911: immediately thereafter a great groundnut boom began, influencing the development of Kano up to the 1960s.

In the years after World War I Kano became a center of the Syro-Lebanese trading capital. The first emigrants from the Near East had reached Senegal in 1860, Lagos in 1890, and the Sokoto empire in 1898. The first "Lebanese" trader to settle down in Kano permanently in 1912 was Ferris George, who had come to Lagos in 1902. He was followed by Saul Raccah, a Tripolitanian Jew, and Joseph Elias, all of whom initially worked, as with Ferris George, for British companies. In 1914 fourteen Lebanese were living in Kano, and by the early 1980s their number had risen to about 6,000 (Willer 1989: 35). In the Second World War, Kano became an Allied supply basis, which stimulated the industrial takeoff of the city. The industrialization of Kano was intensified after the start of the the oil boom in the 1960s. Between 1972 and 1978 alone the number of industrial workers in Kano rose from 20,000 to 32,000. The most important areas of industrial production were textiles, leather processing, chemical industries, machine construction, food processing, and the production of consumer goods (Lubeck 1985: 53).

The economic boom of the city found its expression in Kano's population growth. In 1952 the number of inhabitants was estimated to be about 130,000; in 1963 this count had risen to 256,000 (Becker 1969: 50). Because of the rapid expansion of the town the Kano metropolitan area was established in 1963 (see map 3). This area comprised the old city (Birni) as well as the old traders' quarter of Fagge. In addition, the quarters built by the British after 1903 outside (Waje) the old city walls to the North, East, and South were included: Nasarawa (1903) the British residential and administrative quarter, Bompai (1907) for industry and commerce, Sabon Gari (1912) for the immigrants from the South and Tudun Wada (1940), as well as Gwagwarwa (1954) for the immigrants from other parts of the North. Since the 1960s a series of other quarters at the periphery were included, most of them former farming villages around Kano, such as Bompai Extension, Challawa, Sharada (for industry and commerce), Gandum Albasa, Hotoro, Tarauni, Giginyu, Kurnar Asabe, Kumbotso, Ungogo, Kawo, Jaoji, Hausawa, and Dorayi (for the immigrants who had been settling since the 1960s). In 1986 the Kano metropolitan area had expanded to 550 square kilometers and comprised a population of approximately 832,000 (estimate Statistical Year Book Kano 1983: 45). Together with the surrounding Local Government Areas of the so-called Kano close-settled zone, namely, Dawakin Kudu, Dawakin Tofa, Gezawa, Minjibir, and Rano, which are connected with Kano in a close symbiosis of exchanges, the Greater Kano Agglomeration (6,500 sq. km) had by 1986 reached a population of approximately 3,630,000 people (estimate Statistical Year Book Kano 1983: 39 ff.). The census of November 1991 gave the total population of Kano State (after the exclusion of Jigawa state) at 5.6 million (*West Africa*, 5 Apr. 1992, official census results). Whereas vast areas even within the old city walls continued to be used for agriculture in the early 1960s, by 1988 the entire area within the walls was densely populated. With the exception of a small area in the West close to the Bayero University campus, this latter area had been surrounded by a zone of densely settled immigrant quarters extending between five and twenty-five kilometerss (along the major roads) into the rural hinterland, every year swallowing up old villages and hamlets.

The tremendous expansion of the city since the 1960s led to an increasing scarcity of land for building around Kano. This scarcity was aggravated by the fact that the state reserved large areas at the periphery for the future extension of the airport, industrial development zones, and the army barracks. This expansion of the city and the increasing commercial activity since the beginning of the oil boom led to inceasing speculation with the land belonging to the farmers around Kano. For many Kano traders and bureaucrats land speculation has become a lucrative economic activity. Thus a building plot in the Tudun Wada quarter that in 1970 would have cost approximately 200–300 naira, in 1978 would cost 7,000 naira. The farmers did not, however, get adequate compensation from the state for their land and received a mere 120 naira per acre indemnity referred to as a "disturbance fee," a consequence of their never having held a legal title of property on the land other than the traditional right to cultivate it. After the confiscation of the farmers' land by the state authorities the land was declared building area and then sold off in small plots to private investors who paid up to five times more to the state for their allotments as well as special fees (*laada*) to the respective officials to obtain official registration. The private investors then developed their plots for the construction of houses or resold them for commercial use. Thus in 1976/77 the price for one acre of building land was between 66 and 333 times higher than the original "disturbance fee" paid to the farmer (i.e., between 8,000 and 40,000 naira per acre), whereas the price for commercial areas had risen 200–1,000 times (96,000–480,000 naira per acre). In the course of this land reallocation thousands of farmers around

Kano were deceived and driven from their lands if they refused to go. Most of them were forced to find work as salaried unskilled workers in urban Kano (Lubeck 1986: 68).

Land speculation, however, is only one of many sources of the wealth of the Kano traders. Until the end of the nineteenth century they were active in the kolanut and textile trades. After the British conquest of Kano a series of new occupations were added, namely, the trade in groundnuts, transport business, and the activities as middlemen for the great British or Levantine enterprises. Lovejoy remarks that many of the traders in the groundnut and kolanut sector invested in transport during the colonial period and built up great fleets of trucks. In 1970 about 73 percent of all trucks in Kano were in possession of kolanut traders (Lovejoy 1980: 94). The foundations for much of the wealth of many Kano traders had already been established during their employment as middlemen for the British and Lebanese trading enterprises (Dan Asabe 1987a: 48 ff.). Until 1952 the discriminating system of licensed buying agents (LBAs) was, however, to block the rise of an indigenous trading aristocracy. The LBAs had the task of buying agricultural products like groundnuts or cotton from the local farmers and to transport the goods to the regional market centers where they were bought up by the great enterprises. For this reason many LBAs established transport companies of their own which later became the starting point for their further commercial activities. However, the system of LBAs dictated that only those traders who commanded a sufficient knowledge of the English language as well as the art of bookkeeping were permitted to trade in cotton and groundnuts, the most profitable goods. Further qualifying conditions were the ability to make an annual minimum purchase of five hundred tons of groundnuts and command over an capital basis of 10,000 pounds sterling (Interview Albasu, 28 Apr. 1988).

These harsh conditions meant that out of a total of twenty-two LBAs for groundnut marketing in the early 1950s a mere two indigenous traders were to be found, while in the cotton trade no indigenous trader was represented at all among the thirteen official LBAs (Willer 1989: 43). Only when this system was modified in 1952 and the conditions for obtaining a licence were relaxed by reducing the original capital required to 1,000 pounds sterling and the buying capacity to three hundred tons of groundnuts annually (Interview Albasu, 28 Apr. 1988) were the first two indigenous traders, al-Hassan Dantata and Ibrahim Musa Gashash, able to obtain licences and to extend their commercial enterprises. Thus, by the early 1950s, al-Hassan Dantata commanded some one hundred unlicensed agents purchasing groundnuts for him (Watts 1983: 338). In the late 1950s and in the 1960s more and more indigenous traders registered as LBAs, and in 1969 266 of 268 LBAs in the groundnut sector were indigenous. In the cotton sector the respective numbers were 167 of 174 LBAs (Willer 1989: 43). Nevertheless many indigenous traders were not able to expand their commercial activities and become entrepreneurs. They restricted themselves to the traditional sectors of trade (kolanuts, cattle, textiles). As this market was to become too small for an increasing number of traders, many traders had to accept the role of middlemen for the British, Lebanese, and later Nigerian enterprises. On the other hand, the market in the 1950s was already firmly controlled by the British and Lebanese trading houses, so that in spite of the success of some great traders like Dantata and Gashash only the indigenization decrees of 1972 and 1977 made a further expansion of the Kano trading enterprises possible. The indigenization decrees ("Nigerian enterprises promotion decree") forced all expatriate entrepreneurs in Nigeria either to accept Nigerian citizenship or to sell the majority of their shares and assets to Nigerian investors. These decrees led on the one hand to a partial emigration of the Lebanese and on the other hand to increased industrial activities by Lebanese who were forced out of their trading activities (Interview Albasu, 28 Apr. 1988). Since the enforcement of the indigenization decrees the Kano trading enterprises, now often connected with Lebanese counterparts, push into the sphere of actual production of goods: leather, chemicals, processed food, furniture, textiles, and machinery.

The most famous and greatest of all Kano trading enterprises today is the commercial empire of the Dantata family. It was founded and build up by al-Hassan Dantata. He was born in Bebeji near Kano in 1877 and came to Kano in 1903 with his parents. He laid the foundations for his wealth through the kolanut trade with Gonja in present-day Ghana. After 1918 he acted as a middleman for the British Niger Company but was to set up his own enterprise very early on. In 1922 he was already regarded as the wealthiest Kano trader. When the first bank was opened in Kano in 1929, al-Hassan Dantata is said to have deposited twenty camel loads of silver coins (Dan Asabe 1987a: 88). He was the first to construct a "modern" house out of concrete in the old city of Kano, which made his wealth proverbial: *Gida da zumunti sai da na Alhassan* (the houses of concrete belong only to Alhassan), as the Kano residents used to say. In the 1920s and 1930s he became a business partner of the German trading company G. I. Gaiser, which led to great problems with the British colonial administration in World War II. In 1952 he finally managed together with Ibrahim Musa Gashash to be recognized as an LBA. His career was crowned in 1953 by his being admitted into the influential emir's council where he became the first representative of the Kano trading community. After his death on 17 August 1955 his company with its headquarters in Unguwar Koki was divided according to the Islamic laws of inheritance among his eighteen children. However, his heirs took over the Alhassan Dantata & Sons Company in 1956 under the management of the eldest son, Ahmadu Dantata, thus forestalling fragmentation of the enterprise. They thereby avoided the division of business capital which usually meant the end for many smaller Kano companies like that of Umaru Sha Rubutu Koki (d. 1944) or of Muhammad Nagoda (d. 1965) (Dan Asabe 1987a: 70, 95, 103 ff.).

After the early death of Ahmadu Dantata (1916–60) the family enterprise was taken over by another son, Aminu Dantata (b. 1931), who currently manages the company. Aminu Dantata is one of the most important financiers of the Tijânyya in Kano. He was a close friend of the former President Shehu Shagari and supported him politically. Today he is owner of a number of companies like the Dantata Candle Manufacturing Company, the Grand Industrial Company Ltd., and the Northern Nigeria Flour Mills (Bashir 1983: 397, Williams 1982: 83; Dan Asabe 1987a: 101 ff.). As early as 1959 another son, Sanusi (b. 1917), had founded his own enterprise named Sanusi Dantata & Sons Company. Among other industrial companies he owns the Moukarim Metal Wood Factory, the Dantata Kola Company Ltd., and the Dantata Metal & Wood Factory (Bashir 1983: 377). He withdrew in 1982 from an active role in the business and handed the management to his sons Nasiru Abdulkadir and Usman. A third son of al-Hassan Dantata, Makhmud (1922–83), was less successful in his commercial activities. In 1948 in collaboration with Ibrahim Musa Gashash and Haruna Kashim he founded the West African Pilgrimage Association (WAPA), the first Kano travel tour agency, which specialized in organizing the pilgrimage to Mecca. In 1966 the WAPA was transformed into a hotel with bar and nightclub, managed by the later governor of Kano state, Sabo Bakin Zuwo (Dan Asabe 1987a: 100). In contrast to his brothers Aminu and Sanusi, Makhmud Dantata supported the opposition party NEPU. In 1957 he was arrested and charged with the possession of counterfeit money and held in custody until 1964.

Apart from the Dantata family a number of other big commercial enterprises exist in Kano which are not much smaller than the Dantata's. Among them, for example, exists the enterprise belonging to the afore-mentioned Ibrahim Musa Gashash, the descendant of an Arab family from Ghadâmis, who had created his wealth in the groundnut trade and transport sector. In 1950 he was one of the cofounders of the first joint enterprise of Kano traders, the Kano Citizen Trading Company (KCTC). Like al-Hassan Dantata he was a financier of the NPC and was appointed Minister of Lands and Survey in Ahmadu Bello's cabinet. In 1963 he supported the deposition of Muhammad Sanusi, in this way supporting his business partner and cofounder of the WAPA, Haruna Kassim (1919–86), a Kanuri from Ringim (Dan Asabe 1987a: 117). After his death in 1975/76 his brother Makhmud (b. 1931) took over the family company. Makhmud Gashash is among his other occupations a member of the supervisory board of the Nigerian Bank of Industry and Commerce (Paden 1986: 148, 454; Bashir 1983: 241).

Another very important commercial enterprise is that of Isiaku Rabiu (b. 1928), which is said to be almost as big as that of the Dantata family. Rabiu's father Rabiu Dan Tinki was a religious scholar who also traded in books and sewing machines. Like his father Rabiu is a religious scholar and supports the Tijâniyya-Ibrâhîmiyya in Kano. Until the 1960s he was the personal *malam* of Ibrahim Musa Gashash, who introduced him into the Kaduna Textile Factory as a trading agent for his company. This activity enabled Isiaku Rabiu to set up the foundations for his own enterprise. His major business activity today is the trade in sewing machines and textiles. For example, he owns the Bagauda Textile Company Ltd., the Kano Sugar Company Ltd., and the Rabiu Brothers Metal and Steel Works. In 1986/87 he build a new palace-like residence on Aminu Kano Way near the Goron Dutse Friday Mosque which was also financed by him. He acts as one of the major financiers of the NPC-NPN and was thus able to secure a series of lucrative contracts for his thirteen companies under the Shagari administration. In early 1984 he was arrested by the Buhari military government on account of a large hoarding operation with rice imports, whereby he was able to make a net profit of 140 million naira. He was released only twenty months later after the military takeover of General Babangida (Dan Asabe 1987a: 126 ff.; Othman 1984: 451–52).

Another wealthy trading baron is Uba Abdurrahman Ringim. As with Isiaku Rabiu he is considered to be one of the most influential supporters of the Tijâniyya in Kano and financier of the NPC-NPN. He is a muqaddam and scholar of the Tijâniyya and has constructed a mosque and zâwiya in Kofar Sabuwa Road in the southern part of the old city of Kano. Like Ibrahim Musa Gashash he opposed Emir Muhammad Sanusi and the NEPU and resented the succession of Muhammad Sanusi as khalîfa of Ibrahim Niass in 1963. He was one of the most important shareholders of the Bank of Credit and Commerce International

(Nigeria), of which Ibrahim Dasuki, Sultan of Sokoto, was the chairman until 1989 (Inteview Kane, 18 Jan. 1989).

Of the great Kano trading houses the company belonging to Adamu Jakada (d. 1943) must also be mentioned. He was one of the wealthiest of the early traders of Kano, and who since 1901 had been active as a British informer. When this activity was revealed, the Emir of Kano ordered a boycott of his company, which soon went bankrupt (Bashir 1983: 104). Sani Mashal (b. 1927) from Kura, south of Kano, was more successful. He specialized in the bicycle and car trade and offered transport services for private companies and state-subsidized companies such as the Northern Region Marketing Board. As early as 1964 his trucks already went as far as Accra (Ghana). Finally he engaged in the "estate management" sphere, a euphemism for land speculation. He was one of the few traders of importance who supported the NEPU-PRP. Among his companies are the Kaura Biskuits Company Ltd., the Residential Hotel, a transport company, and a large farm (Dan Asabe 1987a: 51, 122 ff.; Bashir 1983: 315). Also worth mention is the company belonging to Aminu Ahmad who, like many Kano traders, is an Agalawa from the Air region in present-day Niger. He dominated the trade in perfumes and essences. His company is nowadays managed by his son, Sani Ahmad (Interview Dan Asabe, 7 Mar. 1987).

Numerous trading families concentrated on specific products. Thus Hassan Nabadamasi (1880–1970), originally a middleman for Ferris George, later controlled the trade in glass beads and necklaces (Dan Asabe 1987a: 109 ff.), whereas Iliasu Dan Gomba (d. 1952) was active in the kolanut trade with Gonja. His son Musa Iliasu opened the first pharmaceutical company in Kano (ibid.: 65 ff.). Garba Bichi (b. 1926) concentrated on the intermediate trade in groundnuts and bicycles and later established a transport company of his own. He was the third Kano trader who obtained a licence as LBA in 1960 (ibid.: 120). An interesting biography has also Baba Danbaffa (Danbappa, 1919–90), whose father was malam in Bauchi. He himself became malam of the Emir of Kano and in this way acquired the capital for his participation in the KCTC which he cofounded in 1950. From 1954 to 1956 he was a member of the federal House of Representatives and became successor to Ibrahim Musa Gashash as secretary of the KCTC. After 1963 he was LBA for groundnuts. Under the auspices of Kano state governor Audu Bako (1968–75) in 1972 he became Commissioner for Establishments and Service Matters. In addition, until 1983 he was Deputy National President of the Chambers of Commerce and Industry (Bashir 1983: 243, 280; Dan Asabe 1987a: 111 ff.).

The above cited businessmen and a number of smaller trading barons belong to a group of entrepreneurs whom Tahir has named "merchant financiers and patrons" (Tahir 1975: 92, 139). They are active in almost every sphere of trade and manufacture, and their trading enterprises embrace smaller trading companies with their own trading networks. They preside over their own transport companies and have property worth up to several hundred million dollars. They maintain schools and mosques; they own great estates around Kano and call themselves owners of numerous immovables. They are major shareholders of banks and invest in international financial and economic activities. In Kano they are the masters and patrons of one or several *unguwoyi* (wards), which can be regarded as the basis for any political or religious career. Each unguwa usually has its own clubs, school(s), mosque(s), market, associations, and central place, and is represented externally by a *mai unguwa* (master of the ward). The big entrepreneurs are, however, politically active not only on the local level of the unguwa, but also in regional or national politics as power brokers and financiers of parties and power groups. Finally they usually invest great sums of money in the social and religious sector (ibid.: 139).

The social and religious donations (*ṣadaqât*) are spent "in the way of God" (Tahir: fî sabîl Allâh) for the construction and maintainment of schools, hospitals, or mosques, for the costs of the pilgrimage of needy Muslims, for the support of poor malamai, or for the nourishment of beggars and *almajirai* (Hausa: Qur'ânic school pupils). These donations not only have a charitable or religious meaning, but can also be used quite directly and systematically in order to achieve political or economical aims. With the help of such donations voters may, for instance, be influenced favorably or the chances of an applicant for a political office may be enhanced (Interview Kane, 18 Jan. 1989): "For giving charity the businessmen primarily expects God's blessing, but in addition he also expects a reciprocal favor from the recipient of the charity" (Bashir 1983: 49). The concept of "compensating acts" plays an important role in determining the size of these socioreligious donations (Interview Dan Asabe and Moten, 7 Mar. 1987). Many of the wealthy traders are conscious of the dubious ethical grounds upon which they have acquired their wealth, which is neither in accordance with the prescriptions of the sharî'a nor with the laws of the state, irrespective of the fact that only in rare cases are those responsible for semilegal or illegal economic activities punished by the Nigerian state. This point is clearly demonstrated by Ogunnika in his thesis on Kano businessmen (1982). The Kano traders try, however, to balance their sins by giving more or less extensive dontions fî sabîl Allâh (Interview Moten and Dan Asabe, 7 Mar. 1987). At the same time, as a consequence of their charitable activities they expect relief from their moral conflicts. How the traders themselves see the concept of "compensating acts" is indicated by a discussion between 'Abd ar-Rashid Moten and a pious trader with whom he met regularly in the Bayero University mosque. Moten confronted his interlocutor with the question as to why he would on the one hand go to the mosque regularly but on the other hand entertain extramarital relationships and drink alcohol. Was this not an obvious contradiction to his piety? The trader replied that to his mind this was a typically "Western" way of thinking (Moten was a native Bangladeshi). He argued that in Islam the good acts are balanced against the bad ones at the day of judgment. Therefore he would pray and fulfill his obligations and duties as a pious Muslim. But as long as he fulfilled these duties he could also go on to commit his "little sins" (Interview Moten, 7 Mar. 1987). Tahir comments on this behavior: "The most aggressive and successful merchant industrialists and traders are the heaviest investors in religious institutions" (Tahir 1975: 27–28).

In the course of the economic development of Kano and in the context of the growing wealth of the Kano trading community socioreligious donations were also to grow in size. The connection between political ambitions and "bad consciousness" on behalf of the Kano traders on the one hand and the size of their socioreligious investments on the other can be clearly demonstrated by examining the growth of the number of mosques in Kano during the last few decades. In Kano the construction of mosques is regarded as especially meritorious and is seen as an act of charity bringing the donor blessing even after his death (Tahir 1975: 127). While in 1900 there were a mere twelve mosques and only one Friday mosque in Kano (Paden 1973: 51), statistics indicating the growth of mosque construction from the turn of the century until the present are given by Tahir (1975: 396) as follows:

1901–10	21 new mosques
1911–20	34 new mosques
1921–30	37 new mosques
1931–40	37 new mosques
1941–50	68 new mosques
1951–60	97 new mosques
1961–70	112 new mosques

After the release of a *fatwâ* (legal opinion) of the Kano religious scholars in 1970 a number of new Friday mosques were built in and around the old city. Among them are the Murtala Muhammad mosque in Fagge (1970), the Kurnar Asabe mosque (1972), the Bayero University mosque (1979), the Hausawa mosque (1980), the 'Yar Akwa mosque and No Man's Land mosques (1982), the Hotoro mosque (1986), and the Goron Dutse mosque (1987). The mosques were, according to Tahir (1975: 395), financed at a ratio of 58 percent by traders, 19 percent by religious scholars, 8.5 percent by artisan associations, and only 7.5 percent by the old aristocracy.

The big boom in the construction of mosques clearly coincided with the economic expansion of Kano since World War II. In 1973, 446 mosques existed in Kano (metropolitan area), that is, thirty more than in 1970, which clearly shows that the construction boom of the 1960s continued in the 1970s. This indicates that by the mid-1970s each unguwa had per average four mosques (ibid.: 127). If one assumes that this trend has continued at least until the beginning of the economic crisis in 1982/83 it may then be considered as relatively certain that Kano had approximately 650 mosques by 1990. Especially significant in this context, however, are not only the sheer numbers of mosques, but also their attachment to the great Sufi brotherhoods. In 1970 the picture according to Tahir (ibid.) was thus: 329 mosques (72.4%) had a Tijânî imam, 77 mosques (18.7%) had a Qâdirî imam, and 40 mosques (8.9%) had an nonaffiliated imam.

Most mosques are thus closely attached to one of the two great Sufi brotherhoods: They have an imam who is either affiliated with the Qâdiriyya or the Tijâniyya and a steady community of followers also attached to the network of a religious scholar. In the mosque communities of the unguwoyi the faithful practice the dhikr of the Qâdiriyya or Tijâniyya. They are financed by the rich traders of the unguwa and can be regarded as the basis of the respective ṭarîqa in the unguwa. It has to be emphasized, however, that these observations are not valid for the great Friday mosques. Although these can be led by an imam who is ṭarîqa-affiliated, they are nevertheless open to all Muslims, and the rituals of the ṭuruq are not practiced there. Furthermore the appointment of a new imam of a Friday mosque is the duty of the emir and his council and is therefore a complex political decision, whereas the appointment of an imam to a smaller mosque within a given unguwa falls predominantly to the responsibility of the ward. Although the emir has to consent to the appointment of such an imam he is usually not in a position to appoint a candidate who receives little or no support from the community or of the rich financiers of the ward. Aside from these factors the office of the imam in many of the smaller mosques is usually handed down within the families of the scholars, from father to son or brother. Thus outside interference is regarded as a serious violation to intracommunal peace and balance of power and would consequently create much communal trouble.

The above mentioned statistics show that the dynamics of the different trader-scholar networks are very different. The Tijâniyya was in this respect obviously more successful than the Qâdiriyya, which enjoys fewer connections to wealthy farmers and therefore commands a smaller economic basis for the construction and entertainment of mosques. Nevertheless it is significant that the majority of Kano's mosques are attached to either the Qâdiriyya or the Tijâniyya and that the percentage of nonattached mosques is below 10 percent. The fact that the traders are the most important financiers for the construction and maintenance of mosques is a further indication that the majority of Kano traders are affiliated with the two great Sufi brotherhoods. This connection between traders and scholars becomes even more obvious if one takes into account how much influence the traders exert on the appointment of a new imam for one of their own mosques. Thus Sanusi Dantata won one of the greatest scholars of the Qâdiriyya in Kano, 'Ali Kumasi, for his mosque in Unguwar Koki, and in the case of the Makwarari family the network connections between mosque and commercial enterprise are still clearer: The Makwarari family belongs to the most influential financiers of Nasiru Kabara and the Qâdiriyya. The founder of this family enterprise was al-Ḥajj Isa Abdullahi Makwarari who, under the spiritual protection of Kabara in the late 1950s, founded the Bayajidda Amenity Trading Company, the second great joint enterprise of the Kano traders after the KCTC. Isa Abdullahi Makwarari's brother Yusuf Abdullahi Makwarari is the founder and imam of the renowned Makwarari mosque in Unguwar Makwarari, who is concurrently both Kabara's deputy in Kano and spiritual head of the Makwarari family. During periods of Kabara's absence from Kano, it is Yusuf Abdullahi Makwarari who leads the Qâdiriyya in Kano spiritually and acts as its spokesman. His nephew Ibrahim Isa Abdullahi is the present managing director of the Gidan Bayajidda and of the ISAB Petroleum Company Ltd., personal advisor of Kabara in financial affairs, and chairman of the management board of the Qâdiriyya in Kano. He is responsible for press contacts and for the organization of the Maulid 'Abd al-Qâdir (see the overview of the network of the Qâdiriyya in the appendixes) (Interview I. I. Abdullahi, 3 Jan. 1987). It also should be considered that a number of big traders, as Isiaku Rabiu or Uba Ringim in the case of the Tijâniyya, are also scholars of their own and as leaders of their networks important personalities in the power structure of their ṭarîqa.

How substantial the fî sabîl Allâh donations of a single trader can be is shown by the following example of a trader from Kano, who according to Tahir (1975: 165) in 1972 spent the following sums for socioreligious purposes:

Donations for the Masu Sarauta	30,000 naira (37.5%)
Donations for clients	14,400 naira (18.0%)
Donations for politicians	10,000 naira (12.5%)
Financing of the ḥajj for poor Muslims	7,000 naira (8.8%)
Donations to schools and mosques	6,000 naira (7.5%)
Zakât payments to the malamai	4,000 naira (5.0%)
Food donations for poor Muslims	4,000 naira (5.0%)
Ṣalât gifts to malamai	4,000 naira (5.0%)
Sum	79,400 naira

Of these c. 80,000 naira, 25,000 naira (the last five categories) can be regarded as donations fî sabîl Allâh in the sense of the word. Donations which are even bigger than these are not rare, however. Thus on the establishment of an appeal fund for the support of the Council of 'Ulama' in Kano on 12 March 1988, Isiaku Rabiu donated a sum of 100,000 naira on a single day, whereas on the same occasion Aminu Dantata donated 250,000 naira (*The Triumph*, 14 Mar. 1988). Thus in the course of one year great commercial entrepreneurs may donate several million naira fî sabîl Allâh. Further examples of the size of such donations are the

3 million naira which Isiaku Rabiu gave for the construction of the Bayero University mosque, followed by 2 million naira given by Sanusi Danata for the same purpose (Interview Dan Asabe, 7 Mar. 1987). In 1983 Sani Mashal gave another 2 million naira for the construction of the Kura Local Government Senior Islamic Secondary School alone (*The Pen*, 1988, no. 13). He also financed the construction of the Kurnar Asabe Friday mosque in Kurnar Asabe along the Katsina Road. As previously mentioned, Isiaku Rabiu financed the construction of the Goron Dutse Friday mosque along Aminu Kano way and shared the costs of a new mosque at Kofar Mata (Interview Kane, 18 Jan. 1989). Uba Ringim supported the construction of the new major zâwiya of the Tijâniyya in Kofar Nasarawa with a sum of 100,000 naira (Interview Kane, 18 Jan. 1989), and al-Ḥâjj Danbatta financed the construction of the Gwale Islamiyya Primary School as well as that of the Goron Dutse Islamiyya Secondary School which are both attached to the Qâdiriyya (Interview S. U. Kabara, 15 Feb. 1987).

The growing size of socioreligious investments of the Kano traders directly benefited the religious scholars in Kano because these donations achieved their intended purpose only then, when they were really employed fî sabîl Allâh. For this reason, however, the traders need the religious scholars: The religious scholars guarantee that the traders' charitable mandate is fulfilled by accepting the donations of the wealthy men in the name of God and in the name of the Muslim community, especially the needy ones among them. The wealthy men are therefore as dependent on the cooperation of the holy men since the latter need the donations of the rich traders in order to maintain their mosques and schools. Because of this many wealthy men also employ personal malamai who pray exclusively for their economic success as well as their spiritual welfare. For their services the holy men do not receive a salary but ṣadaqât, donations fî sabîl Allâh. The generosity of these ṣadaqât is relative to the size of the donor's property. The wealthier he is, the more malamai he is able to support and the higher his donations are going to be. Extremely successful traders do give their malamai ṣadaqât not only in return for spiritual support but also because they believe that their economic success can be attributed to the baraka of the prayers of their malamai (Cohen 1969: 168).

In this way the influence of certain religous scholars over their affiliated traders can become so great that they are even in a position to influence the economic enterprises of the traders. Thus in 1950, a number of Kano businessmen who were affiliated with the Tijâniyya on the advice of Ibrahim Niass established the KCTC as the first indigenous joint commercial enterprise. The initial capital of the KCTC with its headquarters in Unguwar Gwammaja was raised primarily with a credit of 35,100 pounds sterling from the Northern Regional Development Board on a basis of 3 percent interest and also through a donation of 11,000 pounds sterling from an indigenous trader. To the founders of the KCTC belonged, among others, Ibrahim Musa Gashash, Baba Danbappa, al-Hassan Dantata, Baba Nabegu, and Sule Nababa. The first secretary of the KCTC was Ibrahim Musa Gashash, followed by Baba Danbappa (Bashir 1983: 67). After the withdrawal of Niass from Nigeria in 1963 the company stood under the spiritual protection of Abubakar Atiku, Tijani Usman, and Sani Kafanga, all members of the Salgawa network of the Tijâniyya. In connection to the traders motives with founding this enterprise, Tahir quotes the following: "We did not like mixing our affairs before. Then Shaykh Ibrahim told us that one of us may have baraka and his baraka may make the whole enterprise a success. So we formed our company and approached the Sardauna" (Tahir 1975: 88). The other great joint commercial enterprise of Kano traders of the time was the already mentioned Bayajidda Amenity Trading Company of the Makwarari family, which stood under the spiritual protection of Nasiru Kabara (ibid.: 81).

The alliances between certain trading houses and the religious traders have existed in some cases for several generations and have been carried over until the present day. Thus al-Hassan Dantata supported the Qâdiriyya in Kano, and after his death his son Sanusi Dantata assumed his role (Tahir 1975: 156). The cooperation between traders and malamai in Kano had far-reaching repercussions on the development of income and relationships of dependence on the religious scholars. Whereas as late as the nineteenth century many malamai, with the exception of those who lived at the emir's court, continued to make their living through teaching and an additional handicraft, in the twentieth century financial support through wealthy traders became increasingly important. Tahir (1975: 393) characterizes this development as follows:

> The secularization of taxes [after 1908] ended zakkat payments to the state [and thus also the redistribution of zakât among the malamai, the author] and together with the income revolution made disciple connections highly valued by ulema. . . . Commercial dispora expansion and the general improvement in the availability of wealth extended . . . opportunities for the quasi-commercial agency and liaison activity [of the malamai]. To these must be added the introduction of printing and the sponsorship of the works of ulema whose sale generated another source of income. By 1930 an almost entirely new ulema type completely depending on patronage given "fi sabil Allah" and from the proceeds of scholastic actitiy had come to predominate. . . . By the arrival of Niass . . . Kano ulema had advanced very far in elaborating and entrenching the charitable use of wealth in "sabil Allah" obligations.

In addition to donations from wealthy men and their incomes from the sale of their books, which can be considerable (ibid.: 157), the holy men are also business partners in the economic enterprises of their wealthy supporters. This combination of spiritual and economic influence not only puts a number of religious scholars like Nasiru Kabara in a position to enforce their own spiritual claims within their brotherhoods but also enables them to exert considerable pressure on their business partners. Tahir states in regard to the relationship between holy men and wealth men, "In relation to the merchant aristocracy each Shaykh can and does excommunicate a recalcitrant merchant adherent" (ibid.: 151).

Only very powerful commercial barons such as Sanusi Dantata risked rebellion against the authority of his shaykh. A movement of emancipation also began among the rich traders in connection with the weakening of the ṭuruq only after the foundation of the 'Yan Izala in 1978. Thus Aminu Dantata, one of the most important financiers of the Tijâniyya in Kano, is said to have supported the 'Yan Izala for some years, and similar rumors are reported in connection with Isiaku Rabiu (Interview Kane, 18 Jan. 1989). Since the early 1980s the rich traders have no longer limited their donations to a single religious movement, but have distributed their donations over a greater range of sympathizers and support apart from the Qâdiriyya, the Tijâniyya, or the 'Yan Izala movement. This does not, however, imply that the basic structures of understanding and cooperation between holy men and wealthy men have decisively changed. The network connections have just become more flexible.

3

The Political and Religious Development of the Muslims in Northern Nigeria between 1951 and 1978

In the 1950s the Muslims in Northern Nigeria experienced not only the conflict between the two great Sufi brotherhoods, but also the rapid development of the political parties. It was under these historical conditions that the leader of the Northern People's Congress (NPC), Ahmadu Bello, was to rise and become the most important politician of his time in Northern Nigeria. His ultimate political aim was to conserve and consolidate the unity of the North as a precondition for its dominant role within the Federation of Nigeria. In view of this aim Bello supported the unification of the Muslims in Northern Nigeria in the form of religious organizations like the Jamâ'at Naṣr al-Islâm (Association for the Support of Islam). Politicians, parties, or groups who opposed the politics of Bello were persecuted and suppressed. On the religious level the policy of Bello was supported by Abubakar Gumi, who in 1962 was appointed Grand Kadi of Northern Nigeria. Gumi regarded the ṭuruq as the greatest obstacles to be removed on the way to Muslim unity. After the assassination of Bello in 1966 Gumi lost his political protection, but he won new allies among the heirs of Bello, the so-called Kaduna Mafia. After 1966, this group of politicians, military officers, intellectuals, businessmen, and bureaucrats sought to conserve the legacy of Bello and their own positions of influence. Among them Gumi had his greatest social and political support. Ahmadu Bello is still regarded by many leading personalities the public life as a political idol and a leading figure. His policy and his legacy are therefore the central topic of this chapter.

3.1. The Era of Ahmadu Bello

Ahmadu Bello was born in 1910 in the village of Rabah, about twenty kilometers east of Sokoto. His father, Ibrahim Bello, the "District Head" of Rabah, originated from Usman dan Fodio's family. After having gone through the Qur'ânic school, Bello attended the Sokoto Provincial School and in 1926 left for the Katsina College which at that time was the first high school in Northern Nigeria. It had been established in 1922 for the purpose of raising indigenous administrators and teachers. In 1938 the college, which had rapidly become a school of the Northern elites, was transferred first to Kaduna and in 1949 finally to Zaria, where since then it has been known as Barewa College. After completing his education in 1931 Ahmadu Bello was appointed teacher at the Sokoto Middle School, where he worked until the death of his brother in 1934. The latter had taken over the post of district head of Rabah after the death of their father, and this office was now passed on to Bello himself. As district head he was confronted for the first time in his life with concrete tasks of administration, such as census or the raising of taxes. His actual political career began in 1938 when the Sultan of Sokoto, Hassan, died. As a member of a sideline of the royal family of Sokoto he was thus to become a candidate for the succession to the throne in Sokoto. The succession was, however, decided in favor of the *Sardauna,* the head of the royal guard, Abubakar (1903–88), who as Sultan Abubakar III ruled until his death on 1 November 1988. After his accession to the throne, Ahmado Bello was to replace him in the office of the *sardauna,* a title which was to become the most popular form of addressing him in later years. In order to keep his competitor and threat away from his court, in 1938 the new sultan sent Bello to the distant provincial town of Gusau in the extreme southeast of Sokoto province, where he himself had been in "exile" since 1935 before his own accession to the throne (Boyd 1989: 121). In Gusau Bello was responsible for the administration of fourteen districts. The attempt to get Bello out of the way by transferring him to distant Gusau backfired, however, as a result of Bello's dynamic character. He rapidly became an able administrator and achieved a great deal for this region, which, in contrast to Sokoto, was connected with the national railway grid and had become a major center for the cultivation of groundnuts in Northern Nigeria. Bello's alleged complicity in an incident involving corruption also failed to block his ascension. In 1943 some Fulani cattle holders accused Bello of having collected the cattle tax (*jangali*) from them but of having failed to pay the money into the public treasury. On the basis of this accusation Bello was charged by the court of the Sultan of Sokoto of "misappropriation of monies," a criminal offence. This was the usual way in the Sokoto empire and the British colonial system to depose of troublesome officials or emirs. The British administration in particular could be moved to depose an official of the Native Administration usually only on charges of corruption (Fika 1978: 105–6). The sultan's court declared Bello guilty and condemned him to one year imprisonment (Anwar 1989: 124). Bello lodged an appeal against the judgment, however. He was to make a direct request for a revision of his case to the British colonial courts, an action in which he was supported by among others the future Emir of Kano, Muhammad Sanussi. Whitaker interpretes the action of Bello as follows: "At that time, it was unheard of for a Sokoto subject to appeal to the secular British magistrate against a decision of the court of the Sarkin Musulmai . . . but the Sardauna did so successfully, with the help of a southern Nigerian Christian lawyer [the late Chief Bode Thomas]!" (Whitaker 1970: 350).

After his acquittal and rehabilitation Bello could return unopposed to Sokoto and take over the direction of the Native Administration Office, practically under the nose of the sultan. He began a number of reforms within the administration, and replaced some elder bureaucrats of the administration by younger officials of his choice, thereby raising a following in Sokoto of his own. In this way Bello became the leader of the younger generation of administrators in Sokoto who supported a reform of the existing system of administration and who were no longer to hold an unquestioning belief and acceptance of the absolute authority of the sultan.

After the return from his first journey to Britain in 1948 Bello applied for one of the two Sokoto seats in the House of Assembly of the Northern Region. This seat had become vacant after the death of the Wazirin Sokoto. Although the sultan rejected Bello's candidature, the latter pushed through his claim and thus started his parliamentary career. His first journey was to Southern Nigeria where he held talks with the then leader of the independence movement, Azikiwe, about the future of the country. These talks made him realize that the North had to adapt rapidly to the exigencies of the time if it wanted to secure for itself a place in the future construction of an independent Nigeria (Bello 1962: 66). When the new governor of Nigeria, MacPherson, initiated the debate about the future Nigerian constitution in 1949, Ahmadu Bello was consequently one of the three representatives of the North, including Tafawa Balewa and the Wali of Bornu, in the negotiations that took place in Ibadan.

The establishment of political parties and the politicization of public life in Northern Nigeria began in the context of the transfer of the House of Assembly from Sokoto to Kaduna in 1950/51 and in the course of the preparations for the first parliamentary elections in 1951/52. It was particularly the rapid expansion of the populist Northern Elements Progressive Union (NEPU) and its first victories in the primaries of 1950 that shocked the conservative political establishment. The NEPU was founded in 1950 by Aminu Kano (1920–83) and Sa'd Zungur (1915–58). Both stemmed from families of local notables. Sa'd Zungur attended the Bauchi Provincial School, then Katsina College, and Yaba College in Lagos. As early as 1947 Aminu Kano had founded the Northern Teachers' Association which included Tafawa Balewa and Shehu Shagari, both future heads of state of Nigeria, among its members (Williams 1982: 39). In the same year in Kano, Raji Abdallah and Abubakar Zukogi had founded the Northern People's Progressive Association. These two groups merged in 1950 with the Bauchi General Improvement Union of Sa'd

Zungur to form the NEPU (see Whitaker 1970 and Dudley 1968). The conservative elements in the North feared that the NEPU, which attacked not only the British colonial administration but also the existing establishment, namely, the emirs, would win a majority of seats in the elections for the first parliament of the North. Therefore Ahmadu Bello, Ibrahim Kashim, Tafawa Balewa and other conservative representatives founded, on 1 October 1951, the Northern People's Congress (NPC). The NPC was based on an organization called Jamiyyar Mutanen Arewa, founded in 1948 in Kano and Kaduna by R. A. Dikko, Maitama Sule, and D. A. Rafih. With the massive support of the political establishment and a number of wealthy traders from Kano, the NPC managed to avert the danger of a NEPU victory in 1951 and won a majority of seats in the first parliament of the North (Whitaker 1970: 355 ff.; Osuntokun 1987: 35).

Originally the NPC consisted primarily of graduates from Katsina College, organized in the Katsina Old Boys' Association, as well as the bureaucrats of the Native Administration. They were joined in the next few years by many wealthy traders and most of the emirs, as well as a number of politicians from the Middle Belt areas, who were won over to the NPC by Ahmadu Bello (Paden 1986: 202 ff., 343 ff.). Bello himself was appointed Minister of Works after the elections of 1951 and in 1953 also became responsible for Community Development and Local Government. Thus he controlled the implementation and realization of all development and investment projects in the North as well as the entire apparatus of local and regional administration. This position proved to be especially important in the coming years in the context of the fight of the NPC against the regional opposition movements in Kano (see below), Bornu (see Osuntokun 1987), Ilorin (see Whitaker 1970), and Benue-Plateau (see Paden 1986). Bello, in his function as head of the Native Administration, could distribute the available resources and jobs according to his and the NPC's political strategies and thereby considerably damage the efforts of the opposition movements. The control over the administrative apparatus facilitated Bello's further political career.

After the second parliamentary elections in 1954 he became the first prime minister of the North. In these elections the NPC won eighty of ninety-two seats in the parliament and could thus consolidate itself as the most important political force in the North.

Whereas after the elections of 1954 a number of influential politicians of the NPC, like Tafawa Balewa or Inuwa Wada, went to the South and thus continued their political career on the national level, Bello remained in the North and expanded his regional power base. In the first national elections in 1959 the NPC could win 134 out of 312 seats in the first federal parliament, whereas Awolowo's Action Group (AG) obtained only eighty-three mandates, and the National Congress of Nigeria and the Cameroons (NCNC) of Azikiwe obtained seventy-three seats. Thereby the NPC became the strongest parliamentary group in the first federal parliament. On account of this development the British Governor General of Nigeria, Sir James Robertson, nominated Tafawa Balewa as prime minister of the federation, preventing a coalition between the AG and the NCNC (Coleman 1958: 377). The degree of Bello's influence on national politics was shown by his relationship to the prime minister of the federation, Tafawa Balewa, whom he described twice in 1959 and in 1961 as his "lieutenant in the south" (Whitaker 1970: 352). Thus the North, represented by the NPC, had won on the national level the supreme control of political power. The precondition for the nomination of Tafawa Balewa as prime minister was, however, the fact that Bello had consented to a reform of the existing judiciary system in the North, a reform which resulted among other things in the excision of the penal law from the sharî'a legislation (Abun-Nasr 1988: 38 ff.).

The political dominance of the NPC would be consolidated in the following elections. In 1961 the NPC won 159 out of 170 seats in the parliament of the North, thereby reducing the political importance of the three most relevant opposition movements, the NEPU, the Bornu Youth Movement (BYM), and the United Middle Belt Congress (UMBC) of Joseph Tarka, to almost nothing. Another great personal success for Bello was the vote of the population in the British Trust Territories of the Cameroons. Whereas the southern half of British Cameroons voted for reunification with the Cameroons, a majority of the population in the northern half (146,000 votes against 98,000) voted for incorporation into Northern Nigeria. These areas were thereupon integrated into the North under the name of Sardauna province (Paden 1986: 409). Under the government of Bello the new political capital of the North, Kaduna, was established as the third important center of the region, besides the spiritual center Sokoto and the economic center Kano. Whereas Kaduna in 1939 counted a population of only 4,336, this number had risen by 1960 to 73,346 people, and in the late 1980s Kaduna's population was estimated to surpass half a million people. Furthermore, in 1959 the planning process for the first university in the North began. It was founded in 1960 in Kano as Ahmadu Bello College but transferred in 1962 to Zaria to become Ahmadu Bello University (ABU), today Nigeria's biggest university with an enrollment of about sixteen thousand students.

Apart from his efforts to unite the North politically under his leadership, in the 1950s Bello began to engage himself increasingly in religious affairs. A decisive factor for Bello's interest in the promotion of Islam was his occupation with the problems of organizing the ḥajj. In 1954 two Muslims from Kano, just returned from their pilgrimage, edited a report about the conditions of the ḥajj in the Hijâz, and this report was channeled to Bello's office. In 1955, in response to the findings of the report, Bello, together with the Minister of Works, Isa Kaita, the Emir of Kano, Muhammad Sanusi, and Ibrahim Musa Gashash of the West African Pilgrimage Association, traveled to Saudi Arabia in order to examine the situation of the Nigerian pilgrims personally. In the Hijâz Bello met a young scholar from Sokoto, Abubakar Gumi, whom he already knew and who had undertaken his first pilgrimage that year. On account of his knowledge of Arabic, Gumi became Bello's interpreter in his political and religious talks with the Saudi government. After his return, Bello appointed Gumi Deputy Grand Kadi of Northern Nigeria and first Nigerian liaison officer for the contacts between him and the Saudis. Gumi stayed for about ten months in the Hijâz in 1957 in this function and was thus able to establish numerous contacts with Saudi officials. The contacts to King Sa'ud, but especially to Crown Prince and future King Faisal, were destined to become very important in the 1960s as far as the further expansion of the political and religious links between Northern Nigeria and Saudi Arabia were concerned. After his return to Nigeria Gumi wrote another report about the conditions of the ḥajj in the Hijâz which was handed over to the prime minister of the federation, Tafawa Balewa. In reacton to Gumi's report Tafawa Balewa sent an official Nigerian Pilgrims' Mission to the Sudan and to Saudi Arabia in 1958. Its task was to solve the problem of the organization of the ḥajj in direct negotiations with the respective governments. The political context of the mission was that Saudi Arabia, in response to the British attack on Egypt in 1956, had broken off its diplomatic ties with Britain and threatened to expel all Nigerians living in Saudi Arabia. Members of the Nigerian mission were, apart from Bello himself, Muhammad Sanusi, Abubakar Gumi, and D. S. Adegbenro (Paden 1986: 288). They published their findings in March 1958, and in the same year a resident Nigerian pilgrimage officer was installed in Jidda. His task was to take over the functions of the British consulate in Jidda regarding the diplomatic care for Nigerian pilgrims. Thus Bello, Tafawa Balewa, and Gumi had managed, two years before the actual independence of Nigeria, to nationalize the management of the ḥajj (see Loimeier 1988). In the course of their efforts to reorganize the pilgrimage, close personal ties had developed between Bello and Gumi. These ties were strengthened in the following years as Gumi accompanied Bello on his pilgrimages and journeys to Arab countries. In his function as interpreter and councillor on religious affairs Gumi was able to exert considerable influence on Bello. Gumi himself characterized this influence on Bello as "I was the man behind him" (Interview Gumi, 17 Sept. 1987).

After the successful reorganization of the ḥajj Bello continued to give new initiatives for the development of the Muslims in

Northern Nigeria. In 1962 he appointed Abubakar Gumi first indigenous Grand Kadi of the North and in the same year he supported the establishment of a new Islamic organization called Jamâ'at Naṣr al-Islâm (JNI). This organization was to take on the task of improving Islamic education of the Muslims in the North and to serve as a platform for the promotion of the political and religious aims of Muslims in Nigeria. Furthermore Bello increased his journeys to Arab and Islamic countries and thereby stressed his role as a political and religious leader of international standing. In 1955 and 1956 he had already met with Jamâl 'Abd an-Nâṣir, who at that time was one of the most popular heroes of many anti-imperialist political movements in Africa and Asia. As the Egyptian leader was the political idol of Bello's most important internal opponent, Aminu Kano, his visits to Cairo can also be interpreted as efforts to gain sympathies among Kano's radical followers. In 1961 and 1962 further visits to Egypt followed, and in 1963 Bello undertook a journey to Morocco, Senegal, and Iraq where he visited the centers of the Tijâniyya and the Qâdiriyya, thereby underlining his role as a religious leader of all Muslims in Northern Nigeria.

Bello's attempt to establish in 1962/63 a new religious movement under the name of Usumaniyya also have to be seen in the context of his efforts to unite the North not only politically, but also religiously. In 1962 Bello had published a silsila of his own which depicted him as a descendant of Usman dan Fodio and the Prophet Muhammad. This silsila was consequently disseminated in the North by the praise singers as "lost but found" (Anwar 1989: 104). The Usumaniyya was intended to cultivate the legacy of the leaders of the jihâd and to unite all Muslims in Northern Nigeria under one umbrella, disrespective of their brotherhood affiliations. In order to make this movement acceptable to the Sufi brotherhoods, Abubakar Gumi on Bello's instructions invented a new *wird* (litany) for the Usumaniyya. This wird was laid down in Gumi's treatise *al-Wird al-'aẓîm* (The Mighty Litany) (Interview Kane, 18 Jan. 1989; see also Quadri 1981: 387). As part of the propagation of the Usumaniyya Bello supported the reedition of Usman dan Fodio's works. Thus in 1964 a new edition of the *Iḥyâ' as-sunna wa ikhmâd al-bid'a* and an anthology of his collected works were printed. Gumi and the Wazirin Sokoto Junaidu also translated Usuman dan Fodio's treatise *Uṣûl al-wilâya* (The Roots of Holyness), in which the jihâd leader describes his links with the Qâdiriyya and speaks about his mystical visions (Umar 1988: 185). The foundation and support of the Usumaniyya by Bello was, however, seen by many Muslims as an effort by Bello to undermine the religious authority of the Sultan of Sokoto and to take over the religious lead of the Muslims in the North himself. Therefore the Usumaniyya only gained a short-lived support until Bello's death in Kaduna, Bello's seat of government. The restriction of the Usumaniyya to Kaduna caused Paden to characterize the Usumaniyya as a movement of the "Northern Civil Service" (Paden 1973: 182). By virtue of the fact that a majority of the religious scholars in Northern Nigeria were affiliated in the 1960s with one of the two great Sufi brotherhoods and were not prepared to give up their affiliations in favor of the Usumaniyya, Bello tried to win the collaboration of the malamai by other means. In 1963 he thus supported the foundation of the Kaduna Council of Malamai, an idea inspired by Gumi. The Kaduna Council of Malamai also became known as Advisory Committee on Islamic Affairs (Umar 1988: 182). The Kaduna Council of Malamai was integrated two years later into the JNI and played an important role in its two years of existence only in the context of the Argungu riots of 1965.

One of the central concerns of Ahmadu Bello was the reform of the administrative system. The existing system had been set up by the British in the first decades of the twentieth century. The central elements of the Native Administration were a new system of finance and taxation (introduced in 1909), the Land and Native Rights Proclamation of 1910, and the Native Authority Ordinance of 1916 which recognized the emirs as the supreme authorities in the existing judicial system and gave them the right to appoint, transfer, or dismiss the officials of the Native Administration. This framework was completed in 1925 by the introduction of exactly defined departments in the Native Administration, whereby a rationalized form of administration was created (Fika 1978: 160 ff.). Bello had initiated local reforms during his time as a native authority official in Sokoto in the 1940s. In the 1950s he began, however, an all-embracing reform of the old system which still gave the emirs far-reaching rights in government, administration, and jurisdiction and thus blocked Bello's struggle for political unification and hegemony. In his function as Minister for Local Government and Community Development Bello implemented after 1952 a number of measures aimed at the rejuvenation, rationalization, and improvement of the training of the native authority staff. Stricter financial controls were introduced and administrative procedures were restructured, and administrative tasks were slowly withdrawn from the emirs' courts and transferred to Kaduna, the new political center of the North.

The young bureaucrats in Kaduna, protégés of Bello, were modernizers like him. They regarded the existing emirate system as the source of all evil and tried to systematically weaken it to overcome the stagnation and backwardness of the North. In 1958 Bello approved a reform of the judiciary by which the whole sphere of the administration and execution of penal law was taken away from the sharî'a courts of law. Thus the sharî'a was limited more or less only to the sphere of personal law. Bello seems to have recognized by 1958 that the consolidation of his position as leader of all groups of the population in the North and the effective fight against the demands for an independent Middle Belt state depended on the renunciation of the Islamic criminal law (Abun-Naṣr 1988: 51). The judiciary reforms of 1958 represented a considerable limitation of the powers of the emirs, as they had until this time been the last resort of appeal in the judiciary. Furthermore Bello transformed the emirate councils, which had until then had only consultative functions, into real bodies of administration. They received certain rights of cotermination with the emirs in decision making. Thereby the emirs lost their almost absolute powers to the new central administration in Kaduna and its agents in the provinces. The decisive step in the direction of actual deprivation of the powers of the emirs came, however, only in 1962 with the implementation of the so-called Provincial Administration Bill. This law provided for the appointment of a new supreme head of administration, the provincial commissioner in each province (emirate). The provincial commissioner was to be appointed by the central government in Kaduna, that is, by Ahmadu Bello. He should head the respective provincial administrations and in addition be of higher rank to the respective emir. If any "irregularities" were to occur in the administration of a province, the provincial commissioner was, after consultation with the prime minister of the North, entitled to depose an emir (ibid.: 438–41). Depositions of local rulers had in the past under the British colonial rule been a popular practice in order to bring unruly or corrupt emirs to order. This method of enforcing the policy of the central authority was taken over by Bello and his new administration in Kaduna. Thus in 1954 the Shehu of Dikwa, Mustafa III, was deposed under the pretext of "autocratic bearing, reliance on personal favorites and failure to consult the council" (ibid.: 196). In 1957 Bello appointed a Council of Chiefs which took over the task of deposing, disciplining, appointing, or promoting emirs and of deciding about their succession. Bello himself was chairman of the council and used this body in the following years to enforce his policy of unification. The number of chiefs was raised considerably, and thus an increase of title-bearers occurred, which led to a devaluation of the actual weight of an office in the old system of government. Bello repeatedly intervened in debates over successions to support his own candidates. Thus in 1954 he intervened in favor of Muhammad Sanussi, who was thereupon nominated new Emir of Kano, and in 1959 supported Muhammad Aminu as new Emir of Zaria (ibid.: 195, 199). Thereby the power and respect of the emirs was eroded, and they were subsequently obliged to the prime minister in exchange for his support. In addition, a new Land Tenure Bill was introduced in 1962, which replaced the Land and Native Rights Proclamation of 1910. The new law took away the control of all lands in Northern Nigeria from the emirs and transferred these powers to the new provincial administrations. Thus the emirs lost a decisive tool for the maintenance of power over their subjects, the power to distribute and to reallocate land (Zillikens 1985: 87).

The only emir who tried to resist these reforms and fight against his loss of power was Emir Muhammad Sanusi of Kano, an old friend and ally of Bello. Sanusi had supported Bello in 1943 when the latter had been accused of tax evasion and mismanagement of monies by the Sultan's court in Sokoto but had subsequently been rehabilitated and acquitted by a British court (Paden 1986: 121). In a countermove Bello supported the succession of Sanusi as Emir of Kano in 1954. In the 1950s he became one of the most important politicians of the NPC in Kano and had a considerable share in the establishment of the party in Kano. It was due to his influence that numerous wealthy traders from Kano, like Ibrahim Musa Gashash, became supporters of the NPC and did not join the NEPU, which was very popular in Kano (ibid.: 146). Since 1954 Sanusi was minister "without portfolio" in Bello's first cabinet. As a member of the Nigerian Pilgrims' Mission he traveled together with Bello to the Hijâz in 1955 and 1958 and in 1961 was even appointed acting governor of the North in the absence of the governor, Sir Gawain Bell. For various reasons, however, a conflict had developed between him and Bello. Sanusi's strong support for the Tijâniyya in Kano since 1954 went against Bello's plans for the religious and political unification of the North under his own leadership. Abubakar Gumi, Bello's religious advisor, advised him to fight the Tijâniyya, arguing that this brotherhood would frustrate Bello's efforts to build up the Usumaniyya, which was intended to incorporate all other religious movements (Umar 1988: 182). In addition, parts of the Tijâniyya in Kano sympathized with the NEPU and thereby also questioned Bello's claim for hegemony in the North. Finally Muhammad Sanusi sought to gain acceptance as leader of the Tijâniyya throughout Nigeria and used his office to place members of the Tijâniyya and confidants of his choice in high positions at the court and in the emirate's administration. Thus he achieved greater power than former emirs ever had, but at the same time he gave up the policy of balancing out the diverse interest groups in Kano, a policy practiced successfully by his predecessors. Not only his policy but also his claim for leadership within the Tijâniyya was rejected by the malamai of the Salgawa network of the Tijaniyya in Kano (Interview Kane, 18 Jan. 1989). As Sanusi, like Bello, was a politician with far-reaching ambitions, a conflict between them was inevitable. The discussion about the enactment of the Provincial Administration Bill brought their conflict to a head.

The conflict between Sanusi and Bello was also influenced by a number of other factors. In 1962, for instance, Bello had not appointed Sanusi as successor to the Governor of the North but lifted his confidant Sir Kashim Ibrahim from Bornu to this position, although Sanusi as former acting governor had expected that he himself would become the new governor (Osuntokun 1987: 84). Bello on the other side had the ambition to be recognized as a Grand Emir of the North, after his claim to the office of the Sultan of Sokoto had misfired in 1938. Bello's vanity had been hurt again and again because he was obliged to stand up according to the laws of protocol during public receptions, and that not only before the Sultan of Sokoto, but also before the emirs of Gwandu and Kano as well as the Shehu of Bornu, if the latter arrived at a public ceremony later than himself. Bello could obviously never overcome constant humiliations like these (ibid.: 86). An opportunity to avenge himself was the appointment of the Magajin Garin Sokoto, al-Ḥâjj Aliyu, as new provincial commissioner of Kano in 1962. Al-Ḥâjj Aliyu was a confidant of Bello and came from a family of court slaves of the Sultan of Sokoto. Whitaker summarizes al-Ḥâjj Aliyu's appointment as provincial commissioner in the following words: "In the context of historical claims, that appointment conveyed an unmistakable message that the Emir of Kano was being put in his place by the Sardauna" (Whitaker 1970: 279). In view of his increasing loss of authority Muhammad Sanusi tried to mobilize the NPC in Kano in order to exert pressure on Bello. As he had created numerous enmities in Kano by his own one-sided and arrogant policy, however, his efforts remained futile. A number of scholars of the Tijâniyya, like Muhammad Sani Kafanga, Uba Ringim, and Tijani Usman, who had been excluded by Sanusi from participation in power, supported the downfall of Sanusi and thwarted his efforts to draw the NPC in Kano to his side (Interview Kane, 18 Jan. 1989).

Under these circumstances all resistance by Muhammad Sanusi remained unsuccessful. In late 1962 Bello finally used an administrative board of inquiry under the direction of the British officer Muffet, which had been instituted on account of alleged irregularities in the financial administration of the Kano Native Authority, to force the emir to resign. The Muffet commission established in the course of its inquiries that under Sanusi's rule "misuse" of the land allocation rights of the emir, "fraud," "maladministration and financial mismanagement" had occurred (Quadri 1981: 360; Paden 1986: 446). To escape an impending trial, Sanusi gave up his resistance and on 14 April 1963 handed in his resignation, whereupon he was sent into exile to Azare in Bauchi province. With the deposition of Sanusi Bello's problems in Kano were not yet solved. On 14 April 1963 the followers of Sanusi under the leadership of Ali Wazirichi and Bello Abdulkadri founded a new party in Kano named the Kano People's Party (KPP). Its aims were the rehabilitation of Sanusi and the establishment of an independent Kano state within the Federation of Nigeria. After a few weeks the KPP already numbered about thirty-six thousand members and had thus become a serious danger for the NPC in Kano (Osuntokun 1987: 87). In the same year contacts were established among the KPP, the NEPU, the UMBC, the Northern Youth Movement, which was recruited mainly from young dissidents of the NPC in Kano, and a number of trade unions, and a Northern Progressive Front was formed. This union of opposition movements presented itself as a common platform for the next regional and federal elections, attacked the policy of the NPC, supported the emancipation of women in the North, and demanded the improvement of the economic performance of the North, as well as the creation of more states in the federation and a thorough reform of the judicial system. Sanusi was forced under the threat of a public trial and the raising of his immunity to abstain from any political activity (ibid.: 89). The danger of a further strengthening of this opposition movement in Kano propelled Bello and the NPC to react quickly and along well-tried lines:

> In June 1963 the entire executive committee of the Kano People's Party was tried and committed to prison by the Alkali court for using abusive and "annoying language" in references to the Premier, Sir Ahmadu Bello, the Sardauna of Sokoto. . . . In this way the KPP was stopped in its tracks and the Sardauna's victory over the Emir of Kano was total. This victory signalled to all other Emirs that the Sardauna was a Baban Emir and he would not brook any challenge to his own power which he saw as being independent of the support which the Emirs had previously given him. He also began to see himself as being divinely inspired, driven and directed and that the Emirs must follow his religious and political direction if they wished to retain their position. (ibid.: 89–90)

By late 1963 the KPP was crushed and the position of power of Bello and the NPC asserted. In January 1964 the remainder of the KPP fused with the NEPU of Aminu Kano to become the Kano State Movement (KSM). In the same year Aminu Kano traveled to Kaolack to meet Ibrahim Niass personally and obtained from him the spiritual blessing for the unification of both NEPU and KPP. Thus by July 1965 a factual alliance between the progressive forces in Kano in the form of the NEPU and the supporters of Sanusi within the Tijâniyya came into existence. The chairman of the KSM was a well-known trader, supporter of the Tijâniyya, and follower of Sanusi, Ahmadu Trader, whereas Kano confined himself to the role of political advisor and Tanko Yakasai became the secretary general of the movement. The KSM renewed the demand for the rehabilitation of Sanusi and for the creation of an independent Kano state (Paden 1973: 312). After the 1966 military coup all political activities were suspended, however, and the KSM was thus unable to develop a profile of its own. With the foundation of Kano state in 1967 one of the two major demands of the KSM was fulfilled. When the NEPU's successor party, the People's Redemption Party (PRP), won the first elections in Kano after the end of military rule in 1979 and Sanusi was brought home to Wudil (Kano) from his exile in Azare, the last traces of Bello's policy in Kano had finally been removed.

Many Muslims in the North interpreted the deposition of Muhammad Sanusi not only as a political struggle for power, but also as an effort by Bello to contain the Tijâniyya-Ibrâhîmiyya, which had become too strong in Kano under Sanusi's rule, in order to improve his own religious ambitions (Quadri 1981: 298). Thus Bello not only acted as a political leader but also stressed his religious role and thus threatened the position of the Sultan of Sokoto. In a speech in Argungu on 22 April 1965, for example, he adressed the public with the words "I am here as a leader in [sic] Islam" (Anwar 1989: 174). Bello's policy after Sanusi's resignation in respect to the Tijâniyya seem to confirm his intentions. After his resignation Sanusi was appointed Khalîfa of the Tijâniyya-Ibrâhîmiyya for the whole of Nigeria by Ibrahim Niass. This appointment had become necessary because Abubakar Gumi had, according to Sir Kashim Ibrahim, advised Bello to ban further visits by Niass to Nigeria to hit the Tijâniyya more severely (ibid.: 292). The appointment of Sanusi as overall leader of the Tijâniyya-Ibrâhîmiyya triggered off a crisis of leadership within the Tijâniyya, as many Tijânîs, especially the malamai of the Salgawa network, were not prepared to accept Sanusi's leading role. The ensuing disintegration of the Tijâniyya-Ibrâhîmiyya into several competing networks weakened the brotherhood to such a degree that the Kaduna Council of Malamai, which had also been created by Bello on Gumi's advice, was able to condemn the practice of qabḍ on the basis of a religious argument in the context of the Argungu riots in 1965. The only member of the Tijâniyya-Ibrâhîmiyya in the commission of inquiry on the question of qabḍ was Tijani Usman, and he again belonged to the outspoken enemies of Sanusi within the Salgawa network.

With the deposition of Sanusi it was made clear that the new bureaucratic elite in Kaduna with Bello at its head was stronger than even a Babban Emir. Although Bello had by 1963 already deposed a number of other emirs, the great emirs of Sokoto, Gwandu, Kano, and Bornu had been regarded until then as "untouchable." With Sanusis's deposition Bello had shown that their position was vulnerable. Whitaker stresses the importance of the deposition of Sanusi for Bello's position of power in these words: "An unusual aspect of the Sanusi case, however, was that the Sardauna had succeeded in doing what some traditional heads of the Fulani empire had failed to do: dethrone an Emir of Kano" (Whitaker 1970: 282).

After his crushing victories over Muhammad Sanusi and the KPP in 1963, Ahmadu Bello was adressed, in conscious irony at least, as Sarkin Arewa (King of the North) (Whitaker 1970: 351). Through his assassination on 15 January 1966 the North lost the only politician who had the authority to guarantee the political and religious unity of Muslims in Northern Nigeria and to defend the position of the North within the federation. On the other hand, Bello's policy to make the North the stongest force within the federation also led to the failure of his policy and to the military coup in 1966. The South could not accept the predominance of an arrogant North in the long term, especially in view of the fact that this predominance was not based on a correspondingly strong economic basis or on a appropriately trained apparatus of experts, administrators, or teachers. The oil fields which by the 1960s had become the most important source of Nigeria's export earnings all lay in the South, and in 1960 only 750 of about forty thousand employees of the federal administration came from the North (Williams 1982: 63). Thus the North's position of power was bound to be destroyed by its inherent contradictions and the opposition of external forces from the South.

3.2. Bello's Heirs: The Kaduna Mafia

The policy of Ahmadu Bello, symbolized by the motto "One North, One People," seemed to suffer a setback by his assassination in 1966. No other politician existed who could have taken over Bello's role within the NPC. There was, however, a group of supporters and followers of Bello who were prepared to protect his legacy. This group consisted essentially of the representatives of the new bureaucratic elite, which had been posted by Bello in all important administrative positions in the North, especially in Kaduna. Many among them were, like Bello, members of the Katsina Old Boys' Association and Western educated. With their help, Bello had achieved in the 1950s and 1960s the realization of his administrative reforms, the establishment of the NPC, and the modernization of the economy. They represented the backbone of a new technocratic and bureaucratic elite which became famous under the name the Kaduna Mafia. This expression has been common in Nigeria since the 1970s, especially in the media. Nevertheless I want to emphasize that there are no connections whatsoever between the Kaduna Mafia and the original nineteenth-century Sicilian mafia. The term Kaduna Mafia is therefore not used to imply an unusual criminal energy, but rather to point to the extraordinary efficiency by which this network fought for and often achieved its political and personal aims in many spheres of public life and economy in modern Nigeria. At best the Kaduna Mafia can be characterized as an all-embracing network, consisting of bureaucrats, businessmen, politicians, military officers, and intellectuals from Northern Nigeria, based in Kaduna, which forms a lobby of "the North," exerting pressure on the federal government in Lagos to defend the interests of the modernizing elites of the North within the federation.

Originally the Kaduna Mafia consisted of Bello's closest followers and friends like Ali Akilu, Ibrahim Dasuki, Ahmad Joda, Hassan Lemu, Sunday Awoniyi, Hassan Katsina, Ahmad Talib, and Yahya Gusau. Ali Akilu (1928–71) from Sokoto, studied at the Barewa College in Kaduna, went to London, and after his return became the first director of the northern civil service and in 1958 Nigeria's first pilgrimage officer in Jidda. In 1963 he was appointed Senior Assistant Secretary of the prime minister and thus became the head of the administration of the influential Premier's Office in Kaduna which was organized into four departments: general administration of the Premier's Office, political tasks, finances, ḥajj, and provincial administration (Paden 1986: 472–74). After the coup of 1966, Ali Akilu became one of the leading members of the transition government of Hassan Katsina in the North. Ibrahim Dasuki (b. 1923) from Dogondaji in Sokoto was to become one of the most important figures in the development of the JNI. In 1988 he was nominated Sultan of Sokoto after the death of Abubakar III. Ahmad Joda (b. 1930) from Adamawa was head of Bello's intelligence service and from 1961 to 1966 Permanent Secretary in the Ministry of Information. Until 1976 he served as chairman of Peugeot Automobiles Nigeria (Williams 1982: 133). Hassan Lemu (b. 1930), a Nupe from Niger state, was a private secretary to Bello, whereas Sunday Awoniyi (b. 1932) from Kabba (Kwara state) was responsible since 1961 for security matters in the Premier's Office. After 1966 he worked in the office of the military governor of the North, Hassan Katsina, and between 1968 and 1978 he was Permanent Secretary of Finances (Paden 1986: 242). Hassan Katsina (b. 1933), a member of the emir's family of Katsina attended, like Sunday Awoniyi, Barewa College, later gained an education at Sandhurst as a military officer, entered the Nigerian army, and after 1966 became the military governor of the North. Together with Akilu and Ibrahim he set up an interim government in the North. In the army he swiftly rose to high positions and was thus able to raise other officers from the North, like Shehu Musa Yar'Adua and T. Y. Danjuma, into high positions within the army. In 1971 he was replaced as army chief of staff by David Ejoor from Bendel state (ibid.: 680 ff.). Ahmad Talib (b. 1918) from Yerwa (Bornu) attended Barewa College, studied in England, and after 1953 worked in the treasury in Kaduna; he was thereupon appointed assistant finance secretary and worked from 1961 to 1968 as Permanent Secretary of Finance (Paden 1986: 222, 265 ff.). Finally, Yahya Gusau (b. 1916) from Gusau (Sokoto) founded in 1947, together with Aminu Kano, the Northern Teachers' Association. He went to England in 1954 and was appointed Senior Assistant Secretary in the premier's office in 1959. After 1966 he became head of the Federal Commission of Natural Resources (ibid.: 142).

After the initial shock which followed Ahmadu Bello's assassination this central group tried, for the time being, to get an overview of the developments after the coup and to solve the immediate problem of the succession to Bello. Two options existed: either to find a new political leader who would be able to replace Bello and continue his policies or to set up a collective leadership made up of Bello's closest friends and confidants. As it was not possible to find a new, charismatic political leader acceptable to everybody overnight, the central group of the Kaduna Mafia resolved to constitute a collective leadership. Originally Major Hassan Katsina, Ali Akilu, and Yahya Gusau were the most important members of this group around which the other followers of Bello regrouped. In the months after Bellos's assassination they met either in the Ni'ima club or in Lugard Hall, the Parliament of the North, and in the course of these meetings came to be a sort of Executive Council of the North (Takaya and Tyoden 1987: 97). The above-mentioned friends of Bello were soon joined as members of this inner circle of the Kaduna Mafia by a number of other high-ranking bureaucrats, influential businessmen, wealthy traders, military officers, bankers, and investors, as well as some emirs, who had been close friends of Bello, and last but not least, a number of lecturers from the Institute of Administration of ABU Zaria (Othman 1984: 447). Their first goal was to close the gap which had been created by Bello's assassination and to prevent the North's loss of power within the federation. They achieved this aim in a relatively short period of time (1966/67) by filling key positions in the administration, economy, banking sector, army, and other public institutions with their own confidants, as far as these positions had not already been filled by members of the Kaduna Mafia. The greatest problems could already be solved in July 1966, when the Igbo army officers who had staged the first coup were ousted in a second, internal coup.

The most important of these institutions was the Interim Common Services Agency (ICSA), founded in 1967, which had the task of supervising the allocation of the assets in the dissolved Northern region and to distribute the federal monies among the new federal states of the North. Other organizations apart from the ICSA were the Northern Nigerian Development Corporation (NNDC), an umbrella organization of the Northern industries and enterprises, representing about 120 companies and responsible for the allocation of contracts; the Northern Nigerian Produce Marketing Board (NNPMB), responsible for the distribution of seeds and chemicals, as well as the planning and implementation of rural development projects, and finally the Northern Nigerian Housing Corporation (NNHC), responsible for the construction sector in the North and an umbrella organization for the Northern building industry. After 1966/67 these institutions took over the administration of all assets, shares, estates, and properties of the former Northern region which had been allocated to the six new federal states of the North, according to the respective strength of their population (Paden 1986: 698). Apart from these central institutions the members of the Kaduna Mafia rose in the following years to numerous leading and influential positions in a number of banks, such as the Habib Nigeria Bank (Chairman: Major-General Shehu Musa Yar'adua), the Nigerian Agricultural and Cooperative Bank (Chairman: Group Captain Usman Jibrin), the Universal Trust Bank (Chairman: Lt. General T. Y. Danjuma), the Nigerian Bank of Credit and Commerce International (Chairman: Ibrahim Dasuki), the Federal Mortgage Bank, and the Nigerian Industrial Development Bank. The latter two banks are development banks through which the World Bank carried out most of its project-related financial transactions with Nigeria. Thus in 1985/86 alone $570 million was channeled to Nigeria through these banks (Bergstresser 1988: 187; Othman 1984: 454). Further strongholds of the Kaduna Mafia were the previously mentioned Institute of Administration of ABU Zaria, as well as the three media giants of the North, Radio Kaduna, the daily newspaper *New Nigerian* which had been founded on 1 October 1966 as the "Voice of the North," and the Hausa daily *Gaskiya Ta Fi Kwabo* (Takaya and Tyoden 1987: 63).

The control of these institutions enabled the Kaduna Mafia to exert pressure on other spheres of public life through the allocation (or nonallocation) of monies, contracts, and posts. The Kaduna Mafia was especially successful in its infiltration of the administration of the federal ministries, parts of the army, and the banking sector. Within the army Major Hassan Katsina had a key position as Army Chief of Staff until he was replaced in 1971 by the Gowon confidant David Ejoor who had played a dubious role during the Biafra war (Hussaini 1988: 92). After the coup against Gowon on 27 July 1975 by General Murtala Muhammad and after the assassination of the latter in the abortive coup of 13 February 1976, Lt. General T. Y. Danjuma and Lt. General Shehu Musa Yar'adua took over similar positions of power under the administration of General Obasanjo (1976–79).

The members of the Kaduna Mafia who were recruited or coopted during the civil war and the Gowon years can be characterized as the "second generation" of the network. This group of individuals was still connected with the inner circle of the confidants of Ahmadu Bello. In the early 1970s they had not yet taken part in the informal process of decision making and consultation. In the course of the mid- and late 1970s and early 1980s a number of second-generation network members rose, however, to become members of the inner circle and came to occupy key positions within Nigerian institutions. Apart from the Generals T. Y. Danjuma and Shehu Musa Yar'adua, a number of politicians, intellectuals, businessmen, and bureaucrats, such as Adamu Ciroma (b. 1934) who had served in the Premier's Office from 1961 to 1965, took over the *New Nigerian* in 1966 as first editor-in-chief, and became governor of the Nigerian Central Bank in Lagos (Paden 1986: 242), have to be counted among them. Others include Ibrahim Tahir from Bauchi who rose to be the director of NITEL (Nigerian Telecommunications) from 1979 to 1983, al-Ḥâjj Umaru Shinkafi who was appointed head of the first Nigerian secret service, the Nigerian Security Organization (NSO) in 1976, A. B. U. Hayatudeeen, the Managing Director of the NNPC, Mahmud Tukur (b. 1939) who had worked in the premier's office after 1963 and was appointed Federal Minister for Industry and Commerce in 1984, Liman Ciroma from Bornu who had studied archaeology in England and became head of the Northern History Research Scheme at ABU Zaria after 1966, and Tukur Othman who had worked for Bello as an intelligence officer and later found employment in the Ministry of Information (Takaya and Tyoden 1987: 68–69). The second generation of network members was completed in the 1970s by an outer circle of supporters of the network who were recruited predominantly from the spheres of economy and administration. Members of this group were people who had gained wealth and a high position through the support of the Kaduna Mafia.

The first indigenization decree of 1972 was especially important for the economic sucesses of the network. On the basis of this decree all expatriate entrepreneurs were forced to nationalize their shareholdings and companies. As the Kaduna Mafia controlled numerous key positions in the federal and regional administrations, the banking sector, the ministeries, and organizations like the ICSA or the NNDC, it could execute transactions under favorable conditions and thus acquire large shares of the nationalized enterprises. The major profiteers of these transactions were of course the members of the network themselves. On the other hand, a number of businessmen and entrepreneurs who had hitherto not been connected with the network were thus integrated into the system of services and obligations of the Kaduna Mafia. From a bank connected with the network they were to receive, for instance, credits at low interest rates which enabled them to acquire their own shares in certain companies. Thus ambitious businessmen would be obliged to join the network and be asked for counterservices if the need arose (Takaya and Tyoden 1987: 98).

The first crisis in the development of the Kaduna Mafia occurred when General Gowon started to appoint more and more Christian advisors from the South and his own region (Plateau state) to his government. In 1974 he also initiated the nationalization of a number of organizations and institutions which had been regarded until then by the Kaduna Mafia as their own sinecures. Among these were the nationalization of the *New Nigerian* and of Radio Kaduna in 1975, the most important daily newspaper and radio station in Northern Nigeria, as well as the Nigerian Produce Marketing Board, which was chaired by Ibrahim Dasuki. In the face of this increasing erosion of its power basis the Kaduna Mafia supported the coup of General Murtala Muhammad of Kano who toppled the increasingly unpopular General Gowon in 1975 and established a regime of moral purification, also replacing David Ejoor as army chief of staff by Lt. General T. Y. Danjuma (Husseini 1988: 92). After the assassination of General Murtala Muhammad and the takeover of power by General Obasanjo in the course of the abortive coup of 13 February 1976, the Kaduna Mafia got the chance to regain lost positions. Decisive for the second rise of the network was the fact that Major General Shehu Musa Yar'adua, an important network member, rose to become the strongman of the Obasanjo administration after 1976. These favorable conditions again provided the Kaduna Mafia the opportunity to occupy key posts in the economy, army, and administration.

In the course of the oil boom a tremendous expansion of public investments and state expenditures started in the second half of the 1970s. This boom led to the development of new groups of entrepreneurs who began to question the dominance of the Kaduna Mafia. Especially in the context of the readmission of the political parties in 1978 a number of competing networks appeared on the scene who independently from each other voiced their respective claims to political leadership. Apart from the Kaduna Mafia which had organized itself in the form of the so-called Northern Caucus within the new conservative National Party of Nigeria (NPN), there were networks like the Ibo Caucus, the Yoruba Solidarity Front, and the Ikenne Mafia, in which the supporters of Awolowo especially gathered (Othman 1984: 446–48). The latter founded in competition with the NPN a new party of its own, the Unity Party of Nigeria (UPN), which thus succeeded the old Action Group. Of increasing importance for the development of the new parties was the principle of "zoning," the regional allocation of the most important party positions or future government posts among the representatives of the different ethnic groups within a party. Thus a party like the NPN which had its power basis in the North could try to win representatives in other regions among groups which had not found a foothold in their regional networks on account of animosities within their groups. Thus the most important opponent of Awolowo in Yorubaland, the wealthy entrepreneur M. K. O. Abiola, affiliated himself with the NPN, and in this way helped the party to win a considerable number of voters in Western Nigeria and thus overcome old regional antagonisms (ibid.: 448).

In the race for the office of president of Nigeria in 1979 the candidate of the Kaduna Mafia within the NPN, Adamu Ciroma, was unable to force his way through as a result of his involvement in the Leyland corruption scandal of 1977. Thus the uncompromised Shehu Shagari from Sokoto was nominated candidate of the NPN for the presidency (Othman 1984: 449). Shagari was essentially supported by some wealthy Northern businessmen who were not members of the Kaduna Mafia, and in addition he had the trust of the Southern supporters of the NPN in contrast to his opponent Adamu Ciroma. After the close victory of Shagari against Awolowo (5,689,000 votes to Awolowo's 4,917,000) the Kaduna Mafia saw itself again excluded from its direct access to power. A number of personalities of the younger generation of the network, however, for personal and economic reasons joined forces with the Shagari government so that an actual split within the Kaduna Mafia took place after 1979. The pro-Shagari group within the network again swiftly rose to positions of power and influence. One of them was Ibrahim Tahir who was appointed head of Nigerian Telecommunications (NITEL) in 1979. A number of network members could enrich themselves in an hitherto unknown extent on the basis of lucrative state contracts which were usually connected with highly coveted commission payments (Hausa: Laada). Thus a businessman like Bako Kontagora received 8 million naira for a number of state contracts which were never executed, and the company Fougerole (Nigeria) paid "kickbacks" of about 24 million naira to a number of NPN functionaries to get state contracts worth 746 million naira. Also highly lucrative was the trade with import licences which were sold to the highest bidder by the Ministry of Industry and Commerce. The successful buyer of an import licence then hoarded the imported products, like rice and wheat, in order to increase the marketprices for these goods and was thus able to make high profits. These practices not only accelerated inflation but also increased the costs for state contracts because only a part of the monies were actually used to realize the contracts. Thus a commission of inquiry estimated that as early as in 1980 the costs for comparable state contracts were three times higher in Nigeria than in other African countries. These practices of enrichment at the cost of the state treasury converted the Nigerian balance of payments despite high prices for crude oil until 1982 from a surplus of 5.5 billion naira in October 1980 to a deficit of 11.1 billion naira of internal and about 22 billion naira of external debts by the end of 1983 (Othman 1984: 450–52).

When the economic and financial performance of the Shagari administration deteriorated rapidly after 1981, and the Nigerian economic crisis began in the context of the simultaneous decay of the prices for crude oil after 1982, the group within the Kaduna Mafia critical of Shagari started a campaign against the mismanagement of Nigeria by the Shagari government. Among other things they criticized the president for having surrounded himself increasingly with non-Muslim advisors from the South and thus having neglected the interests of the North. The major aim of the group critical of Shagari within the Kaduna Mafia was thus to prevent confirmation of Shagari as president of Nigeria in the 1983 federal elections. In order to achieve this goal, a "dialogue" was initiated between the Kaduna Mafia and the opposition party PRP. Major General Shehu Musa Yar'adua met the leader of the PRP, Aminu Kano, to set up an alliance of Shagari opponents. In June 1983 a secret agreemeent was concluded between the Kaduna Mafia and the great opposition party of the South, the UPN of Awolowo. In the context of this agreement the Kaduna Mafia promised to support Awolowo as candidate for the presidential elections of that year, whereas in return the UPN accepted the transfer of the capital from Lagos to Abuja, the political boycott of Israel, and establishment of a Federal Islamic Bank, and they were to give the Kaduna Mafia in addition the right to fill all administrative posts in the North (Othman 1984: 455). These agreements were, however, made public in the course of the election campaign, and a scandal resulted. On account of its willingness to cooperate with Awolowo, Ahmadu Bello's greatest opponent in his lifetime, the Kaduna Mafia was discredited and the alliance between the network and the UPN broke up as a consequence. When Shehu Shagari managed to secure his reelection as president in 1983 with 12,047,000 votes against Awolowo's 7,885,000, the Kaduna Mafia had thus lost all hope of regaining its influence in governmental affairs.

Their position changed abruptly, however, when on 31 December 1983 the Nigerian army under General Buhari staged another successful coup against the government of Shehu Shagari on account of its inability to master the economic crisis. The new military regime started a radical purge of the corrupt administration. Numerous businessmen, politicians, and bureaucrats like Isiaku Rabiu, Ibrahim Tahir, and Shehu Shagari were imprisoned under accusations of mismanagement, corruption, fraud, or misappropriation of government monies and sentenced to long terms of imprisonment. Others, like Umaru Dikko, managed to flee abroad. Together with the Buhari-Idiagbon administration the group critical of Shagari within the Kaduna Mafia came back to power and was able to co-opt other representatives of its network into key positions of the new administration. Thus Mahmud Tukur, one of Ahmadu Bello's private secretaries after 1963, was appointed Minister of Industry and Commerce and became responsible for the allocation of import licences (Othman 1984: 456). Lawal Rafindadi, another member of the second generation of the network, rose to become the head of the NSO which had until then been directed by al-Ḥâjj Umaru Shinkafi (Takaya and Tyoden 1987: 141). The policy of economic austerity and disciplinary purges in almost every sphere of public life, as well as the often brutal and arbitrary actions of the Buhari regime and the

NSO, swiftly brought the anti-Buhari forces in administration, industry, commerce, and army together. On 27 August 1985, the Buhari regime was ousted in an internal coup under the leadership of General Ibrahim Babangida. Consequently the imprisoned representatives of the Shagari administration were released and rehabilitated. The NSO was dissolved on account of its arbitrary behavior and reorganized in 1986 bearing the name State Security Service (SSS) after a general revison of its activities by a commission of inquiry led by al-Ḥâjj Umaru Shinkafi (Peters 1987: 185). With General Babangida's succession and the initiation of the program of transition to civilian rule in 1986 the rift and splits within the Kaduna Mafia became apparent, especially when after 1986 the network tried to gain control over the formation of a new conservative party. In the course of the process of political reorientation members of the Kaduna Mafia for the first time appeared in public and described themselves on 15 February 1987 in Kaduna as a Concerned Citizens Committee (or Constitutional Consultation Committee, CCC) in order to influence the discussion of the new constitution of the federation and to form the basis for a future party in the tradition of the NPC-NPN. The constitution of the CCC shows that the internal contradictions within the Kaduna Mafia and the circle of influential personalities have become so great that confidential, internal consultations, debates, and decisions are no longer possible. Thus it has been necessary to shift from an informal and secret entity to a formal and public form of organization in order to coordinate the diverging interests of the different fractions of the Kaduna Mafia. Among the 130 founding members of the CCC were among others Sir Kashim Ibrahim, Hassan Katsina, Shehu Musa Yar'adua, Yahya Gusau, Umaru Shinkafi, T. Y. Danjuma, Maitama Sule, Sunday Awoniyi, and Abubakar Gumi (*The Analyst,* 2 May 1987).

The central political goal of Ahmadu Bello, namely, the unity of the North, was also stressed and followed by the Kaduna Mafia. The network reacted accordingly if the political dominance of the North seemed to be threatened by either external or internal factors, both political and religious. Thus a reconciliation was achieved in 1978/79 among the different quarreling religious movements of the North under the pressure of Shehu Musa Yar'adua, the strongman of the Obasanjo administration. The Kaduna Mafia did not want to risk the victory of a Muslim candidate in the presidential election of 1979 by internal religious rivalries and thus forced the Sufi brotherhoods as well as Abubakar Gumi and his 'Yan Izala followers to conclude an agreement of mutual respect and noninterference. The so-called Committee of Scholars met twice in Lagos and Sokoto on 1 October 1978, and between 3 February and 5 February 1979, and among other things agreed to end the mutual accusation of unbelief (takfîr). The assembled scholars also consented that each scholar should in the future stick to his respective field of knowledge and not interfere with those of other experts (see full text in the appendixes). Although the religious movements shelved their quarrels until after the elections of 1979, another intervention by the Kaduna Mafia became necessary when the heated disputes between the Sufi brotherhoods and the 'Yan Izala resulted in a disastrous defeat of the Muslim candidates in many areas of the Middle Belt during the Local Government elections of 12 December 1987. Thus in January 1988 a second reconciliation between the feuding parties was achieved under the pressure of many Northern politicians led by Ibrahim Dasuki.

It therefore seems as if the unifying forces within the Kaduna Mafia were, despite the diverging interests and despite the internal splits of the 1980s, still stronger than the rivalries of the different fractions within the network, at least as far as major political questions and the overall interests of the elites of the North were concerned. As there was no other network in Northern Nigeria with comparable economic, political, religious, and administrative connections, the Kaduna Mafia was bound to maintain its function as the major broker of connections, monies, and positions in the North at least until the presidential elections of 1993. One of the leading members of the second generation of the network, the managing director of the NNDC, A. B. U. Hayatudeen, explained the secret of the success of the Kaduna Mafia saying, "Because we turn out a large number of people into strategic places on the labour market, we have connections. This enables us to get things done easily" (Takaya and Tyoden 1987: 134).

3.3. The Development of the Jamâ'at Naṣr al-Islâm

The foundation and the development of the Jama'at Naṣr al-Islam (JNI, Association for the Support of Islam) can be regarded as the most important effort to unite the Muslims in Northern Nigeria under one umbrella. In contrast to the Kaduna Council of Malamai and the Usumaniyya, the JNI has survived a number of crisis. It was the only religious organization with a supraregional orientation in which religious scholars and religious movements of different and opposing tendencies have come together in order to discuss and determine their political and religious aims and to present them to the Nigerian public. Thus the JNI was in a position to give important impulses for the development of the Muslims in Nigeria.

The first suggestions to create an umbrella organization for all Muslims were raised in November 1960 by Abubakar Gumi, the religious advisor of the Prime Minister, and by Dr. Abubakar Imam, the treasurer of the NPC. A first meeting of persons interested in the foundation of such an organization took place, however, only on 15 January 1962 in Kaduna. The participants at this meeting were, apart from Abubakar Gumi and Dr. Abubakar Imam, a number of confidants of Ahmadu Bello, including Ali Akilu, Ahmad Talib, Husaini Adamu, Ahmad Joda, Sadiq Abbas, Mallam Musa Bida, Abubakar an-Nafaty from Gombe, and al-Ḥâjj Haliru Binji (b. 1922) from Sokoto. The latter had become successor to Abubakar Gumi as Deputy Grand Kadi to Northern Nigeria in 1962 and was later nominated Grand Kadi of Sokoto state (Paden 1986: 211; Ishaku 1976: 2). Ahmadu Bello also took part in the meeting; he had been convinced of the necessity of such an organization by Gumi and saw the creation of the JNI as a strategy to win the 'ulama' for his religious policy. According to Shehu Galadanci, Nigerian Ambassador to Saudi Arabia, "the

Sardauna knew they [the 'ulama'] had the masses, the students and important people with them; he did all he could to attract, encourage and retain them in Jama'at" (Paden 1986: 582). A personal experience during the ḥajj of 1962 further strenghtened the conviction of Bello to set up such an organization. According to Gumi, the Nigerian VIP delegation was accommodated during the ḥajj at 'Abdullâh Khâlid's residence near the last jamra, close to Mina, where the pilgrims stone Satan, symbolized by the jamra, by throwing small pebbles at this rock. It was there that Gumi noticed, to his indignation, that a number of Nigerian pilgrims out of obvious ignorance of the meaning of this ceremony misbehaved in a very shameful way. They had climbed on the jamra and were beating it with their shoes and cursing it, thinking that it was the real Satan. Asked what ought to be done to prevent such a behavior in the future, Gumi answered the prime minister, "There is nothing except going back to educate the people" (ibid.: 532).

This experience in Mina helped Gumi to convince Bello of the necessity of investing money not only in the construction of splendid new mosques but also in the improvement of Islamic education, arguing that the question was "what is the use of a mosque, if only donkeys are going to it?" (Interview Gumi, 3 Oct. 1987). During the first meeting in Kaduna the participants agreed upon the future name of the organization (JNI) and undertook the first concrete steps to set up the JNI. Bello arranged a credit which enabled the founding committee to buy a piece of land in Kaduna on which the first school of the JNI was to be built. Until the completion of the school, Gumi made his garage at his house in Kaduna available for the teaching of the first classes. Bello and Gumi also initially paid the salaries of the first five teachers of the JNI, whereas the Pakistani businessman Yusuf Gardee donated 12,000 copies of the Qur'ân. The first center of the JNI was the new Sultan Bello Friday mosque in Kaduna close to the residence of the prime minister, Arewa House, in Unguwar Sarki, but later a regular headquarters building was constructed with Saudi financial support (50,000 pounds sterling) along Ali Akilu Road in

Kaduna (Elayo 1984: 4). After the first efforts in 1962, however, a number of financial problems blocked the further development of the JNI for about two years.

To overcome these financial bottlenecks and to speed up the construction of the JNI structure, Ahmadu Bello and Abubakar Gumi used a journey to Kuwait in 1963 in order to ask the Kuwaiti government for financial support. They received a donation of 200,000 pounds sterling for the construction of new mosques and for *da'wa* (missions) (Paden 1986: 543). This money was redirected, however, upon Gumi's intervention and with the consent of the Kuwaitis, to support the construction of a school (Interview Gumi, 3 Oct. 1987). As Saudi Arabia had already donated 100,000 pounds sterling for the construction of the Sultan Bello mosque in Kaduna and added another 100,000 pounds in 1964 for the improvement of Islamic education (Paden 1986: 543), the construction of the first Islamiyya school of the JNI could now be realized very quickly. Work on the so-called Sultan Sabah College had already started in 1963 and could thus be completed in 1967. Renamed Sardauna Memorial College after Bello's death, this secondary school had an enrollment of about four thousand students in 1984 (Elayo 1984: 5).

The financial engagement of a number of wealthy Gulf states, especially Kuwait and Saudi Arabia, can be explained by the fact that these states felt threatened by the expansionist politics of Egypt at that time. Ahmadu Bello had visited Jamâl 'Abd an-Nâṣir several times. In 1960 Egypt had donated 2,000 and in 1961 another 10,000 pounds sterling for the construction of new mosques in Kaduna and Sokoto. In July 1962 Bello received an honorary doctorship from the renowned al-Azhar university in Cairo (Paden 1986: 534). To balance the increasing Egyptian influence on Bello, in 1963 the Gulf states began to channel monies of their own to Northern Nigeria. Thus Kuwait became the greatest donor from 1963 to 1966, whereas Saudi Arabia took over the leading role after 1966. As Egypt was no longer able to continue its ambitious Africa policy after its defeat in the war against Israel in 1967 and after the failure of its military engagement in

Yemen in the same year, Saudi Arabia became the most important power in the financing of religious projects in Northern Nigeria beginning in the 1970s (Interview 'Abd as-Samad Muhammad, 3 Oct. 1987).

To overcome the first phase of stagnation in the development of the JNI, the Kaduna Council of Malamai was created in Kaduna in 1963. The first meeting of the council took place in Kaduna between 23 August and 25 August 1963. The task of the council was to advise the government of the North in all religious matters and thereby to assume a role that the JNI was originally intended to play. Furthermore the Kaduna Council of Malamai was asked to develop concepts for the religious development of the Muslims in Northern Nigeria and to find solutions for the problems within the Muslim community (Paden 1973: 184–85). The council, or Advisory Committee on Islamic Affairs as it was also called, had forty-six malamai from the whole Northern region and from all religious groups as its members. Its first chairman was the Wazirin Sokoto Junaidu b. Muhammad al-Bukhari (b. 1906) who had become advisor to Sultan Abubakar III in 1943 and who rose in 1948 to the office of the Wazirin Sokoto (Chancelor of Sokoto) (Paden 1986: 123). Among the members of the council were scholars such as Nasiru Kabara (Qâdiriyya), Sani Kafanga, Tijani Usman, Shehu Mai Hula (all Tijâniyya), Sa'id b. Hayatu, the leader of the Mahdiyya movement in Northern Nigeria, Shehu Galadanci, Abubakar an-Nafaty, and Haliru Binji (all nonaffiliated and independent): in total twelve scholars from Sokoto alone and six from Kano (Paden 1973: 184–85). The Kaduna Council of Malamai was increasingly integrated into the work of the JNI when the latter's financial problems had been solved in 1964. Thus the council had lost its function as a stimulus for the establishment of the JNI. The Kaduna Council of Malamai finally became obsolete in the context of the qabḍ-sadl dispute in 1965 and was no longer to meet thereafter (Umar 1988: 192). Its functions were taken over by the JNI itself.

The formal foundation of the JNI was proclaimed on 9 March

1964 in Kaduna. The Wazirin Sokoto Junaidu was elected first chairman of the JNI, whereas the prime minister acted as its supreme "Patron." After his death in 1966, the Sultan of Sokoto followed him in this function. The actual work of administration and management was, however, carried out by the secretary general, Abubakar an-Nafaty from Gombe who was succeeded after his death in 1971 by Ibrahim Dasuki from Sokoto.

Ibrahim Dasuki, as a confidant of Bello and close friend of the Grand Kadi of the North, Abubakar Gumi, decisively influenced the development of the JNI as its secretary general after 1971. He was born on 31 December 1923 in Dogondaji (Sokoto). His father, Haliru, was the Sarkin Yamma of Sokoto and belonged to the Bukhari line of the family of Usman dan Fodio. His education began in 1929 with the Qur'ânic school; in 1931 he attended the Dogondaji Primary School; he was admitted to the Sokoto Middle School in 1935 and to Barewa College in Kaduna in 1940, where he completed his education in 1943. Thereupon he worked as a native administration employee in Sokoto for about two years, then accepted a job with the Gaskiya Corporation in 1945, the publishing house of the daily newspaper *Gaskiya Ta Fi Kwabo*. In 1954 Ahmadu Bello appointed him a personal secretary and sent him to Pankshin (Plateau) as assistant district officer in 1956. After one year he returned to Kaduna where he filled the job of Regional Executive Council Deputy Secretary and was then sent to Jidda in Saudi Arabia in 1958 to become the Nigerian pilgrimage officer until 1960. In 1960/61 he worked in the Nigerian embassy in Khartoum (Sudan) and was brought back to Nigeria by Bello in 1962 to work first as Resident in Jos and then as first indigenous official in the function of a Permanent Secretary, in the "Ministry of Local Government." In this function he became one of the prime minister's most important "troubleshooters" (Paden 1986: 239). In 1965 he switched to the Ministry of Commerce where he remained until 1968. In 1966 he became chairman of the influential Northern Nigerian Produce Marketing Board, an office he filled until 1969. After 1968 he concentrated on his business activities and became one of the key figures of the

Kaduna Mafia. Apart from his chairmanship of the NNPMB and his office of secretary general of the JNI, he filled a number of other important posts such as chairman of the Gusau Oil Mills, the United Arewa Stores, and the Nigerian Railway Corporation (all since 1969), and chairman of the Zamfara Textile Industries (since 1971) and of the North-West Trade Development Company (since 1972). He was appointed fourth Baraden Sokoto (General of Sokoto) in 1973 and elected secretary general of the newly established Nigerian Supreme Council of Islamic Affairs (NSCIA). His involvement in Jewish business connections raised much criticism in Northern Nigeria; he was director of the Afro Continental Company, owned by the Jewish entrepreneur Goan, from 1979 to 1981. Aside from this last post his activity as chairman of the Bank of Credit and Commerce International (Nigeria) was attacked repeatedly on account of certain business practices of the bank. From the fact that a large gap existed between the sum of profits (dividends) distributed each year among its shareholders, and the total sum of credits allocated each year to its creditors, the conclusion could be drawn that the bank cultivated unorthodox business practices in the sphere of foreign exchange (*New Nigerian,* 7 Jan. 1989; *New African,* 1989, no. 257). Until his nomination as new Sultan of Sokoto on 8 November 1988, Ibrahim Dasuki filled the post of the secretary general of the JNI. His right hand in this office was his assistant secretary general, Muhammad Kolo Biu from Bornu, who kept his office under the new secretary general, the Grand Kadi of Abuja, Bashir Sambo, whereas Ibrahim Dasuki rose to be the new supreme patron of the JNI.

In the course of the first formal meeting of the JNI on 9 March 1964 in Kaduna, the members agreed to hold a formal meeting of all members of the General Purpose Committee (GPC) of the JNI on the last Tuesday of each month in Kaduna. The GPC was set up to lead the JNI and to manage its everyday affairs. Members of this most important committee within the JNI were, according to Muhammad Kolo Biu (Interview, 21 Sept. 1987), Abubakar Gumi as Chairman, Bashir Sambo (Grand Kadi of

Abuja), Isa Kaita, Ahmad Talib, Yahya Gusau, Nuhu Bamali, Shehu Muhammad, Saidu Labo, Bello Bindama, Muhammad Dodo (Grand Kadi of Kaduna), Mamman Dawa, al-Ḥâjj Armiyau, Usman Mai Riga, Abubakar Shehu, Hamidu Yahya, Ali Keita, Akilu Idris, Ibrahim Dasuki, and Nuru Yahya. The federal states were represented by the following delegates: Sulaiman Onyeama (Anambra), Idris Muhammad (Bendel), Babakura Iman (Bornu, Grand Kadi), Hassan Na Laraba (Benue), Isa Obetam (Cross River), Ibrahim Babawo (Gongola), Hassan Gwarzo and Naibi Sulaiman Wali (both Kano), Abdulkadir Orire (Kwara, Grand Kadi), Bagure Waziri and Ahmad Lemu (both Niger), Yahya Kanem (Plateau, Grand Kadi), Haladu Gano (Rivers), and Haliru Binji (Sokoto, Grand Kadi). During the formal meetings of the GPC organizational and general matters were discussed and decided. Finally the first constitution of the JNI was ratified in 1964, but it was revised in 1975 and again in 1988/89. In the constitution the aims and intentions of the JNI were presented first: the promotion of Islam, the establishment of schools and hospitals, the organization of lectures, conferences, and seminars for the promotion of Islam, as well as propaganda relating to the unity of all Muslims. It was stressed that the JNI was to be open to all Muslims in Nigeria; the members were called upon to pay a monthly contribution which was established by the central council of the JNI from time to time. Apart from the abovementioned positions of chairman (president), supreme patron, and secretary general, a number of committees were instituted. Among them were the Central Council which was to approve changes in the constitution, the General Purpose Committee (GPC), which was responsible for the general management of the JNI, and a series of other committees, like the financial committee and the committee for education. In particular, the financial administration of the JNI was regulated in detail to prevent mismanagement of monies and properties, which was a constant fear within the JNI. Geographically the JNI was organized in state branches for each federal state. The patron of each branch was the respective traditional ruler (emir) of the region. Each state branch delegated one representative to the GPC. The state branches were fully responsible for the work and financing of the JNI in their respective areas. The functionaries of the JNI were reelected or confirmed in their offices every three years by a general assembly of the Central Council. The annual general assembly of this council had the additional task of approving the annual report of the secretary general and the chairman of the finance committee (Elayo 1984: 5 ff.).

The establishment of the state branches which began as early as 1963 developed so quickly that it became necessary to introduce further levels of organization below the state branches. Thus the so-called area councils were created and as the lowest organizational unit the local government branches were set up. In 1976 the JNI commanded about one hundred local government branches in the whole of Nigeria, the majority of them, however, in the North. Apart from the organization of the JNI itself, agreements of cooperation were concluded over time with other Muslim organizations in Nigeria, like the Jamâ'at Nûr ad-Dîn (Association of the Light of Faith) and the Jamâ'at Anwâr ad-Dîn (Association of the Beams of the Faith), organizations which were based in the South (Imam 1980: 2 ff.).

The actual educational and propaganda activities of the JNI were carried out predominantly by the area councils. Each had a *murshid* (guide) who was responsible for information, education, and promotion of Islam (*irshâd*). The propagandists of the JNI, as well as the teachers of the JNI schools, were prepared for their work at three JNI training schools: the JNI Training School in Unguwar Sarki, Kaduna, the Arabic College in Zaria, and the Jos Training Institute in Jos. The JNI Training School in Kaduna was founded in 1974 and was financed by Saudi Arabia. The school housed eight teachers under the lead of Malam Ibrahim Jitari and included two expatriate teachers: Shaykh Jamil Ahmad from India and Shaykh Iqbal Ahmad from Sudan, both paid directly by the Râbiṭat al-'Alam al-Islâmî (Muslim World League) (Elayo 1984: 20). All murshidûn of the JNI, about one hundred persons in 1984, were examined by a special examination committee and received certificates after their successful examinations which allowed them to act in the name of the JNI. The same commission organized teams of preachers for special purposes, handed out directives for methods and pedagogy of irshâd, and fixed the basic qualifications for the admission of new murshidûn. The members of this committee in 1984 were among others Ibrahim Tahir, al-Ḥâjj Sidi Ali, al-Ḥâjj 'Abd al-'Aziz Yusuf, and al-Ḥâjj Ibrahim Arab, a reknowned leader of the 'Yan Izala in Kaduna (ibid.: 28).

The first JNI-financed schools were nationalized in 1967 by the Gowon government, an event which deterred many Arabic donors in the next years from donating money to the JNI. By the mid-1980s however, the JNI were again to command a number of Islamiyya schools, and there also existed a JNI school in Kaduna since 1983 which was reserved for the education of women (Elayo 1984: 20 ff.). Additionally the JNI took over the management of numerous mosques, especially in Kaduna, such as the Sultan Bello Friday mosque in Unguwar Sarki and in other areas where the JNI was represented by local government branches. The JNI used all available modern media for its propaganda and information work. Thus Radio Kaduna used to broadcast twice a week a program called "Islamic Calling." The JNI edited in addition a monthly periodical called *Haske* (Light). These promotional and informational activities were directed exclusively to a Muslim public and were intended to enlighten the faithful about the contents of their religion. The mission to the non-Muslims was of secondary concern and not even mentioned as an aim of the JNI in its constitution.

Since 1975 the JNI commanded its own first-aid organization. This aid group was founded on the advice of Abubakar Gumi and was responsible not only for medical first aid in emergencies but also for the humanitarian care for pilgrims during the ḥajj. Furthermore, the aid group of the JNI acted as a security group during the great rallies of the JNI or on the occasion of Friday prayers. All members of the aid group completed a training course and received identity cards. By the mid-1980s the aid group had about five thousand members (Kudu 1984: 24). There was a plan to establish the aid group as an Islamic alternative to the Red Cross. Its chairman until the late 1970s was the Emir of Katsina, Usman Nagogo (Kusimo 1979: 27).

The financing of JNI projects, the maintenance of its buildings, and the payment of the salaries to its teachers and employees was guaranteed in part by the JNI's own sources of capital and in part by donations from members and supporters. Until 1984, all members contributed a monthly fee of at least ten kwobo. In addition, the JNI received further fees from every new member and also part of the annual zakât payments which could be made through the JNI. A further source of income was the profits derived from the sale of donated books (Ishaku 1976: 13). The JNI drew further income from the rent of its houses and received annual dividends from the shares it owns in a number of companies. Among these were companies such as the pharmaceutical enterprise Chellaram's, the Gaskiya Corporation, and the Blanket Manufacturing Company in Kaduna (Elayo 1984: 18). In 1974 the Pakistani businessman Yusuf Gardee conferred his shares in the Northern Nigerian Textile Mill in Kaduna to the JNI in the course of the implementation of the first indigenization decree. The JNI thus received 74 percent of all shares in this company (Ishaku 1976: 13). Very important for the financing of the JNI were, however, the donations of wealthy national and international donors. Thus Yusuf Gardee annually donated books worth 12,000 pounds sterling to the JNI (ibid.: 13). The considerable flow of monies from the Gulf states was interrupted in 1966 by a decree of General Gowon who was afraid of their growing influence (ibid.: 3). The decree was revoked by the mid-1970s, and in 1973 King Faisal of Saudi Arabia again donated a sum of 37,000 pounds sterling to the JNI. The large number of donations, not only from abroad but also from Nigeria itself, induced the JNI to open a public donations list and to hand out receipts for the donations for the revenue office. The considerable donations from the Gulf states became a great problem for the development of the JNI in the 1970s as these monies were channeled into the JNI through Gumi who had the confidence of the

Saudis. Gumi thus achieved an extraordinary position of power within the JNI. In addition, his internal opponents within the JNI always suspected him of reallocating monies from the Gulf states to destinations other than the JNI (Anwar 1989: 144).

The first existential crisis in the development of the JNI began after the assassination of Ahmadu Bello in 1966. His death removed his unifying and mediating influence on the different groups within the JNI. After 1966 these groups started to carry out their disputes within the JNI. Gumi and his supporters, as well as the ṭuruq and the emirs, each in his own way tried to instrumentalize the JNI for his own religious and political aims. This led to a rapid dissolution of the JNI into a number of regional fractions which were controlled by different networks. Thus Gumi and his supporters in the Kaduna Mafia were able to keep control over the management of the JNI in Kaduna, as well as in Jos, Gongola, and Niger, whereas Kano, Bauchi, Sokoto, Bornu, and Kwara were taken over by alliances between the emirs and ṭarîqa-affiliated religious scholars. Thus Bornu came under the undisputed control of the Shehu of Bornu and the great Tijânî leaders of Maiduguri, Shaykh Abu l-Fâtiḥ, Shaykh Abu Bakr al-Miskin, and Shaykh Ibrahim Ṣâliḥ (Interview Nur Alkali, 21 Mar. 1988). Ilorin-Kwara was taken over by the Emir of Ilorin and an alliance between the Qâdiriyya and the Tijânîyya under the leadership of Shaykh 'Ali Jabata and Shaykh 'Abd as-Salam Pakata (both Tijânîyya) and Muhammad Ibrahim an-Nufawi (Qâdiriyya) (Jabata and an-Nufawi 1978: 2 ff.). Nevertheless a number of nonaffiliated intellectuals always tried to mediate between the different groups, among them Shehu Galadanci, Nigeria's present ambassador to Saudi Arabia, and the Grand Kadis of the federal states, like Hassan Gwarzo (Kano), Bappa Mahmud (Bauchi), and Bashir Sambo (Abuja). None of these groups were able, however, to bring the entire organization of the JNI under its exclusive control. This led to an almost total paralyzation of the activities of the JNI after the late 1960s.

In 1969 Abubakar Gumi tried for the last time to convince the influential Kano 'ulama' of the need to unite within the JNI. He argued that the North had lost respect and honor and the emirs lost their power after the coup of 1966. Only through the unification of all forces under the umbrella of the JNI the could the North "regain its status as a leading political community." The Kano 'ulama' asked for some time to reflect on Gumi's appeal and then accused him of inconsistency: Why did he now appeal to them for help, since before he had rejected them as "unbelievers"? Despite the mediating efforts of the Emir of Kano, Ado Bayero, the Kano 'ulama' finally rejected Gumi's appeal and did not believe his sincerity (Anwar 1989: 175). This led to the continuation of the conflict between Gumi and the ṭuruq and to the final break between the two camps. The Kano 'ulama' concentrated their efforts on the expansion and activation of the Fityân al-Islâm, whereas Gumi started to construe a new strategy in his policy toward the ṭuruq. According to Malam Ibrahim Umar Kabo, a Tijânî scholar from Kano, the final split in the development of the JNI occurred in 1971 when the secretary general of the JNI, Abubakar an-Nafaty from Gombe (Sokoto), was not replaced by the assistant secretary general, Na'ibi S. Wali from Kano, but by Ibrahim Dasuki from Sokoto, a friend of Gumi: "Making Ibrahim Dasuki the Secretary General has really destroyed the organization. As a result of his appointment everybody understood that the whole affair was political and had nothing to do with the religion of Islam at all. He was simply given the post to consolidate the ascendancy of the Sokoto aristocracy within the organization" (ibid.: 136).

The activities of the JNI have been thus confined since the early 1970s to formalities like the fixing of the amount of the annual zakât payments or the sighting of the new moon for the fixing of the month of Ramadhân. Thus the state council of the JNI in Kano resolved in 1988 that the minimum annual income for which zakât had to be paid should be 5,716 naira, whereas the bride price was fixed at 72 naira (*The Triumph*, 6 Apr. 1988). The paralyzation of the JNI had serious effects on the finances of the organization and its further development, as many investors deemed the JNI untrustworthy and as a result either stopped making donations to the JNI all together or transferred them only via individuals whom they were personally able to trust, in particular, Abubakar Gumi (Interview Biu, 21 Sept. 1987). Gumi again channeled these monies, mostly from the Gulf states, only to those state branches and area councils of the JNI which followed his advice. This development led to an undermining of the financial foundations of the JNI which resulted, among other things, in the inability to publish the monthly periodical *Haske*, which has been the case now for a number of years. In addition, a number of cases of financial mismanagement and fraud hit the JNI so that the organization was virtully bankrupt by 1987 (Interview Biu, 21 Sept. 1987). In the face of this dire situation the leading bodies decided to reorganize the JNI (Adekilekun 1989: 115). In 1989 a new constitution with a new system of checks and balances was approved, and the new Sultan of Sokoto, Ibrahim Dasuki, became Supreme Patron of the JNI. His sucessor as secretary general was the Grand Kadi of Abuja, Bashir Sambo, whereas assistant secretary general Muhammad Kolo Biu kept his position (*The Pen*, 29 Sept. 1989).

The stagnation of the JNI since the late 1960s and early 1970s led to a new effort in the 1970s to overcome its stagnation. In 1973 the Nigerian Supreme Council of Islamic Affairs (NSCIA) was set up in Kaduna in the course of a Muslim Unity Conference. The task of the new body was to obtain a national consensus on questions concerning the development of Islam in Nigeria in order to overcome the stagnation of the JNI. The Sultan of Sokoto was elected chairman and national president of the NSCIA, and Ibrahim Dasuki became its secretary general. Thus a personal union at a high level was created between the JNI and the NSCIA. From each federal state four delegates were sent into the NSCIA in order to stress the national character of the organization (Doi 1984: 349–50). In 1974 the NSCIA accepted the appeal of the Râbiṭat al-'Alam al-Islâmî of 18 October 1970, to prosecute the Aḥmadiyya movement, and implemented this decision in Nigeria. This resolution remained the only activity of the new umbrella organization for a long time on account of the internal frictions which continued within this new body of religious scholars and emirs. The old tensions thus proved to be stronger than the efforts to form a common platform for all Muslims.

3.4. Abubakar Gumi and the Unity of the Muslims in Northern Nigeria

Abubakar Gumi was one of the central personalities for the development of Islam in Northern Nigeria during the era of Ahmadu Bello. He decisively influenced not only the religious policy of Bello—according to his own words he was "the man behind Bello" (Interview Gumi, 17 Sept. 1987)—but tried to continue Bello's policy of religious unification and revitalization after the latter's assassination. When Gumi lost his official political backing in Northern Nigeria after Bello's death, he tried to achieve his aims with the external support of the Râbiṭat al-'Alam al-Islâmî. Although he was successful as far as the proscription of the Aḥmadiyya movement was concerned, his external support did not prove to be sufficient enough in his struggle against the Sufi brotherhoods. Thus Gumi, like Ibrahim Niass and Kabara before him, decided to set up a religious mass movement of his own in the 1970s, the Jamâ'at izâlat al-bid'a wa iqâmat as-sunna (Hausa: 'Yan Izala), in order to realize his aims of religious tajdîd in his struggle against the ṭuruq. The conflict between Gumi and the two great Sufi brotherhoods influenced the development of Islam in Northern Nigeria until the late 1980s. Yet Gumi wished not only to realize his concepts of tajdîd of Islam in Nigeria, but also to conserve the political predominance of the Muslims within the federation. This aim was shown, for instance, by his efforts after 1982 to politically mobilize the Muslim women.

Abubakar Mahmud Gumi was born on 7 November 1922 in the small village of Gummi (Sokoto province). His date of birth was advanced in 1960 by Mervyn Hiskett, then vice principal of the School of Arabic Studies in Kano, to 1924 in order to improve Gumi's chances of getting a job at the Northern Regions' Sharî'a Court of Appeal (Tsiga 1992: 72–73). Gumi's education began under the tutelage of his father Mahmud, a religious scholar and *alkali* (judge) of Gummi. After memorizing the Qur'ân he attended the school of Malam Musa in Ambursa (Sokoto) where he received an introduction to fiqh and where he read al-Fazâzî's Ishrînîyât, a famous collection of praise-poems on the Prophet, which are very popular in Hausaland and an essential part of the education in the Qur'ânic schools (Ajani 1987: 87, 287). In 1933 Gumi began his secular education at the Dogondaji Primary School where he was soon appointed Hakimin Salla (Leader in Prayer) for the students on account of his extraordinary knowledge for his young age. As Hakimin Salla he was responsible for the religious activities of his fellow students. In Dogondaji he also met one his most important companions of later years, Ibrahim Dasuki. On account of his great progress in learning he was transferred to the Sokoto Middle School in the same year, where Ahmadu Bello was teaching between 1931 and 1934. At this school Gumi met Haliru Binji, later Deputy Grand Kadi of Northern Nigeria, but also Shehu Shagari, the future president of Nigeria. Among his teachers were personalities such as Junaidu, later Wazirin Sokoto, as well as Malam Yahya Gusau, both cofounders of the JNI. Apart from the regular classes, Gumi set about studying the essential texts of the Maliki school of law, the Risâla of Ibn Abi Zayd al-Qayrawânî and the Mukhtasar of Khalîl. After completing his education at the Sokoto Middle School he passed the entrance examinations at Katsina College. Nevertheless he decided to continue his studies at the Kano Law School. At this school Gumi was trained as alkali between 1942 and 1947 and again had the Wazirin Sokoto Junaidu as his teacher. In 1947 he obtained a job as scribe to Alkali Attahiru in Sokoto. This office did not meet his expectations, and thus he soon began to give private lessons in tafsîr. His teaching attracted a growing number of students, recruited either among the local pupils of the existing Qur'ânic schools, or among the students who attended western-oriented schools in Sokoto and regarded the local malamai as too "primitive" (Shanono 1976: 5). This life was apparently unable to satisfy Gumi entirely so that he returned to Kano in 1947 where he began to teach at the Kano Law School. In the following two years of his stay in Kano he met the young mujaddid of the Qâdiriyya, Nasiru Kabara, whom he later described as one of his most important teachers in Nigeria apart from the Wazirin Sokoto Junaidu (Garba 1983: 49). Abubakar Gumi also came into contact with the leader of the Nigerian Mahdiyya movement, Shaykh Sa'id b. Hayatu, who had just returned from exile in the Cameroons and was regarded as one of the most prominent victims of the British colonial policy. Under his influence Gumi gave up his formal affiliation with the Qâdiriyya and became a follower of the Mahdiyya. He married one of the daughters of Shaykh Sa'id b. Hayatu, Maryamu, who gave birth to a son, but both she and the child died immediately after birth (ibid.: 96–97). The temporary affiliation of Gumi with the Mahdiyya movement, which had always been regarded by the British as a potentially dangerous enemy, can be interpreted as an effort by Gumi to break with the old authorites and to find a new way of his own. That he had already been searching for a new way is shown by his decision to give up his post as scribe in Sokoto and to return to Kano. His acquaintance with Nasiru Kabara, who had started a movement of tajdîd within the Qâdiriyya, also points to that direction.

Abubakar Gumi's first public appearance took place in the small settlement of Maru in Central Sokoto province in 1949. Gumi had accepted a post as teacher at the Teachers' Training College at Maru that year. In Maru he met one of the cofounders of the Northern Teachers' Association, Aminu Kano. In the rural seclusion of Maru a friendly relationship developed between the two teachers. Their conversations and discussions repeatedly centered on the development of Islam in Hausaland, the distortion of the faith as a result of mixing with the traditions of the Hausa society, and the toleration of these bida' by the Sufi brotherhoods. Gumi, influenced by his discussions with Kano, seems to have found in Maru the aim which was to determine his later life decisively: the struggle against the bida' and against the Sufi brotherhoods as the most important agents of the bida'.

The bone of contention in Gumi's first dogmatic dispute with the existing authorities was the practice of *tayammum* (the ritual washing with sand before prayers) which was practiced by the Imam of Maru, although there was no scarcity of water in Maru. Gumi argued that according to the orthodox interpretation of law tayammum was acceptable only if no water was available for the ritual ablutions (*wudu'*) as, for example, is the case in the desert. However, these conditions would not apply in Maru. He therefore appealed to the students of the college to boycott the obligatory Friday prayers until the Imam of Maru abandoned tayammum. This appeal to rebel against the imam would never have had any consequences if the Sultan of Sokoto had taken up the case himself. Gumi had attacked the sultan in a letter to the editor of the daily *Gaskiya Ta Fi Kwabo* on the basis of a speech by the sultan on the last Salla festival ('Id al-fiṭr). For this criticism the sultan obviously wanted to revenge himself on Gumi by attacking him and Aminu Kano directly and demanding that they explain their protest concerning tayammum. In the following inquiry Gumi carried the day by a purely dogmatic argument. The commission of inquiry which had been set up by the sultan acquitted Gumi and even urged the sultan in his function as Amir al-mu'minîn to come to Maru and stop the practice of tayammum in person (Shanono 1976: 10). Although the sultan did not comply with this appeal of the commission of inquiry his dignity suffered as a result of Gumi's acquittal. Gumi, on the other hand, was able to profile himself as a renowned scholar through his open confrontation with the Sultan of Sokoto and take the offensive. He wrote a fatwâ against the acceptance of titles such as Knight of the British Empire by the Sultan of Sokoto and argued that this practice was un-Islamic. On the basis of this fatwâ Kano wrote an article for the daily *Gaskiya Ta Fi Kwabo*, which was not published, however. His article was thus copied mechanically and distributed by hand. This campaign by Gumi and Kano against the sultan was finally stopped by the British who prohibited public preaching in Maru district in 1949 (Umar 1988: 239). That this conflict between Gumi and the Sultan of Sokoto was interpreted by the public as something more than a dogmatic dispute on the question of tayammum is shown by the fact that Gumi was backed by the Emir of Kano, Abdullahi Bayero, who presumably saw in his supporting Gumi an opportunity to show his independence from Sokoto. Gumi was to gain similar support from Bello, who was a member of the parliament of the North at that time and who already had had a number of clashes with the sultan.

Despite this early temporary alliance, Bello and Gumi went different ways for the time being. Gumi, like Aminu Kano, was strongly influenced at that time by the ideas of the first nationalist leader of the North, Sa'd Zungur, who had started to attack the British colonial power, the emirate system, and the Sufi brotherhoods in the late 1940s. He especially criticized the mixing of Islam with the local customs, the system of polygamy, and the seclusion of women. In contrast he appealed for the introduction of women's education and started a translation of the Qur'ân into Hausa to make the contents of the Holy Book better known to the common people. He wrote numerous poems against the Tijâniyya and the Qâdiriyya and asked Muslims to return to the sources of their religion (Umar 1988: 173). Gumi adopted these criticisms of Sa'd Zungur without engaging himself at that time, as Aminu Kano had done, in a more political direction. Rather, he criticized the colonial system on a dogmatic level on account of the abolition of zakât, which would force the religious scholars, according to Gumi, to earn their living through *tsubbu* (sorcery, divination), *damfara* (tricks), *duba* (fortune-telling), *sihiri* (magic), *sha rubutu* (literally, the drinking of the written), and *yawan kadar raba* (literally, leaving home in search for the means of subsistence during the dry season), or simply on the basis of the production of *laya* (charms) and *nakulkula* (either protective or harmful medicine) (Anwar 1989: 95; Umar 1988: 179).

Whereas Sa'd Zungur and Aminu Kano followed their political goals and built up the NEPU in the 1950s, Gumi returned to complete his studies. Between 1950 and 1952 he read courses at the School of Arabic Studies (SAS) in Kano and then took up a teaching assignment at this institution until 1954. The SAS had been established in 1934 by the British with the intention of preventing the spread of radical ideas among the students who had hitherto been forced to go abroad to Arabic countries for higher Arabic studies and to keep the development of Arabic education in Northern Nigeria under British control. The teachers for the SAS were therefore not recruited in Egypt, as the Northern elites had demanded, but in the British Sudan (Interview A. Mustafa, 7 Mar. 1988). With the hiring of the so-called Sudanese Shaykhs, Bashir ar-Rayah, Muhammad Salih Swar ad-Dahab, and Shaykh an-Nur at-Tingari (NAK, Kano Prov. Files 1304 Vol. 1), in 1934, a tradition of educational links between Northern Nigeria and the Sudan was established which would remain dominant during the coming decades. At the new school the students were confronted with a new model of education and a new concept of authority. They learned to ask critical questions and to discuss problems with the teachers. It is therefore no surprise that the majority of critics of the Sufi brotherhoods in Northern Nigeria in the 1970s and 1980s were onetime students of this school (Umar 1988: 170).

In 1954 Abubakar Gumi applied for a grant to continue his studies at the renowned al-Azhar University in Cairo. His request was refused by the British authorities. Abdul writes in his foreword to the 1976 edition of Gumi's *al-'Aqîda aṣ-ṣaḥîḥa* that this decision by the authorities was connected with the fear that Gumi might come into contact with the radical ideas of the Ikhwân al-muslimîn in Cairo and be influenced by them (Gumi 1976: 4). The Emir of Kano, during his visit to Cairo in 1937, had in fact appealed to the scholars of the Azhar to come to Nigeria. However, the British were to block the establishment of contacts to the Azhar (NAK, Kano Prov. Files, no. 2131). On 2 November 1951 the British administration declared that examinations of the Azhar would not be acknowledged in Nigeria. On account of the growing pressure concerning the improvement of the Islamic eduction the British were forced, however, to develop a new system of Arabic education. They instituted a commission of inquiry in 1953 which was to evaluate options for an expansion of the Islamic educational system in Nigeria. The members of this commission were, among others, the British orientalists Arberry, Anderson, and Geary. In their Report of the Committee on Higher Muslim Education (NAK, Zaria Prov. Files, SCH 1: 1) they concluded that studies in Egypt and Morocco could not be recommended on account of the political situation in these countries. Instead they proposed the establishment of a chair for Islamic studies at the University of Ibadan. At the same time and in the context of the procedures of the commission, the Emir of Zaria, the Wazirin Sokoto Junaidu, and representatives of the Northern regional government visited the Sudan in order to evaluate the possibilities of cooperation. After their return to Kano in 1953 they recommended not only the expansion of the SAS in Kano, but also the setting up of grants for studies at the Faculty of Law at the University of Khartoum as well as the establishment of twelve-to-eighteen-month diploma courses at the Bakht ar-Ruda College of Education in the Sudan (NAK, ZPF, SCH 1: 7). Thus Gumi, instead of being sent to al-Azhar, obtained a grant for a course at the Bakht ar-Ruda College of Education in the British Sudan. Other members of this first group of Nigerian students to go there in 1954 included Hassan Gwarzo, Haliru Binji, Shehu Galadanci, Ibrahim Bibi Faruq, and Abdulkadir Orire (Interview Omar, 8 Mar. 1988). In later years they were all to achieve influential positions in government and in the educational and judicial system and can today be regarded as the first members of the group of Western-educated Muslim intellectuals in Northern Nigeria, a group which began to grow rapidly in the 1950s.

In the early 1950s Ahmadu Bello was working on the consolidation of the NPC as the leading political force in Northern Nigeria. Only when both Bello and Gumi met during the ḥajj in Mecca in 1955, and later when Gumi was to assist Bello as interpreter in the latter's contacts with the Saudi government representatives, was a closer personal relationship to develop. The connection with Bello had direct repercussions on Gumi's career: In 1956 Bello appointed him not only first Nigerian Pilgrims' Officer in Jidda, but also to the representative office of Deputy Grand Kadi of the Northern region, at that time subordinate only to the

Grand Kadi, the Sudanese Shaykh 'Awad 'Abdallah al-'Arabi, Dean of the College of Law in Kano. In 1957 Gumi spent ten months in Saudi Arabia and undertook an inquiry into the conditions of the pilgrimage for the Nigerian pilgrims. In numerous talks and meetings with Saudi officials he also prepared the official journey of inspection of the prime minister to Saudi Arabia (Shanono 1976: 12). In the following year Gumi was a member of this official delegation during its visit to Saudi Arabia and was consequently able to lay the basis for many friendships and political links with important Saudi government officials and businessmen. When the problems connected with the organization of the ḥajj were solved, Gumi devoted himself on Bello's instruction to work on the reform of the system of Islamic law as it was practiced in Northern Nigeria. After the completion of this task Gumi was appointed Grand Kadi of Northern Nigeria in 1962, while Haliru Binji became Deputy Grand Kadi. In the following years Gumi further supported the reforms of the Islamic judicial system in Northern Nigeria. He approved of a better selection of the Alkalai by a Judicial Service Committee and supported the institution of diploma courses for Islamic law at Ahmadu Bello University in Zaria. He stressed the importance of the setting up of new Shari'a courts of appeal in the regions and of an Upper Shari'a court of appeal for the whole federation (ibid.: 447). Until the death of Bello in 1966 Gumi devoted himself to the consolidation of the JNI and consequently accompanied Bello on his travels to the Arab countries. In these years not only did Gumi influence the religious policy of Bello in the direction of a stronger emphasis on the improvement of modern Islamic education, but he also established important links abroad.

The most important of these external links was Gumi's connection with the Râbiṭat al-'Alam al-Islâmî (Muslim World League), founded in Mecca in 1962 by Saudi Arabian scholars and politicians as well as a number of representatives of the Ikhwân al-muslimîn who had fled from Egypt after 1954. The Râbiṭa was initially intended to counterbalance ideologically the nationalist and socialist propaganda of Jamâl 'Abd an-Nâṣir. Ahmadu Bello had acquired one of the seats in the Râbiṭa on account of his role as leader of the strongest Muslim community in Black Africa and on account of his efforts concerning the unification of the Muslims in Northern Nigeria. As he himself was too occupied with his work as head of government in Northern Nigeria and as he was not able to speak Arabic he delegated his seat to his confidant Abubakar Gumi. Gumi held since that time one of the fifty-five seats of the original assembly of the Râbiṭa. He also became a member of the Supreme Council of the newly established Islamic University in Madina, which was founded as a counterpart of Azhar University in Cairo, and joined a number of other committees of the Râbiṭa. One of the most important among these was the World Supreme Council for the Affairs of Mosques which was responsible for advice and support in so far as the construction, management, and entertainment of mosques in the Islamic world was concerned. Another body was the Legal Committee of the Râbiṭa which discussed and edited legal opinions (*ahkâm/qararât*) on all aspects of the Islamic law. Between 1962 and 1988 fifty legal opinions were edited. The weight of these legal opinions has considerably increased over the years because they were adopted by a number of Islamic countries, especially Saudi Arabia, Pakistan, and Sudan, and integrated into the respective national legal systems (Schulze 1990: 344). In his function as a member of the legal committee of the Râbiṭa Abubakar Gumi took part in the formulation of all these legal opinions, a fact which increased not only his international fame as an 'âlim, but also his weight as a scholar in Nigeria. Apart from that, his membership in the Râbiṭa and his good connections with the Saudi government paid off in financial terms as well: On 8 March 1987, for instance, Gumi received the "King Faisal Prize," worth 300,000 Saudi riyâl, for his achievements as an Islamic scholar. Although the Râbiṭa is financed not only by the Saudi government, but also the Islamic Development Bank in Jidda and a number of wealthy Hijazi businessmen, the budget of the Râbiṭa is relatively small. In 1986 it comprised c. 18 million riyâl. About 90 percent of that amount was spent on the salaries of the 250 employees of the Râbiṭa (Schulze 1990: 246 ff.). Nevertheless, the Râbiṭa and its members have an important function as counterparts and brokers for numerous institutions, organizations, and individuals from within the entire Islamic world for the investment and channeling of monies for specific purposes. The funds of the Islamic Development Bank in Jidda and of the Bait al-Mâl al-Islâmî (Islamic Banking House) on Cyprus in particular are channeled and mediated by the Râbiṭa and its prominent members. The Islamic Development Bank is a body of the Organization of the Islamic Conference (OIC), founded in 1972, which today includes forty-four member states, responsible for the allocation of interest-free credits, as well as the financing of technical aid, the training of experts, and the subventioning of the export trade of poor third-world countries (Nienhaus and Choudoury 1988: 315–16).

As Abubakar Gumi was regarded as a trustworthy religious scholar from Nigeria with some international standing as a consequence of his close links to Saudi Arabia and his membership in the Râbiṭa, he was also trusted in financial affairs. Thus he became the most important councillor of the Saudis and the Kuwaitis in the 1960s in respect to investment, allocation, and distribution in Nigeria of monies from the Gulf states. Through him the Gulf states channeled their credits and donations for the JNI and since 1978 also for the 'Yan Izala. From Gumi they received direct advice on ways and possibilities to invest funds. If, for instance, a Nigerian institution or a private individual turned to a donor in Saudi Arabia with an appeal for financial support for certain religious or educational projects, the donor usually asked Gumi whether the project in question was trustworthy. In this way Gumi was not only in a position to channel monies to Nigeria, in theory he was also in a position to decide the allocation of these funds. The role of a broker made Gumi a very sought-after counterpart in Nigeria. People had to come to him and develop good relations with him to get monies from the Gulf states for their projects (Interview Biu, 21 Sept. 1987). Thus Gumi was in a position to influence the development of Islamic institutions and organizations in Nigeria as early as the 1960s. He had built up his own basis of power, fed from abroad, and was no longer dependent on the political support of Ahmadu Bello and other politicians. Despite Bello's appeals for moderation, he was thus able to adopt a more radical position toward the ṭuruq than if he had remained dependent on Bello's support alone. After Bello's assassination he was therefore in a position to prevent the takeover of the JNI by the ṭuruq and the conservative emirs in at least some state branches of the JNI (Interview Biu, 21 Sept. 1987).

When Ahmadu Bello was assassinated on 15 January 1966, Gumi was finally free from the moderating influence of the prime minister and could now attack the ṭuruq openly. In an interview with Paden in 1984 (Paden 1986: 565 ff.) Shehu Galadanci, then head of the Department of Arabic at the Bayero University Kano (BUK), described Gumi's role in the 1960s exhaustively:

> The Sardauna knew that Gummi was outspoken and had radical ideas about religion, and radical ideas about traditional rulers. Therefore, the Sardauna allowed Gummi to inject these ideas into the meetings [of the JNI]. The Waziri of Sokoto was the moderator, pushing the traditional ulama to understand modern ideas and trying to push Gummi back more in line with tradition. The Sardauna did not really want Gummi to attack tariqa, but supported him fully. Gummi was more important in the outside world, and was always taken on visits abroad. He was regarded as "a learned man from Nigeria and one who knows modern trends in Islam in other countries." . . . Gummi at the time of Sardauna was the Grand Kadi with great authority, and had the moral support of the Sardauna, thence he would say and do what he wanted. When the Sardauna died, Gummi continued as Grand Kadi, but needed something to support himself. Without such a group, there was no strength. Therefore the Izala group grew up gradually over three to five years. If the Sardauna had lived, Gummi would not have needed the Izala, but the Jama'atu Nasril Islam might have been a more solid platform both religious and political. . . . Gummi attacked the Tijaniyya and the Qadiriyya to weaken them. He [Bello] knew the Sa'udis were part of Gummi, supporting him in the background. If the Sardauna had lived, Gummi would not have been able to magnify the differences. . . . After the death of the Sardauna the mallams [especially from Kano such

> as Nasiru Kabara] felt free to attack Gummi, because Gummi was no longer Grand Kadi. Thus in 1968–69 they attacked him vigourously. Gummi in turn responded and in the process of responding [between 1967–1969] laid the foundation for Izala.

Despite a number of chronological distortions Galadanci's statement clearly shows the repercussions of the assassination of Bello on the further development of the Muslim community in Northern Nigeria. The struggle between Gumi and his opponents started to become increasingly violent. The ṭuruq thought they now had the opportunity to decisively eliminate Gumi, as the latter had lost Bello's political backing. Gumi himself could now attack the ṭuruq without any considerations for Bello's political ideals and strategies. As Gumi's external support was, however, obviously not strong enough for a full-scale confrontation with the Sufi brotherhoods and as Gumi could not yet, at least for the time being, rely on a religious mass movement of his own, he was to initially concentrate on the fight against the Aḥmadiyya movement.

The Aḥmadiyya movement had originated in the Western region of Nigeria in the 1920s and had contributed considerably to the setting up of a modern Islamic system of education as well as the organization of the ḥajj. Jibril Martin, the leader of the Aḥmadiyya movement in Islam, had in the 1950s been one of the cofounders and the chairman of the Pilgrims' Board of the Western region which had taken over the organization of the ḥajj from the British authorities (Fisher 1963: 135). In the early 1960s the Aḥmadiyya movement had started to establish its first centers in the North and was therefore regarded by Gumi as a danger for the future development of Islam in that region. Furthermore the Aḥmadiyya was easy to criticize on account of its heretical views on the alleged prophetship of its founder. Thus Gumi opened his campaign against this weak link in the chain of bida'. He prepared his struggle against the Aḥmadiyya by translating and publishing a number of anti-Aḥmadiyya works by Abû al-A'la al-Maudûdî from Pakistan, Muḥammad al-Khidr Ḥussain, a Hanafite scholar from Tunisia, and Abû l-Ḥasan 'Alî an-Nadwî from

Lucknow (India). On 18 October 1970, at the request of al-Maudûdî, the Râbiṭa decided to declare the Aḥmadiyya heretical. This decision was supported by Gumi. Nevertheless it still took more than two years until the Islamic League adopted the resolution of the Râbiṭa concerning the Aḥmadiyya and asked its member states to enforce the necessary regulations in respects to the Aḥmadiyya. In December 1973 Saudi Arabia imposed a ban on all members of the Aḥmadiyya who wanted to come to Saudi Arabia for the ḥajj. All Saudi embassies and consulates abroad were advised to immediately stop giving visas to members of the Aḥmadiyya. This regulation led to violent protests in Nigeria, in the course of which the Saudi embassy in Lagos was occupied by members of the Aḥmadiyya. Nevertheless their protest was futile. On 9 March 1974, the resolution on the Aḥmadiyya of the Râbiṭa was adopted by the Nigerian Supreme Council of Islamic Affairs and the JNI (*Sunday Times*, 10 Mar. 1974), and regulations were developed to make sure that no Ahmadi would be able to get a Saudi visa in the future. These regulations ruled that any Muslim who wanted to undertake the pilgrimage had to apply to his local imam for a written certificate first, confirming that he was not a member of the Aḥmadiyya. Only on the presentation of this certificate declaring the individual "unobjectionable" would the Saudi embassy release his visa (Doi 1984: 352–53). In reaction to this development a part of the Aḥmadiyya movement in Islam, the Nigeria Branch, which had already split off earlier from the central Aḥmadiyya movement in Rabwah, dissolved its ties with the Aḥmadiyya on 12 May 1974. The group adopted the new name of Anwâr al-Islâm (The Rays of Islam) (Balogun 1977: 3).

The prohibition of the Aḥmadiyya movement and its ensuing split were a major victory for Abubakar Gumi. He was convinced that the split of the Aḥmadiyya into the Anwâr al-Islâm group and a small group of "diehards" was due to his pressure (Interview Gumi, 3 Oct. 1987). As Gumi was appointed first Amîr al-ḥajj (Leader of the Pilgrimage) in 1975 and thus had become responsible for the actual management of the ḥajj, an office which he held until 1978 (Shanono 1976: 12), he was also in the position to supervise and implement the above-cited regulations. Furthermore, he was also able to intensify his efforts to improve the mechanisms of control for admission to the ḥajj. On the basis of his earlier experiences in 1962 with the misbehavior of Nigerian pilgrims in Mecca Gumi wanted to develop an admissions procedure which sought to guarantee that only those Muslims obtained the permission to take part in the pilgrimage who were able to prove their *istiṭâʿa* (preparedness) and furthermore who were able to show a certain basic knowledge of their religion. Istiṭâʿa in the context of the ḥajj means that the prospective pilgrim should not only be a free, responsible, mature person, but also able to finance the ḥajj without ruining himself or his family by undertaking this costly journey to the Hijâz. After the exclusion of the Aḥmadis from the ḥajj in 1974 Gumi achieved his next success when the Nigerian government approved of the official registration of all prospective pilgrims at their respective Local Government Pilgrimage Boards in 1982. This registration was connected with the allocation of a fixed quota of pilgrims for each federal state. Thus Kano state in 1984 received an allocation of 4,211 seats from the National Pilgrimage Board, whereas Anambra state received only fifty seats (*New Nigerian*, 15 May 1984). In 1984 the Buhari administration also introduced a "test" for all pilgrims which had been demanded by Gumi as early as 1982. In this test all aspiring pilgrims were required to demonstrate their command of a number of the essential prayers and knowledge of how the prayers were correctly performed (*New Nigerian*, 6 June 1984). For the Buhari regime, this procedure was also a way to enforce its austerity policy in economic terms on the pilgrimage and to reduce the expenditures during the ḥajj operations. Nevertheless Gumi had managed to create and enforce mechanisms which make it at least theoretically possible to refuse admission to ḥajj not only on the basis of political or economic considerations but also on the basis of religious precepts.

After his successes in the organization of the ḥajj, Gumi tried to implement a similar strategy in the construction of mosques in Nigeria. In the mid-1980s the World Supreme Council for the Affairs of Mosques, a subcommittee of the Râbiṭa, through the Nigerian embassy in Saudi Arabia, proposed the idea of conducting a general census of all mosques in Nigeria. This census should register information such as the name, address, year of construction, present condition, name of the imam, size, and history of each mosque. On the basis of the register it would then be possible to see where new mosques should be constructed, which mosques had to be expanded or renovated, and how much money would be necessary for implementing these tasks. The collected data would be made accessible to prospective donators such as the Islamic Development Bank to help them in their process of deciding which projects they should support and which not. As Abubakar Gumi was not only a member of the World Supreme Council for the Affairs of Mosques, but also an advisor to the Islamic Development Bank in Jidda (*The Analyst*, 1987, no. 5), the census could easily have been transformed into a further instrument of power, and Gumi would have been able to influence the development of mosques in Nigeria to an unprecedented extent (Interview Biu, 21 Sept. 1987). Thus he could have advised potential donors from abroad to finance only those mosques which were not affiliated with a Sufi brotherhood. On account of these obvious implications the plan of a census of the Nigerian mosques was carried out only in Kwara state, where all Muslim groups hoped to gain more external support against the growing pressure of the Christian missions (Interview Biu, 21 Sept. 1987).

Despite his successes in the struggle against the Aḥmadiyya movement in Nigeria, a conflict in which Gumi was supported by the JNI and the NSCIA, he failed to achieve similar successes in his fight against the Sufi brotherhoods. Under the impression that he had not been able to instrumentalize the JNI in the late 1960s for his purposes and that the ṭuruq had set up a vigorous organization of their own, the Fityân al-Islâm, in order to fight him, Gumi began a new initiative against the Sufi brotherhoods. In late 1970 he began to publish in the Hausa daily newspaper *Gaskiya Ta Fi Kwabo* a series of articles under the title "Nasiha ga

Musulmi" (Advice for Muslims) (Anwar 1989: 196) and thus initiated a public campaign which raised many emotions and unrest in Northern Nigeria. In the same year Gumi also began a series of regular tafsîr programs on Radio Kaduna which continued until 1974. He was thus able to reach a much bigger public audience throughout the North than before. By using the modern mass media and by using the Hausa language in his publications Gumi was able to compensate the nonexistence of a mass organization of his own. Apart from that he also ended the era of the predominance of the Arabic language in the religious debates and popularized the use of Hausa (ibid.: 74). To place his attacks against the ṭuruq on a dogmatic basis, Gumi published his major work against the bida' and the ṭuruq in 1972 entitled *al-'Aqîda aṣ-ṣaḥîḥa bi-muwafaqat ash-sharî'a* (The Right Belief According to the Sharî'a). This treatise was answered almost immediately by corresponding counterattacks from Nasiru Kabara and Muhammad Sani Kafanga. As all these publications were still written in Arabic, however, the discussion was confined to a relatively small circle of religious scholars and thus had for the time being no further repercussions on the development of Islam in Northern Nigeria. This situation changed decisively only in 1978 when Gumi supported the establishment of a mass organization of his own, the 'Yan Izala.

Apart from his efforts to revive and to purify the faith, Abubakar Gumi was also very active in the issue of the political unity of the Muslims after the assassination of Ahmadu Bello. The Aḥmadiyya movement and the Sufi brotherhoods were in Gumi's eyes not only agents of the bida', but also movements which blocked the unification of the Muslims. On account of this they had to be fought and crushed. Only if the Muslims in the North would be united could they hope to maintain their predominance within the federation. After the assassination of Bello and Tafawa Balewa and after the military coup against General Ironsi on 27 July 1966, General Gowon, a Christian from Plateau province, had come to power. This situation was acceptable for Gumi as long as the Kaduna Mafia could codetermine the policy of the military regime in a decisive way and as long as a prominent representative of the Kaduna Mafia, Major General Hassan Katsina, remained the military governor of the North and army chief of staff, thus remaining the actual strongman of the Gowon government. This situation began to change, however, when General Gowon replaced Major General Hassan Katsina in 1971 with the Bendelite David Ejoor as army chief of staff and began to fill other important positions of his administration with his own confidants and Christians from the South or from the Plateau area, most of whom were members of the so-called Langtang Mafia. When Gowon began to nationalize a number of important companies and organizations in 1974, which until then had been under the control of the Kaduna Mafia, he increasingly lost his backing in the North (Hussaini 1988: 92). Gumi consequently attacked General Gowon on account of the latter's corrupt policy, administration, and economic mismanagement. After 1974 Gumi and other critics from the North like the Kaduna Mafia ridiculed Gowon as the "Christian missionary's boy from Pankshin" (Usman 1987: 83).

As a result of his biting and constant attacks on Gowon, Gumi was able to boost his popularity considerably, especially in the North. In a time of moral decadence and corruption Gumi acquired an aura of moral integrity and incorruptibility (Usman 1987: 33). When General Murtala Muhammad finally ousted General Gowon in another coup on 27 July 1975, Gumi rose for the first time to become the official advisor on religious affairs to the government. He was consequently appointed Amîr al-ḥajj in 1975 and director of the National Pilgrimage Board of the federation. Furthermore General Murtala Muhammad authorized Gumi, on account of his excellent connections with the Saudis, to prepare the accession of Nigeria to the Organization of the Islamic Conference (OIC), an organization which had been established in 1972 (Nienhaus and Choudoury 1988: 311 ff.). The purpose of joining the OIC was to gain access to the interest-free loans of the Islamic Development Bank in Jidda. Finally Gumi was appointed Grand Mufti of Nigeria in 1976. In this function he was supposed to take over the chairmanship of a future federal Sharî'a Court of Appeal of Nigeria, thus rising to the highest position in the Islamic judicial system of the federation. This plan failed, however, as a result of the assassination of General Murtala Muhammad in the abortive coup on 13 February 1976, and on account of resistence by the Tijânî-shaykh Dahiru Bauchi. The latter had successfully rallied the other leaders of the Sufi brotherhoods and a number of emirs to oppose the proposal to make Gumi supreme head of the federal Islamic judicial system (Umar 1988: 242; Anwar 1989: 311). General Murtala Muhammd's successor, General Obasanjo, a Christian from Abeokuta, shelved the establishment of a federal Sharî'a Court of Appeal, as well as the idea of joining the OIC as full member, projects which were also violently rejected by many Christian politicians and interest groups. Thus the nomination of Gumi as Grand Mufti of Nigeria remained without institutional consequences. Although he drew a salary as Grand Mufti he had no office and was finally retired from the civil service in 1986. Gumi believed that the institution of a federal Sharî'a Court of Appeal did not fail because of the assassination of General Murtala Muhammad, but because of the opposition of the emirs and the ṭuruq (Interview Gumi, 17 Sept. 1987). They could never accept their archenemy Gumi as the highest authority in an Islamic system of jurisdiction.

Despite this personal drawback for Gumi, his relationship to the state relaxed under the administration of General Obasanjo, because representatives of the Kaduna Mafia were able to rise to key positions in the Obasanjo administation and the strongman of the Obasanjo regime, General Shehu Musa Yar'adua, was also a leading member of the Kaduna Mafia and a confidant of Gumi. Apart from that, Gumi was able to present himself as a leader of the Muslims in the North in the so-called "sharî'a debate" between 1976 and 1979 on the basis of his vigorous demands for the integration of the shari'a into the new constitution (Interview Sulaiman, 9 Sept. 1987; Christelow 1983: 231 ff.).

In 1978/79 Gumi had reached the peak of his popularity and influence among the Muslims in the North. At the same time this year constituted a turning point in his career. Through his open support for the militant anti-Sufi organization of the 'Yan Izala which had been founded in February 1978, Gumi had given up the last remnants of impartiality. Furthermore, he publicly supported his old friend Shehu Shagari in the preelection campaign of 1979, and after the latter's victory was appointed the new president's advisor on religious affairs. Thus he had openly taken the side of the ruling NPN, thereby forfeiting the sympathies of his PRP-oriented followers. Aside from this, in 1979, the Iranian revolution began to exercise a growing attraction on young Muslims in the North who had hitherto accepted Gumi as their leader. In particular, the radical groups within the Muslim Students' Society (MSS) were stimulated by the ideas of the Iranian revolution. When the Shagari regime after a short period of time turned out to be as corrupt and inefficient as the Gowon administration had been, and Gumi nevertheless failed to criticize the corruption and decay, many of his young followers turned away from him and the 'Yan Izala movement. Many of these young Muslims who attended a high school or a university were to join the ranks of the MSS and began to denounce Gumi as a "puppet of the Saudis" (Interview Sulaiman, 9 Sept. 1987).

That Abubakar Gumi was much more concerned with the conservation of the political power of the Muslims and not so much with the criticism of certain un-Islamic aspects of the Shagari administration can be demonstrated by his support for Shehu Shagari in the election campaign of 1982/83. In order to ensure a second victory for the president and the NPN, Gumi supported the political mobilization of Muslim women. As the elections of 1979 had been a very tight vote in favor of Shehu Shagari, Gumi and the politicians of the Kaduna Mafia supported more participation by Muslim women in the elections of 1983 to rule out any risks. The elections of 1979 had been the first federal elections in which the women in the North were entitled to vote. In the 1959 elections they had been excluded (Williams 1982: 47). In an interview with the Hausa daily *Gaskiya Ta Fi Kwabo* in 1982 Gumi appealed to the Muslims of the North to allow their wives to be registered as voters for the next federal elections and to allow them to exercise their right to vote. His argument, very similar in structure to Nasiru Kabara's argument in the context of his dispute with 'Ali Kumasi on ikhtilaṭ, was essentially that "politics is more important than prayer" (Siyasa tafi muhimmanci da salla). This argument was often rendered out of context in public and thus violently attacked as a sign of Gumi's turning against a basic pillar of Islam. His actual arguments in favor of the registration of the Muslim women therefore ought to be quoted in full and in context:

GASKIYA: What about the legality of men and women mixing together, especially as the time of elections draw nearer?

GUMI: Well, it is said that if the Muslims rest, the unbelievers will make war on them. So it is a duty for men and women to take up arms. . . . Well [by analogy to this], it is [a duty] to cast a vote. Now since this will be beneficial to oneself, and, moreover, beneficial to the Muslim community, it is Satan who prevents them from going out. . . . As long as a man's wife covers her body properly, well there is no problem. If you hear somebody say that this is a gathering of men and women, we don't want it, this is Satan who urges the unbelievers, men and women, to oppress the Muslims. I personally will go out with my wives, with our children following. If this is not done, even to the point of letting unbelievers predominate, then what is our position? . . . This religion, if you do not protect it, it will not protect you. That is what makes me say that politics is more important than prayer. . . . With politics one stands for prayer and worship together, whereas prayer is only part of this. . . . It is a necessity that every man takes his women and children above the age of eighteen to register so that we can predominate over the Non-Muslims. (Gumi, quoted in Christelow 1987: 232–34)

Aside from his appeal to strengthen the political participation of the Muslim women, Gumi repeated his argument in another interview with *Gaskiya Ta Fi Kwabo* on 12 May 1983, with a similar intent by saying that taking part in the elections was more important than taking part in the pilgrimage (al-intikhabât ahamm min al-ḥajj). He urged Muslims to abstain from going on ḥajj in that year, as the month of the pilgrimage would be at the same time as the elections for parliament and president. Gumi was again severely attacked for this argument by his religious and political opponents, who interpreted his appeal as an obvious sign of his one-sided support for Shehu Shagari and as another attack on a pillar of Islam (Ṣâliḥ 1986: 439). Despite the religious criticism of Gumi's appeals the NPN and Shagari won a decisive victory in 1983, a victory to which the Muslim women had contributed significantly. Shagari won more votes (12,047,000) than his two most important opponents, Azikiwe and Awolowo, together (3,534,000 and 7,885,000, respectively) (*West Africa*, 15 Aug. 1983).

Shehu Shagari's second term of office came to an abrupt end with the coup of Generals Buhari and Idiagbon on 31 December 1983. Gumi fell into disgrace on account of his close connections with the former president. In particular, the Sufi brotherhoods who had until then been constantly under attack by Gumi now saw the opportunity to strike back and consequently tried to eliminate Gumi from the political arena. Only when General Buhari was himself ousted in another coup organized by General Babangida on 27 August 1985 did the tables turn again in favor of Gumi. Gumi immediately proclaimed his support for the new government and publicly prayed for the new rulers. Under General Babangida he regained his old function as religious advisor to the president (Interview Umar, 5 Apr. 1988). In 1986 General Babangida initiated the process of transition to civilian rule. In response, a group of influential and renowned personalities from all spheres of public life, the economic sphere, the military, and the intelligentsia gathered in Kaduna on 15 February 1987, to proclaim themselves the Constitutional Consultation Committee (CCC, also called the Concerned Citizens Committee) to exert influence on the formation and development of the future constitution. This reconstituted forum of the Kaduna Mafia consisted mainly of former NPN members or supporters. Gumi was represented on its Religious Leaders Contact Committee (*The Analyst*, 1987, no. 5: 25–28). In light of General Babangida's decision to introduce a two-party system in the new constitution, the CCC originally had good chances to lay the foundations for a new, conservative, Kaduna-oriented, Muslim-influenced party along the lines of the NPC and the NPN.

In view of these political developments, Abubakar Gumi and his followers again began to promote the political mobilization of Muslim women in 1986. Just before the local government elections of 12 December 1987, the first democratic elections after the Buhari coup of 1983, one of the closest allies of Gumi and leader of the 'Yan Izala in Kaduna, Shaykh Lawal Abubakar, declared in an interview with Radio Kaduna on 14 October 1987 that it would be a "disaster" if Muslims were to prevent their women from registering for the elections under the pretext of ikhtilâṭ. He said that "such people would only live to regret their actions in the future, when the wrong people are voted into power" (*The Reporter*, 16 Oct. 1987). He furthermore argued that the Muslim women could leave their homes without any problem as long as they were dressed properly. Their husbands should accompany them to the registration centers, "so that they can register and vote for all those that would guarantee tranquility and economic prosperity in the country" (*The Reporter*, 16 Oct. 1987). Some days later, Malam Aminu d-Din Abubakar, the leader of the Daawa movement in Kano, during a speech at the opening of a new factory for ḥijâb textiles, appealed to Muslim women to register for the coming elections (*The Triumph*, 20 Oct. 1987), and on the same occasion the chairwoman of the Muslim Mothers Association of Kano, Malama Hassana Maikifa, appealed to women to register, as "it is our fundamental right and we do not want to wake up to see that we are dominated" (*The Triumph*, 20 Oct. 1987).

The interesting point in all these statements was that in their arguments and even in their choice of words, they resembled the appeals Abubakar Gumi made in 1982/83. It could thus be claimed that Gumi's campaign for the political mobilization of

Muslim women in the North was not only an important step in the consolidation of the political power for the Muslims in the Federation of Nigeria, but also—consciously or unconsciously—a considerable stimulus for the development of a politically active Muslim women's movement in Nigeria. That Gumi did not in fact oppose such a movement was demonstrated by the fact that he, as well as Shaykh Lawal Ibrahim, Ibrahim Arab, and other leading representatives of the 'Yan Izala movement, took part in the launching of a new regional branch of the Federation of Muslim Women's Associations of Nigeria (FOMWAN) in February 1988 in Kaduna (*The Pen,* 1988, no. 10).

FOMWAN was founded in October 1985 in Minna (Niger State) with the goal of creating an umbrella organization for all Muslim women and women's organizations in Nigeria. The initial support for FOMWAN came, apart from Gumi and the 'Yan Izala, from organizations like the Râbiṭa, the Islamic Foundation in Kano, the JNI, and the Islamic Education Trust (IET) in Minna, an organization under the leadership of the Grand Kadi of Niger State, Shaykh Ahmad Lemu, whose wife, 'Aisha Lemu, was elected first national president of FOMWAN. The Râbiṭa, for instance, financed together with the IET the "First International Training Seminar for Women in Da'wa and Social Development" which took place in Lagos in September 1988 (*The Reporter,* 27 Sept. 1988). By 1989 FOMWAN commanded regional branches in almost all states of the federation, not only in the North, but also in the South, and has developed an especially strong basis in Yorubaland and among the new group of western-educated women in the North (Interview H. U. Bugaje, 28 Apr. 1988, and B. Yusuf, 11 Apr. 1988). Since its foundation in 1985 FOMWAN has managed to convince the Muslim politicians and the western-educated Muslim intelligentsia in the North of its importance. Thus a number of public personalities, such as the Grand Kadi of Abuja, Bashir Sambo, the Grand Kadi of Kwara, Abdulkadir Orire, and Dr. D. O. S. Noibi, head of the Department of Islamic Studies at the University of Ibadan, agreed in a series of interviews with the FOMWAN paper *The Muslim*

Woman that Muslim women should not only vote in the next federal elections in 1992, but also take part in the political process with equal rights and even be elected to political offices (*The Muslim Woman,* 1 Jan. 1988). Ahmad Lemu, for instance, stated in his interview concerning the role of the Muslim women in the future political process, that

> This situation [the transition to the elections of 1992] is a sort of political jihad between Muslims and non-Muslims. In this jihad situation the Muslims need all the human resources they can mobilize to facilitate their proper representation in all aspects of national life. If women are to be excluded, while voting will be the means of electing future political leaders, the Muslims will reduce the effect of their human resources by at least 50% and consequently make themselves liable to perpetual domination politically and otherwise, by non-Muslims. (*The Muslim Woman,* 1 Jan. 1988)

However, should the mobilization of Muslim women as propagated by Abubakar Gumi not lead to the desired results, namely, the consolidation of the political power of Muslims in the Federation of Nigeria, then Gumi would have supported a division of the country. In an interview with the periodical *Quality,* Gumi expressed himself in 1987 as follows:

QUALITY: What are your views on the two-party system recommended for Nigeria? People fear it will polarize Nigeria into North and South.

GUMI: It will not be South against the North but it will be Islam against Christianity.

QUALITY: Can you explain further?

GUMI: I don't think a Muslim can join a party where a Non-Muslim is leading . . .

QUALITY: What if Christians do not accept Moslems as their leader?

GUMI: Then we have to divide the country . . . " (*Quality,* 1 May 1987)

4

The Dogmatic Discussion

The conflict between Abubakar Gumi and the two great Sufi brotherhoods dominated the intellectual disputes between the Muslims in Northern Nigeria in the 1970s and the 1980s and shall therefore be analyzed extensively in this chapter. Gumi played a central role as the leader of the most recent movement of tajdîd among the Muslims in the North, and his writings, especially his programmatic treatise *al-'Aqîda aṣ-ṣaḥîḥa,* are of paramount interest, as it was this text that has instigated the leaders of the Tijâniyya and the Qâdiriyya to answer Gumi's attacks as they were formulated in *al-'Aqida aṣ-ṣaḥîḥa.* Although Gumi's booklet had already been published by 1972 and although the replies of Nasiru Kabara (Qâdiriyya) and Muhammad Sani Kafanga (Tijâniyya) were published in the same year, *al-'Aqîda aṣ-ṣaḥîḥa* remains the point of reference to which younger scholars such as Ibrahim Ṣâliḥ refer. The fundamental criticism of Gumi, directed especially against the Tijâniyya, led to a reorientation within that Sufi brotherhood, as far as its strategies in the conflict with Gumi and the 'Yan Izala were concerned. While a number of religious scholars began to develop a new and more flexible line of argument to take the wind out of the sails of Gumi and his supporters, a number of older religious scholars still cling to the positions of the Tijaniyya as they are presented in this chapter.

4.1. The Religious Debate as Level of Argumentation in the Political Conflict

The disputes about ikhtilâṭ, the qabḍ-sadl debates, or other ritual problems discussed above have shown that religious scholars prefer to rely on a dogmatic argumentation in order to fight their opponents. This functional reference to religion does not mean, however, that religious debates are just dogmatic quarrels and little else. The above-mentioned discussions rather have documented that religion is still the common platform on which conflicts between religious scholars are being carried out. In these conflicts a multitude of interests are involved: the competition between different trader-scholar networks for a greater clientele, the question of religious and political authority within a network or within a ṭarîqa, or the supersession of an older tradition of teaching and authority by a younger generation of scholars. In these confrontations dogmatic arguments were used functionally as it was required by a given situation. At the same time, however, the religious arguments also indicate the erudition of the respective scholars. Only a master of the religious debate has the chance to assert himself politically and socially as the leader of a religious network. This fact strengthened the weight of the religious scholars and of the importance of a sound and all-embracing Islamic religious education. As the disputes between the different networks were carried out in the form of dogmatic discussions, a strong symbolic reevaluation of rituals and religious learning took place. Deviating behavior in this sphere was thus seen not only as a symbol of delimitation from other religious groups but also afforded a welcome basis for takfîr, the "accusation of unbelief." The qabḍ-sadl dispute of the 1950s and 1960s was thus instrumentalized in order to weaken the Tijâniyya-Ibrâhîmiyya on not only a religious but also a political basis. Despite the tremendous symbolic importance of qabḍ and sadl this question lost its religious significance very rapidly after the assassination of Ahmadu Bello and ceased to be a matter of dispute between the Qâdiriyya and the Tijâniyya in the early 1970s in the context of the new conflict with Gumi and the 'Yan Izala. Today the question of qabḍ or sadl no longer incites emotions in the religious debate anymore, and the greatest enemies of the 1980s, the 'Yan Izala and the Tijâniyya, both practice qabḍ. The qabḍ-sadl dispute was, however, replaced by conflicts turning around other religious rituals, such as the communal dhikr, the beating of the bandiri drums in mosques, and the significance of certain prayers. These manifestions of religious life are now to be understood as the new symbols of deviant behavior and were consequently used as a basis for takfîr.

The most important precondition for carrying out a conflict on the religious level is that a pretext is found which might be used to create a dispute with an opponent. In this context the concept of *ḥusn an-nîya* (acting in good faith) plays an important role. Considering the complex ritual and legal prescriptions of the religion (*dîn*) it cannot usually be expected from a common believer (mu'min) that he is always well informed about all aspects of the religion. Thus it is possible to concede the sinner (ʻâṣî) the benefit of doubt that he has acted or spoken in good faith. Only if a Muslim consciously violates in words and deeds against a prescription of the religion, and states that this violation is in concordance with the prescriptions of Islam, can this person be regarded and defined as an unbeliever (*kâfir*). In this sense Abubakar Gumi could have tolerated the practice of tayammum by the Imam of Maru and granted him the benefit of the doubt under the concept of ḥusn an-nîya. Gumi's behavior during the tayammum debate of 1949 demonstrates, however, that he was not interested in a peaceful solution to the issue, but intent on the conflict with the Imam of Maru and the Sultan of Sokoto. The latter would have been obliged to prevent such practices if no convincing arguments in support of them were found. The tayammum debate thus shows the importance of a sound dogmatic argumentation. If Gumi would not have been able to present his arguments convincingly in dogmatic terms, he would have had no chance in the confrontation with the Sultan of Sokoto despite the political support of Ahmadu Bello and Abdullahi Bayero. If a pretext for a dispute in a certain situation is thus needed, the concept of ḥusn an-nîya ought necessarily to be excluded. This procedure is justified by the scholars usually by arguing that the concept of ḥusn an-nîya can be granted only to the really uneducated Muslims but not to an ʻâlim who is supposed to be well informed about the prescriptions of the religion (Interview Saʻid, 8 Mar. 1988). In a dogmatic conflict the argumentation therefore has to be selective. As far as the majority of the faithful are concerned, no thorough knowledge of the religion can be expected, and the argument thus has to be very simple or even crude. The 'ulamâ', however, have to be measured on a different scale, and disputes between them take place on a much more sophisticated level. If the religious scholars deviate from the norms they become bad examples for the common faithful and have thus to be attacked and condemned as *'ulamâ' as-sû'* (scholars of evil) so that their deviation does not become the norm. If the common faithful do deviate from the norm, the only answer is to provide a better education. This line of argumentation was used in Nigeria not only by Gumi in his fight against the ṭuruq, but also by Usman dan Fodio in his attempts to justify the jihâd.

The instrumentalization of rituals of the religion to delimit and condemn deviating groups shows that the religious system of values in Northern Nigeria is still valid. The accusation of unbelief can be made only when faith in this system of norms and prescripitions is still prevalent. Only then can takfîr be used in the religious, political, and social struggle. The selectivity of arguments in dogmatic disputes concerns, however, not only those addressed but also the argumentation itself. This point becomes clear if one looks at the way in which the ḥadîth collections are used in the religious discourse. All malamai underline their arguments with extensive quotations from the Qur'ân and from the ḥadîth collections. This phenomenon may be regarded as a manifestation of the indirect influence of the Salafiyya and the Ikhwân al-muslimîn who have cultivated the use of the ḥadîth collections in order to strengthen their dogmatic positions. The instrumentalization of the ḥadîth in the dogmatic dispute is problematic, however, if one takes into account that to this day there is no open discussion taking place in Northern Nigeria over the different and often diverging sources on ḥadîth. This situation is exploited by religious scholars who emphasize their respective arguments with suitable ḥadîth which can always be found. They accept that the majority of uneducated Muslims is becoming increasingly confused by this style of argumentation (Interview

Miskin, 18 Mar. 1988). The increasing use of the ḥadîth in the different treatises thus became another symbol of the conflict between Gumi and the ṭuruq.

Another important means of argumentation in the religious dispute is the tafsîr (the interpretation of the Qur'ân). Every religious scholar who strives to spread his fame is intent upon holding public tafsîr meetings during Ramadhân, meetings which are often transmitted by the modern mass media. Leading scholars such as Nasiru Kabara or Abubakar Gumi have already distinguished themselves by translations of the Qur'ân into Hausa and by writing tafsîrs of their own. Their tafsîr meetings during Ramadhân are transmitted live by Radio Kaduna. These scholars thus have the opportunity to address a much greater number of Muslims than during their usual tafsîr classes in their respective schools. The popularity of the tafsîr is based on the fact that the scholars can use the tafsîr in order to supplement the actual text, like the very popular *Tafsîr al-jalâlain* by as-Suyûṭî and al-Maḥallî, with commentaries (sub-tafsîrs) of their own. This commentary often adopts, as with Gumi's tafsîr, the character of a sermon and is usually illustrated with examples from everyday life. This new method of tafsîr had been developed in Egypt during the nineteenth century. In contrast to the traditional tafsîrs like those of as-Suyûṭî and al-Maḥallî who understood the tafsîr as an aid toward a better understanding of the Qur'ân or as a philological exegesis, the nineteenth-century mufassirûn (exegetes), such as Muḥammad ibn Aḥmad al-Iskandarânî, understood the tafsîr either as a practical exegesis of the meaning of the Qur'ân, illustrated by examples from the everyday life of their contemporaries, or as a way of proving the Qur'ânic foundation of the modern scientific innovations. In the twentieth century this "scientific tafsîr" (*tafsîr 'ilmi*) was further developed by some leading representatives of the Salafiyya and later by the Ikhwân al-muslimîn, such as Muḥammad 'Abduh, Rashid Riḍâ, Sayyid Quṭb, 'Abd ar-Raḥmân al-Banna,' and Muḥammad Muṣṭafa al-Maraji, who gave their tafsîrs an increasing political character. In particular the tafsîr of Sayyid Quṭb had a great influence on Gumi's own tafsîr. The interpretation of the tafsîr, by establishing connections with actual everyday life, offers any malam the opportunity to influence his disciples and audience not only religiously but also politically, and in this way provides with the chance to attack his opponents. A whole series of violent clashes between the 'Yan Izala and followers of the ṭuruq have occurred in the last few years as a reaction to tafsîr meetings of famous scholars like Gumi. Thus the Kano riots of 1982 were said to have been instigated by a sermon by Aminu d-Din Abubakar in the Bayero University Mosque in Kano. In this context the tafsîr serves as an authentic basis of interpretation within the framework of an essentially politico-social conflict. Although the dogmatic argumentation of the religious scholars in the struggle between the ṭuruq and their critics has an inherent political and social dimension, it is nevertheless necessary to take a closer look at a number of the most important dogmatic questions to understand the importance of the formal religious debate and to understand the role of the religious scholars in this struggle.

4.2. Abubakar Gumi as a Religious Scholar: His Work

Abubakar Gumi gained his fame not only on account of his efforts to revitalize Islam in Northern Nigeria but also on account of his achievements as a religious scholar. He worked for the reform of the Islamic jurisdiction, for a better organization of the pilgrimage, and for the expansion of modern Islamic education. As an author of a great number of books and treatises he emphasized his efforts of tajdîd. His most important works include numerous translations of Usman dan Fodio's writings into Hausa, a number of booklets about ritual aspects of Islam, a translation of the Qur'ân, and a tafsîr entitled *Radd al-adhhân ilâ ma'ânî al-Qur'ân* (The Intelligent Reply Concerning the Meaning of the Qur'ân). His convictions were closely connected with the developments in the Islamic world as a whole. Although he regarded himself as an heir to the work of Usman dan Fodio, he was also to a great extent influenced by contemporary Muslim thinkers like Sayyid Quṭb. Despite his achievements Abubakar Gumi was considered, on account of his radical views on the Sufi brotherhoods, as one of the most controversial personalities among the Nigerian Muslim scholars. Venerated by his followers as a mujaddid (Shanono 1976: 1), he was attacked by his opponents as the personification of Satan.

Gumi's major religious goal, according to his own writings and numerous public statements, was the tajdîd of the religion and the eradication of all bida' (Interview Gumi, 17 Sept. 1987). He presented himself in the same historical tradition as Usman dan Fodio. Like the leader of the jihâd, Gumi denounced the propagators of the bida' as 'ulamâ' as-sû' (scholars of the evil) or as Mallaman Bid'a and criticized the representatives of the ruling elite who opposed any change as Sarakunan gargajiya (the old kings). Like dan Fodio he tried to make Islamic education for the Muslims accessible and easier by translating important works of Islam into Hausa. He thought that his own efforts for the revitalization of Islam in Northern Nigeria would have been meaningless without the achievements of Usman dan Fodio (Interview Gumi, 17 Sept. 1987). Thus Gumi's concept of the bida' was strongly influenced by dan Fodio's work *Iḥyâ' as-sunna wa Ikhmâd al-Bid'a* in which the latter gives a detailed analysis of what constitutes a bid'a and what does not. The emphasis on Usman dan Fodio's legacy also had the effect of protecting Gumi: On account of his reliance on the work of dan Fodio he could make any attack on his own efforts of tajdîd a very risky enterprise because he was able to denounce such an attack easily as an attack on dan Fodio himself (ibid.). In his strategy of claiming the legacy of Usman dan Fodio as the driving force behind his own activities, Gumi went one step too far, however. In his polemic *Musulunci da abinda ke rushe shi* (Islam and the Things Which Lead to Its Corruption), written originally in 1978 and published in 1981, Gumi claimed that although dan Fodio had originally been a member of the Qâdiriyya, he had later given up that affiliation: "Ya karbi Kadiriyya farkon al'amarinsa, amma daga baya ya barta" (he had faith in the Qâdiriyya before he started his struggle but later he left it). Thus dan Fodio, according to Gumi, implicitly regarded the Qâdiriyya as a bid'a. Gumi tried to prove this claim by quoting from a poem by dan Fodio where he says, "Mai magana ko 'Abd al-Qâdir ne wanda yake shi ne sarkin waliyyai ba'a binsa, sunnan Annabi ake bi" ('Abd al-Qâdir, who is the leader of the saints—it is not him whom [we are going to] follow, but the Sunna of the Prophet). In order to support his argument, Gumi also quoted the Wazirin Sokoto Junaidu who wrote in his work *Ifâdat aṭ-ṭâlibîn* (The Teaching of the Searchers), "Lokacinda muka falka, muka ambaci Allahi shi kadai" (When the time has come to wake up [when we will wake up], then we call only on the name of God [then we will have only God in our mind] Gumi 1981: 41–42).

Even if one assumes that these statements were authentic—Gumi, for instance, did not give information as to where he has found Usman dan Fodio's poem—they do not prove that dan Fodio ever gave up his affiliation with the Qâdiriyya. On the contrary, there is not even a hint at such an action. Rather, one has to assume that such an important step by dan Fodio would have been pronounced publicly by the leader of the jihâd and, considering its consequences, would have been explained by him to his followers in extensio. Gumi's intention was clear: He tried to explain away the unpleasant fact that dan Fodio was member of a Sufi brotherhood. Thus he tried to legitimate his anti-Sufi strategy by the invocation of Usman dan Fodio. Gumi's insistence on his claim has given his opponents, especially among the Qâdiriyya, a welcome opportunity to attack him and to publicly question his reputation as an "objective" scholar, a claim which Gumi himself has raised in *al-'Aqîda aṣ-ṣaḥîḥa* (Gumi 1976: 60). As Gumi did not substantiate his claim, his strategy of making the identificaton with the leaders of the jihâd more difficult for the Sufi brotherhoods by invoking Usman dan Fodio was bound to fail.

After his nomination as Deputy Grand Kadi of Northern Nigeria in 1956 Gumi concentrated on reforming the Islamic legal system in the North. He stressed the necessity of integrating the

Islamic legal system into the existing secular jurisdiction on all levels as well as in the constitution. He regarded the reopening of the process of *ijtihâd,* that is, the effort to develop new legal norms adapted to the exigencies of the time by an independent interpretation of the Qur'ân and the Sunna of the Prophet, as a precondition for the fundamental reform of the Islamic law. According to the predominant opinion of all legal schools, the "door" of ijtihâd was closed after the development of the four established schools of law, the Malikite, Hanbalite, Hanafite, and Shafi'ite. Gumi rejected this idea and thereby adopted a position which is generally identified with the ideals of the Salafiyya and the Ikhwân al-muslimîn. According to Gumi three different forms of ijtihâd exist: the ijtihâd of the *ṣaḥâba* (the companions of the Prophet), the ijtihâd of the *tâbi'în* (the companions of the ṣaḥâba), and the ijtihâd of the four schools of law. Whereas the ijtihâd of the ṣaḥâba and of the tâbi'în is closed due to their demise, the ijtihâd of the four schools of law can never be completed as times are changing and new things which did not exist in the times of the Prophet, of the ṣaḥâba, and of the tâbi'în appear again and again. These new things nevertheless have to be integrated into the system of Islamic law (Interview Gumi, 17 Sept. 1987). To make the reopening of the process of ijtihâd possible, Gumi supported the acceptance and application of the two legal principles of *talfîq* (the solving of a specific legal problem by selecting possibilities of a solution among all four schools of law) and *maṣlaḥa* (having regard for the public interest) (Schacht 1964: 61, 68, 106). As the Maliki school of law is, however, the only accepted one in Nigeria, Gumi de facto practiced neither talfîq nor ijtihâd. Although he personally tended to prefer the Hanbali school of law, he used the corpus of the Maliki school of law for his fatâwa (legal advice) in Nigeria (Shanono 1976: 13). Gumi believed that the process of ijtihâd can be begun in Nigeria only if the Islamic judges were trained more completely and if they had a sufficient knowledge of the corpus of all four schools of law. Only then would they be in the position to practice talfîq (Interview

Gumi, 17 Sept. 1987). Gumi's appeal to reopen the process of ijtihâd thus has to be seen as an appeal to the sense of responsibility of the Muslims.

On the basis of his anti-Sufi ideas Abubakar Gumi was connected with other thinkers of the Islamic world, especially Rashîd Riḍâ and the Wahhâbî movement. He had a number of points in common with the Wahhâbiyya, such as the emphasis on the importance of the *'ibâdât* (ritual practice), *tawḥîd* (the uniqueness of God), and, connected with this, the rejection of a special role of the Prophet as it is understood by the Sufi brotherhoods. The influence of the Wahhâbiyya on Gumi was strengthened by the fact that as a member of the Râbiṭa he was in constant close contact with the religious scholars of the neo-Wahhâbiyya in Saudi Arabia. In Nigeria he was therefore considered as a representative of the Wahhâbî movement. Nasiru Kabara, Muhammad Sani Kafanga, and other malamai from the Sufi brotherhoods denounce him publicly as a "Wahhâbî" in order to discredit him as a puppet of the Saudis.

Finally the influence of Sayyid Quṭb on Gumi ought to be mentioned. Sayyid Quṭb (1906–66) was the most influential thinker of the Egyptian Ikhwân al-muslimîn after the death of their founder, Hasan al-Banna', in 1948. Apart from his tafsîr entitled *Fî ẓilâl al-qur'ân* (In the Shadow of the Qur'ân), which was published between 1955 and 1959 and mostly while in prison, his critical works on modern society are of importance: *al-'Adâla al-ijtimâ'iyya fî l-Islâm* (Social Justice in Islam, Cairo 1949) and *Ma'âlîm fî ṭ-ṭarîq* (Milestones, Cairo 1964). Many Ikhwân had fled during the 1950s to Saudi Arabia as a result of the persecution by Jamâl 'Abd an-Nâṣir. It was at this time and under these circumstances that Gumi came into contact with the ideas of Sayyid Quṭb, as many refugees were among the founders of the Râbiṭa in 1962. Gumi asserted that he has taken over his method of tafsîr from Sayyid Quṭb (Interview Gumi, 17 Sept. 1987). This method is essentially based on the idea that each sûra (chapter) of the Qur'ân has a dominant topic which might reappear in other sûras but then only as an illustration of another major topic (Interview

Gumi, 17 Sept. 1987). However, Hunwick has discovered on the basis of an analysis of Gumi's tafsîr that he was influenced to a much greater extent by the classical tafsîr of Abû Sa'îd al-Baiḍâwî (d. 1286), a Shafi'ite qâḍî from Shirâz in Persia (Interview Hunwick, 31 Oct. 1989). Al-Baiḍâwî was the author of a tafsîr entitled *Anwâr at-tanzîl wa-asrâr at-ta'wîl* (The Rays of the Revelation and the Secrets of the Interpretation) which was again based on an earlier work by al-Zamahsarî. Al-Baiḍâwî's commentary on the Qur'ân is characterized above all by its short and comprehensive presentation (EI Vol. 1: 1129).

Sayyid Quṭb's influence on Gumi can also be shown in other spheres of thinking. Thus Gumi, like Sayyid Quṭb, regarded Christianity as a falsification (*taḥrîf*) of true religion. The gospels are seen as manipulated and constructed. The gospel of Barnabas, on the other hand, which is not accepted by the Christian church, was seen by Gumi as authentic and thus used as a basis for his statements about Christianity (Interview Gumi, 17 Sept. 1987). Sayyid Quṭb's concept of jâhiliyya (ignorance) also was adopted by Gumi. Sayyid Quṭb regards the time of jâhiliyya not as an historical period, that is, the time before the appearance of the Prophet Muhammad, but as a condition in which the whole world including the Islamic states presently finds itself. The point of reference for this definition of jâhiliyya for Quṭb, as well as for Gumi, is the degree of concordance with the Qur'ân and the Sunna of the Prophet that a contemporary society possesses (Cedzich 1982: 12). On the basis of this interpretation of the world Gumi proposed a "fundamentalist" solution to the actual problems of the present-day Islamic societies: "This community will never be able to regulate its life and its affairs in a satisfactory way if it does not return to the sources" (Gumi 1976: 78).

Gumi's efforts to revitalize Islam in Nigeria covered not only the reform of the Islamic judicial system and his struggle against the bida', but the whole sphere of Islamic education. Gumi was chairman of the National Teachers' Institute in Kaduna beginning in 1982, an institute which, since 1978, has had the task of examining and employing the teachers for the state schools on the national level. In the international sphere Gumi was a member of the Supreme Council of the Islamic University of Medina and a member of the Islamic Research Council in Cairo. In these functions he took part in the development and formulation of curricula and new Islamic educational systems (*The Analyst*, 1987, no. 5: 25–28). Apart from these institutional engagements for the improvement of the Islamic eduction, Gumi also gave private lectures. Every afternoon he held a tafsîr meeting in the mosque in his house in Kaduna. His tafsîr is based on his own work *Radd al-adhhân ilâ ma'ânî al-Qur'ân* (The Intelligent Reply Concerning the Meanings of the Qur'ân) and his translation of the Qur'ân into Hausa entitled *Tarjamar Ma'anonin Alkurani Maigirma.* Gumi's Arabic tafsîr was financed in a first edition of 100,000 copies by a Saudi businessman and distributed free of charge in Nigeria. The second edition was financed by his Nigerian supporters al-Ḥâjj Bello Maitama (200,000 naira) and al-Ḥâjj Ibrahim Kano (20,000 naira); the third edition was financed by King Fahd of Saudi Arabia personally (Interview 'Abd âs-Samad Muhammad, 3 Oct. 1987). Gumi also appealed to his followers to establish and to maintain schools of their own. Thus al-Ḥâjj Ahmad Chanchangi founded the Malam Abubakar Mahmoud Gumi Islamiyya School in Kaduna in 1979, where the first graduation ceremony took place in 1987 (*The Reporter*, 28 Dec. 1987). Al-Ḥâjj Ibrahim Kano established the Nûr al-Islâm School in Kaduna, and al-Ḥâjj Garba Dan Shagamu followed his example by founding another Islamiyya school in Kaduna (Gumi 1987: 20 ff.). With the financial support of M. K. O. Abiola, entrepreneur and publisher from the South, Gumi, after 1987, planned the establishment of an 'Uthman b. Fudi-Institute for Higher Islamic Studies in Kaduna. This institute was supposed to be gradually transformed after its completion into an Islamic university (*Quality*, 1 May 1987).

Gumi's educational efforts were supported by his endeavors to spread his ideas through the mass media. Thus his tafsîr in the Sultan Bello Mosque which he has held regularly since 1963 during Ramadhân has been transmitted live by Radio Kaduna since

1966. After the assassination of Ahmadu Bello and the 1966 coup, Gumi received permission to continue the radio tafsîr from the new military governor of the North, Major Hassan Katsina. This was commented on by Gumi in an interview with Umar in 1986: "Thus the respect I enjoyed from Hassan [Katsina] was more than that from the Sardauna. That was how I came to have more powers to speak out" (Umar 1988: 188). Thus Gumi obtained open access to the modern mass media which led to the rapid spread and popularization of his ideas after 1966. Apart from his tafsîr Gumi had two regular radio programs (Islam by Radio and Hasken Musulunci) with Radio Kaduna. Since the mid-1970s, in reaction to Gumi's media activities, the Sufi leaders have demanded their own programs on radio and TV to present their own positions. Finally, Gumi spoke on occasion at public rallies and demonstrations. After 1966 he regularly published articles in the Hausa daily newspaper *Gaskiya Ta Fi Kwabo,* which was founded by the British in 1939 and which is today part of the Northern Nigerian Newspaper Ltd. in Kaduna. In his articles Gumi concentrated on questions of the Islamic law and problems of the ritual.

In comparison with other religious scholars in Northern Nigeria Abubakar Gumi was, as far as his methods in propagating his ideas are concerned, the most versatile scholar among them. He spoke not only Fulfulde, his mother tongue, but also Hausa, English, and Arabic. His initiatives in relation to the development of a modern Islamic educational system put the Sufi brotherhoods under pressure, especially in the sphere of women's education. Since the foundation of the 'Yan Izala Abubakar Gumi Arabic tafsîr malso commanded a mass organization of his own and was thus able to propagate his ideas and to inflict profound damage on the foundations of the Sufi brotherhoods. The support from wealthy members of the Kaduna Mafia and Saudi businessmen has made the construction of numerous new Islamiyya schools under the management of the 'Yan Izala possible. The dogmatic foundation of his policy of tajdîd was laid down in his book *al-'Aqîda aṣ-ṣaḥîḥa.*

4.3. Abubakar Gumi's Major Work against the Sufi Brotherhoods: al-'Aqîda aṣ-Ṣaḥiḥa

Whereas Gumi's translation of the Qur'ân into Hausa and his Arabic tafsîr might be regarded as his major religious works, his treatise *al-'Aqîda aṣ-ṣaḥîḥa bi-muwâfaqat ash-sharî'a* (The Right Faith According to the Prescriptions of the Sharî'a) is without doubt his major programmatic work. The book was first published in Arabic in 1972 and was therefore taken up only by a relatively small circle of religious scholars. The reply to *al-'Aqîda* thus came, for the time being, only from their ranks. In 1976, however, a second edition with an English translation by Musa Abdul was published, and in 1978 an extended and popularized Hausa version followed under the title *Musulunci da abinda ke rushe shi* (Islam and the Things Which Lead to Its Destruction). Although *Musulunci* and *al-'Aqîda* are almost identical in argument and content, they differ considerably in style. *Al-'Aqîda* argues on a predominantly dogmatic level, uses many quotations from the Qur'ân and the ḥadîth collections, and is fairly moderate as far as polemics are concerned. In *Musulunci* a simple, comprehensive language is used, the book has the character of a polemic, and after 1978 it was used by the 'Yan Izala as the basis for their attacks on the ṭuruq. Since that time Gumi's views have found a greater public.

Gumi emphasizes in his introduction to *al-'Aqîda* that he has written the book especially for those who seem to need religious advice on account of the "stagnation in their thinking" (jumûd al-qarîḥa), a clear reference to the thinkers of the Salafiyya who have also used the term *jumûd* to legitimize their criticism of their societies. On the other hand Gumi stresses that he had a great many reservations about writing the book at all on account of the controversies it would trigger. These controversies could lead to a split in the umma. In the end he chose to stick to the verse of the Qur'ân which says, "Those that hide the clear proofs and the guidance We have revealed after We had proclaimed them in the Scriptures shall be cursed by God (Qur'ân 2:159).

This Qur'ânic command had already been used by Usman dan Fodio in order to legitimize his effort of tajdîd (Fodio 1986: 279).

Gumi starts with the actual presentation of his program—the condemnation of the bida'—only after the justification of his intentions. First, he stresses the very meaning of the Islamic confession of faith. The person who has once confessed that there is no god but God and that Muhammad is his messenger has at the same time accepted that nobody and nothing else but Allah and his messenger are to be worshipped. The person who does something else consequently violates this basic dogma of Islam. Second, Gumi emphasizes the importance of the Prophet Muhammad as a bearer of the revelation of God. The Prophet was the "seal of the Prophets," and after his death no further revelations can be transmitted to mankind. On account of the death of the Prophet the "house of Islam" was completed and has since been perfect. The "advantage" of the death of the Prophet is based on this point: On account of his death the number of things which were imposed on mankind to do or to omit were limited. Thus no Muslim should try to introduce something new into the religion which is not in accordance with the revelations transmitted by the Prophet. According to an ḥadîth, other people will appear, however, after the death of the Prophet who will claim the status of a prophet for themselves. Their claims are to be regarded as false: "There shall emerge after my death, thirty persons who shall falsely claim to be prophets whereas I am the seal of the Prophets and there shall be no Prophet after me" (Gumi 1976: 7–8).

This basic argument concerning the role of the Prophet reappears in a number of places in *al-'Aqîda.* It has to be seen as the decisive difference in the interpretation of the role of the Prophet between Gumi and the ṭuruq. Whereas Gumi limits the Prophet to his role as the bearer of the revelation of Allah, the Sufi brotherhoods also consider him a lawgiver in the sense that he has fixed ways of behavior on the basis of his example, his *Sunna,* which was inspired by God. In this way his example would be effective after his death. Gumi, in contrast, sees the death of the Prophet as the final stone in the construction of the revelation of Allah. However, this does not mean that Gumi rejects the Sunna of the Prophet as a source of the religion as such. Rather, he regards him as the undisputed leader of the umma and thus accepts the importance of his Sunna. Gumi mentions several times in *al-'Aqîda* that the Prophet has led an exemplary life and that the focus on his Sunna would thus be a blessing for Muslims (Gumi 1976: 7, 20). He rejects, however, the idea which is presented by the Sufis, namely, that the Prophet continues to be active in a mystical way even after his death by transmitting new instructions or recommendations to mankind through the dreams and visions of the Sufis; thereby the Sufis would extend his Sunna in an inadmissible way. According to Gumi the death of the Prophet has made the religion perfect and mankind is not "burdened" with further obligations or instructions which have to be observed: "This day I have perfected your religion for you and completed My favor to you. I have chosen Islam to be your faith" (Qur'ân 5:3). These statements show how much Gumi was influenced by his experiences as Grand Kadi: He welcomes a simple and comprehensive codex of laws and abhors the unlimited extension of rules of behavior. With this definition of the role of the Prophet, Gumi has also identified the basis of his attack on the ṭuruq: according to his opinion they violate the basic dogma, namely, that all revelation has come to an end after the death of the Prophet.

In a further passage Gumi elaborates on the differences in the meaning of the terms prophet (*nabî*), messenger (*rasûl*), and saint (*walî*). He concentrates especially on the definition of the "saint" and stresses that holiness (*wilâya*) is a relative concept as every person of faith might be regarded as "holy" according to his respective degree of faith. In this respect it would not be important how intensively a Muslim fulfills his religious obligations (*'ibâdât*). Much more important would be how sincere his faith is. Gumi says, quoting the tafsîr of Ibn Kathîr (d. 1372), "The Saint is therefore the pious believer" (Gumi 1976: 11).

On the other hand, Gumi emphasizes that the degree of personal faith (*imân*) is determined by the intensity of a person's practice of his religious obligations. Not all of the faithful possess an equal degree of faith. Whereas the faith of some is "brighter than the sun," the faith of others is "weaker than a lamp." Thus the faithful who support their confession of faith by deeds (*'amal*) show that their faith is greater than the faith of those who are faithful only in their heart (ma'rifa bi-l-qalb) (Gumi 1976: 13–14). This principle is valid not only as far as the daily prayers are concerned but also in respect to all other obligations of the religion: *zakât, ṣaum,* and *ḥajj.* Nevertheless no Muslim can be regarded as a kâfir if he does not show his faith by 'amal, as the faith of each Muslim is a secret between him and God alone. No one except God is able to look into the heart of a person. A Muslim who has committed a sin is thereafter not to be labeled a kâfir merely on account of an act of sinning. His sin is not persistent, and if he repents he returns to the faith: "None of those who turn towards the Qiblah will be unbelievers through sin" (ibid.: 17). Only if a Muslim openly shows in words and deeds that he is sinning consciously and only if he then declares this violation of the Sunna of the Prophet as being in accordance with the Sunna can such a person be regarded as an unbeliever. With this position Gumi takes the same line of argument as Usman dan Fodio or al-Qâdî 'Iyâḍ, a Maghribinian scholar of the twelfth century, whose *Kitâb ash-shifâ'* (The Book of Healing) is widely distributed in Northern Nigeria as a basis for teaching. Both have stressed that a Muslim does not become a kâfir by an act of sinning but has to be regarded as a "disobedient Muslim" (*'aṣî*) ('Iyad 1950: 248). Gumi's position in respect to the definition of holiness and faithfulness shows another fundamental difference in the interpretation of these concepts between him and the Sufi brotherhoods: Whereas the Sufis emphasize the importance of faith (imân), the personal relationship between man and God, Gumi underlines the relativity of personal faith as far as wilâya is concerned and stresses in contrast the overall importance of Islam as a normative system of behavior for the faithful.

Gumi starts to discuss the major question of what has to be regarded as a "blameworthy innovation" (bid'a madhmûma) only after the definition of these basic problems. He regards as such blameworthy innovations all actions which contradict the sunna of the Prophet (Gumi 1976: 18). Among those who practice bida' are, for instance, those Muslims who worship God on the basis of love alone. Gumi calls such a person a *zindîq* (hypocrite). In addition he says that all those who worship God exclusively on the basis of fear are also contradicting the Sunna; he includes in this category all murji'îtes who worship God only on the basis of hope. The correct approach, according to Gumi, is the worship of God based on all three motivations combined. As Muslims who are guilty of practicing bida' he also regards those who are satisfied with the perception of God in their heart alone (ma'rifa bi-l-qalb). Thus, according to Gumi, the Pharaoh of Egypt as well had recognized the truth of God, but nevertheless refused to believe in it. People who act like the Pharaoh are therefore in a condition of jahmiyya. By introducing the term *jahmiyya* Gumi is making recourse to Jahm b. Safwân, a scholar from Tirmîdh (Khorâsân), who regarded only the mere ignorance (*jahl*) of God as an act of unbelief, thus placing himself, according to Gumi, on the same level as the unbelievers, as he had negated the importance of the attributes of God (Gumi 1976: 19). The condemnation of Jahm b. Safwân is a typical Hanbalî position and was, for instance, a central point in Ibn Taimiyya's *al-'Aqîda al-wâsiṭiyya* (Laoust 1939: 261). In West Africa Gumi defines especially those Muslims as adherents of jahmiyya who follow the teaching of tarbiya (Gumi 1976: 19). Gumi particularly addresses the Tijâniyya-Ibrâhîmiyya with this polemical attack, and consequently follows it up by his criticism of the ṣalât al-fâtiḥ and the central work of the Tijâniyya, *Jawâhir al-ma'anî wa-bulûgh al-amânî fî faiḍ sîdî aḥmad at-tijânî* (The Jewels of the Meanings and the Fulfilling of the Wishes in the Grace of Sîdî Aḥmad at-Tijânî), which is a compilation of the sayings and deeds of Aḥmad at-Tijânî written down by his disciple 'Alî Ḥarâzim (Abun-Naṣr 1965: 24). The ṣalât al-fâtiḥ, one of the most important prayers of the Tijâniyya, was revealed according to Sufi belief to the founder of the Khalwatiyya Sufi brotherhood, Muḥammad al-Bakrî, by the Prophet himself. Aḥmad at-Tijânî again is said to have received a revelation from the Prophet that a single recitation of that prayer equals in its blessing six complete recitations of the Qur'ân (ibid.: 61). Gumi particularly attacks a passage in *Jawâhir al-ma'ânî* where the claim is made that the instructions which were revealed by God to the Prophet for transmission to the general public had found their end with the death of the Prophet, whereas the "special instructions" (al-amr al-khâṣṣ) which the Prophet allegedly transmitted only to "specially chosen persons" continued to be transmitted even after his death (Gumi 1976: 19). With his attack on this claim of the Tijâniyya Gumi again attacks the Sufi conception of the Prophet. According to Gumi the message of the Prophet was complete and had been fully transmitted. The revelation is not in need of further amendments, extensions, or changes. The Prophet has also never mentioned the possibility that other revelations would occur after his death. Rather he warned against all bida'. Therefore the ideas as they are expressed in *Jawâhir al-ma'ânî* infringe the limits of the sharî'a and thus have to be regarded as bida'. In addition, the ṣalât al-fâtiḥ was neither mentioned in the Qur'ân, nor in the ḥadîth collections, not to mention its alleged blessing power. Thus, it must also be categorized as a bid'a (ibid.: 21–22).

After this first attack on ṣalât al-fâtiḥ and *Jawâhir al-ma'ânî* Gumi pursues another attack on the leaders of the Sufi brotherhoods. Some of the contemporary leaders would follow the "insinuations of the evil" and would ascribe traditions to the founders of the Qâdiriyya and the Tijâniyya, 'Abd al-Qâdir al-Jilânî and Ahmad at-Tijânî, which had nothing to do with them. In this way they would fill the hearts of the weak with fear so that they followed them in their "unsatiable greed for wordly desires" (Gumi 1976: 25). These so-called religious leaders would make themselves guilty by practicing all kinds of witchcraft (*siḥr*) to confuse the credulous Muslims. Gumi criticizes in particular the practice of Sha Rubutu, a custom widely spread in Hausaland which is also found in other Islamic countries such as Egypt and the Sudan. It can be regarded, like *ḥisâb* (astrology), as an essential part of the magical corpus of Islam. Sha Rubutu, that is, "the drinking of the written," is a magical practice in which a malam writes a sura of the Qur'ân or a part of it which is regarded as especially powerful or a blessing for a specific purpose, on a wooden slate (Hausa: *allo*). The writing is washed off and the liquid then given to the person seeking help to drink or to wash with. Sha Rubutu is practiced by almost all malamai in Northern Nigeria in varying degrees, and many malamai make their living from practicing Sha Rubutu or other religio-magical occupations like the production of charms (*laya, guru*), protecting or harmful medicine (*malakula*), the practice of sorcery (*tsubbu*), fortune-telling (*dubu*), or tricks (*damfara*) (Anwar 1989: 95). In his treatise *Nûr al-albâb* (The Light of the Hearts) Usman dan Fodio had already attacked these practices, and among them Sha Rubutu in particular, as acts constituting *kufr* (unbelief) (Meyer 1975: 102). Gumi's attack on these traditions can thus be regarded both as an effort to rationalize and to demystify the religion and as a negation of these magical practices of Islam.

In the next chapter of *al-'Aqîda* Gumi again returns to the problem of the special instructions. He raises the rhetorical question of why the ṣalât al-fâtiḥ, for instance, which was not yet known at the time of the Prophet and ought therefore to be regarded as an amr khâṣṣ, changed its character after the death of the Prophet and was suddenly made public, although the Prophet had made it very clear that the Muslims should refrain from all bida'. Why had the Prophet failed to mention that all those innovations which were transmitted to the Muslims after his death by some "special chosen persons" were not to be regarded as bida'. And why had the Prophet not explained how one could distinguish these special instructions from others in order to make sure that they were authentic and true? (Gumi 1976: 35–36). With these criticisms Gumi attacks the claim of the Sufis in their being able to see the Prophet in their dreams and visions and to receive instructions from him which they could then transmit to the Muslims as rules of behavior. In this context Gumi opposes the idea that other "special chosen persons" such as Aḥmad at-Tij had ever existed after the death of the Prophet and the f rightly guided khalîfas. Gumi thereby follows the opinion Rashîd Riḍâ who also limited the circle of the "righteous an tors" (as-salaf aṣ-ṣâliḥ) in that sense.

In a further paragraph on the different forms of appearance the bida' Gumi criticizes the practice of reciting the dhikr alo the practice of the bandiri-dhikr, and the practice of the gr dhikr (Gumi 1976: 36–44). There were no hints of such pract either in the Qur'ân nor in the ḥadîth collections, and if th practices were not mentioned in these sources of the religion t one has to accept that they have to be regarded as bida':

> No one denies the fact that reading the Qur'ân, listening to serm and praising God are necessarily religious deeds. . . . But as for p ing with muscial instruments such as tambourines and drums which the law is silent on occasions such as of marriage ceremoni birthday parties of women and children, no one would oppose th they are done within the limits of the shari'ah. . . . But those combine drumming with religion or the recitation of the Qur'ân the praises of Allah in the mosque, such people are considere those who reduce their religion to a play thing and make them mockery of it. They therefore fall within the group of those Qur'ân refers to when it says [Qur'ân 8:35], "Their prayers at the cred House are nothing but whistling and clapping of hands. T shall be punished for their unbelief." (ibid.: 44)

After this passing shot at these practices of the Sufi brotherhc Gumi begins a voluminous critique of the hierarchies of saint the ṭuruq. He attacks the claims of some Sufi leaders, like Aḥı at-Tijânî, Ibrahim Niass, and Nasiru Kabara, who defined th selves as quṭb or ghauth. These ideas should be seen accordin Gumi as a variant of the bida', as the veneration of human be and the belief in their alleged "special capabilities" constitute violation of the basic teachings of Islam. Furthermore the cl of Prophets had found its termination in the person of Muh mad, and since his time no one would be in the position tc ceive divine revelations which could tell mankind who is a ghauth and who is not (Gumi 1976: 45 f., 49). The veneration of such alleged saints also violates the principle of the uniqueness of God (*tawḥîd*): "Say: No one in the heavens or on earth has knowledge of what is hidden except God" [Qur'ân 27:65]. Thus no human being could claim to be a ghauth and to have knowledge of the Hidden.

In the following chapter of *al-'Aqîda* Gumi directs his criticisms again at the Tijâniyya. According to him the prayer Jawharat al-kamâl (The Jewel of Perfection) would be particularly violating the prescriptions of the sharî'a. According to the belief of the Tijânîs this prayer is to be recited just like the five obligatory prayers of the day only after a ritual ablution. In their belief the Prophet and the four rightly guided khalîfas take part in the *waẓîfa* (recitations) after the seventh of twelve recitations of the prayer. During the waẓîfa the Tijânîs therefore spread a white, square piece of cloth, the 'izâr, in their midst, so that the Prophet and the four rightly guided khalîfas can settle down (Abun-Nasr 1965: 53). Gumi attacks the Jawharat al-kamâl also from the linguistic point of view and claims that the prayer can be misunderstood on account of its choice of words. To illuminate his argument he refers to the usage of the word *asqam* (that is, the elative of *saqam,* "sick, defective") in this prayer. The term was used by Aḥmad at-Tijani erroneously, as the correct superlative of the word *mustaqim* (straight) is not asqam but al-aqwam, as the roots of the word mustaqim is q-w-m and not s-q-m (ibid.: 56). The usage of the term asqam as a term denoting the path of the Prophet, according to Gumi, proves that this prayer cannot be regarded as a revelation of the Prophet as Aḥmad at-Tijânî had claimed (Gumi 1976: 54). The discussion of the linguistic mistakes of the Tijâniyya enabled Gumi to place the linguistic competences of his opponents into question. It is obvious how painful such a criticism had to be for those to whom it had been intended, if one takes into account how important the Arabic language is for the religious scholars. Nevertheless, Gumi was not immune to such criticism. In *al-'Aqîda* he also made a mistake which was promptly used by Nasiru Kabara in his argument against Gumi: On page 57 of *al-'Aqîda* the original heading for the chapter—Takhâfât ba'd al-mufassirîn, which makes no sense —was crossed out and replaced by the new heading Tahâfât ba'd al-mufassirîn (The Irregularities of Some Exegetes of the Qur'ân). This mistake was used by Kabara to demonstrate to Gumi his own deficiencies in his command of the Arabic language (Kabara 1972: 24–25).

In the following chapter Gumi extensively discusses the problem of the correct exegesis of the Qur'ân and gives a number of exemples of how traditions have been falsified. Of special interest for the understanding of his perception of society is his interpretation of a tradition about a legal dispute which the Prophet Dâwûd had to solve. In this dispute a rich man and a poor man were opponents. The poor man accused the rich man of having intended to steal his last sheep, whereas the rich man refuted this accusation. Gumi enters the discussion at that point and argues that the very fact of the poor man's accusation already points to a certain compulsion thus exerted on the "generous" Dâwûd. The fact that the accused was rich and powerful failed, according to Gumi, to prove that he was guilty. Rather, the probability would be greater that he, the owner of ninety-nine sheep, was also the owner of the hundredth, the disputed sheep (Gumi 1976: 71). With this interpretation Gumi clearly takes the view of "in dubio pro ricco."

In a further passage Gumi discusses briefly the political dimension of the sharî'a: Only the person who follows the guidelines of the sharî'a can be called a real Muslim. A judge who makes his decisions on the basis of something other than the sharî'a is therefore to be regarded as a *fâsiq* (a deviationer) and in addition a kâfir, if he continues to think that his deviation is in concordance with Islam. This principle would also be valid for every Muslim who would go with his case to a non-Muslim judge (Gumi 1976: 76).

In the last chapter of *al-'Aqîda* Gumi discusses the corruption of the Muslims by "sectarian leaders" (shuyûkh aṭ-ṭawâ'if) and "misleading books" (al-kutub ad-dasîsa). An important reason for the success of the enemies of Islam according to Gumi is based on the fact that they had corrupted the children of the Muslims by subversive education. Thereupon they had infiltrated the community of the Muslims with the help of "sectarian leaders" and offered the latter absolute control over the Muslims. Furthermore they had educated the children of "idolatory unbelievers whose parents walked about naked and who do not realize what is moral, sense of honor or humanness," and elevated them to leading government positions and thus made them rulers over the Muslims, "whose intelligence had wandered away into the arena of superstitions" (Gumi 1976: 78–79). These polemics constitute a violent and insulting attack not only on the leaders of the Sufi brotherhoods but also on the Christians and non-Muslims in Southern Nigeria who, according to Gumi, have a disproportionately large share of power as a consequence of colonial rule and continue to do so. Furthermore Gumi criticizes in this respect the writings which deal with the hierarchies of the saints and claim that the saints are in contact with God. Apart from *Jawâhir al-ma'anî* Gumi identifies *al-Fuyûḍat ar-rabbâniyya fî l-ma'âthir wa-l-awrâd al-qâdiriyya* (The Streams of Divine Grace in the Glorious Deeds and in the Litanies of the Qâdiriyya) by Ismâ'îl b. Muḥammad Sa'îd al-Qâdir, a book which describes the doctrines and practices of the Qâdiriyya. Among these misleading books are included the writings of the contemporary religious scholars "who follow their desires and therefore have gone astray" (ibid.: 79–80).

With this polemical statement Gumi concludes *al-'Aqîda*. The most important aim of the treatise is the definition of his point of view in regards to certain conceptions on religion within the Sufi brotherhoods, especially as far as the role of the Prophet and the bida' are concerned. It ought to be mentioned that Gumi exempts the founders of both the Qâdiriyya and the Tijâniyya in a number of aspects from his criticism and by contrast blames their successors for all deviations and corruptions within their ṭuruq. Their reaction was related directly to Gumi's line of argument in *al-'Aqîda*.

4.4. The Reaction of the Sufi Brotherhoods to Gumi's Attacks

The publication of *al-'Aqîda aṣ-ṣaḥîḥa* in 1972 had far-reaching repercussions on the further development of the Sufi brotherhoods in Northern Nigeria. From then on Abubakar Gumi was their common enemy, and the disputes between the two Sufi brotherhoods were shelved in the interest of their common defense against his attacks. Immediately after the publication of *al-'Aqîda* Muhammad Sani Kafanga wrote a treatise in the name of the Tijâniyya entitled *al-Minaḥ al-ḥamîda fî l-radd 'alâ fâsid al-'Aqîda* (The Praiseworthy Gifts in the Reply to the One Who Is Corrupted in His Faith) in which he answered Gumi's attacks for the Tijâniyya. Nasiru Kabara followed suit on behalf of the Qâdiriyya with a booklet called *an-Naṣîḥa aṣ-ṣarîḥa fî l-radd 'alâ l-'aqîda aṣ-ṣaḥîḥa* (The Frank Advice in the Reply to *al-'Aqîda aṣ-ṣaḥîḥa*). Both works follow a single strategy, namely, to defend the ṭuruq and Sufism in general against Gumi's attacks and to denounce Gumi's arguments as "ignorant chatter" (*kalâm jâhil*) (Kafanga 1972: 52). They are polemical in style and complement each other even in details of presentation. Together with *al-'Aqîda* they form a homogenous complex of topics. The arguments presented in these three works have been taken up and discussed again and again by all parties in the conflict since their publication in 1972.

Neither Muhammad Sani Kafanga nor Nasiru Kabara covers every point of Gumi's criticism in their replies to *al-'Aqîda;* some questions are even left out of consideration entirely. Thus both scholars evade the discussion of sorcery (*siḥr*) which plays an important role in Gumi's book. Although both authors cover a series of criticisms of Gumi which concern their specific ṭarîqa, such as the problem of *Jawâhir al-ma'ânî* in the case of the Tijâniyya of the bandiri-dhikr in the case of the Qâdiriyya, they prefer to discuss more wide-ranging topics like the role of the Prophet or to defend Sufism in general. Usually both Kabara and Sani Kafanga begin by quoting, but not always completely, a point of critique of Gumi. Then they add quotations by a number of authorities who have concerned themselves with the specific point in question, such as the Qur'ân, the ḥadîth collections, and the classic authors of Sufim like Ibn 'Arabî, Shaykh 'Abd al-Wahhâb ash-Sha'rânî (1492–1565), Muḥammad al-Ḥâfiẓ b. 'Abd al-Laṭîf al-Miṣrî (1897–1978), Aḥmad at-Tijani, Ibrahim Niass, Usman dan Fodio, and Muhammad Bello, as well as the legal works of Khalîl b. Isḥâq and Imam Mâlik. Finally they give their own opinion on a specific point. In both works Gumi is characterized repeatedly with polemical and insulting terms. Thus throughout his book Kabara calls him a "Wahhâbî" who wants to seduce people into committing devilish things (*ash-shayṭâniyya*) (Kabara 1972: 4), whereas Kafanga denounces Gumi's arguments as "ignorant chatter" or as "talk producing unbelief" (*kalâm mukaffir*). This strategy aims to depict Gumi as an outsider who in reality does not belong to the community of the ahl as-sunna. His arguments are characterized as biased and thus not credible on account of his affinities to the "Wahhâbî" ideology. A judgment about Sufism could thus not be accepted from him; he would simply not be in a position to judge Sufism at all. With this way of procedure and argument the supporters of the ṭuruq who have become insecure in their positions are to be strengthened, and the stupidity and groundlessness of Gumi's arguments are purported to be demonstrated. Both authors do not attempt a refutation of Gumi's criticisms by a systematic, point-by-point, exact counterargument. Rather, they try to present their own positions with the help of certain questions they have chosen for argument. They do not intend to convince Gumi but to back up the followers of the Tijâniyya and the Qâdiriyya.

In contrast to Muhammad Sani Kafanga Nasiru Kabara introduces his treatise with four points of practical advice which the Muslims should heed in their conflict with Gumi and *al-'Aqîda*. First, he enjoins friends that the love for the Prophet is more important than the love for one's fatherland, for one's own person, for the next of kin, or for money, as one can only turn with prayer to the Prophet. Second, Nasiru Kabara stresses that *al-'Aqîda* is a work which follows a purely "Wahhâbî" strategy. He who would attack the Prophet would also fight against God and seduce people to devilry (Kabara 1972: 4). Therefore Kabara in a third piece of advice attempts to inform the population about the true character of the book through the religious schools, the mosques, and the religious institutions to protect the children in the schools. At the same time it would also be the task of the government to shield the Muslims in the state schools from its influences. This appeal of Kabara was apparently taken very seriously at least by the malamai of the Qâdiriyya. Thus I witnessed during a bandiri-dhikr on 7 January 1987 in one of the Qâdirî mosques of Unguwar Alfindiki in Kano how the imam of the mosque, Malam Sidi, appealed in his final prayer to God to protect the children of the Qâdirîs so that they would not fall into the hands of the "Wahhâbîs and the 'Yan Izala." With his fourth piece of advice Kabara states that it should be an obligation for all Muslims to make themselves free of all that is misleading and to strive to learn the path of the Sufis (ibid.).

After this programmatic introduction Nasiru Kabara emphasizes that Gumi's only interest seemingly is to destroy the Sufi brotherhoods even though scholars agree that Sufism has existed for more than a thousand years (Kabara 1972: 6). Kafanga complements this argument by saying that it could not be characterized as a bid'a on the basis of the fact that it can be traced back to the times of the Prophet (ibid.: 4). After these basic declarations both authors extensively discuss the central problem of the role of the Prophet. Kabara as well as Kafanga refutes Gumi's idea of limiting the role of the Prophet to that of a transmitter of the revelation. Kabara argues that the Prophet had not only been a rasûl but also a "lawgiver with the authority of God" (Shâri' bi-idhn Allâh) (ibid.: 10). On the basis of his intimacy with God his Sunna had a legislative function for the Muslim community. With the idea that the death of the Prophet had been "useful," as the number of things which had to be done or to be avoided had been limited, Gumi, according to Kabara, simply intends to close the door of ijtihâd for the Sufis and the jurists in order to attack the Sufi brotherhoods as bida' with less difficulty. It is, however, unthinkable that mankind is cut off from the benefactions of the Prophet through his death. It should rather be the other way round: The death of the Prophet was useful as the process of ijtihâd in respect to the Sunna of the Prophet could begin only in this way. The religion of Islam was completed through the death of the Prophet and not the process of ijtihâd. The death of the Prophet had, on the other hand, also been useful, as in this way, according to Kabara, the intercession (*ash-shafâ'a*) of the Prophet with God was made possible (Kabara 1972: 6–7). Kafanga follows a similar argument in his work. Gumi's interpretation of the death of the Prophet would mean that the Prophet would no longer be useful after his death. This is false faith. The Muslims followed the Sunna of the Prophet not only as long as he was living but continued to do so after he had died. The Prophet is thus still relevant today as an example and furthermore continues to be useful through his role as an intercessor with God (Kafanga 1972: 6 ff.). The positions of Kabara and Kafanga thus represent a totally different conception of the role of the Prophet than Gumi's ideas about him. For Kafanga and Kabara the Prophet is relevant even after his death as a legislator, on the basis of his Sunna and as an intercessor with God. In their arguments they impute to Gumi, however, a conception of the importance of the Sunna of the Prophet which is too restricted: Gumi does not reject the importance of the Sunna as a fundamental source of the religion, but he refutes the extension of the "interference" of the Prophet after his death through the dreams and visions of the Sufis. He thus rejects the claim of the Sufis to practice ijtihâd on the basis of their alleged spiritual connection with the Prophet.

After the discussion of the role of the Prophet, Nasiru Kabara and Sani Kafanga deal with the problem of defining a saint and defining the bida'. Their presentation is not in contradiction to Gumi's argument, but rather serves as a platform to describe their own positions. Both scholars essentially try to depict their ṭuruq as absolutely "orthodox" in the sense of the Sunna. Sani Kafanga begins the debate with the definition of the "saints." According to him they are formed along the "example set by the Prophet" (Kafanga 1972: 11); they are in contact with the Prophet through their dreams and cannot go astray merely as a result of this. In addition, Sani Kafanga refutes Gumi's criticism of tarbiya which is characterized as a bid'a in *al-'Aqîda* as it limits the perception of God to a partial aspect (*ma'rifa bi-l-qalb*). Kafanga replies with a quotation from Imam Zarruq:

> The fulfilling of the religious obligations [*'ibâdât*] is valid only, if they are fulfilled in the realization of God [*ma'rifa*]. There can be no salvation [*faraj*] on the basis of the fulfillment of the religious obligations alone if this is not based on ascetism [*zuhd*]. The same is valid for zuhd, too: there can be no ascetism except on the basis of the realization of God and on the basis of the fulfullment of the religious obligations. (ibid.: 17)

Kafanga thus stresses that the 'ibâdât which were so stressed by Gumi make sense only if they are fulfilled in the realization and perception of God. This consciousness is, however, to be reached only on the basis of the ascetism of the Sufis. Zuhd again can be reached only if one fulfils the 'ibâdât. Thus Gumi's attack on the followers of tarbiya is not quite to the point: They are characterized by their insistence on the importance of the 'ibâdât as a precondition for zuhd and thereby also the realization of God (Kafanga 1972: 17). The practice of the formal aspects of the religion as it is stressed by Gumi as an indicator of one's personal faith is senseless if that practice is not done in the right imân (personal relationship to God) which again can be achieved only through the ascetism of the Sufis. Apart from that, the followers of Aḥmad at-Tijânî and Ibrahim Niass are known by the fact that they are following the Qur'ân and the sunna of the Prophet, that they are fulfilling all obligations of a faithful Muslim, and that they would in addition render a number of further proofs of their faith: They practice the waẓîfa, they obey the sharî'a, and they build schools. Thus it is not possible to reproach them on the basis of ma'rifa bi-l-qalb bi-dûn 'amal (the realization of God in the heart alone without the fulfillment of the "works of faith") (ibid.: 18). Only people who do not know Sufism would spread lies and untruths. Gumi would thus lead his followers into kufr (ibid.: 20). Kabara confines himself, in the context of the discussion of tarbiya, to the simple statement that tarbiya has been practiced in West Africa since time immemorial by renowned scholars such as al-Maghîlî, Shaykh Sîdî al-Mukhtar al-Kuntî, and the leaders of the jihâd (Kabara 1972: 8). The discussion of tarbiya in the three treatises by Gumi, Kabara, and Kafanga suffers, however, as none of the three disputants is willing to exactly define his specific concept of tarbiya. This of course makes it easier to condemn the alleged positions of the respective opponent.

After the discussion of this topic Nasiru Kabara begins an extensive debate of the bida' (Kabara 1972: 11–16), in which he explains that sound chains of transmission (*isnâd*) exist for all those prayers and traditions which were criticized by Gumi, so that they cannot be characterized as bida' (ibid.: 14). Kafanga, however, concentrates on Gumi's criticism of the ṣalât al-fâtiḥ and the *Jawâhir al-ma'ânî.* The essence of Kafanga's discourse is condensed in the argument that the criticized prayers are not "special instructions" as Gumi has claimed but rather "additional" works of faith which might be practiced in addition to the obligatory prayers. They have to be seen as an appeal to praise the Prophet and to worship God and thus could not be regarded as bida' (Kafanga 1972: 32, 44). Apart from that the ṣalât al-fâtiḥ would not be a pure Tijânî affair but be accepted as a prayer by many Sufis, including the Qâdiriyya (ibid.: 39). This argument is supported by Kabara in a similar way. He also characterizes the ṣalât al-fâtiḥ as an additional, not obligatory, manifestation of faith (Kabara 1972: 22). At this point the different conceptions of religion become clear again. Whereas Gumi depicts the ṣalât al-fâtiḥ as a "special instruction" connected with a "special obligation," transmitted to "special persons," Kabara and Kafanga in their counterarguments describe it as a general appeal for additional prayers. The problem of the character of the ṣalât al-fâtiḥ as a "special instruction" or as a "general recommendation" points to a basic problem of authority within the Sufi brotherhoods. Speaking to the public they stress that a prayer like ṣalât al-fâtiḥ is only an additional, not an obligatory, work of faith. Of their own followers they demand, however, that they still accept these prayers as a "special instruction" of the Prophet revealed to the leader of the ṭarîqa and connected with a special obligation for his followers. Thus two levels of authority and of dispute are created. With the help of a strategy, such as to say, "What we do is done only in the praise of God and thus constitutes nothing special," any external attack can be refuted. On the other hand, however, the credibility of the Sufi shuyûkh suffers in respect to the support they enjoy among their followers on account of this argument as they still ask their followers to accept the special obligation and the special position connected with the ṣalât al-fâtiḥ.

A further fundamental difference between Gumi and his two opponents comes out in the definition of the "rightly guided successors" (al-khulafâ' ar-râshidûn) of the Prophet. Whereas Gumi recognizes only the first four caliphs of the Prophet as "rightly guided," Kafanga extends this term considerably. According to him all those companions, contemporaries, and followers of the Prophet who were living in the spirit of the Sunna of the Prophet have to be regarded as "rightly guided." If one accepts this extended definition then one also has to accept not only the first four caliphs and the ṣaḥâba of the Prophet as "rightly guided" but also persons like Usman dan Fodio, Muhammad Bello, and Aḥmad at-Tijânî and all those who have followed his teachings as they had observed the Sunna of the Prophet and lived and acted in his spirit (Kafanga 1972: 47). At this point the contrast to the ideas of the Salafiyya becomes very clear. Kafanga explicitly emphasizes the importance of the historical tradition of Islam in Northern Nigeria.

Kafanga as well as Kabara then concentrate on the linguistic problems in the context of Gumi's criticism of the term *asqam* in the prayer jawharat al-kamâl. Both scholars point out that Gumi's interpretation of this term cannot be derived by his method. Gumi has not taken into account that this term has a different meaning in the Maghribinian dialect of Arabic, the language of the author of Jawâhir al-ma'ânî, 'Alî Ḥarâzim, than in the Eastern Arabic dialects. Gumi has thus committed the mistake of failing to take into consideration the change of meaning of this term in the context of a regionally different usage. In addition he has not realized that the term asqam might be understood, apart from its literal meaning, in an allegorical way. In this way Gumi shows that he himself in reality does not know the Arabic language well enough to criticize its usage (Kabara 1972: 23). Kafanga enforces the criticism of Gumi's interpretation of the Jawharat al-kamâl. He says that an understanding of this prayer is closed to everybody who tries to analyze it only with the help of the Qur'ân and the ḥadîth and at the same time does not have the additional knowledge of the Sufis. The real understanding of the writings of Usman dan Fodio, Abdullahi dan Fodio, and Muhammad Bello would be forever inaccessible to them as the external meaning of a certain term is limited (Kafanga 1972: 58). The important point here is the insistence of Kabara and Kafanga on the allegorical interpretation of religious terms which gives them more room for an understanding of the texts.

Following this line of argument Kabara and Kafanga deal with Gumi's criticism of the "misleading books" and the "sectarian leaders." Nasiru Kabara especially criticizes Gumi for having included in his list of kutub dasîsa a number of books which were originally not mentioned in Muhammad Bello's list of "misleading books" which he quoted in his treatise *Infâq al-maisûr,* such as *Jawâhir al-ma'ânî* or *al-Fuyûḍât ar-rabbâniyya.* On the other hand, he does not include the writings of the Aḥmadiyya or the Wahhâbiyya which again demonstrates the one-sidedness in Gumi's criticism. Thus he is bound to fail in his understanding of the Sufi brotherhoods (Kabara 1972: 27).

The lines of argument followed by Nasiru Kabara and Sani Kafanga in relation to Gumi's attacks are essentially identical and can be summarize in a number of basic points:

1. Gumi and his supporters are representatives of the Wahhâbiyya; their sense of judgment in respect to ideas

of Sufism is distorted by their hate of the Sufi brotherhoods.

2. The ṭuruq represent the real "orthodoxy" in the sense of the Sunna of the Prophet. Attacks on them are thus at the same time attacks on the Prophet himself.
3. The positions attacked by Gumi are not given up, as controversial as they might appear in the eyes of the critics. Rather the ṭuruq, in their uncompromising attitude, symbolize the stability and continuity of the religion.
4. He who wants to understand the language of the Sufis has to accept their allegorical interpretation of the texts. He who fails to understand this entirely misses the point with his criticism.

Both sides set out from totally different assumptions as far as the role of the Prophet or the role of the Sufi saints is concerned. Whereas Nasiru Kabara and Sani Kafanga regard Sufism as an obligatory practice of the religion and as an essential part of the Sunna of the Prophet, such as the schools of law, Gumi, on the other hand, sees the ṭuruq as bida' which have to be destroyed. Kabara as well as Kafanga defend their own positions. They do not consider Gumi's argument in order to convince him, but they want to make him ridiculous in the eyes of their own followers. The positions criticized by Gumi are not questioned in isolation as that could lead to a breakdown of their own conceptions of the religion. The most important aim of Kabara and Kafanga is to strengthen the convictions of their own followers. The debate between Kabara and Kafanga on one side and Gumi on the other is thus not only a sideshow in a more encompassing political, economic, or historic conflict between the Sufi brotherhoods and the "fundamentalists" around Gumi. The dogmatic dispute rather shows the deep-seated contrasts in the understanding of the religion of the two parties in the conflict. The Sufis essentially want to defend their "community of grace" (Hiskett 1980: 99). After the publication of the writings of Gumi, Kabara, and Kafanga in 1972 the dogmatic framework of the future struggle was staked out. The escalation of the conflict began only when the movement of the 'Yan Izala, inspired and led by Abubakar Gumi, began its fight against the Sufi brotherhoods at the grassroots level in 1978 and in so doing did not merely criticize the networks of the ṭuruq on a dogmatic level but was to turn to more palpable means of dispute.

5

The 'Yan Izala Movement

In 1978, with the foundation of the Jamâ'at Izâlat al-Bid'a wa Iqâmat as-Sunna (Association for the Removal of the Innovation and for the Establishment of the Sunna), better known under their Hausa acronym 'Yan Izala, a new phase in the development of Islam in Northern Nigeria began. This recent development is characterized not only by the escalation of the conflict between the Sufi brotherhoods and their critics but also by a greater participation of the Muslims, especially the Muslim women in the political process, and by the intensification of the efforts to expand Islamic education. In the first years after their establishment, the 'Yan Izala put the ṭuruq under heavy pressure. Numerous members of the Sufi brotherhoods, especially the Tijâniyya, discontinued their affiliations or abstained from further activities within their respective ṭarîqa. Only in the early 1980s did the Sufi brotherhoods begin to overcome their shock and initiate a counter-offensive. The struggle with the 'Yan Izala forced the ṭuruq to accept a number of compromises and changes, not only on the level of dogmatic argumentation, but also as far as their organization was concerned. The most significant effect produced by the 'Yan Izala's attack was that the Tijâniyya and the Qâdiriyya shelved their old disputes so as to form a united opposition against the "fundamentalists." On the other side, this conflict has led to great changes in the sphere of social life. In respect to women's education, the activities of the 'Yan Izala had pioneering effects. In addition, the engagement within the 'Yan Izala was for many young people an expression of their protest against established structures of authority. Finally, the 'Yan Izala movement has overcome the prevalent type and structure of informal religious networks and organized itself as an organization with a constitution of its own.

Whereas the 'Yan Izala have officially defined as their aim the revival of the Sunna, the abolishing of all bida', and the achievement of Muslim unity, their factual appearance and propaganda had a decisively polarizing character on the Muslim community in Northern Nigeria. Thus, the question to be raised is whether the 'Yan Izala will be able to maintain their protracted struggle against the Sufi brotherhoods, particularily in view of the renewed emphasis on Muslim unity since the late 1980s.

5.1. The Structure and Development of the 'Yan Izala

The establishment and development of the 'Yan Izala movement is closely connected with the political and religious strategies of Abubakar Gumi. On failing to enlist the support of the JNI for his political program following the assassination of Ahmadu Bello in 1966, it became evident to Gumi that the JNI was no longer an adequate platform for his own efforts of tajdîd: Since the mid-1970s the JNI had been dominated by the Sufi shuyûkh and the traditional political establishment (Umar 1988: 191). Furthermore he was forced to accept that the financial support of his Saudi friends and supporters alone was not enough to enable him to maintain the struggle against the ṭuruq for a long period of time. Aside from this, Gumi's career in the national jurisdiction had been blocked despite initial support from Bello and later General Murtala Muhammad. This was on account of the resistance to the introduction of a federal Sharî'a Court of Appeal with Gumi as Grand Mufti of Nigeria after 1976. Like the ṭuruq in the 1940s and 1950s Gumi was thus forced to change his strategy by obtaining support not only by means of personal patronage but also by attempting to gain access to a broader public. In view of these various factors, after 1976, Gumi began to lay the foundation for a mass movement of his own. By this achievement Gumi would then be in a position to shift the struggle against the ṭuruq from a mere scholarly dispute between the malamai to a struggle at grassroots level. In fact, Gumi himself told me that he founded the 'Yan Izala in response to the efforts of the Fityân al-Islâm to bring the JNI under its control (Interview Gumi, 3 Oct. 1987). Until Gumi's death in late 1992 the 'Yan Izala remained under his dominating influence. All efforts to develop alternative orientations within the movement have failed. Thus, the 'Yan Izala were exclusively dependent on Gumi both dogmatically and politically. His death threw them into a serious crisis of orientation.

Abubakar Gumi had begun his struggle against the ṭuruq on the dogmatic level as early as 1972 with his treatise *al-'Aqîda aṣ-ṣaḥîḥa.* This was complemented in 1978 by the Hausa version *Musulunci da abinda ke rushe shi.* On the organizational level Gumi preferentially used former students to disseminate his ideas. These had attended either the School of Arabic Studies in Kano or the schools of the JNI in Kaduna in the 1960s and 1970s and had been educated there by Gumi personally. After the completion of their education Gumi sent them to the different parts of the North to take jobs within the JNI, in the sphere of education, or in the legislative apparatus, where they were to preach "the pure Islam" (Quadri 1985: 96). Thus, well before the formal foundation of the 'Yan Izala in 1978 a number of activities took place which were directed against the Sufi brotherhoods. In 1976, for instance, "fundamentalist" elements expelled Malam Sani, the Chief Imam of the Sabo Sagamu Friday mosque in Sagamu (Ogun State), who was affiliated with the Tijânîya, from the mosque. They instituted a new chief imam who had no affiliation with a Sufi brotherhood. The followers of the Tijânîya under the leadership of Malam Sani thereupon shifted their activities to the old Friday mosque of Sabo Sagamu (Quadri 1981: 397). Gumi further escalated the conflict on 11 April 1977, when he declared during a sermon in the Sultan Bello Friday mosque in Kaduna that any person who recited the ṣalât al-fâtiḥ was to be regarded as a kâfir. It would be legal to kill or to get a divorce from such a person. A remarriage would be possible only after that respective party had given up all brotherhood affiliations and paid a second bride-price (Quadri 1985: 102). This declaration of war was the appeal to start a militant struggle against the Sufi brotherhoods.

The exclusion of the followers of the ṭuruq from the Muslim community became one of the major strategies of the 'Yan Izala when they founded their organization ten months later. In an immediate reaction to Gumi's sermon in Kaduna, seventy malamai of the Qâdirîya and the Tijânîya published a pamphlet called "Hakika nasiha ita ce addini" (Correct Advice Concerning the Religion) in which they listed their criticisms. Among other things they accused Gumi of practicing tafsîr in a self-styled fashion, basing his interpretation on his own views instead of the Sunna, giving zakât to the wrong persons, destroying the peaceful coexistence between Mulisms and non-Muslims, instigating children against their parents, supporting the disobedience of women, ridiculing the emirs, falsifying ḥadîths, and monopolizing the mass media with evil intentions (Umar 1988: 192). The religious scholars challenged Gumi to a public dicussion in response to these criticisms and published a further list of forty-two topics for discussion. These included the old qabḍ-sadl dispute, the controversy concerning the spreading of the izâr, as well as the practice of tarbiya (ibid.: 197). Gumi refused to take part in the debate, justifying his absence on grounds of security, and instead sent two of his closest followers, Isma'ila Idris and Ahmad Muhammad Sanusi Gumbi. Nevertheless the debate failed to materialize. The heated atmosphere threatened to turn violent, and under such circumstances Gumi's delegates decided against taking part (ibid.: 198). These conflicts in Kaduna and the formation of organized resistance against him by the ṭuruq confirmed Gumi and his supporters in their belief that the establishment of an organization of their own was a prerequisite for any effective opposition to the Sufi brotherhoods.

A student and protégé of Abubakar Gumi, Malam Isma'ila Idris became the organizer of the 'Yan Izala movement and its nominal leader (for his biography see Umar 1983). He was born in 1937 in Goskorom near Katagum in Zungur Local Government (Bauchi province). He began his education with the traditional Qur'ân school under the tutelage of his father who was a religious scholar. In 1952 he moved to Bauchi where he studied under Malam Yakubu Mai Dajin, Malam Ahmad Kankasuwa, and later the Chief Imam of Bauchi, Malam Makhmud Bello. In Bauchi he learned Hausa, the language of communication of the North. Besides Fulfulde, his mother tongue, and Hausa, he possesses a partial knowledge of Arabic and English (Interview Idris, 7 Oct. 1987). He also affiliated himself with the Qâdirîya. However, as an indication that he was already searching for new inspiration, he left this Sufi brotherhood after two years. After the completion of his education under Imam Makhmud Bello in 1959, he acquired work as teacher of Islamic Religious Knowledge at the Tulu Provincial School. In 1963 he gave up his occupation as teacher and went to Kano where he continued his education at the School of Arabic Studies. At the SAS, Idris for the first time came into contact with teachers who held explicitly anti-ṭarîqa ideas. Among them were the Grand Kadi of the Northern Region, Abubakar Gumi, and Shaykh Hassan Khalil. In 1968 he completed his education at the SAS with the Higher Malam Certificate and in 1969 returned to Bauchi where he was again employed as a teacher in Tulu. Clearly dissatisfied with both his profession and the region in which he was living, Idris left, within a year of his appointment, for Kaduna where he was to join the JNI. He was appointed teacher of Arabic by the Kaduna Local Government at the Sultan Bello Islamiyya Primary School. The school had been founded originally by Bello and Gumi and had been part of the JNI network of schools until the nationalization of the educational system. As a teacher at this school he was in constant contact with Gumi who lived about two kilometers away.

Already during this period Isma'ila Idris had been taking part in the disputes between Gumi and his opponents. He was soon dismissed from the Sultan Bello School on account of his "inflammatory preaching" and transferred to the Kakuri prison in Kaduna, a clear punishment of his propagandistic activities. In 1974 Isma'ila Idris finally gave up his membership in the JNI and started a short but turbulent career as an army imam in the Nigerian military. The reason for this new shift in his career is not clear, and Isma'ila Idris himself has made very contradictory statements about this period of his life (Umar 1983; Interview Idris, 7 Oct. 1987). He was posted originally to Ibadan in the South but was transferred only three months later to Kontagora (Niger state) in the North. In Ibadan he had incited the disfavor of his superiors by protesting publicly against the obligatory deduction of the zakât from the pay of the Muslim soldiers by the divisional imam. Recurrent manifestations of protest and rebellion as shown in Ibadan seem to have been a constant feature in his life and career. In Kontagora a conflict was also soon to break out, this time with the civilian imam of the town who was a member of a Sufi brotherhood. As a consequence of this new quarrel, Idris was dismissed from his office as army imam and was to be further demoted from the rank of staff sergeant to that of Warrant Officer I. This time Gumi intervened, and on the basis of his mediation a discussion was arranged between Isma'ila Idris and some malamai from Kontagora in an effort to clarify a number of problems and misunderstandings. Immediately after this talk the Imam of Kontagora as well as the Emir of Kontagora relinguished their ṭarîqa affiliations (Umar 1983: 51).

This about-face of renowned religious and political personalities signified a tremendous success for Isma'ila Idris. It is, however, possible that the "conversion" of the Imam and the Emir of Kontagora was instigated not only by the arguments of Idris but also by the activities of the Islamic Education Trust (IET), an Islamic educational organization which had been founded in 1969 in Sokoto by the present-day Grand Kadi of Niger state, Dr. Ahmad Lemu. As the IET had its headquarters in Minna (Niger state) and had already been active in the region for some years, a possible connection between Idris's activities and the IET cannot be overlooked. After the Kontagora affair Isma'ila Idris was again transferred to Jos, the capital city of the ethnically and religiously very heterogenous Plateau state. After a short time in Jos he was also successful in convincing the imam of the army division, Major Alhassan, to discontinue his brotherhood affiliations. These propaganda activities led to protests from the side of the Sufi brotherhoods, especially the Tijâniyya which predominated in Jos as well as in Kontagora. On account of these protests yet another order was issued for Idris to be transferred, this time to faraway Potiskum in Bornu state. However, this transfer was not executed, as the lobby which became active in his support in Jos and Kaduna was influential enough to overcome the protests of the ṭuruq in Jos. Thus he could stay in Jos, continue his propaganda activities, and gather a small but growing group of supporters and preachers around him.

The public appearances of Isma'ila Idris in the Dogon Dutse barracks in Jos were so successful that he was soon invited to hold lectures in the city of Jos itself. His sermons against the ṭuruq were recorded on cassettes and disseminated in this way. During the course of his lectures in Jos disputes with other malamai broke out again and again. In these disputes Isma'ila Idris would elaborate his ideas and could thus sharpen his rhetorical capabilities. Over time he succeeded in building up a growing core group of followers in Jos. These followers were recruited predominantly from the Tijâniyya, which can be explained simply by the fact that the Tijâniyya was numerically much stronger than the Qâdiriyya in the Plateau area. This group of followers supported the efforts of Idris to establish a regular organization for the campaign against the Sufi brotherhoods. Thus on 8 February 1978, the Jamâ'at Izâlat al-Bid'a was finally founded in Jos. Abubakar Gumi sent his best wishes on the occasion of the foundation ceremony of the new organization and proposed to complement the name of the organzation by adding "wa Iqâmat as-Sunna," which was consequently accepted by the delegates (Umar 1988: 199). This gesture again demonstrates how important Gumi's influence was. At the same time Idris published a polemical treatise which appeared in 1978 under the title *A gane bambanci gaskiya da karya* (Toward an Understanding of the Difference between Truth and

Lie). In this treatise he presented the basic outline of his arguments against the Sufi brotherhoods and attacked the ṭuruq especially on the issue of *shirk* (polytheism): "all that the ṭariqah brotherhoods teach is associating somebody else with Allah in worship" (quoted in Umar 1983: 47).

As a response to the establishment of the 'Yan Izala, Isma'ila Idris was dismissed from the Nigerian army on 7 April 1978. His supporters in Jos quickly procured a house for him at 96/6 Dodo Street near the 'Id praying ground in Jos where he continued to live. On 25 May 1978, the Jamâ'at Izâlat al-Bid'a wa Iqâmat as-Sunna was finally established officially in their first mass rally in the Jos Township Stadium. In the course of his activities for the 'Yan Izala Idris had already been imprisoned and interrogated by the Nigeran State Security Service in 1975. After the establishment of the 'Yan Izala the Nigerian security forces remained vigilant. He was imprisoned again in April 1978 after his dismissal from the Nigerian army and was liberated only after Gumi's intervention. A third arrest by the same security officer followed in February 1979 in Kano and lasted thirty-nine days. Again, intervention by Gumi brought about his release (Umar 1983: 55). The effective protection of Idris by Gumi suggests much about the relationship between them. Without Gumi's support Isma'ila Idris's campaign would have been crushed quickly by the Nigerian security forces.

After the formal establishment of the 'Yan Izala the organization experienced an initial boomlike growth. This widespread public interest at that point in time can be explained by the ban on the political parties which was still in force in 1978. Many politically interested Muslims sought for alternative ways to express their political energies and thus engaged themselves in religious organizations. Thus the 'Yan Izala movement in 1978 rapidly spread throughout Northern Nigeria. The expansion was based predominantly on the organizational structure built up by Abubakar Gumi and was usually carried out in the course of preaching campaigns. During these campaigns new local groups were founded. Their leaders usually were former students and followers of Gumi. In some regions like Kaduna, Niger, Gongola, and Plateau the 'Yan Izala movement could also rely on the existing JNI networks. By way of protest against this development the leaders of the Tijâniyya in Jos, Shaykh Nakande, and in Yola, Shaykh Modibo Jailani, left the respective regional organizations of the JNI (Quadri 1985: 102). However, the expansion of the 'Yan Izala was also to meet resistance from the Sufi brotherhoods. Thus in 1978 an effort by some preachers of the 'Yan Izala to establish a foothold in Ilorin (Kwara state) failed. The ṭuruq of the town mobilized the Muslim opposition to counteract their activities, and the Emir of Ilorin, al-Ḥâjj Sule Gamberi, a member of the Qâdiriyya and local Patron of the JNI, expelled the 'Yan Izala from Ilorin (Quadri 1981: 396). Clashes between the 'Yan Izala and the supporters of the Sufi brotherhoods occurred, however, not only in Ilorin. Between 1978 and 1980 an escalation of violent conflicts took place throughout Northern Nigeria. Most of these conflicts occurred during the preaching campaigns of the 'Yan Izala in the rural areas of the North and were often connected with the group's constant efforts to disturb or interrupt the religious activities of the ṭuruq and gain control over the local Friday mosques. As the Tijâniyya was represented in most regions of the North, especially in the rural areas, in much greater numbers than the Qâdiriyya, the conflicts between the 'Yan Izala and the followers of the ṭuruq were usually clashes between the 'Yan Izala and the Tijâniyya. Quadri describes the method of procedure of the 'Yan Izala in these first years of their expansion until late 1980 in the following way: "In places where they are not welcome such as Zaria City, Funtua, some parts of Kaduna and Jos, they usually go about to preach armed with knives. In these places they attempt to prevent the Tijanis from holding their waẓîfah or remove the izar from their midst while the waẓîfah is in progress" (ibid.: 400–401).

Many violent clashes between the 'Yan Izala and the Sufi brotherhoods were registered until late 1980. These confrontations were to deeply influence the political and religious climate in Northern Nigeria. The chain of violent clashes started in the spring of 1978 immediately after the foundation of the 'Yan Izala. The chronology of the conflicts shows a clear connection between the political developments of the time. In 1978, when the political parties were still banned or only in the process of formation, a great number of clashes occurred. It has to be assumed that many were essentially political confrontations carried out in the framework of the 'Yan Izala–ṭarîqa conflict. In 1979 when the interest was directed increasingly toward political developments due to the elections and the return to civilian rule, many Muslims who had become active in the 'Yan Izala movement once again turned to politics, and the number of violent "religious" clashes diminished considerably. After the elections the scenario changed again: The 'Yan Izala took up their struggle with renewed energies and with a less politically, more religiously oriented following. Politics became less important, and the number of clashes rose anew (see the chronological chart of the clashes between the 'Yan Izala and the Sufi brotherhoods in the appendix). This phenomenon repeated itself after the coup of General Buhari on 31 December 1983; because of the ban on the political parties the religious organizations experienced a considerable boost in their numbers and activities. Conflicts in the religious sphere became more important than political discussions until General Babangida, Buhari's successor as head of state in late 1986, once more began the process of a return to civilian rule.

As mentioned above, the strategy of the 'Yan Izala was to bring as many mosques as possible under their control. The mosque, especially the Friday mosque, in Northern Nigeria was not only a place for prayer and teaching but also one for the dissemination of political and religious propaganda. The imam of the Friday mosque acted at the same time as local leader of the faithful. The struggle for the imamate of a mosque was thus not only a question of religious dimensions but also a political problem. The political importance of a movement could be deduced from the number of mosques it controls. The struggle for the control of the mosques remained an essential feature for the spread of the 'Yan Izala. As early as 1976 "fundamentalist" elements had taken over the control of the Sabo Sagamu Friday mosque (Quadri 1981: 397). In Kaduna the most important Friday mosques—Sultan Bello, Tudun Wada, Barnawi, Maiduguri Road, Sarkin Rimi—were under control of Gumi's followers by 1978 or rapidly came under the influence of the 'Yan Izala after 1978. In Jos the 'Yan Izala succeeded very quickly after 1978 in gaining control over most of the important Friday mosques (Interview Aliyu, 7 Oct. 1987). In Idah (Benue state) the chief imam of the local Friday mosque, Malam Muhammad Lawan Sidi, relinguished his affiliation with the Tijâniyya in order to keep his office (Quadri 1981: 398). Similar events occurred in Gombe (Bauchi state) where the imam of the central mosque, a Qâdiri, gave up his office because he was afraid of the violent methods of the 'Yan Izala (Ahmed 1986: 307). In Funtua (Kaduna state), however, the Imam al-'Id, Malam Muhammad Mustafa Jibril, who had relinguished his affiliation with the Tijâniyya and gone over to the 'Yan Izala, was dismissed from his office by the local representative of the Emir of Zaria, the Sarkin Maska. Thus, the takeover of this important and prestigious post by the 'Yan Izala was prevented (Quadri 1981: 399). In some cities like Kano, Zaria (old city), or Bauchi, where the 'Yan Izala did not succeed in taking over the control of the Friday mosques, they constructed their own. These new mosques were usually financed by wealthy traders and entrepreneurs or by external (Saudi) donors. Thus in Zaria one of the wealthiest supporters of the 'Yan Izala, al-Ḥâjj Haruna Danja, financed the construction of a new Friday mosque for the 'Yan Izala just opposite the Congo Campus (Institute of Administration) of the ABU Zaria (ibid.). In Kano the Bayero University Friday mosque under Imam 'Abbas as well as the new Friday mosque in Sulayman Crescent (Nasarawa) under Imam Malam Aminu d-Din Abubakar were regarded as centers of the 'Yan Izala or related groups (Interview Dan Asabe, 6 Sept. 1987).

The aggression of the 'Yan Izala in its early years especially affected the Tijâniyya which was already internally divided into many competing networks. Many Tijânis in Kaduna and Plateau ceased to attend the festivities of the Maulid an-nabî for fear of

'Yan Izala attacks. These festivities were criticized by the 'Yan Izala as a bid'a (Quadri 1985: 100). At the same time the number of participants in the waẓîfa of the Tijâniyya was also greatly reduced in these areas. Other groups of the Tijâniyya ceased spreading the izâr during the waẓîfa to avoid provoking an attack by the 'Yan Izala. Many Tijâniyya mosques were abandoned, and numerous Tijânis denied affiliation with the Tijâniyya at all and have consequently gone over to the 'Yan Izala (Quadri 1981: 401; Interview Dan Asabe, 6 Sept. 1987). In particular the Tijâniyya in the Plateau area was hit by the activities of the 'Yan Izala. The situation was similar in the religiously and ethnically mixed areas of Kaduna, Southern Zaria, Gongola, Niger, and Benue in the early 1980s. The confrontation between the 'Yan Izala and the ṭuruq even led to the situation that recent converts to Islam in the Plateau area after 1978 gave up their faith and reverted to their former religion, while, according to Shaykh Nakande, "they see Muslims as troublesome, dangerous and enemies from themselves" (Quadri 1981: 402). As Shaykh Nakande was the leader of the Tijâniyya in Plateau until his death in 1985 this information may be interpreted as a sort of counterpropaganda by the Tijâniyya with the intention of documenting the nefarious influence of the 'Yan Izala on the development of Islam in Northern Nigeria. The 'Yan Izala, for their part, argue that it is better to have a small group of convinced and faithful Muslims than to refer to a great number of ill-educated believers who practice only bida'. Isma'ila Idris compared the situation of the 'Yan Izala with the position of the Prophet when, with a small group of about three hundred Muslims, he defeated a numerically much stronger army of about one thousand Mekkans in the battle of Badr (Interview Idris, 7 Oct. 1987).

The expansive push and dynamic of the 'Yan Izala experienced a heavy blow when the so-called Maitatsine riots broke out in Kano in late 1980. The Maitatsine movement was formed in the 1970s in Kano under the leadership of the tafsîr-malam Muhammad Marwa whose Hausa nickname was Mai Tatsine (the master of condemnation). Marwa, who had originally immigrated from the Cameroons, had settled in Kano in the 1960s. In his sermons he rejected the usage of Western consumer goods such as watches and bicycles and condemned in his tafsîr certain customs and traditions of the indigenous Hausa population like the utilization of *kuka* (baobab leaves) for sauces as there is a Qur'ânic verse that says "wa tara*kuka* qâ'iman" (. . . leaving you [i.e., Muhammad] standing all alone). Eating kuka leaves according to Marwa thus meant committing a similar sin as those companions of the Prophet had committed when they had left him "all alone" in a moment of distress (Hiskett 1987: 219). In addition, he introduced a number of innovations to the practice of the religion such as the reduction of the number of the obligatory prayers from five to three, and he rejected all sources of the religion except the Qur'ân. Thus he was regarded by the local religious scholars not only as an outsider but also as a heretic. During the late 1970s, however, Marwa won an increasing number of followers among the 'Yan Cirani (the eaters of the dry season), migrants who streamed into Kano during the dry season from distant places like Cameroon, Chad, Niger, or the Middle Belt in the hope of finding work in the economic center of the North. Because of the increasing economic difficulties in the late 1970s—growing prices and unemployment—the number of malcontents among the 'Yan Cirani grew constantly. As they were also despised as *gwari* (barbarians) by the local Hausa population on account of their rudimentary knowledge of the Hausa language and because of their superficial degree of Islamization, many of them joined Marwa's movement—himself originally a Dan Cirani—who managed to channel their resentments for his religious movement (Hiskett 1987: 213–14). The situation deteriorated in October 1980 when his only son was killed in Sabon Gari and the first clashes with the security forces occurred. Finally the governor of Kano state, Abubakar Rimi, set a deadline for Marwa and ordered him to leave his lodgings (Unguwar Ayagi) at the periphery of the old city of Kano. Marwa answered this ultimatum by mobilizing his followers throughout Northern Nigeria and on Friday, 19 December 1980, attempted to occupy the central mosque in Kano. The ensuing conflict with the police forces continued for some days until the Nigerian army intervened and crushed the resistence of the 'Yan Tatsine with tanks and heavy firepower. Apart from Marwa himself, about six thousand people were killed in the battle between 18 and 29 December, while the material damage amounted to several million naira. The size of the Maitatsine riot and the brutality of its suppression not only inspired a number of research studies about this religious movement (Nicolas 1981; Hickey 1984; Lubeck 1985; Jami'u 1986; Na Ayuba 1986; Hiskett 1987; Isichei 1987), but also led to the institution of the Aniagolu commission of inquiry. In the heated aftermath of the riots the task of the commission was to inquire into the reasons for the riot and to penalize those responsible.

The hearings of the Aniagolu commission were used by the leaders of the ṭuruq as a platform to accuse the 'Yan Izala that they were themselves either identical with the 'Yan Tatsine or had cooperated with them. The 'Yan Izala consequently sought to divert this accusation. In order to dissociate themselves from the Maitatsine movement they were forced to adopt a more peaceful strategy and for the time being resist violent activities. Thus after 1981 they concentrated increasingly on the promotion and expansion of Islamic education. This change of strategy as well as the blatant support of Abubakar Gumi for the corrupt Shagari administration caused many militant followers of the 'Yan Izala to cease association with the movement and turn to the MSS which they considered more radical and more consequent in political terms. Thus after 1981 the 'Yan Izala lost its expansive dynamic and, faced with the recurrence of Maitatsine rebellions (1982 Maiduguri and Kaduna, 1984 Yola, 1985 Gombe, 1993 Funtua; see Loimeier 1993: 149–51), were forced to disassociate themselves at least formally from the use of violence as a means of confrontation. In order not to offer the Sufi brotherhoods an opening for counterarguments, this approach seemed the most appropriate.

After the fall of Shehu Shagari and the takeover of power by General Buhari on 31 December 1983, the 'Yan Izala experienced a wave of repression as a result of the close connection between

Abubakar Gumi and the Shagari administration. Many members of the 'Yan Izala were imprisoned and tortured by the secret service. Its agents could now operate without restrictions against the 'Yan Izala, which had lost Gumi's protection. Numerous 'Yan Izala donors like al-Ḥâjj Haruna Danja were imprisoned under charges of corruption and thereby reduced the 'Yan Izala's effective support (Interview Umar, 5 Apr. 1988). Only after the internal coup of General Babangida against General Buhari on 27 August 1985 did the political context for the activities of the 'Yan Izala begin to improve. Gumi was reinstated in his old position as religious advisor to the Nigerian government, the imprisoned members and supporters of the 'Yan Izala were released, and the movement again took up its offensive against the ṭuruq. In the face of the ban on political activities they could count on increased public attention as in 1978. Their second offensive broke down, however, after a short time when in March 1987 the conflict between Muslims and Christians became the major topic after the Kafancan riots. In the aftermath of Kafancan the 'Yan Izala were again accused by the ṭuruq of being troublemakers and responsible for the divisions within the Muslim community. After Kafancan the 'Yan Izala were not able to overcome this dilemma and win back the initiative.

Although Isma'ila Idris can be regarded as the most important organizer of the 'Yan Izala, the real leadership in a spiritual and political sense was in the hands of Abubakar Gumi. He protected Idris in a number of cases when he was arrested by the security forces, he proposed the idea of setting up an organization such as the 'Yan Izala, and he influenced its program and constitution in a decisive way. Furthermore Gumi received and distributed the financial contributions from Saudi Arabia and the Râbiṭa within the 'Yan Izala, and he dominated the religious debates and determined the general strategy (Interviews Baba, 9 Sept. 1987; Sulaiman, 9 Sept. 1987). Gumi also decided the filling of all important posts within the organization. According to 'Yan Izala members the most important criteria for being nominated to important positions is the religious knowledge of the respective candidate

(Interview Baba, 9 Sept. 1987). Gumi's dominating influence was based on the fact that he always had direct and personal relations with all heads of state—except General Buhari—and with other members of the respective governments and administrations in Nigeria, and he was thus in a position to intervene in certain problematic situations in support of his protégés. Second, Gumi was the only religious scholar in Nigeria who was regarded by the Saudi and Kuwaiti donors both inside and outside the Râbiṭa as a confidant as far as the investment of monies in Nigeria was concerned. Gumi could either distribute these financial influxes directly to the 'Yan Izala or to those groups within the JNI who followed his authority (Interview Sulaiman, 9 Sept. 1987). Finally, Gumi was also the most important confidant for many Nigerian donors in the investment of monies fî sabîl Allâh. The combination of these factors strengthened Gumi's weight within the 'Yan Izala to such an extent that it was not necessary for him to occupy a formal leading position personally. No policy was possible without or even against his will within the 'Yan Izala. Thus it was not Gumi who went to conferences or meetings of the 'Yan Izala at the headquarters of the organization in Jos, but, as I could observe myself, the leading personalities within the 'Yan Izala rather came to his house in Kaduna, asked for an audience, and received guidance, advice, and instructions from him (Interview Doi, 7 Sept. 1987). Malamai who were not prepared to accept the position and power of Gumi within the 'Yan Izala and who had themselves entertained ambitions to lead the organization, like Malam Aminu d-Din Abubakar, and Malam Sidi Attahiru Sokoto, were forced to leave the organization. As dissidents with similar aims and strategies to those of the 'Yan Izala they have founded organizations of their own.

That the 'Yan Izala were not immune to the dynamics and structures of political, religious, and social developments was shown by the internal disputes within the 'Yan Izala in the 1980s and 1990s. They have come under serious stress, when Isma'ila Idris was accused by other members of his organization in 1991 of embezzling large sums from the 'Yan Izala funds. He was consequently removed from the ranks of the organization. Isma'ila Idris, however, refused to accept this move. He renewed his claim to leadership of the 'Yan Izala, thus splitting it temporarily into two groups (Interview Kane, 1 Apr. 1993). A further blow for the development of the 'Yan Izala was Abubakar Gumi's death on 11 September 1992. By Gumi's demise the Islamic reform movement in Northern Nigeria was deprived of its most charismatic leader. The process of fragmentation that has affected the Sufi brotherhoods so far, and the Tijâniyya in particular, may thus spread to the 'Yan Izala as well. Existing tensions within the 'Yan Izala could, after Gumi's death, become transformed into open conflicts of power and authority between different regional or political networks within the 'Yan Izala. Political feuds and personal rivalries may thus again trigger religious debates even within the Islamic reform movement.

Since 1978 the formal headquarters of the 'Yan Izala have been in the home of Isma'ila Idris in Jos. Only on 5 March 1988 was a campaign by the 'Yan Izala initiated to collect money for the construction of a regular headquarters building in Jos. The formal leadership of the 'Yan Izala consisted of a hierarchy of cadres as was laid down in the constitution of the organization, namely, the president (Isma'ila Idris), two vice presidents, a secretary general (Malam Sule Adamu) and his representatives, as well as the members of the National Executive Council which was made up by the chairmen of the different working groups and committees of the 'Yan Izala. In 1983 the members of the executive council of the 'Yan Izala were Malam Sule Adamu, Malam Yakusa Abdullahi (his representative), Malam Muhammad Tanimu, Malam Yaya Agba Abubakar, Malam Ibrahim Duduwa, Malam Tsoho Mai Maigani, Malam Garba Muhammad, and Malam Adamu Husaini (Umar 1983: 61–63). The candidates for these posts were not elected but nominated by the secretary general and were required to have the consent of Abubakar Gumi. They represented a collective leadership group. Apart from the central administration in Jos a number of regional branches existed. In 1983 thirteen of the then nineteen Federal states had branches of the 'Yan Izala:

Plateau, Kaduna, Kano, Sokoto, Bornu, Gongola, Bauchi, Niger, Kwara, Oyo, Lagos, Rivers, and Benin (ibid.: 47). The regional branches were usually founded by the local friends and supporters of Gumi during a campaign. The regional branches were responsible for the application of the strategies of the 'Yan Izala on the local level, the administration of the organization's schools, the implementation of the Muslim women's education program, and the organization of regional preaching campaigns.

Like the JNI the 'Yan Izala have founded an "aid group" of their own, the 'Yan Agaji (People of Help). Their headquarters were established in Bukuru near Jos, and like the JNI aid group they had the task of providing first aid and acting as security personnel during mass rallies and Friday prayers (Umar 1983: 95). The most important forms of activity of the 'Yan Izala were, as already mentioned, special campaigns which were carried out when new local or regional branches of the 'Yan Izala were to be established. On such occasions the best and most popular preachers of the 'Yan Izala were called in to assist giving the new local branch the necessary public support. The sermons of Abubakar Gumi and other important 'Yan Izala campaigners were recorded on cassette and subsequently distributed by the 'Yan Izala. That the 'Yan Izala concentrated on the utilization of the modern mass media to spread their ideas and that they scarcely published books again demonstrate the modern outlook of the organization in comparison with the Sufi brotherhoods. Cassettes were bound to reach a greater number of people than books if one takes into account that illiteracy continued to be widespread in Northern Nigeria, especially in the countryside. The ṭuruq had no other choice than to follow the 'Yan Izala in their methods of disseminating information and propaganda. On the other hand, the massive utilization of the modern mass media in religious politics has resulted in religious leaders becoming increasingly diplomatic when issuing statements, as they had to take into account that their sometimes insulting and inflammatory utterances might be misinterpreted by their religious or political opponents. Some malamai like Abubakar Gumi, however, became masters of the instrumentalization of the modern mass media for their own political and religious aims. The propaganda activities of the 'Yan Izala were complemented by lectures, public seminars, interviews for newspapers or radio, articles for newspapers, the tafsîr meetings during Ramadhân, and the regular teaching and preaching lectures of the 'Yan Izala in their own mosques, as well as the sometimes violent "actions" directed against the Sufi brotherhoods. These actions included the occupation of mosques, disturbing the activities and meetings of the ṭuruq, distribution of leaflets, and carrying out demonstrations and other mass rallies to intimidate followers of the ṭuruq. The rapid expansion of the 'Yan Izala throughout Nigeria was celebrated at a national symposium of the organization between 14 and 16 November 1986 in Jos. The assistant secretary general of the 'Yan Izala, S. M. Muhammad, stated in his report on the activities of the past eight years:

> It has now become imperative to mention the achievements of the movement as of today. In the beginning, we had only one mosque for 'Id prayers which was located in Jos. And then in 1979 we got a Friday mosque. But today we have, without doubt, these places of religious worship nearly everywhere in this country. It is either that we have constructed new ones for ourselves or the imams in the old ones have seen the light. But our great achievement has been teaching in Modern Schools. We have reached the stage whereby in every corner of this country today we have schools for adult classes, primary evening schools, and also schools for married women. Our branches by 1977/78 were only four, today we have branches in 99% of the local government areas in the country—insofar as there are Muslim residents there. There is nowhere in this country where Izala has not preached. (quoted in Umar 1988: 203)

The leadership of the 'Yan Izala consisted not only of the administration cadres in Jos, nominated or confirmed by Gumi, but also of the leaders of the different regional branches of the organization. Most prominent among them were Malam Ibrahim Arab (Imam of the Tudun Wada Friday Mosque) and Shaykh Lawal Abubakar (Imam of the Sultan Bello Friday Mosque) in Kaduna, al-Ḥâjj Sidi Attahiru Sokoto (expelled in 1985) and al-Ḥâjj Abubakar Jibrin in Sokoto, Malam Muhammad Ba'are and Malam Hudu Akaji in Zaria, Malam Muhammad Abba Aji in Maiduguri, and al-Ḥâjj Ibrahim Bibi Faruq in Kano (Umar 1983: 48; Funtua 1980: 3–4). They did not derive their authority from elections but were instituted, nominated, or confirmed by Gumi. They had direct access to Gumi and were not subject to the directives from the central administration in Jos.

Apart from the central hierarchy of the administration and the leaders of the regional branches existed a third leadership group which was recruited among the Muslim intellectuals of the universities and high schools in the North. Sympathizers with the aims of the 'Yan Izala or direct supporters, they included Malam Dahiru Maigari, Malam Abdullahi Baba, Shaykh Ahmad Ibrahim, and Shaykh Abubakar Jibril. Whereas Malam Abdullahi Baba was one of the most important leaders of the 'Yan Izala in Zaria and worked at the Center of Islamic Legal Studies (CILS) of ABU Zaria, Shaykh Ahmad Ibrahim, Shaykh Abubakar Jibril, and Malam Dahiru Maigari were all employed by BUK Kano. An outstanding example for this group of intellectual leaders of the 'Yan Izala was Malam Dahiru Maigari, who had a high position within the Tijâniyya in Northern Nigeria before he went over to the 'Yan Izala. He originally stemmed from Bauchi and was a close friend of Shaykh Dahiru Bauchi. Within the Tijâniyya he had achieved the rank of shaykh murabbi and was thus authorized to supervise the secret process of tarbiya (Interview Maigari, 2 Mar. 1987). He met Ibrahim Niass in Kaolack personally and wrote an M.A. thesis at BUK Kano about the Tijâniyya and Niass in the late 1970s entitled *Shaykh ibrâhîm niass as-sunughâlî: ḥayâtuhu wa arâ'uhu wa ta'lîmuhu* (Shaykh Ibrahim Niass of Senegal: His Life, Ideas and Teachings). This work was supervised by Ahmad Ghorab at the Department of Islamic Studies at BUK and read after its completion by Gumi who sent it to the Islamic University of Medina where it was finally published in a revised version. Under Gumi's influence, Maigari left the Tijâniyya in 1980 and became a staunch supporter of the 'Yan Izala. In another work, titled *at-Tuḥfât as-sanîya bi-tawḍîḥ aṭ-ṭarîqa at-tijâniyya* (The Precious Gift Explaining the Tijâniyya), he attacked the Tijâniyya openly as a bid'a. On account of Maigari's inside knowledge of the Tijâniyya both works have become reference books for the 'Yan Izala as far as their arguments concerning the Tijâniyya are concerned (ibid.). The intellectuals of the 'Yan Izala were not subject to the directives of the central administration in Jos or of one of the regional branches but did have a direct and independent access to Gumi. They propagated his ideas in the intellectual circles of the high schools and thus directly or indirectly influenced the Muslim students.

Finally, the group of indigenous financiers has to be mentioned as the fourth pillar supporting the leadership of the 'Yan Izala. They operated within various spheres of trade, industry, and banking. The most prominent personalities to be mentioned were al-Ḥâjj Haruna Danja and al-Ḥâjj Ibrahim Kano. Al-Ḥâjj Haruna Danja had been the most important supporter of the 'Yan Izala until his death in 1985. He resided in Zaria and financed the construction of the Congo Campus Friday mosque in Zaria. He was the owner of substantial estates and numerous tenement blocks in Zaria, heavily involved in the fertilizer trade, and owner of a transport fleet. Politically he had been active in the NPN-NPC. Since 1979 he had a seat in the State House of Assembly in Kaduna. As early as 1976 he had been found guilty by the Shehu Muhammad Judicial Commission of having undertaken a number of speculative business transactions of considerable size in the fertilizer trade (Usman 1987: 91). After the Buhari coup of 1983 he was imprisoned on account of his business practices but released by General Babangida after the latter's takeover of power in 1985.

Al-Ḥâjj Ibrahim Kano from Kaduna became active for the 'Yan Izala especially in the sphere of education, and he sponsored the construction of a number of Islamiyya schools. Other traders and entrepreneurs to be mentioned here are al-Ḥâjj Ahmad Chanchangi and al-Ḥâjj M. A. S. Gumbi in Kaduna, the latter a close confidant and personal biographer of Gumi; al-Ḥâjj Shehu

Tabacco in Jos who gave Isma'ila Idris his house in Dodo Street (Umar 1983: 74); al-Ḥâjj Yusufu Abdullahi, a PZ retailer; al-Ḥâjj Ado Dandolo; al-Ḥâjj Bello Maitama, a former minister for industry and commerce; al-Ḥâjj Baba Dan Agundi Mai Tuta, an influential member of the Kano emir's council; and al-Ḥâjj Garba Dan Shagamu, these last named all from Kano (Interview Dan Asabe, 6 Sept. 1987). Finally, al-Ḥâjj Aminu Dantata from Kano has to be mentioned; he seems to have started to support the 'Yan Izala and, in a spectacular action, freely distributed Gumi's tafsîr to all Tijâni mosques in Kano (Interview Kane, 18 Jan. 1989). For many traders Gumi had a similar function as Nasiru Kabara or Ibrahim Niass had for the traders who were affiliated with either the Qâdiriyya or the Tijâniyya. He guaranteed their spiritual well-being by channeling their sadaqât and donations fî sabîl Allâh into projects of public interest to the 'Yan Izala.

The leadership of the 'Yan Izala thus essentially consisted of four coexisting pillars of authority: the administrative cadres of the organization based in Jos, the leaders of the regional branches, the intellectuals in the universities, and the supporters of the organization in trade, banking, and industry. These four pillars of authority were not connected with each other organizationally. They were each oriented directly toward Abubakar Gumi who presided as inspiration, advisor, leader, guide, mediator, and "National Patron" above the whole movement. The 'Yan Izala were, however, in a structural way different from the informal networks of the Sufi brotherhoods: In addition to the regional networks, the intellectual sympathizers, and the financial supporters, they have built up a formal organization with a regular constitution and statutes. Thus the Jamâ'at Izâlat al-Bid'a wa-Iqâmat as-Sunna was comparable with the JNI rather than with the ṭuruq.

The program of the 'Yan Izala as laid down in the statutes of 1978 (see appendixes) and as presented in the pamphlets of the organization is comparatively simple and reads like a shortened version of Gumi's *al-'Aqîda aṣ-ṣaḥîḥa.* The three fundamental points of the message of the 'Yan Izala are the following:

1. Every Muslim can become a member of the 'Yan Izala under the precondition that he or she gives up an existing affiliation with a Sufi brotherhood, that he or she accepts the five pillars of Islam and the principle that Muhammad is the "seal of the prophets," and that he or she finally rejects all bida' which are not in concordance with the Sunna of the Prophet (Funtua 1980: 5).
2. The 'Yan Izala do regard themselves not as a "sect"; they reject any form of racism, tribalism, or sectionalism (Funtua 1980: 5).
3. In addition to the religious foundations of the Qur'ân and the Sunna, the 'Yan Izala recognize the Nigerian Constitution of 1979 and place especial emphasis on article 25, section 2, chapter 10, which states

> The government of the federation of States shall not adopt any religion as a state religion. . . . Everbody shall be entitled to freedom of thought, conscience and religion, including the fredom to change his religion or beliefs and freedom whether alone or in a community and in public or in private to manifest and propagate his religion or belief in worship, teaching, practice and observance.

The major themes of the program of the 'Yan Izala can be summarized in the following points:

1. There are no saints in Islam; all Muslims are equally "holy."
2. The belief in a special role of the Prophet and of his familiy is un-Islamic; all Muslims are equal.
3. The practice of intercession (tawassul) is un-Islamic; prayer at the tombs of the dead is permited only for the dead themselves.
4. The pilgrimage to Mecca is more important than the *ziyâra* (visit) to the tombs of the saints.
5. Nobody except the Prophet himself is able to bring about miracles.
6. Nobody except God himself knows the Hidden. The claim of the Sufis to be able to see the Hidden is a trick to lead the faithful astray.

7. The Jinn do exist. They cannot be seen, however.
8. It is not possible to see God, neither in dreams, in visions, nor while awake.
9. The reciting of praise songs for the Prophet (*madḥ an-nabî*) is un-Islamic.
10. Sufism itself is un-Islamic as the veneration of the Sufi shuyûkh might lead to polytheism (shirk). Thus all Sufi brotherhoods have to be regarded as shirk. Sufism cannot draw its legitimization from the Qur'ân. The origin of the term tasawwuf is the term *ṣûf* (wool) and is not derived from the Qur'ân where the *ahl aṣ-ṣafâ'* (the people of purity) are mentioned. As the Sufi brotherhoods have to be regarded as un-Islamic, no follower of a ṭarîqa should exercise the profession of a butcher or occupy the office of the imam of a Friday mosque.
11. The imams of the Friday mosques should end the practice of appealing to the faithful to conduct further prayers after the conclusion of the obligatory prayers. This practice is a bid'a. Additional prayers should be the free decision of the individual Muslim.
12. The members of the ṭuruq should give up their un-Islamic practices in the Friday mosques.
13. The ṭuruq are the major source for disunity among Muslims.

Apart from the constant condemnation of the Sufi brotherhoods and of Sufism generally the stress on the Qur'ân and the Sunna of the Prophet as the supreme sources of authority have to be mentioned: "Izalatil Bid'a is a purely religious organization based on the Qur'ân and the authentic ḥadîth traditions" (Constitution 1c/d); "our aim is the spreading of the religion of Allah as it is laid down in the Qur'ân and in the ḥadîth traditions" (Constitution 2a). By going back to the Qur'ân and the Sunna of the Prophet the 'Yan Izala aim to reopen the door of ijtihâd which had been closed after the formation of the four legal schools of Islam. The sharî'a is to be adapted to the expediences of the present time by way of reopening the process of interpretation of the sources of the religion (Qur'ân and ḥadîth). Significantly, the sharî'a is mentioned only once in the constitution of the 'Yan Izala: "All future members, male or female, have to reject all innovations which are not in concordance with the sharî'a" (Constitution 3b). The Prophet is recognized as the mediator of the revelation, as the leader of the umma, and as a outstanding example for all Muslims by way of his Sunna. However, he does not receive a special role as an intercessor and the idea that the process of revelation continues after his death through visions and dreams is repeatedly rejected: "It is necessary for all future members of the Izala to acknowledge the role of the Prophet (p.b.u.h) as a leader and to accept that he was the last prophet and that he has transmitted the revelation such as God told him to do" (Constitution 2c/d/e, 3c). The special emphasis on the Qur'ân as the supreme source of the religion (Constitution 2d) was revised after 1980 in the context of the Maitatsine riots in Kano. The Maitatsine movement had publicly adopted the slogan "Qur'ân only" as the foundation of the religion. After the riots of December 1980 the ṭuruq claimed that the stress laid upon the importance of the Qur'ân by the 'Yan Izala constituted a clear sign of the identity of 'Yan Izala and 'Yan Tatsine. Although the 'Yan Izala have never rejected the Sunna of the Prophet, since 1981 they have laid particular emphasis on the importance of the Sunna as a guide for Muslims. In addition, the identity of the programmatic statements of the 'Yan Izala and those of Gumi was pointed out by the 'Yan Izala themselves. Thus Isma'ila Idris underlined in an interview with the author that there were no differences at all between himself and Gumi in their dogmatic orientation and in their ideas (Interview Idris, 7 Oct. 1987).

The acknowledgment of the 1979 Nigerian constitution signifies another important point in the program of the 'Yan Izala. Despite this probably being done for ulterior motives, the reference to article 25 of the constitution demonstrates the principal willingness by the leadership of the 'Yan Izala to coexist with non-Muslim groups in Nigeria. The major enemies of the 'Yan Izala are not the Christians but the "Muslim sects." They have to be fought until the unity of the Muslims is reestablished. This anti-ṭarîqa orientation of the 'Yan Izala became clear in the context of the intense confrontations in many cities of the North which were provoked by Christian students at the Advanced Teachers' College in Kafancan in March 1987. Whereas pogrom-like riots against the local Christian populations occurred in Kaduna and Zaria, the centers of the radical MSS groups in the North, Jos, the center of the 'Yan Izala, remained quiet and peaceful, although Jos was at least as heterogenous in religious terms as Kaduna or Zaria.

5.2. The Regional Development of the 'Yan Izala: Case Studies of Kaura-Namoda, Argungu, Sokoto, and Kano

The rapid spread of the 'Yan Izala throughout Northern Nigeria in the initial years of its foundation provoked violent clashes with the Sufi brotherhoods in a number of incidents. The establishment of regional branches of the 'Yan Izala was accompanied by campaigns usually carried out by the local protégés and followers of Abubakar Gumi. In addition to their anti-ṭuruq propaganda activities the 'Yan Izala concentrated their efforts on the establishment of new Islamiyya schools. Thus they pushed forward into a social vacuum in the rural regions of the North. In particular the campaign for an improved education for Muslim women brought the 'Yan Izala a great number of female followers. They also gained a following from the young who had experienced modern school education and were frustrated by the existing conditions of life and wished to escape the structures of village society. The organization of the 'Yan Izala offered the young a means by which they were able to translate these diffuse frustrations into clear political forms of protest against the religious establishment, the elder generation, and the dominating local authorities. They streamed into the new organization thus increasing the threat for the established networks of the Sufi brotherhoods.

With the growth of the regional branches their respective

weight within the organization increased. After some years, however, a number of religious scholars who had achieved high levels of merit within the 'Yan Izala, and who had developed ambitions for leadership of their own, were no longer willing to accept the undisputed single leadership of Abubakar Gumi. In particular after the years of stagnation between 1980 and 1985 these religious leaders began to demand a certain right of cotermination in respect to the strategy and development of the organization. Gumi, however, was not prepared to let his most important tool for the fight against the ṭuruq slip into someone else's hands. His critics and competitors within the 'Yan Izala were therefore forced to keep quiet or leave. Some of them, like Sidi Attahiru Sokoto, left the 'Yan Izala and established organizations of their own which subscribed to similar aims and strategies but did not submit to Gumi's authority. They were excluded from his financial support and consequently had to search for new donors. In particular, the Kano-based scholar Aminu d-Din Abubakar managed to cultivate new sources of finance in Libya, Kuwait, and the Emirates. Although the dissident groups managed to set up autonomous networks with some importance of their own in certain areas, none of them achieved the size of the 'Yan Izala. In the following case studies the establishment of the 'Yan Izala will be examined in four towns in the North. These are two great cities of supra-regional importance (Kano and Sokoto) and two small towns (Kaura-Namoda and Argungu), which are rather typical of the development of the 'Yan Izala in the rural areas. Unfortunately there are only a few studies of the regional development of the 'Yan Izala. I thus refer in this chapter mainly to the work of Mai Sa'ida (on Kaura-Namoda), Sanusi (on Argungu), and Khalid (on Sokoto) which was carried out between 1985 and 1987 at the University of Sokoto, as well as my own research in Kano and Sokoto and a number of interviews I held with colleagues in Kano and Sokoto. In the studies concerning the development of the 'Yan Izala in Kaura-Namoda and Argungu—where unfortunately I did not have the time to do research personally—the basic social conditions of the establishment of the 'Yan Izala will be treated with special emphasis. These studies may be regarded as an important key to understanding the success of the 'Yan Izala in the whole of Northern Nigeria.

Kaura-Namoda

The small town of Kaura-Namoda is situated at the northern terminal of a railway line which was originally planned to connect Sokoto with Zaria in order to integrate Nigeria's Northwest into the national railway grid. Today Kaura-Namoda is the center of a small but not insignificant rural development area. Historically the region of Kaura-Namoda was part of the ancient Hausa state of Zamfara before the area was integrated into the Sokoto empire in the course of the jihâd. The town of Kaura-Namoda itself was founded as late as 1809 by Muhammad Bello and was ruled during the Sokoto empire by the Sarkin Kiyawa. The Qâdiriya was established in Kaura-Namoda at the same time as the town itself. The Tijâniyya was introduced only in 1952 by Malam Buhari and Malam Sani in the course of the extension of the scholar-trader networks of the Tijâniyya-Ibrâhîmiyya in Sokoto province. Both malamai were followers of Ibrahim Niass. With the coming of the Tijâniyya the conflict with the established Qâdiriyya in Kaura-Namoda began. The major issue of the conflict was the question of smoking. The Tijânis rejected smoking as a matter of principle and condemned all smokers as "unbelievers." They refused to buy meat from butchers who were known to smoke. During the 1960's the Qâdiriyya in Kaura-Namoda came under the influence of Nasiru Kabara and dissociated itself from the former central authority in Sokoto. Originally Kabara had appointed Malam Male as his first local muqaddam. Together with Malam Dan Kwaido, Malam Sidi Aba, and Malam al-Ḥâjj Almu he built up the new network of the Qâdiriyya (Mai Sa'ida 1987: 36). Since the 1970s the Qâdiriyya in Kaura-Nmoda has been led by a son-in-law of Kabara, Malam Abubakar Bello Kaura-Namoda, who was originally an Inspector of Education in the Sokoto State Ministry of Education. He was responsible for Kaura-Namoda becoming one of the most important centers of the Qâdiriyya-Nâṣiriyya in Sokoto (Interview Ahmad, 23 Jan. 1987). The last great confrontation between the Qâdiriyya and the Tijâniyya occurred in 1977 when the Tijâniyya protested against the celebrations of the Maulid 'Abd al-Qâdir. These animosities were reconciled only after the establishment of the 'Yan Izala in Kaura-Namoda in 1979.

The 'Yan Izala movement was originally founded in Kaura-Namoda in 1979 under the pseudonym Iḥyâ' ad-Dîn al-Islâmî (The Establishment of Islamic Religion). Its first leaders were the Sarkin Pawa (master butcher) of Gusau, Malam Zakariyya, and Malam Hassan Muhammad. The role of the Sarkin Pawa Malam Zakariyya Gusau is a very interesting aspect of the establishment of the 'Yan Izala in Kaura-Namoda, and it signifies the important role of the butchers in the local and regional systems of communication in Northern Nigeria. Owing to their profession, butchers meet many people every day and thus belong, together with lorry drivers, taxi chauffeurs, and traders, to a section of the population which is usually well informed about developments going on beyond a purely local level. At the same time they may exert considerable influence on the forming of opinions. The influence of the 'Yan Izala among the butchers—and other "mobile" professions—had in this way a significantly large role to play in the growth of the movement (Lubeck 1986: 93).

The activities of the new group were originally restricted to preaching and propaganda for the 'Yan Izala. Only in 1980 did the group publicly begin to act as a local branch of the 'Yan Izala. On 16 November 1980 they held their first public rally, which degenerated into a confrontation with followers of the ṭuruq. In these skirmishes one person was killed. Immediately after this event the local branch of the 'Yan Izala was officially founded in the town. Since then the office of the president (*shugaba*) has been filled by al-Ḥâjj Sani Haidara; his representative was al-Ḥâjj Abbas Buhari. Secretary of the 'Yan Izala was Malam Muhammad Yusuf; his representative was Malam Sa'adu Aliyu. The office of treasurer was occupied by Malam Zakariyya Gusau. As in other regions the appearance of the 'Yan Izala in Kaura-Namoda led to the formation of a coalition of interests between the Tijâniyya and the Qâdiriyya and to the outbreak of a new conflict between the ṭuruq and the "fundamentalists."

As the 'Yan Izala refused to pray behind an imam who was affiliated with one of the ṭuruq, a number of mosque communities split into two sections at the very outset of the 'Yan Izala's appearance in Kaura-Namoda. These problems increased when the 'Yan Izala, after the death of the old chief imam of Kaura-Namoda, managed to push through one of their own members as new chief imam of the central mosque. The success of this move indicates how strong they had become in their short time in Kaura-Namoda. The followers of the ṭuruq could not accept this defeat and founded a second Friday mosque for themselves in the recently built quarters of Sabon Gari/Kaura-Namoda (Mai Sa'ida 1987: 49). The conflict over the control of the 'Id praying ground developed on similar lines: this was also taken over by the 'Yan Izala, whereupon the ṭuruq withdrew to a new location of their own.

The conflict between the 'Yan Izala and the Sufi brotherhoods not only touched the organization of the mosques and that of the rituals but was carried over into the sphere of familiy life. Thus Mai Sa'ida recounts that in Kaura-Namoda numerous marriages were dissolved or not even concluded after the appearance of the 'Yan Izala due to one of the two partners being a supporter of the 'Yan Izala (Mai Sa'ida 1987: 49). In other cases family heads have expelled their sons after they joined the 'Yan Izala. The sons in turn were no longer willing to submit to the authority of their fathers (Interview Kaura-Namoda, 15 Oct. 1987).

Despite the intense confrontation between both camps, during the following years the 'Yan Izala were to become the most dynamic group in Kaura-Namoda. Particularly decisive for their success were their efforts in the sphere of education, especially in the field of women's education. Even while driving by car through the southeastern part of Sokoto state one will notice the remarkable number of schools the 'Yan Izala have built in the small rural settlements along the road. A similar density of schools in the rural areas of the North could be found only in the Christian mission areas of southern Kaduna and Plateau. By 1987 the 'Yan Izala had already established in Kaura-Namoda twenty-five Islamiyya schools of different sizes which, as with all schools of the 'Yan Izala, were free. Most did belong to the category of Islamiyya primary schools, but there were also nine Islamiyya secondary schools and schools which concentrated on adult education. The most important of these schools were the Irshadu school (1987: 728 students, among them 127 married women and 12 teachers), the Aminci school (1987: 245 students, among them 100 married women), and the Zamfara school (1987: 558 students, among them 127 married women and 7 teachers) (Mai Sa'ida 1987: 57–58). Taking into account a total population of probably forty thousand, the 'Yan Izala managed to convince a considerable part of this population of their objectives. Particularly through the propagation of women's education have they gained access to a section of the population which up until this point in time had been almost completely neglected by the Sufi brotherhoods and the state. Owing to their seclusion (*purdah*) married women in particular until then had had almost no opportunity to communicate with many other women.

A number of studies (Watts 1983; Hill 1972, 1977; Pittin 1979) have shown that seclusion had been increasingly enforced in the rural areas in the twentieth century. Purdah, which was practiced in former times only by the religious scholars and the nobility, is accepted today by an increasing proportion of farmers. Thus Watts writes in reference to the village of Kaita (Katsina state), "Virtually all married, premenopausal women in Kaita village were secluded in 1977" (Watts 1983: 404). Hill explains the almost universal adoption of purdah in the village of Batagarawa (Katsina state) by arguing that the women are no longer needed as "beasts of burden" because of the high level of ground water which made the drilling of wells in almost every single compound possible. Besides this, the seclusion of the wives has become a question of prestige for the husbands. Thus the lifestyle of the "wealthy" and the "holy" in the cities who could economically afford to free their wives from the harsh work in the fields could be imitated by the farmers (Hill 1972: 24). Pittin confirms the almost total observance of purdah in the case of Katsina City. On the one hand purdah was supported there by the women because they were able to carry out their own economic activities in their homes; on the other hand, "conspicuous leisure" has become a sign of a higher social status (Pittin 1979: 376). In the case of Kaura-Namoda the system of sexually separated classes in the schools of the 'Yan Izala made the temporary raising of seclusion possible: The husbands were not in a position to oppose their women attending one of these schools on the basis of the old argument of ikhtilâṭ (mixing). In fact, many women in the new schools of the 'Yan Izala were the wives of the followers of the 'Yan Izala themselves. The fact that they now had access to education exerted, however, considerable social pressure on the followers of the ṭuruq to lift seclusion for their own wives as well, and grant them access to education. In addition the non-fee-paying schools of the 'Yan Izala organized special meetings for the dissmination of information and irshâd every Friday, Saturday, and Tuesday between four o'clock in the afternoon and ten o'clock in the evening. In the course of these meetings the religious and programmatic positions of the 'Yan Izala were explained or specific problems of the community discussed.

By mobilizing the youth and the women the 'Yan Izala struck the Sufi brotherhoods in Kaura-Namoda to the very bone. The latter's reaction was correspondingly violent. The house of al-Ḥâjj Sani Haidara was stoned one night, and mocking songs were sung in front of the houses of other prominent followers of the 'Yan Izala. The Sarkin Kiyawa, the local representative of the Sultan of Sokoto who had become a member of the 'Yan Izala, was a major target of this method of ridiculing religious or political opponents. The supporters of the ṭuruq destroyed cassettes of the 'Yan Izala, and they repeatedly tried to disturb the teaching in the new Islamiyya schools and provoked violent clashes with the 'Yan Izala during the 'Id celebrations (Mai Sa'ida 1987: 60). The animosities demonstrated by the followers of the Sufi brotherhoods were, however, unable to stop the spread of the 'Yan Izala. Instead, a growing consciousness among many Muslims in Kaura-Namoda concerning problems and questions of their faith developed. Mai Sa'ida describes that this change of consciousness has been leading to a more serious and more consequent application of the sharî'a concerning divorce or the rejection of practices such as sha rubutu (ibid.: 62). On account of their social initiatives and program of education the 'Yan Izala were supported by a growing part of the population in Kaura-Namoda. The ṭuruq, on the other hand, have not learned from their defeats and have failed to develop initiatives of their own in the sphere of education as an alternative to their violent rejection of the 'Yan Izala. In the long term, they are bound to lose ground.

Argungu

The town of Argungu is situated in the geographical region of Kebbi about ninety kilometers southwest of Sokoto. Like Kaura-Namoda, Argungu is a small rural development center. In Argungu the population had, however, resisted the jihâd, and the Qâdiriyya had thus only a tiny following in Argungu. The first Tijânis, followers of Ibrahim Niass, settled in Argungu in 1952, but it was as late as 1985 when the first Tijâni who actually died in Argungu was also buried there. After 1952 the Tijâniyya rapidly became the most dynamic and the dominant ṭarîqa. This success stimulated the resitance of the Qâdiriyya and especially of the Sultan of Sokoto. In particular the practices of qabḍ during prayer and the communal reciting of the waẓîfa aloud were criticized by the Qâdiris. In 1955 thirty members of the Tijâniyya were imprisoned by order of the sultan on account of their "troublemaking."

The 'Yan Izala reached Argungu in 1980, and, as in other towns, the Qâdiriyya and the Tijâniyya for the time reconciled their old quarrels. In 1982 the followers of the Qâdiriyya and the Tijâniyya for the first time since 1952 prayed together in the central mosque (Sanusi 1987: 44). In contrast to Kaura-Namoda the 'Yan Izala in Argungu had considerable difficulty gaining a foothold in the town. Sanusi explains these difficulties by pointing to the effects of the so-called "kufr debate" of 1979. The leaders of the ṭuruq and the 'Yan Izala had in that year agreed on a mutual truce and promised each other to put an end to the mutual accusation of kufr. However, after the elections of 1979 the 'Yan Izala broke this agreement and continued their aggressive expansion. This change of policy was to cost the 'Yan Izala in Argungu a large amount of support (ibid.: 18). The initial difficulties of the 'Yan Izala were swiftly overcome, however, as they concentrated on the promotion of Islamic education and setting up a network of Islamiyya schools such as in other towns. Sanusi reports that the 'Yan Izala drove the ṭuruq into a defensive position and finally forced them to give up their internal animosities. In Argungu the conflict between the 'Yan Izala and the Sufi brotherhoods also spread into the social sphere and penetrated deeply into familiy life. Thus, the number of divorce cases rapidly increased where one of the partners within a marriage was a member of the 'Yan Izala: "many cases on family issues have been congested at the Argungu area court" (ibid.: 3).

The aggressive demeanor of the 'Yan Izala led to corresponding reactions in the counterpropaganda of the Sufi brotherhoods. These attacked in particular the hostile attitudes of the young 'Yan Izala members toward the elder generation. Thus the followers of the ṭuruq quoted the example of a young Dan Izala who had allegedly brought his mother a piece of cloth and some milk in order "to recompense her for the costs of his upraising." The 'Yan Izala were accused of treating their mothers like "envelopes" which would lose their value if one had removed their content (the child) (Sanusi 19087: 47). To take the wind out of the sails of the ṭuruq the 'Yan Izala have mellowed their aggressive rhetoric in Argungu in the past years. Their change of strategy facilitated a development in Argungu which led to a number of marriages of convenience between the 'Yan Izala and the Qâdiriyya. As a result of the old conflict with the Tijâniyya the Qâdiriyya was prepared to ally itself from time to time with the 'Yan Izala in order to push back the overwhelming influence of the Tijâniyya (ibid.: 69).

This situation can be explained only by the fact that the 'Yan Izala movement in Argungu has not reached the strength that it has in other towns and has thus not categorically and a priori excluded certain convenient alliances. Obviously the influence of the Tijâniyya was so predominant that this ṭarîqa was regarded not only by the 'Yan Izala but also by the Qâdiriyya as their common major enemy. On the other hand, the Qâdiriyya in Argungu was not oriented toward Nasiru Kabara's movement in Kano but still connected with the older center in Sokoto. The Qâdiriyya in Argungu hence has neither practiced bandiri-dhikr nor the communal dhikr and in addition did not celebrate the Maulid 'Abd al-Qâdir. Thus the most important points of criticism of the 'Yan Izala toward the Qâdiriyya did not exist in Argungu, which again contributed to the willingness of the 'Yan Izala to accept a certain amount of cooperation with the Qâdiriyya. Whether an enduring relationship develops out of this constellation depends, however, not only on the local conditions but also on the development of both the 'Yan Izala and Qâdiriyya on the national level.

Sokoto

The old center of the Sokoto empire and the present-day capital of the federal state of Sokoto is presently the only urban agglomeration in Northwestern Nigeria of more than regional importance. Even if on a smaller scale than in Kano, a number of numerically significant immigrant groups from other parts of the North or from Southern Nigeria live in Sokoto. In contrast to Argungu and Kaura-Namoda a considerable number of western-educated employees in the diverse branches of administration and regional government have settled in Sokoto. In addition there is a new university and a number of institutes of higher education. Thus, like Kano, Sokoto houses a considerable number of Muslims who feel neither bound by the authority of the sultan nor by their being affiliated to a Sufi brotherhood. It is exactly this group of persons among which the 'Yan Izala won its greatest number of followers in the city. In contrast to Kano, a significant basis of the Tijâniyya has never existed in Sokoto. Since the jihâd the town has been a center of the Qâdiriyya. On the other hand, Nasiru Kabara had only attracted a small number of followers in Sokoto, and thus the Qâdiriyya in this town has preserved its character as a movement of religious scholars. In the sphere of Islamic education no initiatives worth mentioning existed. The 'Yan Izala thus found a vacuum in which they could easily expand. Furthermore the Sultan of Sokoto, although being a member of the Qâdiriyya, as the nominal Amîr al-mu'minîn (Leader of the Faithful) of all Muslims in Nigeria was hardly in a position to openly fight the 'Yan Izala. The sultan had undertaken his first pilgrimage to Mecca in 1974. Immediately after his return from the ḥajj in his function as national Supreme Patron of the Nigerian Supreme Council for Islamic Affairs (NSCIA) he had tolerated and supported the condemnation of the Aḥmadiyya movement. As the campaign against the Aḥmadiyya was carried out essentially by Abubakar Gumi and the Râbiṭa, certain points of convergence must have existed between the sultan and Gumi. It may also be possible that the sultan discreetly sympathized with the fight of the 'Yan Izala against the Tijâniyya-Ibrâhîmiyya and to a lesser extent against the Qâdiriyya-Nâṣiriyya as both organizations during the last decades had infringed upon his spiritual influence in Northern Nigeria.

For the establishment of the 'Yan Izala in Sokoto, Malam Ibrahim Gusau, al-Ḥâjj Abubakar Maiwada, and Shaykh Abubakar Jibrin in particular were responsible. Shaykh Abubakar Jibrin, the imam of the important Farfaru Friday mosque in Sokoto, had officially founded the 'Yan Izala movement in Sokoto in 1979. This again is a sign that there was no resistance from the sultan against the establishment of the 'Yan Izala in Sokoto because otherwise the imam of the Farfaru mosque would have been deposed or forced to give up his post for being a member of the 'Yan Izala as had occurred in other towns. On the regional level the 'Yan Izala were essentially set up as an organization by Shaykh Sidi Attahiru Sokoto. He was born in Saudi Arabia as a son of Nigerian immigrants and came to Sokoto as late as the 1960s. He found employment as a teacher at a secondary school.

When the 'Yan Izala movement was founded in 1978 he renounced his affiliation with the Qâdiriyya to which he had belonged formally and joined Gumi's movement. On account of his rhetorical skills he rapidly rose within the ranks of the 'Yan Izala to a leading position. In particular, he succeeded in establishing a vigorous branch of the 'Yan Izala in Gusau, an important town in the southeastern part of Sokoto, and in placing the ṭuruq there under heavy pressure. In the mid-1980s (c. 1985) a serious conflict over the issue of overall leadership broke out between Sidi Attahiru Sokoto as leader of the regional branch of the 'Yan Izala in Sokoto and Abubakar Jibrin, the leader of the movement in Sokoto town. The dispute between the two scholars was finally brought to a court of arbitration established by the 'Yan Izala in Jos. This court decided in favor of Jibrin. Sidi Attahiru Sokoto was excluded from the organization on corruption charges, although there were others who said that he left the movement on his own account because he sought independence. He had been accused of misappropriating for his private use a car which had been bought from 'Yan Izala funds for transport purposes only (Interview Kaura-Namoda, 15 Oct. 1987).

The case of Sidi Attahiru Sokoto had not been the first case of corruption and embezzlement in the history of the 'Yan Izala: "There are instances of officials embezzling the movement's funds. Other officials collect money from the wealthy followers of the movement in the name of the movement, but use the money for themselves" (Umar 1983: 74). As these cases of corruption did not lead to any direct consequences it may be assumed that the charge of corruption in the case of Sidi Attahiru Sokoto was used as a pretext to carry out an internal struggle for power. Shaykh Sidi Attahiru Sokoto had become too ambitious and too influential, and his fame as a malam had spread over the whole of Northern Nigeria by 1985. In particular he had turned against the new strategy in the struggle against the Sufi brotherhoods which was propagated by Abubakar Gumi and which can be described as a more cautious and less aggressive approach by the 'Yan Izala. By contrast, Shaykh Attahiru Sokoto demanded the maintenance of a hard and uncompromising line of confrontation against the Sufi brotherhoods (Interview Kaura-Namoda, 15 Oct. 1987). Thus he questioned not only the guiding directives and competence of Gumi but also the formal leadership of Isma'ila Idris. As he was not prepared to submit forever to Gumi's authority he was compelled to leave. After his exclusion or withdrawal from the organization, Shaykh Sidi Attahiru Sokoto founded a new organization of his own in Sokoto under the name Ahl as-Sunna (People of the Sunna) (Interview Umar, 21 Aug. 1987). Many of his supporters followed him and left the 'Yan Izala. As a result he established a new center in the Gusau Road Friday mosque in Sokoto's Government Residential Area (GRA) and founded an Islamiyya school of his own (Interview Umar, 21 Aug. 1987). Apart from his stronghold of support in Sokoto, he failed in his attempts to expand his organization to a movement of more than local importance nor did he find or cultivate wealthy Nigerian or external donors who were willing to support him. His Saudi connections had presumably been cut off by Gumi. Thus in 1988 he made another turnabout and allied himself once more with the Qâdiriyya (Interview Kane, 18 Jan. 1989). In late 1988 he even appeared in a mass meeting against the 'Yan Izala in the mosque and zâwiya of Uba Ringim in Kano, together with the chief propagandist of the Tijâniyya, Shaykh Dahiru Bauchi. During his stay in Kano he was accomodated by Uba Waru, one of the major supporters of the Tijâniyya in Kano (Interview Kane, 18 Jan. 1989).

The withdrawal of Shaykh Sidi Attahiru Sokoto hit the 'Yan Izala in Sokoto severely because many of the most active members of the 'Yan Izala in Sokoto left with him. He was succeeded as leader of the regional branch of the organization by al-Ḥâjj Abubakar Maiwada, whereas Shaykh Abubakar Jibrin and Malam Ibrahim Gusau kept the leadership of the 'Yan Izala in Sokoto town. This affair indicated that the 'Yan Izala movement was also not immune to internal rivalries and power struggles. It was interesting to see that this conflict within the organization was not carried out on the level of a dogmatic dispute as in the cases of inter- or intra-ṭarîqa quarrels, but solved very formally on a legal basis, namely, on the charge of corruption. This fact points again to a basic difference between the 'Yan Izala and the ṭuruq: The 'Yan Izala organized themselves as a modern mass organization with a constitution, statutes, and formalized administrative structures, whereas the Sufi brotherhoods still had an informal network character and were therefore not in a position to carry out internal conflicts on the level of the constitutional regulations or statutes.

Kano

Kano, the economic heart of the North, has among all great cities in the North the greatest number of immigrants from other parts of the country. Thus a ring of satellite towns, Sabon Garis, has formed outside (*waje*) the old city (*birni*). These immigrant populations do not generally feel subject to the authority of the emir and are usually also not organized by the Sufi brotherhoods. The vast majority of the indigenous population in the old city has in contrast remained affiliated to either Qâdiriyya or Tijâniyya. The community of traders in Kano has for some decades been regarded as among the most active and generous supporters of the ṭuruq. Apart from this, the development of Islamic education in Kano since the 1950s has been connected with the movements of tajdîd of both Sufi brotherhoods. Thus it was extremely difficult for the 'Yan Izala to find any supporters in the old city of Kano. All efforts of the organization to get a foothold within the old city have until recently failed on account of the opposition of the Sufi brotherhoods. Thus in June 1987 some militant followers of the Qâdiriyya dispersed a group of 'Yan Izala who had tried—perhaps with the support of Aminu Dantata—to establish a mosque of their own in the Koki quarters. In September 1987 supporters of the Tijâniyya carried out a similar action in the Sani Mai Nagge quarter where, for some months, a group of 'Yan Izala had managed to occupy an old empty mosque of the Tijâniyya (Interview Dan Asabe, 6 Sept. 1987).

Only since 1987 have new developments seemed to change the situation in the old city in favor of the 'Yan Izala. These recent developments were connected with the fact that some trading barons have obviously decided to support not only the ṭuruq but also the 'Yan Izala. Thus Aminu Dantata, until recently one of the most important supporters of the Tijâniyya in Kano, bought a number of copies of the translation of the Qur'ân by Abubakar Gumi and distributed them free of charge to all mosques of the Tijâniyya in Kano (Interview Kane, 18 Jan. 1989). Isiaku Rabi'u also openly showed his sympathies for the 'Yan Izala. With his toleration and support the first mass rally of the 'Yan Izala in the old city of Kano took place on 16 January 1988 in front of his residence along Aminu Kano way in Goron Dutse (Interview Dan Asabe, 6 Mar. 1988). This mass rally provoked a great deal of irritation because a formal reconciliation ceremony between the 'Yan Izala and the ṭuruq had simultaneously taken place in Kaduna (see section 5.5). In addition, Isiaku Rabi'u participated together with Saudi donors in the financing of a new mosque in Unguwar Kofar Wambai (interview Kane, 18 Jan. 1989) a quarter dominated by al-Ḥâjj Yusufu Abdullahi, one of the most active supporters of the 'Yan Izala among the Kano traders (Kane 1990: 11–12). After its completion this mosque became the first mosque in the old city to be controlled by the 'Yan Izala. These events may be interpreted as a sign that in certain sections of the Kano trading population a process of reorientation of religious affiliations has been initiated: a process from which the 'Yan Izala would profit most. The causes for this reorientation by some Kano traders can so far only be guessed. As with Sanusi Dantata's quest for more autonomy in the early 1970s it may be assumed that many wealthy traders have over the last few years developed the feeling that their affiliations with one ṭarîqa only are too close and too exclusive. The 'Yan Izala were accepted by the traders for a number of reasons. For one thing, they have shown that they are not just short-lived and a transient phenomenon. On the other hand, the 'Yan Izala also represented a new interpretation of religion which was more attractive to the more Western-oriented, worldly minded, and economically flexible traders. Finally, the traders might also exert pressure on their present partners among the ṭuruq by establishing relations with the 'Yan Izala who have been stigmatized before. Thus it is possible that the structures of patronage in Kano will become even more diverse and complex. Ousmane Kanes's article (Kane 1990) as well as his research and Ph.D. thesis already point in this direction.

Whereas the efforts by the 'Yan Izala movement to establish a foothold in the old city of Kano failed until the late 1980s, they were by comparison more successful in the new quarters bordering the old city walls. In 1989 there existed three mosques in Kano which could be classified as supporting the 'Yan Izala. These mosques were the Bayero University Friday mosque under Imam Abbas, a small mosque in the traders' quarter of Fagge, and the Nasarawa Friday mosque in Sulaiman Crescent. The last mosque was situated in the immediate neighborhood of the regional office of the JNI in the Government Residential Area of Kano. The mosque was administered by Imam Aminu d-Din Abubakar and was constructed in the early 1980s with Saudi and Kuwaiti financial support. These three mosques did serve those groups of the population in the town among whom the 'Yan Izala have found their greatest number of supporters: the western-educated Muslims of the Bayero University, the dynamic traders in the "Sabon Gari" quarter, and the modern-oriented employees and functionaries of the local and regional administration based in Kano.

The specific conditions in Kano, especially the strong position of the Sufi brotherhoods, have made the rise of another "fundamentalist" group possible. Although this group, which was founded under the name Daawa (mission), had similar aims as the 'Yan Izala, it has been more successful in its choice of strategies and procedure and has thus managed to attract a considerable portion of the "fundamentalist" potential in Kano. Jami'u explains the development of Daawa as follows: "There is another group which can be described as being still in the making for it has not clearly come out with a name yet, it performs functions as a distinct group. Some refer to them as the Wahhabists for their teachings and preachings are akin to that of al-Wahhabi in perspective. Unlike the ''Yan Izala' it is a non-militant group against the tariqah brotherhoods, however, disinterested in the Sufi performances" (Jami'u 1986: 113–14).

The development of Daawa was closely connected with the personality of Malam Aminu d-Din Abubakar. In the late 1970s he had become one of the most versatile speakers of the MSS in Kano at Bayero University in Kano and was regarded as the leader of the pro-Iranian students at the university. Since 1979 he had translated the Friday sermon (*khutba*) at the Bayero University Friday mosque from Arabic into Hausa (Interview Abubakar, 19 Oct. 1987). As the leader of the pro-Iranian students in Kano Aminu d-Din Abubakar preached openly against the pro-Saudi positions of Abubakar Gumi. In 1981, however, a reconciliation took place between him and Gumi under Saudi mediation (Interview Abdullahi, 26 Mar. 1987). As a compensation for giving up his pro-Iranian stance Saudi and Kuwaiti donors financed the construction of a new Friday mosque and an Islamiyya school in Nasarawa and confided the management of these institutions to Abubakar. Jami'u explains this sudden support of the Saudis for Abubakar by arguing "that his teachings were in perfect conformity with their Wahhabi tendencies" (Jami'u 1986: 114). After his change of affiliations Abubakar openly supported Gumi and, for instance, quoted from the latter's writings. In November 1982 a commission of inquiry held him responsible for the heavy rioting in Fagge. These riots had allegedly taken place on 30 October 1982 due to Abubakar having quoted from Gumi's polemic booklet *Musulunci da abinda ke rushe shi* after the Friday prayers and thereby inciting the students. In the ensuing riots the Muslim students failed to destroy the major object of their protest, a Christian church in Fagge (*New Nigerian*, 13 Nov. 1982), but they destroyed a number of churches and hotels in the immediate neighborhood of Sabon Gari. During these riots three people were killed. The commission of inquiry accused the MSS of having been behind the riots. The MSS denied any participation (*New Nigerian*, 13 Nov. 1982). In the following years the relationship between Abubakar and Gumi cooled off again. Gumi did not succeed in completely integrating Abubakar into the 'Yan Izala movement. The latter established independent contacts in Kuwait and in the United Arab Emirates (Interview Abubakar, 19 Oct. 1987), thus successfully dissociating himself from financial dependence on Gumi. Abubakar's ambitions were obviously not compatible with Gumi's claim to supreme authority within the organization. A number of my colleagues in Kano characterized Abubakar's strategy by laconically remarking that "he wants to lead himself" (Interviews Dan Asabe, 19 Oct. 1987, Anwar, 28 Mar. 1988, and Umar, 5 Apr. 1988).

In fact, Aminu d-Din Abubakar established an organization of his own named Daawa in the mid-1980s. Its center and headquarters were his new mosque and school in Nasarawa. After the foundation of his own movement Abubakar became particularly engaged in the sphere of women's education. He claimed that the efforts of the Sufi brotherhoods for the education of Muslim women in Kano started only after he had established a women's class in his school in 1986 (Interview Abubakar, 19 Oct. 1987), an assertion which was false, as the Imam of the Muhammad Murtala Friday mosque, Malam Isa Waziri, had set up a women's class by 1983. Apart from his efforts for the improvement of the education of Muslim women he also has taken part in the political development of the Muslim women's movement in Kano. Thus he supported the formation of a FOMWAN-managed factory for ḥijâb clothing in Shahuci in 1987 (*The Triumph*, 20 Oct. 1987). At the opening ceremony he appealed to women to participate more in the political process. Abubakar also seemed to become one of the first religious scholars in Kano who publicly supported the interests of the handicapped. Thus in December 1987 he participated in a seminar on the future of the handicapped in Kano (*The Triumph*, 19 Dec. 1987). Finally, he acted as vice-principal of the Arabic Teachers' College in Kano. In 1987 he was working at the Department of Islamic Studies at BUK on a dissertation on Usman dan Fodio's *Nûr al-albâb*, a work in which the leader of the jihâd argued among other things for improved education for Muslim women (Interview Abubakar, 19 Oct. 1987). With this thesis Abubakar not only wanted to show his bonds with the legacy of dan Fodio but also to emphasize his role as a religious scholar with respect to Gumi (Interview Kane, 18 Jan. 1989). Nevertheless, the differences between the scholars were not as major as Abubakar presented them to be. Like Gumi he stresses the necessity of a better education for Muslims as a precondition for the tajdîd of Islam in Nigeria. He emphasizes the importance of dan Fodio and in particular his treatise *Iḥyâ' as-sunna* as a model for his own efforts of tajdîd. In contrast to Gumi he thinks, however, that dan Fodio never left the Qâdiriyya. Dan Fodio's concept of Sufism has been different, however, from that of Nasiru Kabara who has introduced a number of bida' into the Qâdiriyya (Interview Abubakar, 19 Oct. 1987). With this position Abubakar has evaded a serious tactical error that Gumi was unable to avoid and at the same time expressly limited his criticism of the Qâdiriyya to the personality of Kabara.

In contrast to the 'Yan Izala, members of the Sufi brotherhoods may become active in Daawa as long as they accept the Qur'ân and the Sunna of the Prophet as the foundations of the religion (Interview Abubakar, 19 Oct. 1987). Since Aminu d-Din Abubakar disassociated himself from violence as a means of conflict (Interview Abubakar, 19 Oct. 1987), one may regard Daawa as pacifistic and a dissident group of the 'Yan Izala especially adapted to the conditions in Kano. The aggressive strategy of the 'Yan Izala which had proved to be futile in Kano was replaced by Abubakar with a more complex concept which does not condemn the ṭuruq a priori. This interpretation was particularly attractive to the Western-educated Muslim intellectuals in Kano who were not prepared to sympathize with the simplified arguments and uncompromising approach of the 'Yan Izala. In the late 1980s Abubakar broke completely with Gumi and took up relations with Libya (Interviews Kane, 18 Jan. 1989, Dan Asabe, 6 Mar. 1988).

Since 1987, other changes have affected the 'Yan Izala in Kano. In that year the first steps were undertaken to get a foothold in the old city of Kano, and, as has already been mentioned, a reorientation of some members of the Kano trading elite may be observed. This vitalization of the 'Yan Izala was connected in particular with the personality of al-Ḥâjj Ibrahim Bibi Faruq of Gezawa who has taken over the leadership of the 'Yan Izala in Kano. Together with Gumi and Hassan Gwarzo he belonged to the first group of Nigerians who attended the Bakht ar-Ruda College of Education in the Sudan in 1954. Later he joined the diplomatic corps and for some time became a Nigerian ambassador. In the late 1970s he joined the PRP and rose to the position of representative of the State Governor Abubakar Rimi after the PRP's victory in the 1979 regional elections. In 1981 he was dismissed, however, from his office as a result of the intraparty dispute between the factions of Rimi and Aminu Kano. After his dismissal he concentrated on teaching, and since 1987 he has devoted his time to the reconstruction of the 'Yan Izala in Kano (Interview Sa'id, 8 Mar. 1988). He was connected with Gumi by their old bonds of friendship. Kane has shown that the 'Yan Izala since 1987/88 were indeed able to establish themselves not only in the new quarters of Kano but also within the old city. Thus they have acquired control not only over two new mosques in Sabon Gari and a considerable number of mosques in Fagge (Kane 1990: 24); they have also set up a number of new places for prayer (majâlis) within the old city walls (ibid.: 17).

The case studies of Kaura-Namoda, Argungu, Sokoto, and Kano show that the local conditions under which the 'Yan Izala had to operate were different in every case, but that they had a decisive influence on the way in which the movement established itself in these towns. In all cases the stress on modern Islamic education has proved to be the most important reason for the success and the rapid expansion of the 'Yan Izala. As a result of their efforts to promote education for Muslim women, the 'Yan Izala have cultivated a huge reservoir of potential supporters and at the same time exerted increasing pressure on the Sufi brotherhoods to follow suit. Today no religious movement in Northern Nigeria can afford to ignore or even to reject the issue of education for Muslim women. Apart from women and the young, the 'Yan

Izala have also gained a considerable number of followers among the Western-educated Muslims in the big cities. Thus the greatest proportion of the mass following of the 'Yan Izala is made up of these three groups.

5.3. The 'Yan Izala as a Protest Movement

The 'Yan Izala stressed again and again in their program, statutes, and pamphlets that their most important aim was the tajdîd of Islam in Nigeria and that all their efforts were directed toward the eradication of all bida' and the establishment of a modern Islamic system of education (Constitution 1b, 2c,e,f,g). If one focuses, however, on the effects of their actions and the religious, social, and political impacts of the movement, the character of the 'Yan Izala as a protest movement, which was directed against the established social and religious structures of the society in Northern Nigeria, becomes evident. By their protest against the establishment the 'Yan Izala have indeed won a significant number of followers among those groups in society that suffer the most from the constraints of the existing social system: women and the young. On the other hand, the 'Yan Izala have also offered a new platform for religious engagement to the group of Western-educated Muslims, traders, bureaucrats, and intellectuals who were dissatisfied with the existing religious structures and whose numbers have grown considerably recently. Last but not least, many of the immigrant Muslims in the big cities of the North have found a new home in the 'Yan Izala movement as they themselves were often rejected as outsiders by the Sufi brotherhoods.

In the very beginning of their development in 1978 the 'Yan Izala had more or less the function of a political protest movement. In a time when political parties were still banned, many politically motivated Muslims used the 'Yan Izala as a platform to carry out political discussions. When the political parties were readmitted the politically motivated growth of the 'Yan Izala was again reduced or, as Umar states in his thesis, "Now people attend political rallies rather than the preaching sessions of the movement" (Umar 1983: 76). The lifting of the ban on political parties had influenced the politicoreligious development of the 'Yan Izala in two ways: First, many of the rather politically oriented Muslims turned to the new political parties. Second, the 'Yan Izala reduced their militant activities on account of political considerations in order not to endanger the chances for a political victory by the Muslim presidential candidate, Shehu Shagari, by unnecessary internal conflicts. The open collaboration between Abubakar Gumi and Shagari incited many young Muslims within the 'Yan Izala movement, in particular those who attended a high school or a university, to leave the movement, and to turn to the radical, pro-Iranian groups of the MSS. They rejected Gumi and the 'Yan Izala after 1979 on the grounds of being reactionary and Saudi-influenced. The alliance between Gumi and the 'Yan Izala on the one side and the political establishment on the other held good until Gumi's death in 1992 with the exception of General Buhari's short-lived regime in 1984/85. Thus the 'Yan Izala did not play a major role as a movement of political protest. The political protest against the existing establishment was voiced rather by elements within the MSS and some independent Muslim intellectuals.

The character of the 'Yan Izala as a socioreligious movement of protest was much more evident. This protest was usually propagated in the form of religious argumentation even if the aim of the protest was of a specific social character. The Sufi brotherhoods with their hierarchies of authority were particularly subject to attack, as well as a number of popular traditions and customs in Northern Nigeria which were resented by the 'Yan Izala on grounds of their being un-Islamic. Thus in reference to a sermon given by Abubakar Gumi, Isma'ila Idris condemned the Sufi brotherhoods in a speech in Jos on 20 October 1978. He appealed to the followers of the 'Yan Izala not to give their daughters away in marriage to members of the ṭuruq as these had to be regarded as unbelievers (Aniagolu Report 1981: 74–76). Many of the violent clashes between the 'Yan Izala and the ṭuruq have broken out during such socioreligious sermons of the 'Yan Izala. These conflicts were carried over into the fabric of family life. The appeal by the 'Yan Izala to their followers that they dissociate themselves from members of their families who were affiliated with a Sufi brotherhood has led to serious crises of authority in many families. The development of the 'Yan Izala in Kaura-Namoda and Argungu has shown that the appearance of the movement in these towns has a socially liberating effect. Many youths and many women were enabled to legitimate their rebellion and their emancipation against their fathers or husbands on the basis of religious arguments. The 'Yan Izala gave this protest the necessary organizational backing by offering alternatives and by establishing a new social network with the help of their schools. The movement propagated not only the necessity of women's education but also informed women in the new schools about their rights according to the sharî'a, about questions of inheritance or divorce. The remarks of Mai Sa'ida and Sanusi claiming that the law courts in Argungu and Kaura-Namoda were flooded with divorce cases after the appearance of the 'Yan Izala were thus more understandable in view of these developments. It must be taken into account, however, that the divorce rate in Hausa society was traditionally very high. Pittin found that 8–10 percent of all marriages in Katsina are dissolved in their first year and 50 percent by the fifth year. Most cases of divorce were decided on the legal principle of *ṭalâq* (repudiation), and only a few cases were decided by legal process by means of *khul'* (divorce at the demand of the wife who usually has to pay the husband compensation). If, however, a case of divorce was brought to court, the initiative usually came from the wife (Pittin 1979: 184 ff.). This fact supports Mai Sa'ida's and Sanusi's argument and confirms the assumption that the 'Yan Izala movement has triggered this movement of emancipation among Hausa women.

The social protest of the 'Yan Izala had to be based on religious argumentation to be successful. The dogmatic foundation was provided by Abubakar Gumi in his writings against the bida' of the Sufi brotherhoods. His teachings were taken over and popularized by the 'Yan Izala. Thus they condemned bowing or lying down in front of the shuyûkh of the ṭuruq because this act of veneration violated the principle of equality among the faithful. They rejected the appeals of the imams for additional prayers after the obligatory prayers and argued that the decision for or against additional prayers should be left to the free will of each person. They also rejected submission to the authority of the Sufi shuyûkh, particularly in matters relating to the organization of professional or business matters. Their protest included the obligation of the faithful to make donations to the shuyûkh. In particular they accused the shuyûkh of collecting, in addition to the customary *ṣadaqât* (donations), the obligatory *zakât* (alms), and the voluntary *hadiyya* (gifts), the so-called *kudin laraba* (Wednesday money) on a weekly basis. Furthermore the 'Yan Izala blamed the shuyûkh for deceiving their followers by claiming to have special spiritual powers "through which they could command for the services of ruhanai [special creatures that fall between spirits and angels] and aljanu [spirits, jinns]" (Anwar 1989: 96–97). Finally, the 'Yan Izala rejected the pilgrimages to the tombs of the saints (ziyâra) as there was a danger that this may lead to shirk (polytheism). They stigmatized the long-winded religious rites of the ṭuruq as bida' and condemned the magical practices of the shuyûkh like sha rubutu as un-Islamic (Umar 1983: 74).

The religiously authorized protest against a series of costly social obligations and customs from which the shuyûkh, directly or indirectly, were to benefit from, was to be a major reason for the success of the 'Yan Izala. Their criticism found a warm reception among the poor and the socially disadvantaged. In reference to the arguments of the 'Yan Izala, which were usually explained in a comprehensive and easily understandable language, they were able to disassociate themselves from certain social obligations which until then had limited their financial and economic possibilities. Thus they could stop the customs of the kudin laraba, the ṣadaqa donations, or other gifts to the shuyûkh, and, with the backing of the 'Yan Izala, they could reduce or totally stop the costly expenditures for certain social events like naming ceremonies, 'Id festivities, burial rites, and marriages.

These social and ceremonial expenditures occupied a very high position in the value system of the traditional Hausa society and were usually accompanied by a number of additional financial obligations. Thus *ṣadaqât* were donations with a specific religious intention, whereas *gaisuwa* were gifts to a person of higher rank in the social hierarchy. *Biki* were gifts which are exchanged during certain formal social events, and *kori* were obligatory countergifts exchanged, for instance, during the preparations for a marriage (Watts 1983: 124 ff.). These ceremonial expenditures were complemented by the alms given to the beggars who attended these ceremonies as well as the fees for the malamai who carried out the formal act of a marriage (Pittin 1979: 405–14). The financial burden on poor families through these ceremonies has greatly increased during the twentieth century as a result of the rising prices for imported goods such as clothes, garments, and household utensils (Watts 1983: 219). The costs of a marriage increased in particular during the colonial era and continued to do so after independence. Thus the expenditures for an average marriage in Zaria ran to about 1 pound sterling at the end of the nineteenth century, but had increased to about 10 pounds sterling by 1949 and in some cases has even risen to 80 pounds sterling. These expenditures represented between one-third and 50 percent of the annual income of an average farmer in Zaria (ibid.: 360–61). In Batagarawa (Katsina) the costs of a marriage in 1967 ran to about 30–40 pounds sterling for the groom and his parents and about 10–15 pounds for the parents of the bride. The costs for a naming ceremony during the same period ran to about 15–35 pounds for the father of the child, and funeral expenses varied between 12 and 29 pounds (Hill 1972: 150). Ten years later (1977) the costs of a marriage in Kaita (Katsina) already amounted to about 400 naira, whereas it cost only 60 naira in 1969 and only 1 pound sterling in 1900. Twelve sacks of millet had to be sold in 1940 to finance the marriage, whereas twenty sacks had to be sacrificed by 1978 for the same ceremony in Kaita (Watts 1983: 459).

In an economic crisis as was the case in Nigeria beginning in the late 1970s, these ceremonial expenditures meant a considerable economic strain for many family heads. The religious arguments of the 'Yan Izala provided them with the necessary reasons for stopping or reducing these expenditures or to entirely renounce their affiliation with their respective ṭarîqa without necessarily acquiring a bad conscience on account of this behavior. Thus the conversion to the 'Yan Izala for many poor Muslims meant a considerable allevation of their economic constraints. The 'Yan Izala movement was also characterized by the fact that its members did not pay any membership fees, they were not morally obliged to give any donations, and many of the social services of the movement, such as attendance at a 'Yan Izala school, were free of charge. Khalil b. Sa'id pointedly remarked in this connection that "the ṭuruq ask for contributions, the Izala refuse contributions" (Interview Sa'id, 8 Mar. 1988). Umar sees in these economic factors one of the major reasons for the success of the 'Yan Izala: "In fact, I believe this is one of the strongest factors that attracted the vast majority of the followers of the movement from the lower classes. It is not uncommon that such people will welcome anything that will lighten their financial burden" (Umar 1983: 74).

In the meantime the Sufi brotherhoods have recognized the destructive power this economic change has exercised on their networks and try to counterbalance the economic enticements of the 'Yan Izala. Thus Dan Asabe reports that at least in Kano the leaders of the ṭuruq have started recompensing certain costly expenditures of their poorer followers such as the expenses for buying a sheep (70–100 naira in 1987) for the celebrations of their sons' graduation from the Qur'ânic school. Thus they consolidated not only the loyalty of their own followers but also acted as the guardians of the tradition (Interview Dan Asabe, 6 Mar. 1988). The appearance of the 'Yan Izala movement in this respect meant an allevation for the poorer Muslims in two ways: They could either become members of the 'Yan Izala and thus liberate themselves entirely from their socioreligious obligations, or they could remain affiliated with their respective ṭarîqa and profit indirectly from the social pressure the 'Yan Izala were able to exercise on the ṭuruq, as their shuyûkh were now more willing than before to help in situations of ecomomic constraint to prevent the loss of followers.

The members of the 'Yan Izala movement were able to profit from their membership in a number of ways. The less fortunate among them were given financial support from wealthy donors to the organization after Friday prayer which allowed them to construct a house or make other investments. In addition to this they gained income from selling the pamphlets, treatises, and cassettes (price 50 kwobo to 1 naira) of the movement or supplemented their income by offering transport to other members of the movement (Umar 1983: 74). Thus the 'Yan Izala, like the Sufi brotherhoods, essentially constituted—in a socioeconomic respect—a sophisticated network whose members were related to each other and were able to profit from these relations in a number of ways.

The constant criticism by the 'Yan Izala which was directed against the Sufi brotherhoods and legitimated by religious arguments against the practices of the ṭuruq has led since the late 1970s, particularly in connection with a number of economic and social factors, to an increasing questioning of the existing religious authorities by many Muslims. Many followers of the 'Yan Izala, in particular from the poorer strata of society, came to the movement out of economic considerations. Others, however, left the Qâdiriyya and the Tijâniyya because they accepted the principal soundness and logic in the arguments of the 'Yan Izala. Many of these critical Muslims had experienced a secular, western education and were themselves in search of a more rational religion. They used the arguments of the 'Yan Izala to disassociate themselves from their ties with their respective Sufi shuyûkh (Interview Yola, 21 Dec. 1986). The criticism of the existing system of values and authorities also engaged many Muslims who until then had not been questioning this system. They nevertheless regarded the attacks of the 'Yan Izala against certain practices of the ṭuruq as being right and thus became aware of the contradictions in their own religious and social system of values. The 'Yan Izala did not, however, only destroy the old established value system but also offered an alternative by promoting new ethics that particularly stressed equality among Muslims and orientation toward the Sunna of the Prophet. In addition the 'Yan Izala erected a new social network. Thus this movement under the leadership of Abubakar Gumi was in a position to offer many Muslims a solution to their religious crisis. The 'Yan Izala, through their dogmatic condemnation of the practices of the ṭuruq, conveyed the feeling to the employees within the administration, the traders, artisans, youths, women, Western-educated intellectuals, and workers in the new industrial and commercial areas, as well as in the Government Residential Areas, that their personal protest was a positive action in an all-encompassing struggle against the bidaʿ (ibid.). The protest of the 'Yan Izala movement in Northern Nigeria thus led to a revolution of the existing models of explanation. This new social development was characterized particularly by its unwillingness to compromise. The new followers of the 'Yan Izala did not want to preserve parts of the old system of values which they had condemned as "un-Islamic" but rather rejected this system outright. For the 'Yan Izala the process of reorientation could contain no half-truths. A system of explanation was either right or wrong. Thus Abubakar Gumi and Nasiru Kabara or Ibrahim Niass could not all simultaneously claim to be in the possession of the one and only truth. The radical rejection of former social and religious values is an explanation for the aggressivity and militant character that the actions of the young 'Yan Izala took in their struggle with the representatives of the old system. This brutality also characterized the reactions of followers of the ṭuruq to the attacks of the 'Yan Izala (Interview Umar, 21 Aug. 1987). To what extent the supporters of the 'Yan Izala despised the existing social system is indicated by Khalid in his thesis on the 'Yan Izala in Sokoto:

> Like [they were] in which Dan Fodio met them, the bulk of the Muslim populace today are ignorant of the manifest teachings of Islam. Consequently, the religion is pitifully confused with the local customs, blended with superstition and survivals of the pagan Hausa usage. This attitude pervades and permeates virtually in [sic] every as-

> pect of life and is knitted to life, [so] that to an average Muslim the line of demarcation between his religion and what constitutes innovation and unworthy traditional values appears blurred. It is even more disgusting when one realizes that this trend of things perpetuated by the society are [sic] actually justified and legitimated by the largely materially oriented ulema in order to maintain the established order and to protect their personal interests. (Khalid 1985: 1)

The conflict between the 'Yan Izala and the Sufi brotherhoods has led to a deep division within the Muslim community in Northern Nigeria. Many families—in the countryside as well as in the cities, in professional groups, and at all levels of society—are affected by this split. The new division was more profound than the dispute between the Qâdiriyya and the Tijâniyya in the 1950s and 1960s because it was not only a religious and political conflict but a manifestation of the general religious and social reorientation within society as a whole since the late 1970s. All efforts of reaching an agreement between the two sides have failed since then, and a real conciliation seemed to be unlikely: "The two sides cannot interact religiously, they are incompatible and regard each other as non-Muslims" (Umar 1983: 86).

The volatile nature of the religious and social argumentation put forward by the 'Yan Izala was so strong that many Muslims did not wish to openly show their affiliation with the 'Yan Izala, particularly in towns like Kano where the ṭuruq maintained their influence. Outwardly, they therefore acted as nonaffiliated Muslims and kept their sympathies toward the 'Yan Izala secret as they feared reprisals from the Sufi brotherhoods. This fear extended far into the sphere of family life: "There are some or rather many of the Muslims who intend to give up all these innovations and follow the way of the Qur'ân and Hadîth, however, due to fear about ther parents who still remain conservative they cannot show their true identity" (Funtua 1980: 17). The pressure of conformity within the existing norms not only affected the young followers of the 'Yan Izala but also the modern, Western-educated bureaucrats in the administration, of whom one might expect they were less constrained by the existing social norms.

Umar says that among the employees and functionaries of the modern administration the reluctance to confess one's affiliation with the 'Yan Izala is considerable. Although people would show certain sympathies they were often not prepared to support the 'Yan Izala openly and without any reservations, especially in areas where ṭarîqa influence was strong (Interview Umar, 21 Aug. 1987).

However, these factors only partially explain the character of the expansion of the 'Yan Izala. They are necessary to understand the success of their influence within the existing Hausa-Fulbe society in the North, but are not relevant to the influence of the movement among other social groups. If one examines the major areas of expansion of the 'Yan Izala, the strong points of the movement are situated rather in areas outside the centers of the Hausa-Fulbe society (Interviews Sa'id, 8 Mar. 1988, Anwar, 28 Mar. 1988, Umar, 5 Apr. 1988, Nur, Alkali, 23 Mar. 1988, Yola, 14 Oct. 1986): These include the Jos plateau, in the new federal state of Kaduna, in Gongola, Benue, parts of Niger state, and in Zuru Local Government in Sokoto, where, if any, only a small Muslim majority exists. These regions have considerable Christian and other non-Muslim populations, groups which generally belong to numerous smaller ethnic groups which were either not or only marginally integrated into or controlled by the Sokoto empire during the nineteenth century and formed the focal points of the Christian missionary churches in the twentieth century. The 'Yan Izala are nevertheless strong in the old Hausa-Fulbe center of Zaria where, although the seat of an emir, the impact of the Sufi brotherhoods has in the past been rather weak. Zaria is, besides Ilorin, the only emirate of the Sokoto empire where the Tijâniyya-Ibrâhîmiyya has had only marginal success. Furthermore Zaria accommodates the Ahmadu Bello University and its Institute of Administration, an institution which has influenced the religious development of the Muslims in Zaria to a great extent. Only a small number of Islamiyya schools existed in Zaria so that the 'Yan Izala were able, as in Sokoto, Kaura-Namoda, Argungu, and other comparable towns in the North, to gain new territory in the area of Islamic education. Apart from Zaria the

'Yan Izala managed to acquire a considerable following in the new development centers of the North like Kaduna, Jos, and Gusau. They were particularly sucessful in the new immigration centers. The Sabon Garis and Government Residential Areas in the Northern urban agglomerations of Kano, Sokoto, Maiduguri, and Bauchi are areas in which a considerable number of Muslim immigrants from other parts of Nigeria live and where many functionaries have settled. The 'Yan Izala also succeeded in gaining followers in a number of smaller rural centers like Argungu, Kaura-Namoda, Funtua, Malumfashi, and Gombe. These are areas that are situated as an outcome of a number of different historical developments at the periphery of their former emirates or which had even rebelled against the central authority in Sokoto. Finally, the 'Yan Izala were able to win many followers in the settler colonies (Sabo or Sango) of the Hausa migrant workers in the South, especially in Ibadan-Sabo, Sabo Sagamu, Lagos-Agege, and Benin City (Ahmed 1986: 306).

The focal points of the expansion of the 'Yan Izala have two major characteristics: first, they are ethnically or religiously heterogenous areas which did not belong to the central areas of the Sokoto empire. Second, the centers of the 'Yan Izala are characterized by the fact that they are not, like the Sabon Garis of the northern cities, directly answerable to the authority of an emir. Also, the networks of the Sufi brotherhoods have not achieved significant positions of influence in these new centers of settlement and immigration. The Sabon Garis in particular were named by the established malamai of the old cities as *unguwar shege* (the bastards' quarter) and ostracized by the rest of the community. Even today the Sabon Garis are regarded as *waje* (outside), as places of prostitution, alcoholism, and criminal activity, in short, areas of general corruption and decay. Muslims who stay there voluntarily or who even live there, are, in accordance with the opinion of the malamai, not be regarded as being really Muslim (Interviews Sa'id, 8 Mar. 1988, Anwar, 28 Mar. 1988). In addition, the recently immigrated Muslims from Yorubaland, Nupe, Bornu, or the Middle Belt usually worked in one of the "new professions": the administration, banking sector, transport (railway), police forces or army, or the new commercial or industrial enterprises. Working in these new professions implied not only a certain acquaintance and experience of a Western system of education and a certain contact with secular and Christian ideas, but also rigidly fixed hours of work. These rigid regulations concerning the organization of work, including constant transfers to other places or changes in the organization of the shift, made it almost impossible for the Muslims working in the new professions to take part in the often very time-consuming activities of the ṭuruq (Interview Anwar, 28 Mar. 1988). The immigrant Muslims in the Sabon Garis therefore usually had nothing left but the weekly Friday prayer as a communal religious activity. Nevertheless they were looking for ways to practice their faith despite these unfavorable conditions. Many Muslims from Yorubaland living in the Sabon Garis thus established Islamic clubs and societies of their own which were oriented toward educational activities. As these associations had a strong ethnic character, the other Muslims of the Sabon Garis were not able to find a home in them. Only when the 'Yan Izala began to preach in all parts of the North in the late 1970s did these neglected Muslims in the Sabon Garis see a possibility of organizing themselves. In the face of the contempt with which they were treated by the malamai of the old cities, the principle of equality between all Muslims propagated by the 'Yan Izala was particularly attractive for them.

The contempt of the established religious scholars of the old cities was directed not only against the 'Yan Shege but also against the 'Yan Boko, literally the "Sons of the Latin Script," meaning "Sons of Fraud." With this expression the established malamai characterized the modern elite of Hausaland, bureaucrats, Muslim intellectuals in the universities, army officers, and the younger generation of Western-educated entrepreneurs, traders, and bankers. These new social groups had acquired a great part of their political and economic influence under the government of Ahmadu Bello and had experienced in their career and their education an intellectualized and "de-mystified" interpretation of the religion. They were consequently no longer willing to submit themselves to the spiritual authority of a Sufi shaykh and to renounce, even partially, their own free will. They thus supported the policy of tajdîd of Ahmadu Bello and Abubakar Gumi in the 1960s and later the establishment and consolidation of the 'Yan Izala to give their own new religious orientation a kind of organizational backing. As these modern elites were rejected by the established scholars they could not hope to find followers for their reform movement in the centers of authority of these malamai. Thus the 'Yan Boko turned to the 'Yan Shege of the Sabon Garis as their quasi natural clientele and mobilized among them the supporters of the 'Yan Izala in the great cities of the North (Interviews Sa'id, 8 Mar. 1988, Anwar, 28 Mar. 1988, Umar, 5 Apr. 1988, and Nur Alkali, 23 Mar. 1988).

The above-cited factors concerning the expansion of the 'Yan Izala explain why the movement has been unable until recently to gain a foothold in the old cities of the North: The 'Yan Izala have retained the character of being a movement of the modern elites and of the Muslim immigrants in the urban agglomerations of the North. In places where a strong established authority in the form of an emir, a Sufi brotherhood, or established Islamic associations (Kano, Maiduguri, Ilorin) was present and in places where the majority of the Muslims in the old cities were already integrated, the 'Yan Izala have failed to make inroads into the educational and social networks of the Sufi brotherhoods and of the Islamic educational associations (Kano, Maiduguri, Ilorin). In the old city of Kano, for instance, Islamic education is still associated with the activities of the ṭuruq (Interviews Yola, 14 Oct. 1986, 21 Dec. 1986). In Kano the strength of the ties between traders and entrepreneurs and the ṭuruq was so strong that the 'Yan Izala had little possibility of gaining supporters among them. The situation was similar in Maiduguri where the Shehu of Bornu formed an alliance with the ṭuruq under the leadership of Shaykh al-Miskin and Shaykh Abu l-Fatih (both Tijâniyya-Ibrâhîmiyya) including the imams of all Friday mosques and managed to prevent until recently the establishment of the 'Yan Izala within the city area (Interview Nur Alkali, 23 Mar. 1988). In Ilorin the efforts of the 'Yan Izala to gain a foothold in the town failed by 1978 as a result of the united opposition of the emir, Sule Gamberi, and the Islamic educational associations. The situation was complicated here by the fact that the Sango ("new town") was not controlled by Muslims but by Christian immigrants. The Muslims of Ilorin thus already in their early development developed common counterstrategies against the Christians' missionary activities and school societies to prevent their being pushed to the wall by the Christian expansion. In Ilorin the religious scholars had therefore established a considerable educational network of their own so that the 'Yan Izala did not encounter a vacuum as in other towns. Their attempt to gain a foothold in Ilorin was also condemned by the established religious scholars as an action dividing the unity of the Muslims in Ilorin, the resulting situation being one that only the Christians would be able to benefit from.

The fact that the 'Yan Izala were able to win a considerable number of followers in some areas and among some groups of the population since 1978 signified a constant threat for the Sufi brotherhoods, but it also constituted a constant incentive not to relax in their efforts in maintaining the well-being of their own followers. The great effort that has been exerted to establish modern Islamic education in Northern Nigeria since 1978 can only thus be appreciated. The expansion and activities of the 'Yan Izala not only led to the crisis of authority and orientation among the ṭuruq and in particular the Tijâniyya but has also given a number of neglected social groups certain advantages. Many costly social and religious rites were given up or limited in the extent to which they were practiced. The Islamic educational network was extended to many parts of the rural hinterland. Muslim women gained the possibility of improving their for the most part rudimentary education and acquiring a better understanding of their rights and even suing for them. They managed to achieve this as a result of the efforts by the 'Yan Izala to mobilize Muslim women and improve their education. Broadly speaking, the conflict between the 'Yan Izala and the ṭuruq had the effect that many Muslims acquired a greater understanding of the actual meaning of their faith. The religious debate in the 1970s and the 1980s also led to a demystification of religion in Northern Nigeria. This process of demystification was pushed ahead by the violent attacks of Gumi and the 'Yan Izala on any form of siḥr (sorcery). Thus the all-encompassing protest of the 'Yan Izala against the existing religious and social structures not only has increased the political mobilization of the Muslims in Northern Nigeria and contributed to a stimulation of the intellectual discussion but has also led to a revitalization of Islam on a number of different levels.

5.4. The Reaction of the Sufi Brotherhoods to the Challenge of the 'Yan Izala

The publication of Gumi's treatise *al-'Aqîda aṣ-ṣaḥîḥa* in 1972 and the attacks by the 'Yan Izala on the two great Sufi brotherhoods affected the ṭuruq in such a way that they shelved their internal disputes after 1972 and increasingly concentrated on the struggle with the 'Yan Izala. The community of interests between the Tijâniyya and the Qâdiriyya have led to a growing number of common initiatives in the religious and organizational spheres since 1978. As the attacks by the 'Yan Izala concentrated in many areas on the Tijâniyya and as this ṭarîqa lost a great number of followers to the 'Yan Izala after 1978 the development of new strategies became a question of survival for the Tijâniyya. In the early 1980s a number of malamai of the Tijâniyya thus began to look for new ways to defend their ṭarîqa against the attacks of the 'Yan Izala. Shaykh Dahiru Bauchi and Shaykh Ibrahim Ṣâliḥ may be regarded as the two most important exponents of this counteroffensive by the Tijâniyya. However, their different ideas for a solution to the crisis within the Tijâniyya threaten to split the ṭarîqa once again into two factions. Apart from the effort to develop new arguments in the struggle against the 'Yan Izala the ṭuruq also undertook a number of political counteroffensives which aimed at presenting the 'Yan Izala as the destructive force responsible for destroying the unity of the Muslims. These political initiatives were not only more dangerous for the development of the 'Yan Izala but also more successful than the purely religious debate.

Whereas the writings of Muhammad Sani Kafanga and Nasiru Kabara which answered *al-'Aqîda aṣ-ṣaḥîḥa* in 1972 were still published independently of each other, the first united religious counterattack by both Sufi brotherhoods was undertaken in 1978 in Ilorin after the initial appearance of the 'Yan Izala. This took the form of the publication of a treatise called *Raf' ash-shubuhât 'ammâ fî l-qâdiriyya wa-t-tijâniyya min ash-shaṭaḥât* (The Lifting of the Doubts about the Deviations of the Qâdiriyya and the Tijâniyya). This work was inspired by the Emir of Ilorin and, as the authors stated in their foreword, was written on account of the appearance of some preachers in Ilorin who had characterized the members of the ṭuruq as "unbelievers" and who had presented themselves as members of the JNI in Kaduna. In the course of an assembly of the emir's council the decision had been taken to publish a book in which the positions of the Qâdiriyya and the Tijâniyya should be defended. This task was taken on by the reknowned scholar Adam al-Iluri from Agege/Lagos who wrote an introduction and who revised the whole treatise after its completion. The major contributors were, however, al-Ḥâjj 'Ali Abubakar Jabata (Tijâniyya) and al-Ḥâjj Muhammad b. Ibrahim an-Nufawi (Qâdiriyya). They became cochairmen of the Ilorin-based Jamâ'at aṣ-ṣufiyya (Association of Sufism), an organization of both ṭarîqas founded for the fight against the 'Yan Izala in 1978. After the completion of the work the booklet was printed in Lagos and distributed to all zawâya of both Sufi brotherhoods in Nigeria, Senegal, and Ghana. In the introduction a short history of both Sufi brotherhoods in Ilorin as well as a list of the members of the Jamâ'at aṣ-ṣufiyya is presented.

In their treatise the two malamai stress that their aim is to prevent the spreading of kufr in Ilorin. The critics of the ṭuruq must be be regarded as propagators of *fitna* (revolt, unrest) and would have no idea of the history of Islam in Ilorin. The Muslims of Ilorin would not need their advice: Why didn't these critics go to the bars and preach to the Christians? The authors accuse the 'Yan Izala in the same context of hating the Muslims more than the Christians. In addition, many critics of the Sufi brotherhoods had studied in Europe; there they had given up praying and rejected the teachings of Islam. In short they had become *jâhiliyûn* (ignorant of God) themselves (Jabata and Nufawi 1978: 17–18).

With this polemic against the 'Yan Izala the authors insert some new aspects into the religious debate which had not yet been developed in Nasiru Kabara's and Muhammad Sani Kafanga's works. Thus they stress the importance of the local history of Islam: not only the foreign models (i.e., "Wahhabism") from abroad should be taken into account but also the local traditions (i.e., Usman dan Fodio) and the local conditions. On the other hand they attack the 'Yan Izala at a very important point: especially in Ilorin would the struggle against the Christians be more important than carrying out internal conflicts among the Muslims. By acting in such a way the "Wahhabis" would be attacking a false party. Instead of spreading fitna among the faithful the 'Yan Izala should rather deal with the real enemy, the Christians. The fact is also highlighted that many of the leading representatives of the 'Yan Izala had experienced a Western education and allegedly given up their faith. Thus they had become untrustworthy to the Muslims. These ideas have become standard arguments of the ṭuruq in their fight against the 'Yan Izala during the 1980s and have been repeatedly quoted in disputes.

Another important point is the hint at the problem of the *mutashâbihât* (the ambiguous passages in the Qur'ân). The Muslims tried to solve this problem in two different ways: one group such as the Mu'tazilites supported the allegorical interpretation of the ambiguous passages, whereas others make reference to a verse in the Qur'ân which stresses the importance of accepting the mutashâbihât as they are without trying to interpret them: "It is He who has revealed to you the Book. Some of its verses are precise in meaning—they are the foundation of the Book—and others ambiguous. Those whose hearts are infected with disbelief follow the ambiguous part, so as to create dissension by seeking to explain it. But no one knows its meaning except God. Those who are well-grounded in knowledge say: 'We believe in it: it is all from our Lord'" (Qur'ân 3:7).

The authors of *Raf' ash-shubuhât* stress that the acceptance of the mutashâbihât was as obligatory as the acceptance of the rest of the Qur'ân (Jabata and Nufawi 1978: 22). Only God himself and the religious scholars were in a position to understand the mutashâbihât. To explain the ambiguous passages the scholars have to use allegorical exegesis (ibid.: 25). With the hint at the problem of the mutashâbihât as well as at the necessity of an allegorical interpretation of seemingly ambiguous or even contradictory passages in the Qur'ân the authors are thus in a position to reject any attack of the 'Yan Izala on the controversial texts of the Qâdiriyya and the Tijâniyya. These texts can be understood only on the basis of an allegorical interpretation and were thus closed to the understanding of the "Wahhabis" who reject allegorical interpretation. Thus the critics of the ṭuruq could also not claim to understand or to judge a book like *Jawâhir al-ma'ânî* (ibid.: 32). Whereas the argumentation of the *Raf' ash-shubuhât* is almost identical with the arguments of Nasiru Kabara and Muhammad Sani Kafanga in a number of points such as the importance of the 'ibadât for the religion or the correct interpretation of the term asqam, the above-mentioned positions constituted new approaches in the further development of the conflict.

In *al-'Aqîda aṣ-ṣaḥîḥa* Gumi had already vehemently attacked the major book of the Tijâniyya, *Jawâhir al-ma'ânî*. In the years after 1978 the attacks of the 'Yan Izala also concentrated on this book which was originally written by 'Ali Ḥarâzim b. al-'Arabî Barada from Fez who had met Aḥmad at-Tijânî in 1778/79 in Wujda and who had become one of his closest students. Around 1800 Aḥmad at-Tijânî began to dictate the text to his student until its completion in 1802. The work is a biography of Aḥmad at-Tijânî and a collection of his discourses. 'Ali Ḥarâzim, whose Arabic was not very refined, based his stylistics on a biography of the Moroccan scholar Aḥmad b. 'Abdallah Ma'n al-Andalûsî (d. 1708) which had been written by Muḥammad b. 'Abd as-Salâm al-

Qâdirî without, however, quoting this reference. Aḥmad at-Tijânî himself later ascribed *Jawâhir al-ma'ânî* to a revelation he had received from the Prophet (Abun-Naṣr 1965: 24). Although copies of *Jawâhir al-ma'ânî* were distributed as far as the Hijaz as early as the nineteenth century, the first edition was reprinted as late as 1927. As a result of the book's publication, violent attacks against the Tijâniyya by the North African Salafis broke out. A leader of the Moroccan Tijâniyya, Shaykh Aḥmad Sukairij, initially took up the defense against these critics. He held the opinion that all ideas and sayings by Aḥmad at-Tijânî laid down in *Jawâhir al-ma'ânî* were authentic and correct (ibid.: 25). In 1932, however, the leader of the Tijâniyya in Egypt, Muḥammad al-Ḥâfiẓ b. 'Abd al-Laṭîf al-Miṣrî (1897–1978), started a revision of the positions of the Tijâniyya. In the newspaper *al-Intiṣâf* (The Quest for Justice) he published his first efforts at defending the Tijâniyya from the criticisms of the Egyptian Salafis (Karsani 1985: 84–90). His intention was to show the conformity of the teachings of Aḥmad at-Tijânî with the Sunna and to put the Tijâniyya on the same footing as the other Sufi brotherhoods in this regard (Karsani 1988: 16–17). Thus Muḥammad al-Ḥâfiẓ argued by reference to the ṣalât al-fâtiḥ that Aḥmad at-Tijânî had never claimed that this prayer was revealed to him by God himself through the Prophet but that he had said rather that the ṣalât al-fâtiḥ was to be traced back to its author Muḥammad al-Bakrî (ibid.: 18).

The line of compromise designed by Muḥammad al-Ḥâfiẓ found no response in Nigeria until the late 1970s. The leading malamai of the Tijâniyya such as Muhammad Sani Kafanga, Tijani Usman, Abubakar Atiku, and Dahiru Bauchi identified themselves rather with the uncompromising stance of Shaykh Aḥmad Sukairij and were not willing to give up or even to revise the positions of the Tijâniyya as they were laid down in the *Jawâhir al-ma'ânî*. Their defense is based mainly on the argument that the writings of the Sufis are kept in a special language and were thus comprehensible only on the basis of allegorical interpretation. In contrast to the initiated core of the ṭarîqa, the external critics were not in a position to understand this special language, and consequently their criticisms should be regarded as null and void (Interview Kani, 1 Sept. 1987). Furthermore it would not be possible to defeat an opponent in a dispute by making concessions to him. In that way one would indirectly recognize the justification of his argument (Interview Anwar, 28 Mar. 1988). Although the strategy of ignoring the criticsm of Abubakar Gumi was rather successful among the older generation of the supporters of the Tijâniyya, it failed to attract the young and increasingly critical members of the Tijâniyya. They therefore left the ṭarîqa after 1978 in great numbers, and some even joined the 'Yan Izala. Some of the most reknowned critics of the Tijâniyya like Malam Dahiru Maigari stem from this group of Tijânis.

The uncompromising arguments of the old shuyûkh of the Tijâniyya also failed to convince many nonaffiliated Muslims. They regarded their statements as an attempt to draw attention away from the real critique. Many nonaffiliated Muslims were of the opinion that the teachings of the Tijâniyya have been laid down in a written form and that their rituals are public and thus comprehensible and clear for every Muslim. The positions of the Tijâniyya could therefore be verified objectively, and the argument of the Tijâniyya that their teachings are *bâṭin* (hidden, esoteric) would thus not be correct (Interview Umar, 8 Mar. 1988). In the face of these arguments it became increasingly necessary for the Tijâniyya during the early 1980s to develop, independently from the established strategy of defense, a new initiative to resume the offensive on the dogmatic level. This task was finally taken over by the Borno-born scholar Shaykh Ibrahim Ṣâliḥ al-Ḥusainî.

Ibrahim Ṣâliḥ originated from a family of Shuwa Arabs. His father and grandfather had been affiliated with the Tijâniyya and earlier ties to the Qâdiriyya had existed. His family claims to be able to retrace its genealogy to the family of the Prophet himself (Interview Ṣâliḥ, 27 Mar. 1988). Ibrahim Ṣâliḥ was born on 12 May 1939, in Dikwa (Bornu). He began his education in 1945 in the Qur'ânic school his father ran; he continued his education after his father's death under a student of his father, Muhammad Sayyid. After the completion of his Qur'ânic studies he went to Maiduguri where he continued his higher Islamic studies from 1956/57 under the tutelage of Shaykh Muḥammad al-Muṣṭafa 'Alamîn from Mauretania. He obtained his first ijâza as muqaddam of the Tijâniyya from Shaykh Muḥammad al-Ḥabîb b. 'Allâl b. Aḥmad b. 'Ammâr b. Muḥammad al-Ḥabîb al-Kabîr b. ash-Shaykh Aḥmad at-Tijânî, who was resident in Maiduguri during the same period. Furthermore he became a student of Shaykh Abu l-Fatih, one of the leading representatives of the Tijâniyya in Maiduguri and Bornu. After the conclusion of these studies he went to Cairo where he again studied for two years under Shaykh Muḥammad al-Muṣṭafa. After his return to Maiduguri in 1959 Ṣâliḥ received a second silsila of the Tijâniyya from Shaykh Abu l-Fatih which was to put him in direct contact, through Abubakar Atiku, with Ibrahim Niass. Shaykh Abu l-Fatih not only was for Ṣâliḥ the most important connection with the Tijâniyya-Ibrâhîmiyya but also was important for other Bornu scholars like Shaykh Abu Bakr al-Miskin. In 1960 Ibrahim Ṣâliḥ visited Cairo again and established a contact with the Egyptian leader of the Tijâniyya, Muḥammad al-Ḥâfiẓ al-Miṣrî, from whom he received his third ijâza of the Tijâniyya. In 1970 Ṣâliḥ visited Kaolack where he met Niass personally and received his fourth silsila which shortened his earlier link through Shaykh Abu l-Fatih considerably. After his visit to Senegal Ṣâliḥ travelled to Fez and there obtained his fifth silsila from Maula Idrîs al-'Irâqî, one of the leaders of the Moroccan Tijâniyya (Interview Ṣâliḥ, 27 Mar. 1988).

In the 1960s and 1970s Ibrahim Ṣâliḥ concentrated on establishing his trade in books and his publishing house in Maiduguri, as well as on extending his trading contacts with Egypt, the Sudan, and the Central African Republic (Interview Karsani, 29 Nov. 1988). Today he is regarded, not only in Nigeria but also in the Sudan and in Central Africa, as a master of *ḥisâb* (numerology, astrology) and as an expert in producing amulets (Interviews ibid., Kane, 18 Jan. 1989). In 1966 he established an Islamiyya school of his own in Maiduguri. His efforts to collect as many salâsil of the Tijâniyya as possible, with the aim of establishing contact with different centers of authority of the ṭarîqa, show that he like other ambitious scholars tries to disassociate himself from the local sources of authority and to establish an independent position. By the late 1960s Ṣâliḥ had successfully set up an independent spiritual network of his own, and on account of his commercial activities he was able to establish an economically sound basis for his activities. In the early 1980s he finally started to improve his image as a religious scholar by publishing a number of treatises and books such as *al-Islâm fî Nijiriyya* (Islam in Nigeria) or *Ta'rîkh al-islâm wa ḥayât al-'arab fî salṭanât kânim-barnû* (The History of Islam and of the Arabs in the Sultanate of Kanem-Bornu). Ṣâliḥ himself claimed in an interview with the Islamic periodical *The Pen* to have written 132 "books" (*The Pen,* 1989, no. 1), but presumably most of these works have not been published. He raised special attention with his study *at-Takfîr akhṭar bid'a tuhaddid as-salâm* (The Accusation of Unbelief Constitutes a Blameworthy Innovation and Threatens the Peace) in which he made the ideas of Muḥammad al-Ḥâfiẓ al-Miṣrî concerning the defense of the Tijâniyya better known in Nigeria (Interview Umar, 8 Mar. 1988). This book initiated violent reactions from the 'Yan Izala, whereupon Ṣâliḥ published another work entitled *al-Mughîr 'ala shubuhât ahl al-ahwâ'* (The Aggressor on the Doubts of the Sectarians) in 1986, which he defended his earlier line of argument and expanded his ideas. He gives an exhausting presentation of the development and the teachings of the Tijâniyya and extensively quotes Muḥammad al-Ḥâfiẓ and Shaykh Aḥmad Sukairij. The presentation of the history of the compilation and of the spread of *Jawâhir al-ma'ânî* play a central role in his argumentation and strategy (Ṣâliḥ 1986: 68 ff.).

According to Ibrahim Ṣâliḥ *Jawâhir al-ma'ânî* was compiled in a number of versions. The first version was written by 'Ali Ḥarâzim under the direct instruction of Aḥmad at-Tijânî. Thereby Ḥarâzim took pains to remain faithful to at-Tijânî's own formulations. After the completion of his work at-Tijânî found this compilation too unsystematic and ordered its destruction. Thereupon

Ḥarâzim wrote a second version which was again based on at-Tijânî's own formulations as he had heard them from him personally. The second text was written down in Ḥarâzim's own style and complemented with a commentary of his own. This version was later followed by a third version in which Ḥarâzim collected the sayings of at-Tijânî which had been reported to him by other students of the shaykh. The second as well as the third versions were again rejected by at-Tijânî as he found Ḥarâzim's Arabic faulty and too influenced by his Moroccan dialect (Interview Ṣâliḥ, 27 Mar. 1988). As a result of this, Ḥarâzim sent the second version of the book to the renowned Tunisian scholar Shaikh Ibrahim ar-Riyâḥî and asked him to improve the language. Ḥarâzim already knew ar-Riyâḥî from an earlier visit to Tunis in 1796/97. Ibrahim ar-Riyâḥî himself had visited Fez for the first time in 1804, two years after the end of the work on *Jawâhir al-ma'ânî*. In Fez he was initiated into the Tijâniyya, and after his return to Tunis he introduced the ṭarîqa into Tunisia (Abun-Naṣr 1965: 83–84). Although ar-Riyâḥî knew Ḥarâzim from this earlier visit he nevertheless rejected Ḥarâzim's request by arguing that he would need to revise the whole book. Some students of ar-Riyâḥî nevertheless copied the faulty text and brought it to Cairo and Mecca in the next few years. Further copies of the text were produced in different versions and distributed in these cities. According to Ṣâliḥ, in Cairo there are approximately ten different versions in circulation alone at the present time. All are based on the second, nonauthorized version by 'Ali Ḥarâzim. This confusion was increased by the fact that Aḥmad at-Tijânî had a number of influential enemies who tried to discredit him. Thus there have been attempts made to ascribe to at-Tijânî a treatise about his alleged miracles entitled *Buyût as-sirr ar-rabbânî fî karamât ash-shaykh Aḥmad at-Tijânî* (The Verses of the Divine Secret in the Miracles of Shaykh Aḥmad at-Tijânî). This work was recognized as a falsification by the family of at-Tijânî and consequently rejected. The leadership of the Tijâniyya was thus forced to concentrate much time and energy on the discovery and refuting of such intrigues (Interview Ṣâliḥ, 27 Mar. 1988).

The first attempt to clear up the problem of the authenticity of the *Jawâhir al-ma'ânî* was undertaken, according to Ibrahim Şâliḥ, by Muḥammad al-Ḥâfiẓ al-Miṣrî in a newspaper called *Tarîq al-ḥaqq* (The Way of Truth) which has been published in Cairo since 1950. Besides him a number of other scholars such as 'Ali ad-Dakkir, a scholar of the Tijâniyya from the Hijaz, as well as Aḥmad Sukairij, Ibrahim Niass, and Ibrahim Şâliḥ have tried to solve the problem. Finally, a research team was set up by a number of Tijânî scholars from Morocco and Nigeria under the chairmanship of Şâliḥ in 1988. It has then started to find an "authentic" version of the *Jawâhir al-ma'ânî* and edit it (Interview Şâliḥ, 27 Mar. 1988). The result of the work of this research team will be published, however, only when all work has been completed. The basis for the work, according to Şâliḥ, is a saying of at-Tijânî: "Examine everything that is reported [about me] with what is written about it [in the sharî'a] and if it is contradictory to the purity of the sharî'a, then reject it" (Şâliḥ 1986: 68).

This principle had already been adopted in the arguments of Muḥammad al-Ḥâfiẓ and Aḥmad Sukairij to prove the reliability of the sayings of Aḥmad at-Tijânî (Karsani 1988: 17). The reference to this principle affords the scholars of the Tijâniyya who follow Ibrahim Şâliḥ wide room for interpretation in their efforts to find an "authentic" version of the *Jawâhir al-ma'ânî.* In this way they are in a position to eliminate all controversial statements from the book and to make it very difficult in the future for the critics of the Tijânyya to attack the ṭarîqa on the basis of the text of *Jawâhir al-ma'ânî.* By arguing that none of the presently circulating copies of the book are really authentic, Şâliḥ is in a position to take the wind out of the sails of the 'Yan Izala. Their criticism of the Tijâniyya is based, according to Şâliḥ, on erroneous assumptions about the authenticity of *Jawâhir al-ma'ânî.* With the help of this argument Şâliḥ has successfully developed over the last years a new and more flexible strategy for the defense of the Tijâniyya which cannot be be easily refuted by the 'Yan Izala.

At this point the question arises as to what extent Ibrahim Şâliḥ and the other scholars of the Tijâniyya who presently reject the circulating versions of the *Jawâhir al-ma'ânî* for purely tactical reasons are prepared to give up positions in their future "authentic" version of the book which are still regarded by the majority of the the Tijânis, particularly by the older generation of Tijânî scholars, as absolutely undispensable. If Ṣâliḥ would really want to eliminate all controversial points in *Jawâhir al-ma'ânî* to deprive the 'Yan Izala of their arguments for their critique of the book, then the question is what would remain of the teachings of the Tijâniyya and would this tactical line be accepted at all by the majority of the Tijânis.

Ibrahim Ṣâliḥ's strategy over the last few years has led to a new division among the Tijânis in Northern Nigeria because the supporters of the uncompromising line around Muhammad Sani Kafanga and Shaykh Dahiru Bauchi regarded the strategy of Ibrahim Ṣâliḥ as suicidal and as capitulating to the enemies of the Tijâniyya (Interview Kani, 1 Sept. 1987, Anwar, 28 Mar. 1988). Whereas this strategy was thus rejected by the older generation of the Tijâniyya in Nigeria, Ṣâliḥ has on the other hand gained a considerable number of followers among the Western-educated and young Tijânis with this line of argument. He has gained particular support among the students organized within the MSS in the universities and high schools. I thus observed that Ṣâliḥ was the only speaker during a rally of a Council of 'Ulama' in Kano on 3 March 1988 who received the applause of the delegations of the MSS which were taking part. Other speakers, such as Nasiru Kabara, Dahiru Bauchi, Ibrahim Dasuki, Hassan Gwarzo, Khalifa Isma'il, and the Emir of Kano, were simply ignored by the mass of young Muslims. The sympathies of the young intellectuals for Ṣâliḥ were even more astonishing as it is known that Ṣâliḥ entertained close relations with the head of state, General Babangida, and has held the official tafsîr during Ramadhân in the statehouse in Lagos for years (Interview Umar, 5 Apr. 1988). The popularity of Ṣâliḥ among the Muslim intellectuals may be explained by the fact that he emphasizes the importance of the highly respected Arabic language. Also, he stresses his ties with Bornu as far as the conflict between the 'Yan Izala and the ṭuruq is concerned and is thus regarded by many intellectuals as neutral despite his affiliation with the Tijâniyya (Interview Miskin, 18 Mar. 1988). But even if scholars like Ṣâliḥ are able to gain the support of the Muslims intellectuals it does not mean that they are also able to swing the struggle for the sympathies of the Muslim majority in their favor.

Whereas the attacks of the 'Yan Izala concentrated on the Tijâniyya after 1978 and were quite successful on account of the many problematic aspects of the teachings of this Sufi brotherhood and on account of the numerous internal conflicts, the Qâdiriyya was only marginally affected by the attacks of the 'Yan Izala. This circumstance has several explanations. First, the Qâdiriyya in almost all of Northern Nigeria was smaller in numbers than the Tijâniyya and thus automatically less of an object of attacks by the 'Yan Izala. Second, the Qâdiriyya, under the undisputed leadership of Nasiru Kabara, was a relatively homogenous and united movement, whereas the Tijâniyya was split up into many different networks which even fight each other for influence. For the Qâdiriyya the identification with the leaders of the jihâd was much easier than for the Tijâniyya, as these were members of the Qâdiriyya who established this ṭarîqa as the dominant Sufi brotherhood in the Sokoto empire. An attack on the Qâdiriyya therefore constituted for the 'Yan Izala a special risk. Abubakar Gumi had made himself ridiculous by claiming that Usman dan Fodio had left the Qâdiriyya without being able to prove his assertion. Finally, the Qâdiriyya in contrast to the Tijâniyya did not possess a significant number of controversial dogmatic positions so that attacks of the 'Yan Izala on the Qâdiriyya were not very effective. Professors Maikarfi and Muhammad, leading representatives of the Muslim Forum, a union of non-affiliated Muslims at ABU Zaria, unanimously answered my question as to why the Qâdiriyya was seldom attacked by the 'Yan Izala by claiming that "there are almost no mistakes" (Interviews Maikarfi and Muhammad, 5 Feb. 1987). The 'Yan Izala undertook their first direct attack on the Qâdiriyya in Kano only in February 1987. In a leaflet in Hausa they particularly attacked a book entitled *Tafrîḥ al-khâṭir* (The Edification of the Thought) which is ascribed to 'Abd al-Qâdir al-Jîlânî. According to the 'Yan Izala the book contains a statement to the effect that 'Abd al-Qâdir had "seen" God. This claim would imply that the founder of the Qâdiriyya is associated with divine attributes, a fact that violates the principle of *tawḥîd*. Because of this all followers of the Qâdiriyya were to be regarded as unbelievers. Kabara personally answered this attack during two sermons after the Friday dhikr on 13 February and 20 February 1987. His argument was principally that any person who attacked 'Abd al-Qâdir al-Jîlânî implicitly attacked the Prophet himself, as the founder of the Qâdiriyya was connected with the Prophet through his silsila. However, a person who attacked the Prophet had to be regarded as a kâfir. The capability ascribed to 'Abd al-Qâdir to "see" God was defended by Nasiru Kabara with the argument that the Sufis talk in a "special" language (*lisân al-arwâḥ*, literally "angels' tongues," spiritual language) and would thereby also use "special terms" (*iṣṭilâḥ*, literally "technical terms"). The meaning of these special terms can be understood only in an allegorical way and not literally: "When someone is in the position [sic] of iṣṭilâḥ he acquires the ability to say whatever he feels to say except saying that he is Allah. In this regard Shaykh 'Abd al-Qadir excelled in iṣṭilâḥ and karâma" (N. Kabara, 20 Feb. 1987, translation by Yola). This special language according to Nasiru Kabara is comprehensible only to the initiated few, the mystics (*ruhanai*). How could a "dirty and wicked he-goat" claim that he could understand the language of the Sufis (Sermon, N. Kabara, 20 Feb. 1987)?

In contrast to the Tijâniyya the Qâdiriyya increased its unity in the face of the attacks by the 'Yan Izala and stuck to the criticized rites like the communal bandiri-dhikr. Only a few Qâdiris like Shaykh Sidi Attahiru Sokoto renounced their affiliations with the Qâdiriyya, and even the latter returned to it in 1988 after his break with the 'Yan Izala. At least in Kano the activities of the members of the Qâdiriyya were continuing as before and Nasiru Kabara has succeeded, in contrast to the competing networks of the Tijâniyya, to satisfy not only the spiritual but also the socioeconomic needs of his followers. All the traders who have shown sympathies toward the 'Yan Izala in the last years originally supported networks of the Tijâniyya, whereas the traders affiliated with the Qâdiriyya have remained loyal. Whereas the Qâdiriyya attracts public attention in Kano every night through the noisy bandiri meetings, the number of mosques in which the wazîfa of the Tijâniyya is still practiced has decreased significantly. Thus in Unguwar Sani Mai Nagge the number of Tijâni mosques still in use has decreased from an original number of six to a mere two by 1988. When members of the 'Yan Izala tried to build a mosque of their own in Koki, a Qâdiri-dominated quarter of Kano, in the summer of 1987, they were driven away immediately with the use of force by militant followers of the Qâdiriyya. In Sani Mai Nagge, a Tijâni-dominated quarter, the 'Yan Izala were by contrast able to occupy an old mosque of the Tijâniyya for several months until the Tijâniyya finally brought about a similar eviction (Interview Dan Asabe, 6 Sept. 1987). It is therefore not surprising that Kabara was able to act not merely as a protector of the Qâdiriyya in the years after 1978 and to be recognized in this function by the Sultan of Sokoto, but also to put himself forward as a defender of Sufism in general.

The Qâdiriyya owes this development not only to its own strength and unity but also to the permanent weakness and disunity of the Tijâniyya whose defense strategies were scarcely efficient so long as the rivalries between the different networks of the ṭarîqa continued to exist. Thus apart from the above-mentioned recent split between the supporters and the opponents of Ibrahim Ṣâliḥ the old rivalries between the supporters and opponents of Muhammad Sanusi still exist, and two leaders of the Tijâniyya in Kano, Muhammad Sani Kafanga and Khalifa Isma'il Ibrahim, have been engaged in mutual hostilities for years (Interview Kane, 18 Jan. 1989). Despite the disintegration of the Tijâniyya, Nasiru Kabara has not exploited the weakness of the Tijâniyya to continue his own fight against the ṭarîqa. He not only refuses to criticize the Tijâniyya but no longer even comments on the former conflicts (Interview N. Kabara, 21 Feb. 1987). Kabara regards the Tijâniyya as a vital buffer which has often protected the Qâdiriyya from the direct attacks of the 'Yan Izala. Thus he is not interested in the further weakening of the Tijâniyya as the Qâdiriyya would thus become the next target of the "Wahhabis" (Interview I. I. Abdulahi, 14 Jan. 1987). On numerous occasions, particularly during the celebrations of the Maulid 'Abd al-Qâdir, Kabara has stressed the necessity of cooperation between both ṭarîqas to be in a better position to deter the attacks of the 'Yan Izala. The presence of high representatives of the Tijâniyya at the celebrations of the Maulid 'Abd al-Qâdir, like that of Khalifa Isma'il Ibrahim in 1986, shows that the Tijâniyya scholars also prefer cooperation with the Qâdiriyya instead of leading a war on two fronts.

The cooperation between the Qâdiriyya and the Tijaniyya not only covers the sphere of dogmatic argumentation but also includes organizational forms of cooperation. Thus a common organization of both Sufi brotherhoods was founded in Kaduna as early as 1977 under the name Jamâ'at Ahl as-Sunna (Association of the People of the Sunna). Its chairman was al-Ḥâjj Zubair Sirajo (Ahmed 1986: 308–9). This organization was complemented shortly afterwards by another Kaduna-based group with the name Kungiyar Dakarun Dan Fodio (Association of the Soldiers of Dan Fodio) (Quadri 1985: 102). In 1978 the foundation of the Jamâ'at aṣ-ṣûfiyya in Ilorin followed, and in the early 1980s a number of local organizations was established in Kano in order to fight the 'Yan Izala. The most important among these were the following:

1. Jund Allâh (Jundullahi; the "Army of God"), established in Kano on 9 April 1980, by Malam Kamal ud-Din Adamu Na Ma'agi (d. 1986), the Imam of the Marmara mosque of the Qâdiriyya in Unguwar Alfindiki. Kamal ud-Din was a student of Nasiru Kabara. After his death the group, which had been the most important Qâdiri organization opposing the 'Yan Izala in Kano, began to decline in significance (Anwar 1989: 253).

2. Raḥt al-Islâm wa-l-Ḥajj (The Group of Islam and the Ḥajj), an organization founded by Kabara himself. This group has remained a purely Qâdiri organization (Interview S. U. Kabara, 10 Jan. 1987).
3. Awliyya' Allâh (The Friends of God), another Kano-based organization including Tijâni followers (Interview S. U. Kabara, 10 Jan. 1987).

The only organization of both Sufi brotherhoods which has obtained more than local importance, however, is Fityân al-Islâm. After 1978 Fityân al-Islâm was expanded under the leadership of Shaykh Dahiru Bauchi, Mudi Salga, and the new secretary general Zubair Kassim (Qâdiriyya) to become a truly national organization of both Sufi brotherhoods for their fight against the 'Yan Izala (Quadri 1981: 477). Fityân al-Islâm thus became the only organization of both Sufi brotherhoods which was present throughout the North. Consequently most clashes between the 'Yan Izala and supporters of the ṭuruq are in reality clashes between the 'Yan Izala and the Fityân al-Islâm.

Among the local organizations the Jundullahi group in particular became notorious on account of its aggressiveness. Thus in 1981 the leader of the 'Yan Izala, Isma'ila Idris, during his testimony before the Aniagolu commission of inquiry on the Maitatsine riots in Kano of December 1980, presented two Jundullahi placards which propagated "total war" against the 'Yan Izala (Aniagolu report 1981: 73). The Aniagolu commission of inquiry thereupon declared in its final report, "The Kadiriyya and the Tijaniyya movements, faced by one common antagonist, the Izala movement, have now temporarily forgotten their differences to unite under one umbrella of Jundullahi against the Izala movement" (ibid.: 74).

The attacks by the 'Yan Izala on the Qâdiriyya and the Tijâniyya not only brought about an alliance of interests between both Sufi brotherhoods but very soon triggered efforts of reconciliation and mediation with the aim of restoring the unity between Muslims. Thus a number of representatives of the conflicting parties and of the Nigerian government met at the recommendation of a subcommittee on darika under the chairmanship of Brigadier Shehu Musa Yar'adua to discuss ways of solving the conflict in late 1978. This committee of scholars consisted of the following persons: Brigadier Shehu Musa Yar'adua (Chief of Staff, Army Headquarters) and al-Ḥâjj M. D. Yusuf (Chief Police Superintendant) for the federal government, Nasiru Kabara, Ibrahim Ṣâliḥ, Khalifa Isma'il Ibrahim, and Abubakar Gumi for the conflicting parties, S. A. S. Galadanci and M. S. Zahradeen as neutral intermediaries, as well as Hamidu Alkali as chairman. After two meetings in Sokoto and Lagos in early 1979 an agreement was reached which became known as the "Kufr agreement." The conflicting parties agreed to renounce any mutual accusations of kufr (takfîr) and stated, "Any Muslim who calls another Muslim an unbeliever is a kâfir himself" (see the complete text in the appendix).

The number of clashes between the 'Yan Izala and the ṭuruq decreased in 1979, the year of the federal elections. It was particularly in Abubakar Gumi's interest not to endanger the chances of the Muslim presidential candidate Shehu Shagari by unnecessary internal conflicts. After the elections the struggle broke out again in an unmitigated intensity. However, the 'Yan Izala offensive was stopped in connection with the Maitatsine riots in Kano in December 1980. These riots were a clear sign that the economical and religious networks of the city of Kano were no longer capable of absorbing the growing numbers of unemployed 'Yan Cirani and of the Almajirai, Qur'ânic school students from the rural hinterland who were sent by their parents in the dry season to Kano to give them an opportunity to learn and to earn some money (Hiskett 1987: 213–14). The attacks of the 'Yan Izala had weakened the Sufi brotherhoods and in particular the Tijâniyya to such an extent that they could only partially accomplish their social functions. On the other hand, the 'Yan Izala were also not able to integrate the Muslim immigrants in Kano fast enough. These people thus constituted a potential element of protest which could be mobilized to a certain extent by Muhammad Marwa (Interview Kane, 18 Jan. 1989).

For the ṭuruq the Maitatsine riots constituted a welcome chance to win back the initiative, as the 'Yan Izala had to limit their activities considerably after the riots in order to prevent being thrown into one pot with the Maitatsine. The Sufi brotherhoods used this opportunity to launch a counterattack on their critics. They accused the 'Yan Izala of in reality being followers of Maitatsine (Interview Yola, 14 Oct. 1986). The platform for the ensuing dispute was the Aniagolu commission of inquiry which had been instituted to examine the causes of the riots and which had invited the leading opponents of the ṭarîqa–'Yan Izala conflict as witnesses. Abubakar Gumi (witness no. 40) originally reacted very moderately to the accusations of the ṭuruq and stated in front of the commission that, in his own opinion, the Qâdiriyya and the Tijâniyya were no "sects" and that the differences between both movements had originated from ignorance (Aniagolu report 1981: 83). Both Sufi brotherhoods registered this statement of Gumi with a certain relief and hoped that Gumi had changed his mind under the pressure of the events. However, some days later Gumi characterized the Qâdiriyya in an interview with Radio Kaduna as an "un-Islamic phenomenon" and thus contradicted the statement which he had made some days before. Nasiru Kabara (witness no. 48) thereupon appealed to the Aniagolu commission to impose on Gumi and his supporters a ban on preaching for one year, after which a new agreement would be worked out by the conflicting parties (ibid.). Nasiru Kabara's proposal was not adopted by the commission of inquiry. The majority of the commission had close affinities with Shehu Shagari and the NPN government. As a result the first attack on Gumi by the brotherhoods failed.

In 1982 the Sufi brotherhoods started a new phase in their struggle with the 'Yan Izala. The Fityân al-Islâm were mobilized, and their leader, Shaykh Dahiru Bauchi, initiated an extended campaign against the 'Yan Izala. Like Abubakar Gumi he obtained a program of his own at Radio Kaduna in which he could effectively present the positions of the ṭuruq, particularly of the Tijâniyya. Although Bauchi did not succeed in halting the further expansion of the 'Yan Izala by imitating Gumi's methods he was able to give back to the Tijâniyya some of its former self-confidence (Interview Malumfashi, 9 Feb. 1987). Bauchi even claims that through his campaign he was able to win back a number of Tijânis who had gone over to the 'Yan Izala (Interview Umar, 8 Mar. 1988). As in 1978, so in 1983 efforts of mediation were resumed before the federal elections to bring about a similar agreement of reconciliation or at least achieve a formal unity between the religious scholars to support Shehu Shagari's candidacy for a second term as president. Two meetings of scholars without the attendance of Abubakar Gumi and Nasiru Kabara took place in Yankari (Bauchi) on 15 February and 31 May 1983. The meetings did not succeed, and finally these efforts failed because the representatives of the Tijâniyya, in particular Bauchi, demanded that the Shagari administration place a ban on the 'Yan Izala movement as it had on the Maitatsine movement (Anwar 1989: 302–3). Shagari refused, however, to condemn Gumi and was supported in this position by Shaykh Ibrahim Ṣâliḥ, who opposed Bauchi's claim for a leading position within the Tijâniyya (ibid.: 305).

The development of the conflict between the ṭuruq and the 'Yan Izala came to a turning point when General Buhari ousted President Shehu Shagari on 31 December 1983 and established Nigeria's second military government. At the same time a turnabout in the religious policy of the new miltary government took place. As Abubakar Gumi had unconditionally supported Shagari, he now fell out of favor with the new administration. The Buhari government turned toward the ṭuruq, and the Nigerian Security Organization (NSO) imprisoned numerous members of the 'Yan Izala as well as a number of wealthy supporters of the movement such as al-Ḥâjj Haruna Danja (Interview Umar, 5 Apr. 1988). In 1984 a number of initiatives were taken up with the aim of eliminating Gumi from Nigerian politics forever. Thus a investigative panel was established to examine his "performance" as Grand Kadi of the northern region and Gumi's salary was suspended (Anwar 1989: 306). This led to heavy counterattacks by

Gumi against General Buhari and the military government. In consequence General Buhari supported a third meeting of the religious scholars and of some emirs in Yankari on 10 April 1984. This meeting was organized as a conference of the JNI under the chairmanship of the Shehu of Bornu and had the goal of excluding Gumi from the JNI on account of his known anti-ṭarîqa positions and his close affiliation with the 'Yan Izala. Gumi was urged to "either concentrate his attention on the activities of the Jamâ'at or to quit for Izala." He should also submit to a board of inquiry which would examine his anti-ṭarîqa ideas. Gumi refuted both proposals, arguing that he was not a member of the 'Yan Izala, that he was only an advisor to the 'Yan Izala, and that he would not attend 'Yan Izala meetings (Anwar 1989: 143–44). He would furthermore submit to a commission of inquiry and its judgment only if all other members of the committee had to submit to such an commisssion of inquiry as well. This reply was not acceptable to the Council of 'Ulama' in Yankari so their meeting ended without any results (Interview Gumi, 3 Oct. 1987). After this futile attempt by the ṭuruq to stigmatize Gumi on the dogmatic and organizational level, an attempt on Gumi's life took place in Kano on 30 Sepember 1984. According to Gumi the house of a friend in Kano where he slept that night was attacked by a mob and stoned. After the arrival of the police, thirty-two "suspects" were taken prisoner but acquitted in the ensuing trial for "want of evidence" (*New Nigerian,* 24 Dec. 1984). Gumi himself confessed that this attack was orchestrated by ṭarîqa circles in Kano (Interview Gumi, 3 Oct. 1987).

The negative political conditions changed again after the successful coup of General Babangida against the Buhari regime on 27 August 1985. Abubakar Gumi regained his former position as an advisor on religious affairs to the government and celebrated the new government of General Babangida in a public prayer of thanksgiving. The persecution of the 'Yan Izala by the NSO was stopped, and the imprisoned supporters of the movement including al-Ḥâjj Haruna Danja were released. Isma'ila Idris even distributed a cassette on which he attacked Shehu Shagari and General Buhari. The attack on Shagari may be interpreted as a late disassociation from his corrupt administration, whereas the attack on General Buhari was a reaction to the totalitarian politics of the latter under which the 'Yan Izala in particular had suffered (Interview Umar, 5 Apr. 1988). After the takeover of power by General Babangida the 'Yan Izala reopened their offensive against the ṭuruq and again began to attack the followers of the Sufi brotherhoods on the grounds of their unbelief. Dahiru Bauchi, who turned out to be an extremely dangerous enemy, was particularly attacked, and a number of violent polemics were exchanged between him and Gumi. Thus Bauchi was increasingly presented in public as the "leader" of the Tijâniyya. This provoked the anger of a considerable number of Tijânis. They criticized Bauchi's eagerness in promoting himself in public and accused him of self-enrichment as well as "collaboration" with the politicians (Anwar 1989: 313). These internal animosities led to another split within the Tijâniyya after 1985. On the other hand, the attacks of the 'Yan Izala against the ṭuruq were now turned increasingly into arguments against the 'Yan Izala themselves. Whereas Gumi and the 'Yan Izala had characterized the ṭuruq until then as sectarians who had split the unity of the Muslims, the Sufi brotherhoods now started to depict the 'Yan Izala as an obstacle on the road to Muslim unity. This was chiefly due to the fact that the 'Yan Izala would accuse the followers of the ṭuruq as kâfirûn or as mushrikûn and because they would refuse to pray behind an imam of the Tijâniyya or the Qâdiriyya. Even Muslims who were not affiliated with one of the conflicting parties rejected the mutual accusation of unbelief (takfîr). Their arguments may sound somewhat sophistic, but it is nevertheless interesting to hear what they say: Although Sufism has to be regarded as a bid'a it would not be correct to characterize Sufis as kâfirûn. Although the Prophet had said that the Muslim community would split up into seventy-three sects of which only one would pass into paradise whereas the others would go to hell, he did not say that the followers of the seventy-two sects bound for hell were kâfirûn. Even in hell their followers have thus to be regarded as mere sinners who might be saved by God. Only those about whose status as kâfirûn a unanimous consensus exists can be regarded as kâfirûn. This had been the case with the Aḥmadiyya movement. No such consensus existed regarding the ṭuruq, and thus the accusation of unbelief on their behalf was not justified (Interviews Kurawa and Amir, 1 Mar. 1987). Since about 1985 the ṭuruq, in respect to the conflict with the 'Yan Izala, refer to the fact that the 'Yan Izala violate two Qur'ânic commands in their attacks against the Sufi brotherhoods: "Obey God and his apostle and do not dispute with one another, lest you lose courage and your resolve weaken" (Qur'ân 8:46), and "Your religion is but one religion, and I am Your only Lord. Therefore serve me" (Qur'ân 21:92).

In their reaction to the attacks of the 'Yan Izala the Sufi brotherhoods have not only developed and modified their dogmatic argumentation or tried to find an organizational answer to the strategies of the 'Yan Izala, they have also, like Abubakar Gumi and the 'Yan Izala, started to develop their international relations to balance the support of the 'Yan Izala and of Gumi by the Saudis and Kuwaitis. In light of the tensions within the Islamic world between the different centers of power, Libya and Iran offered themselves as partners. Both states maintain a foreign policy which is directed at counterbalancing the foreign policy of Saudi Arabia and the other conservative Gulf states. Both countries had started to extend their contacts to Nigeria in the late 1970s and early 1980s. Iran began with a worldwide campaign of propaganda for its policy in 1979. The Iranian state supported these programs of propaganda on the one hand by the allocation of monies to finance trips to Iran with the aim of giving information on the Iranian revolution as well as offering some revolutionary training (Aniagolu report 1981: 88). On the other hand, in other countries as well as in Nigeria, Iran supported political groups which either sympathized with the so-called Khatt-e-Imam (the Line of the Imam) or were direct offsprings of the Iranian revolutionary organization Hezbollah (Party of God) (Duran 1985: 37). Libya had established an organization for the dissemination of its own propaganda called Jam'îyat ad-Da'wa al-Islâmîya (Islamic Call Society) on 12 December 1970. This organization had the function of acting as a counterorganization to the Saudi-influenced Râbiṭa. The actual work of the organization started only as late as 1972. The program includes the training of propagandists, the publication of informational material, the organization of information trips to Libya, the giving of technical and humanitarian aid, and the carrying out of courses in the Arabic language. In addition the Islamic university of al-Bayḍâ' is connected with the Jam'îya and has offered courses since 1974. In 1977/78 eighteen Nigerian students were matriculated at this university (Mattes 1986: 80 ff.). Libya succeeded in concluding its first agreement of cooperation with a black African country (Ghana) in 1981, and in 1986 thirty-six states throughout the world were members in the Jam'îya.

Initially Iran was more successful in its propaganda in Nigeria than Libya had been. In particular, many students within the MSS turned to the ideals of the Iranian revolution after 1979. Since 1979 ABU Zaria (Ibrahim al-Zakzaki) and BUK Kano (Aminu d-Din Abubakar) have become the most important centers of pro-Iranian activities. Ibrahim al-Zakzaki was imprisoned several times by the Nigerian security forces on account of his alleged revolutionary agitation (see the next section), whereas Aminu d-Din Abubakar, under the influence of Saudi and Kuwaiti donors, adopted a more moderate policy. The nonimplementation of the promised social reforms in Iran and the stagnation in the first Gulf war led to a sobering of the pro-Iranian students in Zaria and Kano, and many of them used the serious riots in Mecca in 1987 during the ḥajj as a pretext to disassociate themselves from Iran. Some of them turned to the Libyan model; others stress the importance of the Nigerian traditions as far as the tajdîd of Islam is concerned (Interviews Sulaiman, 9 Sept. 1987, Kurawa and Amir, 1 Mar. 1987). On account of these setbacks Iran tried to find new partners in Nigeria and in 1986 established contact with the most important propagandist of the Tijâniyya, Shaykh Dahiru Bauchi (Interview Doi, 19 Apr. 1988). He was invited to Iran on the occasion of the eighth anniversary of the Iranian revolution in 1987 and during this visit was granted a number of interviews which were published in the newspaper *Sakon Islam* (*The Message of Islam*) (No. 4, 1987, pp. 30–33) (Umar 1988: 216). In these interviews he defended the Iranian regime as orthodox in the sense of the Sunna (Amana 15 Jan. 1988). The connection between Iran and Dahiru Bauchi has, however not proved to be very reliable and has not been pushed by Iran further than the primary stage of informal contacts. After the termination of the first Gulf war in 1988 Iran has been much more concerned with its internal problems and the management of its economic crisis so that Iranian influence in Nigeria has consequently decreased.

In contrast, the efforts of Libya to find partners in Nigeria have turned out to be much more successful. Libya originally tried to establish contact with Isma'ila Idris in 1980. During that year the leader of the 'Yan Izala visited Libya twice. Both journeys were financed by the Libyan embassy in Lagos (Aniagolu report 1981: 54). This connection broke down in the following year as a result of the escalation of the conflict between Mu'ammar al-Qadhdhâfî and Saudi Arabia: In 1978 the leading Saudi scholar 'Abd al-'Azîz Bâz had condemned the positions of al-Qadhdhâfî concerning the interpretation of the Qur'ân and the Sunna of the Prophet. In 1980 the Râbiṭa also accused al-Qadhdhâfî of being a "heretic" as he had publicly declared that the Sunna of the Prophet was "not authoritative for the faith." The condemnation of al-Qadhdhâfî led to the break-off of diplomatic relations between Libya and Saudi Arabia in 1981, and al-Qadhdhâfî attacked the Saudis as the "enemy number one of Islam" and as "lackeys of the USA." He himself was condemned in retaliation by the Saudis as a kâfir and as a zindîq. Thereupon al-Qadhdhâfî appealed to the Muslims "to liberate the Ka'ba" on 20 August 1982 (Mattes 1986: 79–80). After some years of stagnation the Libyans succeeded in attracting a number of students of the MSS who had turned away from Iran. With Libyan financial support an organization called Young Muslims was founded at BUK Kano under the leadership of one Malam Aminu 'Abd ar-Rahman (Interviews Kurawa and Amir, 1 Mar. 1987). Another confidant of the Libyans in Kano at the neighboring Advanced Teachers' College started to organize journeys for Nigerian Muslims to Libya via Ghana. In Libya the participants absorbed a three-month training course (Interview Dan Asabe, 6 Mar. 1988). Above all, the Libyans established a connection to the leader of the Daawa group in Kano, Aminu d-Din Abubakar, who had started to distance himself from Gumi in the mid-1980s. The Libyan support since 1987 has become more important for Aminu di-Din Abubakar than the support he obtained from Kuwait and the Emirates (Interviews Dan Asabe, 6 Mar. 1988, Doi, 19 Apr. 1989). In this context it is interesting to note that the name of Aminu d-Din's organization Daawa closely resembles the Libyan Jam'îyat ad-Da'wa al-Islâmîya.

Despite the relations with Aminu d-Din Abubakar and parts of the MSS in Kano these connections did not seem important enough in the eyes of the Libyans. They therefore established an additional contact to the Qâdiriyya in Kano. In late 1986 Dr. Salim Warfalli, a member of the Qâdiryya and a leading representative of the Jam'îya, visited Nasiru Kabara in Kano and held initial talks with him on the publication of Kabara's translation of the Qur'ân into Hausa in Libya (Interview S. U. Kabara, 9 Mar. 1988). In 1987 a visit by an official delegation of the Jam'îya in Kano again under the leadership of Dr. Warfalli was to follow. This delegation participated in the Maulid 'Abd al-Qâdir celebrations, and met Aminu d-Din Abubakar and the editor-in-chief of the new Islamic weekly paper *The Pen*. In addition, the foundation of a local office of the Jam'îya was announced (*The Pen*, 1987, no. 9). In the spring of 1988 Nasiru Kabara traveled to Libya, visited the centers of the Qâdiriyya-'Arûsiyya in Fezzan, and met the Libyan head of state Mu'ammar al-Qadhdhâfî (Interview S. U. Kabara, 9 Mar. 1988). Although these connections between Libya and the Qâdiryya in Kano were legitimated on the basis of the traditional bonds between the Qâdiriyya in Kano and the Qâdiriyya-'Arûsiyya in Fezzan, significant economic and political interests formed the background of this alliance. Thus the Jam'îya was willing to finance the publication of the translation of the Qur'ân by Kabara and quite possibly also an edition of his collected writings (Interview Kabara, 23 Feb. 1987). On the other hand, al-Qadhdhâfî has found an important ally in the person of Nasiru Kabara against Saudi influence in Nigeria. The increasing importance of the Libyan connection was also shown by the fact that in February 1989 BUK Kano conferred an honorary doctorate on al-Qadhdhâfî (*Süddeutsche Zeitung*, 11 Feb. 1989).

The competition between the 'Yan Izala and the ṭuruq facilitated the intervention of external political forces. It is doubtful, however, whether these external forces will have a significant influence on the development of Islam in Nigeria in the long term. In respect to the strong economic basis of the ṭuruq as well as of the 'Yan Izala in Nigeria itself it seems more likely that the different external interests will be played off against each other by the Nigerian movements and thus instrumentalized for their own aims.

5.5. Unity Instead of Division: The Way to an Agreement between the Sufi Brotherhoods and Their Opponents

The conflict between the Sufi brotherhoods and the 'Yan Izala had led to a serious split in the Muslim community in Nigeria after 1978. Attempts to solve this conflict by negotiations had failed several times, and organizations like the JNI and the Nigerian Supreme Council for Islamic Affairs (NSCIA) were paralyzed and thus were not in a position to overcome their divisions. These political conditions began to change only in the course of the national debate about Nigeria's membership in the Organization of the Islamic Conference (OIC) in 1986. The Muslim intelligentsia in the North formed a new forum called Council of 'Ulama' under the influence of this debate and started to exert pressure on the conflicting parties to shelve their disagreements. The severe riots in Kafancan and other Northern cities in March 1987 had the effect that the appeals of the Council of 'Ulama' could acquire additional political weight. Finally the first local government elections since the military takeover in 1983 in December 1987, which brough disastrous results for the Muslims, was to lead to the formal reconciliation of the feuding parties in Kaduna in January 1988. Thus the conflict between the ṭuruq and the 'Yan Izala has slowly been pushed into the background since 1986. The new dominating topic is, as in Ahmadu Bello's days, the unity of the Muslims. In this altered social and political context the Council of 'Ulama' has shown itself to be the force with the greatest dynamic and was thus able, with the support of the JNI and the NSCIA, to bring about at least a temporary agreement to end the conflict between the ṭuruq and the 'Yan Izala. This internal political development led, as with the Maitatsine riots of December 1980, to a paralyzation of the activities of the 'Yan Izala. They were forced to stop their attacks on the Sufi brotherhoods to avoid being attacked and condemned as the "dividers" of the new-found unity of the Muslims. As long as these new political conditions prevail and so long as the Council of 'Ulama' is able to maintain its efforts to unify the Muslims in Northern Nigeria it is unlikely that the remaining contradictions between the 'Yan Izala and the Sufi brotherhoods will likely break out into a new confrontation.

In the course of the efforts to overcome the conflict between the 'Yan Izala and the ṭuruq and to establish a new and efficient umbrella organization for all Muslims, a Council of 'Ulama' had been founded as early as 1979. During a conference on the topic of "Sharī'ah" at the Centre of Islamic Legal Studies (CILS) at ABU Zaria the participants had set up a forum under the abovementioned name. The most important task of the council of scholars was to give directions for the revitalization of the JNI and to become the mouthpiece for the aspirations and demands of the Muslim community (Interview Kafawi, 11 Sept. 1987). In the new forum only Muslim scholars were represented, and traditional rulers as well as Muslim politicians were not asked to join in order to guarantee a smooth and efficient working atmosphere (Interview Kafawi, 11 Sept. 1987). The hopes which were connected with this Council of 'Ulama' were to be very shortly afterwards disappointed. After the elections of 1979 and the victory of Shehu Shagari the pressure on the ṭuruq and the 'Yan Izala to keep a low profile decreased, and the violent struggle between both religious camps soon broke out again. This pattern of political and religious development continued to be evident until 1986: as soon as a real or seemingly real threat was exerted on the Muslim community from the direction of the Christians or from secularistic tendencies, the representatives of the conflicting parties cooled off their dispute to establish a united front against the external danger. As soon as this external threat had passed the internal fighting was resumed. This pattern can be shown very clearly in the context of the Pope's visit to Kaduna in February 1982. During his visit the Fityân al-Islâm together with the 'Yan Izala edited a declaration which read, "There has not been any friction between Muslims and Christians in this country. There is therefore no need for the Pope to mediate between the two religious groups since there has never been any misunderstanding" (*New Nigerian,* 14 Feb. 1982).

In the summer of 1986 a political crisis once again developed which forced the Muslim factions to find a common position and to shelve their quarrels: In the face of the serious and increasing economic problems of the country the Babangida administration decided to think about making Nigeria a full member of the Organization of the Islamic Conference (OIC) in which Nigeria had obtained an observer's status under General Gowon in 1975. On account of the serious protests among Christian groups the Obasanjo government as well as the Shagari administration had never applied for full membership status. Full membership status in this Islamic organization would have given Nigeria access to the interest-free credits of the Islamic Development Bank in Jidda. The Christian interest groups, in particular the Christian Association of Nigeria (CAN) which had become very active in Northern Nigeria, denounced the plans of the Babangida administration and agitated against the "sellout" of Nigeria to the Islamic states of the Near East. The attacks by the Christians led to a certain solidarity between the different Muslim factions in the course of the so-called "OIC-debate." The necessity of developing a common position toward the Christians finally led to a meeting of the representatives of the different political and religious groups in Zaria and at Lake Tiga (Kano state) in November 1986. In the course of this meeting the participating Muslim scholars, including Dahiru Bauchi, Nasiru Kabara, Abubakar Gumi, Khalifa Isma'il Ibrahim, and Hassan Gwarzo, not merely outlined their political intentions but were also to revive the obsolete Council of 'Ulama'. As the first concrete measures a secretariat was established with Dr. Umar Bello as first secretary and Muhammad Sadiq al-Kafawi as administrative secretary. This secretariat obtained the task of coordinating the further work of the Council of 'Ulama' (Afkar Inquiry: 11 Mar. 1986). Muhammad Sadiq al-Kafawi was working as a lecturer in the CILS of ABU Zaria, and Dr. Umar Bello was the Director of the Center of Islamic Studies in Sokoto which has organized four conferences on the jihâd since 1983. It was founded in 1983 and has the task of collecting all materials and works on the jihâd, maintaining a library, and to organizing conferences on the jihâd. The center is financed through donations and through funds of the University of Sokoto and serves as a sort of research center of the Sokoto jihâd (Interview Tukur, 14 Oct. 1987). Both Bello and al-Kafawi as well as Ibrahim Sulaiman belong to the new generation of Muslim intellectuals in Northern Nigeria. Soon after the meeting at Lake Tiga a second conference of the Council of 'Ulama' took place in Kano on 25 January 1987. During this meeting the scholars agreed upon a common political platform and set up a list of demands which were addressed to the federal government. The most important points were as follows:

1. Nigeria's joining the OIC as a full member.
2. The acknowledgment of the Islamic festivals as national holidays.
3. The revision of the foreign policy of Foreign Affairs Minister Akinyemi, which was too strongly Western oriented.

4. The acknowledgment of Friday as a holiday.
5. The posting of the security forces in their respective areas of origin: no Christian security forces in Muslim areas. (*The Triumph*, 22 Feb. 1987)

The new political unity of the Muslims in the North which was brought about by the Council of 'Ulama' would have been of short duration despite the external pressure of the OIC debate had not a number of other events occurred in 1987 which made the further extension of a united front of the Muslims necessary.

On Friday, 6 March 1987, heavy riots between Muslim and Christian students at the Kafancan Advanced Teachers' Training College broke out in Kafancan, a predominantly Christian area situated about three hundred kilometers southeast of Kaduna. The immediate cause of the riot was a seminar of the Fellowship of Christian Students which took place in the context of a mission campaign called Mission '87. The Christian students had re-christened the area of the campus Jesus Campus and thus raised the anger of the Muslim minority. On the evening of 6 March a converted Muslim named Abubakar Bako who was employed at ABU Zaria gave a lecture in which he quoted from the Qur'ân and thereby insulted the Prophet according to the mood of the present representatives of the MSS. A heated discussion followed, and in its course a MSS student named Hajiya 'Ali tried to get the microphone, turning the quarrel into a skirmish that escalated into fighting and spread over the whole campus. As the Muslim students were a minority they were driven off the campus. On the following day the campus was closed, and the situation calmed down. The Emir of Kafancan, Isa Muhammadu, appealed to the students to keep the peace and to go home. On Sunday, 8 March, the rumor spread in the churches of Kafancan that Muslim rioters had attacked a church belonging to the Episcopal Church of West Africa (ECWA). Indeed, a group of men, armed with bows and arrows and clubs, had gathered in front of the Kafancan Motel. A fight broke out between this group and the Christian churchgoers which, owing to the numerical superiority of the

Christians, once again led to the defeat of the Muslims. In less than one hour nine people had died and fifteen had been wounded (*Newswatch*, 30 Mar. 1987). The victorious Christians then marched through Kafancan and terrorized the Muslims wherever they could find them. By the end of the riots two mosques were burned down, numerous houses and cars were destroyed, and according to an eyewitness about two hundred people had been killed (Interview Yola, 11 Mar. 1987). Only in the evening were the police able to restore the peace in Kafancan.

On the following day Radio Kaduna began broadcasting the news of the Kafancan riots thoughout Northern Nigeria, referring to a regular "crusade" by the Christians against the Muslims and of a bloody massacre of Muslims in Kafancan. The radio also claimed that copies of the Qur'ân had been burned and that the name of the Prophet had been insulted. Thereupon new riots broke out on 10 March in other Northern cities such as Kaduna, Zaria, Katsina, Funtua, Kankia, and Ikara. During the day the predominantly young rioters had taken over control over the streets and business quarters of Kaduna and Zaria and started to destroy churches, hotels, bars, and houses of known Christians. On Wednesday, 11 March, the city centers of Kaduna and Zaria had come under the total control of the rioters, the police forces had given up their resistance and had withdrawn, and the Christian quarters in Zaria (Sabon Gari and Wusasa) were looted and terrorized. The attempts of the Muslim Forum at ABU Zaria to keep the radical MSS students back failed. Even the refusal of Ibrahim al-Zakzaki, the former leader of the radical MSS students in Zaria, to proclaim a jihâd as his young supporters had demanded remained without effect (Interview Maikarfi, 3 Sept. 1987). The situation in Kaduna and Zaria calmed down only when the military governor of the state, Abubakar Umar, imposed a curfew and martial law on Wednesday afternoon over the whole state of Kaduna. The army was ordered to shoot on sight rioters who violated these regulations. Numerous rioters and looters were imprisoned until the situation had come under control on Thursday, 12 March. During its police actions in Kaduna and Zaria the Nigerian army committed a number of excessively violent actions against innocent Muslims so that the press (*New Nigerian, The Triumph*) were able to convey the impression that the army had used the riots in order to punish and intimidate the Muslims (*Newswatch,* 30 Mar. 1987). In Kano the first demonstrations of MSS students started on 10 March and on the following day a peaceful protest march of about three thousand students and sympathizers took place from the BUK campus to the emir's palace in the old city. In Kano two members of a Christian sect which had before held very noisy sermons in front of the MSS mosque on the campus were beaten up, but not killed, by some MSS activists. In the evening of 11 March the army closed the campus and the next day evacuated the whole area. The official statistics of the riots claimed that by the end of the rioting twenty-five people were killed, sixty-one wounded, six hundred imprisoned, forty churches burned, forty-six houses and thirty hotels destroyed, and numerous cars wrecked. In reaction to the massive participation of many MSS members in the riots the MSS and all other religious groups were banned at the universities and high schools (ibid.).

The brutality of the security forces in the supression of the riots and the fact that the majority of the imprisoned rioters were Muslims again led to a rapid solidarization of the Muslims in Northern Nigeria and to continuing protests by the MSS against the procedures of the so-called Karibi-Whyte Tribunal which was set up on 24 March 1987 with the task of investigating the Kafancan riots and carrying out the court trials against the imprisoned rioters. Demonstrations against the Karibi-Whyte Tribunal took place in Kaduna on 6 November 1987, in Kaduna, Yola, Sokoto, and Zaria on 23 November 1987, in Sokoto on 15 January 1988, once again in Kaduna on 4 March 1988, and in Kano on 12 March 1988. The slogan of these demonstrations organized by the MSS was, as I was able to witness, "Allah is our aim, the messenger is our leader, the Qur'ân is our constitution, jihâd is our principle."

Just a few months after the riots in Kafancan another religious dispute broke out in Kaduna. Since June 1987 female Muslim students of Queen Amina College, one of the largest high schools for girls in the North, had been calling for new school uniforms conforming to Islamic norms. In addition to a school skirt they asked for the introduction of trousers. Their demands were supported by the Muslim Sisters' Organization (MSO), the female wing of the MSS, which at the the same time led a campaign for the introduction of an "Islamic women's outfit" in public places. This MSS campaign was backed by the 'Yan Izala, who exerted pressure on the Kaduna state government for an official recognition of such an Islamic women's wear. However, before the state government could react, the first students started to come to the college in their new dress. The Christian students of the college immediately reacted and initiated a counter-campaign in support of the old uniform. On 14 June 1987 the college was closed down for a period of two weeks on account of the prevailing tension. Although the state government finally conceded to the demands of the Muslim students and accepted the "Islamic" school-dress on a nonobligatory basis, the dispute did not end: Both groups now refused to use the same buildings on the campus. The Muslim students called for a total segregation of Muslims and Christians in classrooms and dormitories. Within a week, tension had again built up to such an extent that on 7 July 1987 police forces had to be called in to separate the quarreling parties by the use of tear gas, wounding twenty students (Ibrahim 1988: 103). The Kaduna disputes as well as the Kafancan riots again demonstrated how seemingly minor religious symbols may acquire importance in the process of the formation of identities, in the definition of distinctive positions, in the mobilization of people for certain religiopolitical ends, and in the exclusion of others.

The Kafancan riots and their aftermath also indicated that a group of radicals had formed within the MSS. These radical elements increasingly influenced the political development of the MSS in the 1980s and 1990s. The radicalization of the MSS had started in the 1970s in the form of rallies at different universities in the North, in particular ABU Zaria and BUK Kano. The leadership of the radical MSS group in Kano had been taken over by Aminu d-Din Abubakar, whereas Ibrahim az-Zakzaki turned out to be the most outspoken MSS leader at ABU Zaria. In 1978 MSS radicals had attacked the "Palm Wine Drinkers Club" on the ABU campus, a major center of the left-wing staff and student groups of the university. On 18 March 1979, MSS students carried out their first demonstration on ABU campus, attacked the house of the vice chancellor and the staff club of the university, finally seeking refuge in the mosque on the campus. Only the personal intervention of Abubakar Gumi brought about their capitulation, thus preventing further bloodshed and damage. On 4 May and 20 April 1980, Ibrahim az-Zakzaki led the first MSS demonstration outside the campus, calling for a second jihâd, condemning the Nigerian constitution as un-Islamic, and demanding the acknowledgment of the sharî'a on a national level (Aniagolu report 1981: 88–89).

Ibrahim az-Zakzaki was finally dismissed form ABU-Zaria on account of his radical actions, and in December 1980 he was imprisoned by Nigerian security forces. According to the report of the Aniagolu commission of inquiry into the Maitatsine riots, he had not only turned out to be the leader of the Zaria radicals but had also undergone several training courses in Iran before 1980 (Aniagolu report 1980: 8). However, Ibrahim az-Zakzaki's detention did not stop MSS activism. Thus in May 1981, students of the Federal Government College in Sokoto refused to sing the national anthem; they argued that the text would violate Islam. In the course of a subsequent demonstration fifty-five students were imprisoned by the security forces (*West Africa,* 1 June 1981). The MSS was also thought to be responsible for the religious riots in Fagge, Kano, in 1982 (*New Nigerian,* 3 Nov. 1982). When General Buhari and the Nigerian army took over power on 31 December 1983, the MSS was not able to act as unrestrictedly as before. Nevertheless radical MSS groups could increase their influence in schools and universities. The massive participation of MSS groups in the Kafancan riots and the Kaduna incidents in 1987 was proof of their increased strength in these institutions. On account of their "Islamic" dress, their radical behavior, and their sympathies toward the Iranian revolution, the young MSS radicals in the 1980s came to be labeled "mini-Ayatollahs" or "Shi'ites" by the Nigerian press (Loimeier 1992: 73).

Since the 1970s several generations of MSS activists have left schools and universities with or without formal degrees. In the context of the Nigerian economic crisis only a few of them were able or lucky enough to get a suitable job. Many former MSS members have thus returned to their hometowns and set up independent schools of their own, education being their only capital. However, their basic willingness to form a radical opposition to the different relay-racing military regimes has not decreased. Their latent radicality and preparedness to fight a government which was made responsible for all social and economic problems of the country was thus repeatedly expressed in skirmishes and riots between them and the security forces.

Thus, in 1991 Northern Nigeria again witnessed religious disturbances involving a group of mysterious "Shi'ites" in Katsina. The Katsina riots were triggered by a cartoon in the *Daily Times*. Under the caption "Fun Times" the cartoon depicted the prophet Muhammad in a satirical way and implied that he had married a prostitute. After the publication of the cartoon the Katsina bureau of the *Daily Times* was stormed on 27 March 1991 by angry Muslims, and all copies of the cartoon were burned. After some days of lingering tension, these verbal exchanges turned into violent action. On Friday, 5 April 1991, security forces tried to stop a demonstration of a Muslim crowd. After the first encounter between security forces and demonstrators, the participants of the rally spread into the city of Katsina and attacked a number of government installations (*West Africa*, 29 Sept. 1991). In the course of street-fighting twenty-nine civilians and eight police agents were wounded, and 102 persons imprisoned (*West Africa*, 26 May 1991). In the legal proceedings following the riots it turned out that one Malam Yakubu Yahaya, leader of an "Islamic movement," had organized Muslim action in Katsina against the

Daily Times as well as against the security forces. Press imputations that the group was connected with the pro-Iranian Hezbullahi movement in Lagos were, however, quickly rejected by Yakubu Yahaya. He denied any connection with Iranian Shi'ites and stressed that there were no Shi'ites in Nigeria, "but only Islam" (*West Africa,* 26 May 1991).

The "Islamic movement" had been registered as early as 1985 in Katsina. Its program from the very beginning had been aimed at the establishment of an Islamic state in Nigeria. After 1985 the movement steadily expanded, in particular among young Muslims in Katsina, both male and female: Two of the twenty-five defendants in the 1991 lawsuit were women. By 1989, the growth of the "Islamic movement" had attracted the attention of the military governor, Colonel L. Onoja. He claimed that the state government was well informed about the "subversive activities of some religious fanatics" and was planning to undertake action against them very soon (*The Democrat,* 23 Dec. 1989). Colonel Onoja's successor, Colonel Yahaya John Madaki, again warned all religious leaders in Katsina not to undertake any political action (*The Triumph,* 16 May 1990). Shortly afterwards he instituted a religious board under the chairmanship of the Grand Kadi of Katsina, al-Ḥâjj Usman Muhammad, which was asked to control the activities of all Islamic preachers in Katsina and to issue them licences (*New Nigerian,* 22 June 1990).

On account of his authoritarian and undiplomatic style of government, Colonel Madaki became a symbol of the Nigerian military regime that the "Islamic movement" in Katsina intended to overthrow (*West Africa,* 29 Sept. 1991). By March 1991 Yakubu Yahaya's group seemingly felt strong and desperate enough to start direct confrontation with the state government. The scandal created by the *Daily Times* cartoon provided a welcome pretext to legitimate the first militant move of the group. In the week after the occupation of the *Daily Times* bureau the public dispute between Colonel Madaki and Yakubu Yahaya increased in intensity and sharpness. Thus Madaki publicly warned Yahaya that he was not afraid of him and that Yahaya should be prepared to go into exile if he wanted to create further trouble. In that case "we would go to his house, bring him to the Polo field and execute him publicly" (*West Africa,* 26 May 1991). Yahaya retorted that he regarded himself as truly Muslim, guided by the principles of Islam, and that he did not acknowledge any authority apart from the Holy Qur'ân. He would be prepared to die for the holy cause (*West Africa,* 25 May 1991). Yakubu Yahaya's position was publicly supported by Ibrahim az-Zakzaki who had called for the assassination of Colonal Madaki and had accused him of having tolerated "blasphemy against the prophet" (*West Africa,* 25 May 1991).

The Katsina riots have demonstrated that frustrations of radical Muslims have risen to such an extent that persons and organizations such as Ibrahim Sulaiman or the Council of 'Ulama, known for their uncompromising positions toward the respective military regimes, have increasing difficulties in restraining them. Even Ibrahim az-Zakzaki, who was said to have been "the man behind" the Katsina riots, has lost his former influence among the young radicals. In the context of the Kafancan riots of 1987, az-Zakzaki had already refused to call upon his followers to start a jihâd, thus showing his increasing moderation (Interview U. Maikarfi, 3 Sept. 1987). After his release from prison in December 1989 he had been put under strict surveillance by the security forces. Connections of any kind between him and the Katsina rioters could thus not be substantiated. Repeated reference to az-Zakzaki in the context of religious riots of Northern Nigeria has to be seen in a similar perspective as the 'Yan Izala incidents of the 1970s or the Maitatsine riots of the 1980s: On account of his revolutionary career az-Zakzaki has acquired the image of "the mysterious instigator" and has therefore been made responsible for of all kinds of violent politicoreligious disputes in Northern Nigeria. However, economic crisis and political authoritarianism have always been a sufficient reason to create revolutionaries, and Islam has never ceased to provide the ideological basis.

In the volatile atmosphere after the Kafancan riots the Council of 'Ulama' under the leadership of Dr. Umar Bello and supported by the MSS was still able to put itself forward as the mouthpiece of all Muslims in the North. This role of the Council of 'Ulama' had become possible as the members of the executive committee (the "General Purpose Committee") which was meeting regularly under the leadership of Dr. Bello could act regardless of the diverging interests of the traditional rulers and Muslim politicians and thus influence public opinion with rapid efficiency. The emirs, politicians, and religious dignitaries thus had no other choice than to support the demands and the statements of the Council of 'Ulama' in the name of all Muslims (Interview Kafawi, 11 Sept. 1987). Under these conditions in 1987 the Council of 'Ulama' developed into the religious and political spearhead of the Muslims in Northern Nigeria.

In 1987 the dispute between the Council of 'Ulama' and the Nigerian government escalated further when the daily newspaper *New Nigerian* published a communique of the Council of 'Ulama', signed by Dr. Umar Bello (see appendix), in which the Nigerian government was strongly attacked. Immediately afterwards Dr. Bello and the publisher of the *New Nigerian*, Haruna Muhammad, were detained by the Nigerian State Security Service and interrogated. Although both were set free after a short time the atmosphere took longer to cool down. The attacks by the Council of 'Ulama' and the radical intellectuals concentrated on the editor-in-chief of the *New Nigerian*, Innocent Oparadike. The latter, an Igbo and a Christian, had somewhat surprisingly been appointed in November 1985, obviously because he had good relations to the head of state, General Babangida, as new editor-in-chief of the *New Nigerian*. On account of his alleged propagation of Christian interests within the *New Nigerian* and because of his original refusal to publish Dr. Bello's statement in the newspaper, a conflict developed between him and Haruna Muhammad, the publisher and chairman of the publishing company of the *New Nigerian*. On 8 September 1987 Oparadike was dismissed (*National Concord*, 10 Nov. 1987) and replaced by Mrs. Bilkisu Yusuf, a leading representative of FOMWAN and formerly employed by the Kano daily *The Triumph*. Bilkisu Yusuf had studied political science at ABU Zaria and became the first woman to edit a Northern Nigerian newspaper (Interview Yusuf, 11 Apr. 1988). After gaining the upper hand in the quarrel over the *New Nigerian* the attention of the Council of 'Ulama' was directed to the policy and the person of the Christian foreign affairs minister, Bolaji Akinyemi, in the second half of 1987. He was accused of having planned to restablish diplomatic contacts with Israel and to have prevented the full membership of Nigeria in the OIC. Akinyemi became a symbol of the influence of the Christians in the state and was heavily criticized in this regard in late 1987. On 28 December 1987 President Babangida dismissed Akinyemi in the context of a general cabinet reshuffling (*Newswatch*, 14 Mar. 1988).

The third major activity of the Council of 'Ulama' in 1987 was the campaign against the procedures of the Karibi-Whyte Tribunal which had begun to investigate the Kafancan riots on 2 June 1987, and which had the task of bringing about six hundred detainees to trial. The court procedures were terminated on 20 January 1988. Most of the six hundred detainees were released on lack of evidence, and only 159 were finally tried (145 Muslims, 14 Christians). Among these seventy-five were found guilty and sentenced to terms of imprisonment (71 Muslims, 4 Christians). The prison terms in one case reached 22½ years for the main defendant, Danjuma Idi, whereas Ibrahim al-Zakzaki who had not even taken part in the riots, was sentenced to 4½ years of imprisonment. The sentences for the Christian detainees in contrast were very light (*New Nigerian*, 7 Nov. and 29 Dec. 1987, 28 Jan. and 5 Mar. 1988). The protest against the procedures of the Karibi-Whyte Tribunal and the anouncement of the sentences became an important factor in the mobilization campaign of the Council of 'Ulama' in 1987/88 in its efforts to unify the Muslim community in Northern Nigeria. Apart from the very one-sided measures of punishment for Christian and Muslim detainees, the Muslims repeatedly pointed out that the person who had triggered off the riots in Kafancan, the Reverend Abubakar Bako, had been allowed to disappear after the riots together with his family and has never been brought to court. In the course of the above-mentioned demonstrations as a result of the dealings of the Karibi-Whyte Tribunal, the Council of 'Ulama' once again became the spearhead of the Muslim protest movement. The Council of 'Ulama' proclaimed a three-day solidarity fast for the imprisoned Muslims on 4 January 1988, and appealed to the Babangida government to revoke the ban on the MSS (*New Nigerian*, 25 Jan. and 28 Jan. 1988). The protests of the Council of 'Ulama' over the decisions made by the Karibi-Whyte Tribunal for the time being remained unsuccessful. The Council of 'Ulama' nevertheless maintained, by means of its policy of direct action, the initiative in its efforts to unite the Muslims.

The public reconciliation between the ṭuruq and the 'Yan Izala was not achieved by these events but by the results of the local government elections on 12 December 1987. These elections on the lowest level of administration were the first democratic elections since the military coup of 31 December 1983 and were thus regarded as a test for the future development of political parties. Although no political parties were yet admitted, the different interest groups could nominate their candidates and support them. In addition, the Babangida administration had suspended the old politicians and thus opened the door for a young generation of politicans, not compromised by old scandals. The question therefore was whether new developments would occur or whether the candidates of the old power blocks would prevail.

The election results in Northern Nigeria came as a shock for most Muslim politcians and dignitaries: In wide areas of the Middle Belt (Kaduna, Niger, Benue, Gongola, Plateau), which had been regarded as a more or less safe haven of the NPC-NPN in former elections, Christian candidates who either had the support of the Christian Association of Nigeria (CAN) or sympathized with it won the elections. These candidates had been presented in the churches of the North as the "right" candidates and had also been allowed to speak during preaching campaigns by the CAN. The CAN had also arranged that in important constituencies only one Christian candidate was nominated for the office of the Local Government Chairman. Thus a second Christian candidate was beaten up in Kaduna by the supporters of the CAN's candidate, John Aboki, as he had refused to step back in favor of Aboki. Once in the hospital he announced his retirement from his campaign (Inteview Kafawi, 20 Apr. 1988). The Muslims, by contrast, in most constituencies had the choice between two or even more candidates. This led to a splitting of the Muslim vote and had the effect that even in areas where the Muslims had a majority of the population, the Christian candidate could obtain the simple majority of the votes. The splitting of the Muslim vote not only had political grounds but was also caused by the religious conflict between the Sufi brotherhoods and the 'Yan Izala. A a statement by Shaykh Dahiru Bauchi on the radio in particular had serious repercussions on the voting behavior of the Muslims. His appeal was expressed in the following terms:

> Thus as far as what he [Gumi] has said, namely that one should vote only for a good Muslim not for a Christian, it has to be said that according to his [Gumi's] opinion a good Muslim is a follower of the 'Yan Izala group. According to our own opinion and in the faith of all Muslims in this country we should, when we come together [to vote], not vote for one of Gumi's men, because he would be a member of the 'Yan Izala group. If in one place there are three candidates, one Muslim, one Christian and one Izala, then one can make one's choice among all three of them but one should not vote for the candidate of the Izala. (Amana, 15 Jan. 1988: 8, translation by Asma'u Garba Saeed)

What was remarkable in this appeal by Shaykh Dahiru Bauchi was not only that he made a clear distinction between "Muslims," "Christians," and "Izala," thereby implicitly categorizing the 'Yan Izala as non-Muslims, but that he expressly referred to another appeal by Abubakar Gumi. The latter had appealed to the voters to vote only for "Muslim" candidates. According to the understanding of the 'Yan Izala the followers of the Sufi brotherhoods could not be regarded as Muslims, and thus this appeal of Gumi in reality meant to vote only for candidates of the 'Yan Izala. These statements by Gumi and Bauchi had the effect that the supporters of the two conflict parties either abstained or voted for the Christian candidate if their own candidate had only a poor chance to win the local elections or if they did not have a candidate of their own at all, to prevent the victory by the candidate of the opposite group. In Kaduna Local Government (LG), an area with a tiny Muslim majority within the population, the candidate of the CAN, John Aboki, thus won the elections as many supporters of the Tijâniyya, which had only a weak base in Kaduna, preferred to vote for him rather than to give their votes to Malam Sule Bako, the candidate of the 'Yan Izala (*Newswatch*, 28 Dec. 1987; *New Nigerian*, 8 Jan. 1988). The victory of the Gwari Aboki in Kaduna, one of the most important centers of the 'Yan Izala in Northern Nigeria, was such a shock that immediately after the elections influential circles of the Kaduna Mafia under the leadership of the editor-in-chief of the conservative weekly *Hotline* (Hausa edition: *Rana*), Malam Hassan Sani Kontagora demanded an inquiry into the elections with the intention of declaring the results and the election of Aboki as void (*The Reporter*, 12 Apr. 1988).

This kind of vote determined the result not only in Kaduna but also in other Middle Belt areas. Thus in Numan LG (Gongola) Christian candidates won nine of eleven ward districts, in Zing LG (Gongola) five of eight ward districts were won by Christian candidates, and even in Yola, a traditional center of Islam in Gongola state, three of seven wards fell to Christian candidates (*This Week*, 8 Feb. 1988; *Nigerian Economist*, 1 June 1987). The result of the elections in Ali Kazaure ward of Jos LG can be regarded as typical: Of a total number of about 7,000 votes, 3,138 (44%) fell to the only Christian candidate. The remainder of about 3,900 votes (56%) were split up among four Muslim candidates, the strongest among them obtaining 2,053 votes (29%) and the second strongest 1,557 votes (22%) (*Newswatch*, 28 Dec. 1987).

Election results of this kind had the effect that wide areas of the Middle Belt, and here regions even with a Muslim majority, fell to Christian candidates. As the victories of the NPC and the NPN until the 1983 federal elections had been possible only with the support of the votes won in this part of the country, the victory of the Christian candidates meant that these votes would not so easily fall to the dominant party in the North in the future. Therefore the chances of a victory of a NPC-NPN type of party in the next federal elections were put into question. This again could mean that for the first time in the history of Nigeria an elected president of the country would not be a Muslim from the North as Tafawa Balewa and Shehu Shagari had been. In fact, Ibrahim Ṣâliḥ commented on the lesson of the LG elections of 1987 with the following words: "What happened in Kaduna during the local government elections is enough lesson to us and unless something is done to achieve unity in the Ummah something worse may happen in the rest of the elections" (*The Pen,* 1989, no. 1). The election results of December 1987 and the possible consequences shocked the politically influential circles in the North to such a degree that they started to exert pressure on the ṭuruq and the 'Yan Izala to terminate their quarrels for good. Under the mediation of Ibrahim Dasuki, the secretary general of the JNI, the NSCIA, and the Council of 'Ulama' a mass rally was organized in Kaduna on 2 January 1988, with the intention of establishing a support fund for the Muslim victims of the Kafancan riots. About 1,500,000 people took part in this first mass rally of the Council of 'Ulama'. Before the eyes of the Muslims present, Abubakar Gumi and Dahiru Bauchi embraced each other and thus demonstrated the formal reconciliation of both sides in public. This reconciliation was sealed under the auspices of the Council of 'Ulama' during another rally for the establishment of a support fund for the extension of the Sultan Bello mosque in Kaduna on 16 January 1988. The major opponents, Gumi, Nasiru Kabara, Ibrahim Ṣâliḥ, Bauchi, and Khalifa Isma'il Ibrahim, agreed to end their disputes. The formula of compromise was: "No one person could claim to know everything in Islam and should therefore restrict themselves to the areas of their specialization" (*New Nigerian,* 19 Jan. 1988).

This resolution of mutual noninterference and of respect for the respective positions was then signed by these scholars in presence of Ahmad Lemu, Bashir Sambo, and Abdulkadir Orire, all members of the Council of 'Ulama', Ibrahim Dasuki (JNI,

NSCIA, Council of 'Ulama'), as well as the emirs of Kano, Zaria, Daura, and Yauri. Thus for the first time the influence of the Council of 'Ulama' had proved stronger than the religious divisions in Northern Nigeria. In the following months the Council of 'Ulama' started a series of further mass rallies in several cities of the North (Kano, Maiduguri, Jos, Sokoto) to gather support for the further expansion of the Council of 'Ulama' and the support fund. During these rallies the different speakers repeatedly demanded a revision of the judgments of the Karibi-Whyte Tribunal and the liberation of the Muslim detainees (see communique of the Council of 'Ulama', appendix 6). These rallies were characterized in particular by the presence of many MSS groups, a broad spectrum of political and religious dignitaries, and the elite of the new generation of Muslim intellectuals. With the support of these mass rallies the Council of 'Ulama' was able to strengthen its claim to lead the Muslims in the North politically and religiously. The public reconciliation of the leading religious scholars in Northern Nigeria was strengthened by a series of "private" visits: On 6 May 1990, Abubakar Gumi paid a surprise visit to his old adversary Nasiru Kabara in his house in Kano. This sudden end of their feud led Bature Idris Gana, reporter of the Kano daily *The Triumph,* to comment, "Dare daya Allah kanyi Bature" (If God wishes, he may turn [a black man] into a white man) (*The Triumph,* 27 May 1990). Kabara continued this policy of private contacts by visiting a number of Tijâni scholars, such as Dahiru Bauchi and Ibrahim Ṣâliḥ (*The Triumph,* 14 June 1990). In this way the political reconciliation between the different religious movements in Northern Nigeria was deepened and the notion of Muslim unity enhanced.

The energetic appearance of the Council of 'Ulama' and its gradual ascendancy over the political and religious demands of the Muslims in Northern Nigeria since late 1986 also led to a revitalization of the NSCIA. Through the policy of the Council of 'Ulama' not only the Sufi brotherhoods and the 'Yan Izala were put under pressure, but also the emirs who were united with the NSCIA (Interview Kafawi, 20 Apr. 1988). In April 1988 a meeting of the NSCIA under the chairmanship of the Shehu of Bornu, al-Ḥâjj Muhammad al-Kanimi, took place during which the emirs adopted an updated list of the demands of the Council of 'Ulama' of 1986. Among other things they asked for the implementation of the following points:

1. The introduction of the Islamic calendar.
2. The establishment of "Sharî'a Courts of Appeal" in all Muslim areas.
3. The reshuffling of the directorate of the mass mobilization campaign of the Babangida administration (MAMSER) which was under the management of Dr. Jerry Gana.
4. The introduction of Islamic religious education for all Muslim pupils.
5. The revision of the judgments of the Karibi-Whyte Tribunal.
6. The introduction of school uniforms which would conform with Islamic prescriptions of ḥijâb for all Muslim children.

With these demands the NSCIA subsequently adopted the political line of the Council of 'Ulama'. Apart from this, the emirs at that time would most likely not have had the power to oppose the movement of unity initiated by the Council of 'Ulama' even if they had wished to do so. If they did not want to be accused of blocking or preventing the unity of the Muslims the emirs had no choice but to recognize the positions of the Council of 'Ulama' and to jump on the bandwagon.

Although the success of the Council of 'Ulama' since 1986 is connected primarily with the changing political conditions in Nigeria, it was also favored by the social evolution in Northern Nigeria since the 1970s. One of the most important factors in this social change apart from the political mobilization of Muslim women is the numerical growth of the Western-educated Muslims who are not affiliated with one of the existing religious movements and who furthermore reject the religious conflict on account of its political implications. These nonaffiliated Muslims are recruited among a number of different social and religious groups of the population. There are, first, the bureaucrats in Kaduna who were groomed by Ahmadu Bello, the Grand Kadis of the "Sharî'a Courts of Appeal," and the young entrepreneurs and businessmen in Northern Nigeria. They may, due to their usually conservative political and social orientation, be regarded as the real heirs of Ahmadu Bello. Among them are personalities such as the Grand Kadis of Abuja (Bashir Sambo), Niger (Ahmad Lemu), and Kano (Hassan Gwarzo), the secretary general of the JNI and the NSCIA (Ibrahim Dasuki), and the new Nigerian Ambassador to Saudi Arabia (S. A. S. Galadanci) (Interview Nur Alkali, 23 Mar. 1988). In the last few years a group of young and radical Muslim intellectuals emerging from the ranks of the MSS have joined this first group. These young men have their centers mainly in the high schools and universities in Sokoto, Kano, and Zaria in particular; Maiduguri, Jos, and Ilorin are centers of lesser importance. They stressed the relevance of the jihâd of Usman dan Fodio as an example of the development of a new Islamic social model for Nigeria since the 1980s, and they rejected the religious conflict between the 'Yan Izala and the Sufi brotherhoods because it weakened the unity of the Muslims. Leading personalities of this second group of nonaffiliated Muslims were Ibrahim Sulaiman (CILS, ABU Zaria), Usman Muhammad Bugaje (Islamic Trust of Nigeria, Zaria), Muhammad Sadiq al-Kafawi (CILS, ABU Zaria), I. N. Sada (CILS, ABU Zaria), Dr. Umar Bello (Center of Islamic Studies, Sokoto), Aliyu Dauda (School of General Studies, BUK), and Danjuma Maiwada (Faculty of Education, BUK) (Interviews Sulaiman, 9 Sept. 1987, Sada, 20 Apr. 1988, and Bugaje, 7 Sept. 1987). Ibrahim Sulaiman in particular has acquired a leading role among the Muslim intellectuals in the North as one of their spokesmen. Sulaiman was national president of the MSS in 1973/74 and continued to speak for the MSS. In many newspaper articles and lectures he has formulated ideas which were later adopted by the MSS, the Council of 'Ulama', Muslim politicians, and the FOMWAN. Thus in a lecture on the topic of "women and society" which he gave in Kano in 1978 he supported the emancipation of Muslim women within the framework of Islam and thereby voiced ideas which were adopted by FOMWAN almost to the word seven years later: "The reconstruction of the society . . . must begin with the re-assessment of the role of the Muslim women. It is to be noted here, that any emergent social order . . . has to undertake bold and energetic steps to raise the status of women and free them from the chains of custom and tradition invented by men for their own gratification" (Sulaiman 1978: 1). In other speeches and articles Ibrahim Sulaiman openly criticized the collaboration of the religious scholars with the regime, the corruption of the ruling elite, the decay of morals and values, and the division of the Muslims in numerous factions. Recently Ibrahim Sulaiman has boosted his image as a historian by publishing two books on the history and legacy of the Sokoto jihâd (see also his article on the development of Islam in Nigeria in the appendix). The group of nonaffiliated Muslims finally experienced a further boost by the dissidents from the conflicting parties themselves. Not all Muslims who have given up their affiliation with one of the Sufi brotherhoods automatically joined the 'Yan Izala. Some of them disassociated themselves from the authority structures and practices of the ṭuruq and subsequently subscribed to a more intellectual form of Sufism (Interview Karfi, 10 Sept. 1987). These dissidents from the ranks of the ṭuruq were joined in the 1980s by a number of former 'Yan Izala supporters who refused to rejoin their former Sufi brotherhoods. They had left the 'Yan Izala for different reasons: either because their hopes for a rapid career within the organization were disappointed, or because the strategies of the 'Yan Izala were regarded by them as being too militant, too unreflected, or too compromising, or because they were not willing to accept the undisputed authority of Abubakar Gumi and his open support for Shehu Shagari and General Babangida (Interview Umar, 8 Mar. 1988).

These social developments have also influenced the structure of the Council of 'Ulama': It attracted primarily representatives of the new Muslim intelligentsia from the universities, the administration, and the judiciary. Besides the latter there were some representatives of the religious movements, but they did not have a majority. The emirs were not represented at all in the Council of 'Ulama'. The majority of the Western-educated Muslim functionaries and intellectuals were able to develop under the pressure of the events since 1987, a dynamism from which the other religious and political groups could no longer disassociate themselves. In the face of this, the Council of 'Ulama' succeeded in propagating the unity of the Muslims as the supreme and most important aim of the Muslims in Northern Nigeria and in denouncing the conflict between the 'Yan Izala and the Sufi brotherhoods as a dangerous division of the Muslims and as a serious threat to the legacy of Ahmadu Bello's politics. The dynamism of the Council of 'Ulama' was made possible not only by the fact that the council was able to act rapidly and without having to make special references to the interests of other influential pressure groups like the emirs, but also because many members of the council were at the same time represented in the JNI and in the NSCIA. Thus not only did Abubakar Gumi have a seat in the General Purpose Committee (GPC) of the Council of 'Ulama', but he was also the National Chairman of the JNI and a member of the NSCIA. Likewise the Grand Kadi of Abuja, Bashir Sambo, was a member in all three organizations (Interview Biu, 21 Aug. 1987). In late 1987 about one hundred scholars were represented in the Council of 'Ulama' and about thirty of them had seats in the most important working committee of the council, the GPC. The organization of membership to this committee shows that the council was able to successfully bring together representatives of the different religious groups under one roof and has thus evaded the danger of delimiting specific groups. The chairman of the GPC was Hassan Gwarzo (Grand Kadi Kano), and his representative was Ibrahim Ṣâliḥ (Maiduguri). The office of the secretary-general was held by Dr. Umar Bello (Sokoto), and his representative was Muhammad Sadiq al-Kafawi (Zaria). Apart from these individuals, Gumi, Nasiru Kabara, and Dahiru Bauchi, as religious leaders also had seats in the GPC, as well as the S. A. S. Galadanci and all Grand Kadis of the exisiting Sharî'a Courts of

Appeal in Nigeria (Interview Kafawi, 11 Sept. 1987). Thus the representatives of the modern Muslim intelligentsia and of the national Islamic judiciary had a clear majority in the council without excluding the representatives of the religious movements.

The Council of 'Ulama' will be able to maintain its guiding role only as long as the Muslims in the North have the impression that the external pressures on them from the Christians and from a secular government continue to exist. Only under these frame conditions will the council be in a position to condemn the conflict between the 'Yan Izala and the Sufi brotherhoods as an actual threat to the unity of the Muslims. If these external pressures should decrease the principal still-existing tensions and contradictions between the conflicting religious parties will break out again and thus destroy the superficial illusion of Muslim unity. How easily such a conflict may erupt has been shown by the events which took place in Zuru LG in Sokoto state: The followers of the 'Yan Izala and of the ṭuruq had agreed upon a common utilization of the only Friday mosque of Zuru in turn for the holding of their tafsîr meetings during Ramadhân. On 23 April 1988 a clash took place between the followers of both groups as both sides had erroneously assumed that it was their own turn on that specific day. In the ensuing fight three people were killed, one hundred wounded, and fifty houses and numerous cars burned (*The Guardian,* 24 Apr. 1988). In contrast to the Argungu riots of 1965 and the Kafancan riots of 1987 the conflict in Zuru was not used for political means, either by the Northern media or by the religious leaders. This shows that a new internal conflict was not intended or welcomed by any camp at that specific point of time. The commitment to unity was stronger than the will to continue the old conflict.

Developments since 1986 show that a growing group of Western-educated Muslim intellectuals took an increasing part in the political and religious life of Nigeria. Many of the Muslims who could be counted among this new group of nonaffiliated Muslims have originated from the MSS or have disassociated themselves from either the ṭuruq or the 'Yan Izala. For them the religious conflict was no longer of much importance, but they emphasized the need for political unity of the Muslims. In this respect they could be characterized as the real heirs of Ahmadu Bello.

The Muslims' striving for unity received a further stimulation by the succession of Ibrahim Dasuki as seventeenth Sultan of Sokoto in 1988. When the sixteenth sultan, Sir Abubakar Siddiq, died on 1 November 1988, after a reign of almost fifty years, Ibrahim Dasuki was included in the inner circle of aspirants for the succession on account of his good connections with the military goverment of General Babangida. Other candidates were Muazu Lamido, the Sarkin Gabas of Sokoto, Shehu Malami, the Sarkin Sudan, as well as Muhammadu Maccido, the Sarkin Kudu and eldest son of the deceased Sultan. The latter was also favored by the population of Sokoto (*New Nigerian,* 7 Nov. 1988). When the electoral council met on 3 November 1988, and when the local radio station Rima Radio announced the election of Muhammadu Maccido as new Sultan of Sokoto on 4 November, people thus began to celebrate. This soon turned out to be false, and on 6 December Ibrahim Dasuki was officially proclaimed legal successor to Sir Abubakar Siddiq as seventeenth sultan. As a result riots broke out in Sokoto, and heavy clashes took place between rioters and the security forces over the next two days. The rioters demonstrated in the streets of Sokoto chanting the slogan "Bamuso" ("We do not want him"). They attacked the Rima Radio station, the market, the Sokoto Urban Development Authority, Dasuki's house, the Bank of Credit and Commerce International (BCCI), the Dasuki Primary School, and the central prison of Sokoto where they liberated about eight hundred detainees (ibid.). Only after the intervention of the army and the imposition of a dawn-to-dawn curfew could peace be restored. Officially ten people were counted dead, and the material damage ran to millions of naira (ibid.: 10 Nov. 1988). In a commentary on Dasuki's enthronization on 14 November 1988, his unpopularity was explained: "The popular impression was that Alhaji Ibrahim Dasuki . . . was imposed on the Sokoto kingmakers and the Sokoto State Council of Chiefs from Lagos. . . . The aversion to him especially among the Muslim intelligentsia, [is] based on his strong Zionist business connections and on the impression . . . that the Bank of which he is chairman, the "Bank of Credit and Commerce International," has a somewhat dubious reputation for sharp practice" (ibid.: 15 Nov. 1988).

After his takeover Ibrahim Dasuki started to shake off the burden of his past and to unite the Muslims throughout Nigeria with a new, dynamic policy. He stepped back as chairman of BCCI, engaged himself in numerous public declarations for the reconciliation of the hostile camps in Sokoto, visited all local governments in Sokoto state, protested publicly against the inflated expenditures for the bride price and the naming ceremonies, and started a thorough reorganization of the JNI and the NSCIA whose national president he had become by his accession to the throne of the Sultan of Sokoto. Dasuki also tried to silence his internal enemies in Sokoto by deposing Shehu Malami, one of his competitors in the contest for the throne, as district head of Wurno and Sarkin Sudan in September 1989. The deposition of Shehu Malami was justified on grounds of "high-level indiscipline" as he had allegedly refused to lead the village heads from his district to Sokoto in order to honor the new sultan (*Newswatch,* 16 Oct. 1989). In the place of Shehu Malami, Sultan Ibrahim Dasuki appointed a son of the deceased sultan, Abubakar Cika Soro, who had the confidence of the local population. This appointment temporarily contributed to the reconciliation between Dasuki and the family of the deceased sultan and his supporters. Dasuki also started to actively intervene in the Nigerian national politics. Thus, on account of his pressure the importation of Salman Rushdie's book *The Satanic Verses* was prohibited in April 1989 (*West Africa,* 3 Apr. 1989), and at the national conference of the NSCIA in early November 1989 in Ibadan, Dasuki again demanded the release of the Muslim prisoners who had been detained after the Kafancan riots, as well as the prohibition of "inciting and inflammatory publications" (*The Reporter,* 9 Nov. 1989). It was a notable success for Dasuki when the radical MSS leader Ibrahim al-Zakzaki was prematurely released from detention in December 1989 (*The Democrat,* 10 Dec. 1989). With the election of Lateef Adegbite as secretary general of the NSCIA as successor of Dasuki, for the first time a Muslim from Southern Nigeria was elected into this prestigious position, thus enforcing the national character of the NSCIA.

Only three weeks later, in early December 1989, the first conference on "Islam in Africa" took place under the auspicies of Ibrahim Dasuki in Abuja. Numerous delegations from many West African countries took part, as well as delegates from Saudi Arabia, Libya, Egypt (the Shaykh al-Azhar), Iran, Great Britain (Islamic Council), the Sudan, Tunisia (Rashid Ghanoushi of the Mouvement du Tendance Islamique), and even the Caribbean. The aim of the conference was to discuss problems and perspectives of Islam in Africa, to improve the continental communication networks and the exchange of ideas, knowledge, and information, and to set up an institutional forum for discussion for all African Muslims (*The Reporter,* 1 Dec. 1989). A resolution agreed on by all participants was passed to transform the conference into a permanent institution with Abuja as the seat of the conference. For this purpose a secretariat was established which was managed by among others Ibrahim Sulaiman and Usman Bugaje as Nigerian representatives (*Today,* 3 Dec. 1989). Among the Nigerian participants of the conference were, aside from Dasuki and General Babangida and the above-mentioned scholars, Ibrahim Ṣâliḥ, Dahiru Bauchi, Nasiru Kabara, and Abubakar Gumi. In this way the unity of the Muslims in Nigeria was emphasized once more (*The Reporter,* 2 Dec. 1989). In February 1990 Dasuki again underlined his role as leader of the Muslims in Nigeria by heading a national delegation of the NSCIA to Cairo during a conference of the Higher Council of Islamic Affairs.

Nigeria's religious and political development since the late 1980s has not only witnessed a certain détente in the relationship between ṭuruq and reformers but also a remarkable increase in Muslim-Christian tensions. These tensions had already surfaced in the Kafancan riots of 1987 and were stirred up again in the context of the "Islam in Africa" Conference. A few months after the conference a fake communique was published, which listed a number of alleged Muslim demands for the further development of the "member nations of the Islam in Africa Conference," namely:

> To ensure that the appointment of only Muslims into strategic national and international posts of member nations.
>
> To eradicate in all its forms and ramifications all non-Muslim religions in member nations (such religions include Christianity, Aḥmadiyya, and other tribal modes of worship unacceptable to Muslims).
>
> To ensure that only Muslims are elected to all political posts of member nations.
>
> To ensure the declaration of Nigeria (the 24th African and 46th world member of the OIC) as a Federal Islamic Sultanate, at a convenient date at any time after 28 March, 1990, with the Sultan of Sokoto enthroned as the Sultan and Supreme Sovereign of Nigeria.
>
> To ensure the ultimate replacement of all Western forms of legal and judicial systems with the Sharia in all member nations before the next Islam in Africa conference. (quoted in *The Reporter*, 11 June 1990)

These demands were in clear contradiction to the official communique of the conference. The choice of words furthermore suggests that Christian groups wanted to use the occasion of the Islam in Africa Conference not only to discredit the conference itself, but also to point out to Nigeria's Christians the radicality and intolerance of the Muslims. In particular, the call for the eradication of all non-Muslim religions violated all existing Islamic norms defining the relationship between Muslims and non-Muslims. In a denial by the permanent bureau of the Islam in Africa Conference "some irresponsible organizations and individuals" were made responsible for the fake communiqué. They were accused of instigating disputes between the religious communities and of misleading the public as well as intending to create chaos (*The Republican*, 11 June 1990). The fake communiqué of the Islam in African Conference spotlighted the preoccupations of Christian groups in Nigeria in the face of Muslim efforts to unite and develop a sort of Muslim political unity. In times of stress these Christian preoccupations were obviously easy to mobilize and instrumentalize for religiopolitical purposes by radical Christian organizations. Tensions between Christian and Muslim communities consequently developed into further Kafancan-style riots in Northern Nigeria, such as the disturbances in Bauchi in April 1991 and the riots in Kano in October 1991 (see Loimeier 1992: 74–77).

The development of Muslim unity in Nigeria was shaken by an abortive coup d'état by a group of army officers. On the night of 22 April 1990 units of the Nigerian army under the command of Major Gideon G. Orkar, a Tiv from Benue state, attacked the seat of the government in Lagos, the Dodan Barracks, and for some time occupied the Federal Radio Corporation of Nigeria in Lagos. In their public announcement the rebels demanded, among a number of issues, an end to the discrimination against the populations in the Middle Belt and of Southern Nigeria by the Northern Muslims, and proclaimed the temporary excision of the five Northern states—Sokoto, Katsina, Kano, Bauchi, and Bornu—from the federation, the deposition of Sultan Ibrahim Dasuki, and the installation of his competitor Muhammadu Maccido as new sultan (*Newswatch,* 7 May 1990). In addition they criticized the dismissal of army generals Domkat Bali and Dogonyaro, both Langtang from Plateau state, from the cabinet of General Babangida on 29 December 1989, and the alleged takeover of the ruling Armed Forces Ruling Council by Muslim officers (*West Africa,* 30 Apr. 1990). Although loyal units of the army succeeded after some hours of fighting in crushing the coup, the fact that a large number of the rebels stemmed from Bendel, Benue, and other Middle Belt areas, together with the specific demands they made, showed how great the preoccupation in this region still was about the alleged growth of power of the Muslims in Nigeria.

In the course of the ongoing process of transition to civilian rule in 1992 and 1993 religious issues have increasingly lost their appeal to both the public and politicians. This development parallels the political development of the late 1970s when, in the context of the establishment of the second republic, religious issues were de-emphazized in the public debate, while political activity gained in importance. Nigeria's second transition period from military to civilian rule was carefully prepared by a number of communal and regional elections for local government councils and state assemblies in 1990 and 1991, thus giving a new generation of politicians the opportunity to form alliances. After the lifting of the ban on political parties in 1989 numerous new political organizations had formed. Only thirteen of them, though, met the requirements for the formation of political parties imposed by the National Electoral Commission (NEC). After a period of party disputes President Babangida, on 7 October 1989, decided to dissolve all of them. On 9 October the president surprised the Nigerian public again by announcing the foundation of two artificial parties, the "progressive" Social Democratic Party and the "conservative" National Republican Convention, which were to be the only parties permitted. This decision was influenced by the latent regionalistic and religious disputes in Nigeria and had the objective of forcing politicians from different religious and ethnic backgrounds to come together and form interregional as well as interreligious alliances (Abun-Nasr 1993: 36–37). Political developments after 1991 confirmed Babangida's political strategies as the two artificial parties in fact overcame regional and religious strife and started to incorporate political alliances from all parts of the federation irrespective of ethnic or religious affiliations. In 1992 and 1993 no major religious riots among Muslims or between Muslims and Christians were recorded in Nigeria. The decrease in religious disputes in 1992 and 1993 does not, however, imply that religious differences have suddenly disappeared from Nigeria. They have just become dormant due to the new political conditions and may easily be reactivated should the need arise and political conditions change.

Nigeria's second transition to civilian rule was accompanied by a number of administrative measures such as the creation of a further nine federal states, thus dividing Kano state, for instance, into old Kano and new Jigawa, as well as the creation of additional local governments, raising their number to about six hundred (*West Africa,* 8 Sept. 1991). After a long and meticulous preparation a new census was carried out in November 1991. The census results were published by the National Population Commission in March 1992 and came as a surprise for many observers familiar with the United Nations population statistics on Nigeria, which had put Nigeria's population in 1988 at about 112 million. The new census revealed that there were only 88.5 million Nigerians. However, the census results were accepted by the overwhelming majority of Nigerians on several accounts. The previous censuses had vastly exaggerated Nigeria's population, as federal government allocations to state budgets had been connected to their respective populations. This link had been abolished by the Babangida administration. In contrast to former censuses, questions about religious and ethnic affiliation were not included in the new census. Thus incentives to artificially boost population figures in order to show one's ethnic or religious strength did not exist. Finally, the census was carried out by a comparatively great number of counters and a curfew had been imposed during the counting process, thus preventing double-counts due to migration (*West Africa,* 5 April 1992).

On 4 July 1992, general elections were held for the two new chambers of the future Nigerian parliament, the House of Representatives and the Senate. The elections confirmed the consolidation of the two existing parties and gave the SDP a clear lead over the NRC in both houses. In the House of Representatives the SDP won 315 seats against the NRC's 260, and in the Senate the SDP could lay claim to 51 out of 88 seats (*West Africa,* 19 July 1992). Again, when the candidates of both parties for the presidential elections were finally elected, the two-party system was able to overcome past ethnoreligious disputes. Both candidates for the presidential elections turned out to be Muslim, Alhaji Bashir Tofa from Kano for the NRC and M. K. O. Abiola from Abeokuta for the SDP. Both candidates had succeeded in their quest for leadership within their respective parties as they had managed to win support from other political networks from all parts of the federation. In particular, Abiola was able to win over politicians and supporters of the former NEPU-PRP networks in the North. By naming Baba Gana Kingibe of Maiduguri to be his running mate he also gained important support from Bornu.

Abiola had begun his career as the Nigerian representative of the International Telephone and Telegraph Corporation (ITT) in 1971. During the return to civilian rule in the late 1970s he had switched over to politics and turned out to be the most important supporter of the NPN and Shehu Shagari in the Yoruba area. In 1980 he set up a newspaper of his own, the *National Concord.* His hopes to be nominated Shagari's successor in the 1983 presidential elections were disappointed, however. After the Buhari coup on 31 December 1983, Abiola started to emphazize his Muslim identity, initiating, for instance, another campaign for sharî'a courts of appeal in Yorubaland in his newspaper. Thus he intended to increase his political chances as a "Southern Muslim" politician in the next presidential elections in anticipation of prospective "Northern Muslim" or "Southern Christian" candidates (Loimeier and Reichmuth 1993: 63). As the NRC presidential candidate in fact turned out to be a Northern Muslim, Abiola's chances to win the presidency grew considerably. Also, Tofa was regarded not only as an extremely rich business tycoon from Kano, but also as a very conservative politican, and, in addition, many Nigerians thought him to be "Babangida's candidate" (*West Africa,* 18 April 1993). His effort to instrumentalize Islam for his political purposes in the preelection period misfired, as Abiola had already built up an image as a sponsor of numerous Muslim religious and educational projects. Also, the League of Imams and Alfas had in 1984 conferred the title of "Baba Adini of Yorubaland" on Abiola on account of his efforts for the advancement of Islam (Loimeier and Reichmuth 1993: 63–64). Abiola's strategies seemed to bear fruit when the national electoral commission, on Monday, 14 June 1993, published interim results of the presidential elections, which had taken place on 12 June. The official figures gave Abiola a "commanding" lead of 4.3 million votes against Tofa's 2.3 million. Abiola had also swept the polls in eleven out of fifteen declared states and he had won a comfortable 52.8 percent majority in Tofa's own state, Kano (*West Africa,* 27 June and 4 July 1993).

However, on 23 June 1993, General Babangida, who obviously saw his hopes to enthrone his candidate foiled, canceled the presidential elections and declared the preliminary results unvalid. The widespread protest that supported Abiola's claim to the presidency forced Babangida, however, to hand over power to a so-called interim government under Ernest Shonekan on 27 August 1993, exactly eight years after he had come to power on 27 August 1985. Shonekan's unwillingness to accept Abiola's claims to the presidency and to acknowledge the results of the presidential elections kept tensions in Nigiera alive. This impasse was finally settled by yet another military coup on 17 November 1993, when General Sani Abacha took power. Abacha soon disappointed all hopes of an impending return to civilian rule; he immediately dissolved all institutions created by the Babangida administration: local government councils, state governments and state houses, ministries, and the federal parliament, as well as both parties and the national electoral commission (*West Africa,* 5 Dec. 1993). Abacha's takeover of power and harsh style in his first public announcement on 27 November 1993 was commented on by Nigeria's well-known musician Fela Anikulapo-Kuti with irony: "This is the first time that a military leader told the truth to Nigerians: 'Ah tire for oona. I sack efybody. All of oona deh form fool. I close down evythin'. Efybody go home. Ah takin' charge. Thank you.' That is what Nigerian politicians understand. E'good for them" (*West Africa,* 12 Dec. 1993).

The elimination of members of the influential Babangida network from all commanding positions within the army has been one of the major preoccupations of General Abacha. In a first round of army reshuffles in 1993, a son of the Sultan of Sokoto, Colonel M. Sambo Dasuki, former aide-de-camp of the president, was among the dismissed officers (*West Africa,* 12 Dec. 1993). Thus a personal conflict with the Sultan of Sokoto was created. The Abacha-Dasuki conflict was aggravated by the fact that

Abacha supported a lawsuit against the sultan because of Ibrahim Dasuki's long-standing involvement in dubious business activities. He was accused of having embezzled a considerable sum of money in his capacity as chairman of Nigercafe Food (West Africa) Ltd. and as a board member of Afro Continental (Nigeria) Ltd. These companies were alleged to have borrowed about 775 million naira in local and foreign currencies from the Alpha Merchant Bank and the Republican Bank and to have failed to repay the loans (*West Africa*, 5 May 1996). The conflict with the Sultan of Sokoto was finally terminated by Dasukis deposition on 20 April 1996. His successor as nineteenth Sultan of Sokoto was Alhaji Muhammadu Maccido. Ibrahim Dasuki's deposition was justified with a number of charges, namely, "conduct unbecoming of the exalted position of the sultan, poor leadership, unauthorized diplomatic shuttles, alleged misuse of mosque funds, causing disaffection among Muslims, and demeaning the exalted throne through failed bank trials" (*West Africa*, 5 May 1996). Yet these charges have to be regarded as a pretense disguising Abacha's efforts to consolidate his power by removing a powerful representative of the old regime. Dasuki's deposition demonstrated that Nigeria's federal government in the 1990s had acquired such power that it was in a position, instrumentalizing the antagonisms within Sokoto's religiopolitical establishment, to depose even the *Amîr al-mu'minîn*, the Sultan of Sokoto.

6

Conclusion

The Muslim society of Northern Nigeria has experienced a rapid and thorough change in the last decades. After the conquest of the Sokoto empire by the British, the Muslims of Northern Nigeria found themselves living in a secular and Western-oriented system that continues to exist in its basic features. In the new state of Nigeria Muslims are numerically only marginally stronger than other religious groups. As long as they held far-reaching autonomy in the Northern region of Nigeria and as long as they could shape this part of the federation according to their own ideas, the integration of Northern Nigeria into a secular state presented no serious difficulties for the Muslims. The clever policy of Ahmadu Bello even managed to strengthen the dominant conservative party of the North, the Northern People's Congress (NPC), to such an extent that the northern region was able to decisively influence the federal policy after Nigeria's independence in 1960.

Bello's administration was characterized in particular by the efforts of the prime minister to modernize the North. Bello saw in the modernization of the underdeveloped North a precondition for the consolidation of the Jama'ar Arewa, the "Community of the North." Bello's modernization policy involved not only far-reaching administrative reforms, the formation of an efficient bureaucracy, the realization of judicial reforms, and the establishment of new high schools, but also the religious mobilization of the population. New religious organizations, like the Usumaniyya, the Kaduna Council of Malamai, or the Jamâ'at Naṣr al-Islâm (JNI), which were either inspired or founded by Bello, had the aim of overcoming the existing religious contradictions among the Muslims and strengthening their unity. Only a politically and religiously united North could preserve its power to control the economically more dynamic South. Bello knew that the conflicts between the two great Sufi brotherhoods, the Tijâniyya and the Qâdiriyya, could be exploited by the competing political parties. Thus the political unification of the North would be threatened, too. When large parts of the Tijâniyya-Ibrâhîmiyya sympathized with the opposition Northern Elements' Progressive Union (NEPU) party in the 1950s and when a political alliance between the NEPU and parts of the Tijâniyya finally came into being in the 1960s, Bello attempted every means of obstructing this development which endangered his policy of unification: the Emir of Kano, whose connections with the Tijâniyya were particularily close, was forced to step down, the regionalistic Kano People's Party (KPP) was smashed with bureaucratic and other means, and qabḍ, the Tijâniyya-Ibrâhîmiyya's practice of prayer with arms folded, was religiously stigmatized by the qabḍ resolution of the Kaduna Council of Malamai.

The social development of the northern region also led to the development of religious reform movements within both Sufi brotherhoods. These reform movements within the Tijâniyya-Ibrâhîmiyya and the Qâdiriyya-Nâṣiriyya tried to find answers to the multiple challenges of the new era. In a bitter struggle for supremacy the networks of the Tijâniyya-Ibrâhîmiyya and the Qâdiriyya-Nâṣiriyya strove to extend their networks for a modern Islamic education of the Muslims. Both reform movements established connections to external centers of authority and thus enhanced the integration of the Muslims into the religious and political development of a greater Islamic world. The competition between the movements and their respective networks led to not only the religious but also the political mobilization of the Muslims in Northern Nigeria. Since the 1950s the religious scholars together with their supporters have taken active part in politics and become sought-after partners for the political parties. Bello, who hoped to win the support of the religious scholars for his own political aims, increased the political reevaluation of the religious scholars.

These conditions were destroyed by the military coup and Bello's assassination in 1966. The regions were dissolved and replaced by federal states whose political weight was small in comparison to the old regions. With Bello's assassination, Northern Nigeria had lost the only politician who had had the authority and the power to unite the North under his leadership. Nevertheless the new bureaucratic elite that had been raised by Bello relatively successfully tried to conserve his legacy and maintain the political unity of the North. With the election of Shehu Shagari as president and the victory of the National Party of Nigeria (NPN) in the 1979 elections, the North again gained control of the political leadership in the federation. In the religious sphere, however, the superficial unity that had been maintained with great difficulties by Bello rapidly disintegrated. Immediately after Bello's death the Grand Kadi of the northern region, Abubakar Gumi, began to attack the Sufi brotherhoods as carriers of the bida' (evil innovations) in Islam. He initiated an ambitious campaign to reform Islam in Nigeria with an aim, among others, of destroying the Sufi brotherhoods. Under the pressure of Gumi's attacks the ṭarîqas stopped their internal quarrels and in the late 1970s formed a common front against Gumi and his supporters. The Sufi brotherhoods managed to prevent the takeover of the JNI by Gumi and his followers and to thwart his ambitions of a career in the national judicial system. In reaction, Gumi's supporters in 1978 established an organization of their own, the Jamâ'at Izâlat al-Bid'a wa-Iqâmat as-Sunna (Hausa: 'Yan Izala) in order to transfer the struggle against the ṭarîqas to the grassroots level. In their religious orientation the 'Yan Izala were essentially based on Gumi's major programmatic work, *al-'Aqîda aṣ-ṣaḥîḥa,* in which Gumi carried out a vigorous religious attack against the bida'.

The conflicts of the 1950s and the 1960s had already demonstrated the importance of the mastery of religious argumentation for the carrying out of internal power struggles. The qabḍ-sadl dispute between the Tijâniyya-Ibrâhîmiyya and the Qâdiriyya-Nâṣiriyya as well as the question of ikhtilâṭ (mixing of men and women in public) in the conflict between Nasiru Kabara and 'Ali Kumasi (both leaders of the Qâdiriyya) or the quarrel about tayammum (ritual ablution with sand) with the Sultan of Sokoto triggered by Abubakar Gumi were religious conflicts. In all of them the realization of political, social, and personal ambitions was an important motivating factor. As argumentation was based on religious issues, these conflicts have shown that religious teaching and the symbolic system of Islam, as well as religious arguments, were still a hot area for dispute even after several decades of colonization and modernization. This also holds true for the more recent conflict between the ṭuruq and the 'Yan Izala. Gumi and the 'Yan Izala have legitimated their attacks on the Sufi brotherhoods with the argument for the necessity of reforming Islam. The criticism of certain practices or teachings of the ṭuruq is consistently supported by religious arguments. Nevertheless the effect of Gumi's campaign had an essentially social character and thus threatened the interests of the leaders of the Sufi brotherhoods and their networks in a very direct way. They therefore reacted not only with religious treatises but also defended their movements on the political and social level.

The ferocious attacks of the 'Yan Izala, based on the religious arguments of Abubakar Gumi, have put the Sufi brotherhoods, especially the Tijâniyya, under heavy pressure since 1978. Numerous members of the ṭuruq have left their religious leaders and joined either the 'Yan Izala or the growing movement of non-affiliated Muslims. In many regions the social and religious activities of the Tijâniyya have decreased in number and intensity or were entirely given up. The criticism by the 'Yan Izala of certain costly social customs by which the leaders of the ṭuruq profited considerably have in particular engaged Muslims. In the face of the present economic crisis many Muslims have reduced their contributions for marriage or naming ceremonies or have ceased to donate money to their shuyûkh by pointing to the incompability of these customs with the teachings of Islam. The 'Yan Izala did not merely cease to attack the Sufi brotherhoods religiously or to deprive them of the control over the major mosques.

In the context of their educational efforts they set up new Islamic schools and thus created a new social network. The policy of the 'Yan Izala made it easier for many Muslims to give up existing spiritual bonds and to carry out a socioreligious about-face. The young and women in particular used the arguments of the 'Yan Izala in order to legitimate their own emancipation, their rebellion against fathers and husbands, on a religious basis. The protest of the 'Yan Izala against the establishment thus not only destroyed existing structures of authority, but it also created new processes of social emancipation. Since the early 1980s, in opposition to the efforts of the 'Yan Izala, the ṭuruq have increased their own efforts in education and the participation of women. In addition the 'Yan Izala found numerous supporters among the Muslim immigrants to the Sabon Garis (new towns) of the North and among the Western-educated elites in administration, the economy, and the banking sector, which had until then not been accepted by the ṭuruq. The 'Yan Izala offered these social groups new possibilities of orientation and a modern understanding of the faith that was free of mystical bonds to a Sufi-shaikh.

The changes in the Muslim society of Northern Nigeria since the 1950s were legitimated by the religious scholars with religious arguments. The reform efforts of the Tijâniyya-Ibrâhîmiyya, the Qâdiriyya-Nâṣiriyya, and later the 'Yan Izala led to the increasing sensibility among Muslims concerning religious questions and to a general debate about the correctness of certain rites. Emerging from the context of religious disputes, religious arguments were, however, also developed for the modernization of society in Northern Nigeria. Another consequence of the religious conflict of the last few years was the increasing politicization of Islam in Northern Nigeria, and a further, perhaps even more important, development was the activation and mobilization of Muslim women. Muslim politicians and Western-educated Muslim intellectuals of the North have realized that a political predominance of the Muslims in Nigeria is possible only if the potential of Muslim women's voting power is used. Thus in 1988 they forced the parties of religious conflict to shelve their disputes; they have also supported the development of the first Muslim women's organization in Nigeria. The social changes that had been initiated and supported by these political processes are presumably very difficult to turn back. Muslim women in Northern Nigeria have realized their political strength and are willing to use it.

In this respect the conflict between the reformers such as Gumi and the 'Yan Izala and the networks of the Sufi brotherhoods had a positive effect in the sense of a social and political emancipation of groups that until recently have been suppressed or marginalized. This process of emancipation will retain its dynamic as long as the present conditions prevail. The reform of religion and society are thus intrinsically connected with the striving for unity among Muslims which is in return seen as the basis for the conservation of their political power. Islam has in this way taken over a decisive role as a political ideology and as a vehicle of the political identity of its adherents in Northern Nigeria. The programs for the reform of the society as well as the concepts for political unification of the Muslims were formulated with reference to Islam. Leading religious scholars like Abubakar Gumi, Nasiru Kabara, Ibrahim Ṣâliḥ, and Dahiru Bauchi were on account of these general developments able to gain extraordinary influence in Northern Nigeria. Their word was heard and might turn out to be decisive in elections. The future political developments will thus be decisive for the further development of Muslims in Northern Nigeria. In this context Gumi's controversial dictum hits the point: "Siyasa ta fi muhimmanci da salla" (politics is more important than prayer).

Appendix 1

An Example of a Religious Network: The Followers and Supporters of Nasiru Kabara

The following overview of the network of Nasiru Kabara may not be complete, but it gives a relatively comprehensive listing of his most important muqaddamûn and supporters. I begin from the inner circle of followers around Kabara himself: his family and his most important muqaddamûn in Kano. I then present his muqaddamûn in Northern Nigeria, in the rest of Nigeria, and finally those abroad. Data on the followers and muqaddamûn of Kabara up to no. 75 were collected during my fieldwork in Nigeria. Information on his supporters and muqaddamûn in the South (nos. 76–99) were taken from A. E. Ahmed's thesis, and all data concerning his muqaddamûn outside Nigeria (nos. 100–120) were communicated to me by Kabara himself. Qâdiriyya is abbreviated as "Q." and Nasiru Kabara as "N.K." All data refer to the situation as it was in 1988.

1. *Malam Nasiru Kabara.* (For his biography see section 2.3.) He is not only the leader of the Q. in Kano, but also imam of the Dâr al-Q. mosque in Unguwar Kabara. The mosque was constructed in the early nineteenth century by Malam Na Kabara. In the early twentieth century Ibrahim Natsuguni became imam of the mosque, and N.K. was his successor. Since 1968 the mosque has been gradually extended and modernized. Presently the mosque has room for about six hundred people, whereas one thousand may find a place in the compound. On every day of the week, except Thursday and Friday, teaching takes place in the mosque. N.K. himself gives lessons

in tafsîr and ḥadîth (Saturday and Sunday). The majority of his audience are other religious scholars from Kano and the surrounding region. Apart from the regular Friday dhikr, a solemn recitation of the Qur'ân is conducted in the mosque which continues from sundown to sunrise on the last Friday of each month. The Dâr al-Q. mosque is the center for all activities of the Q. in Kano and the base for the celebrations of the Maulid 'Abd al-Qâdir.

2. *M. Shehu Usman Kabara.* A nephew, disciple, and muqaddam of N.K., in 1969/70 Principal of the Gwale Islamiyya Primary School of N.K. He studied in Khartoum, Sudan, and wrote an M.A. thesis on Nasiru Kabara's works. Presently he is a lecturer in the Department of Arabic at BUK. In addition he teaches at the Dâr al-Q. mosque Mondays to Wednesdays.
3. *M. Mukhtar Haruna Kabara.* Teacher at a secondary school in Rano (Kano state), another nephew and muqaddam of N.K.
4. *M. 'Abd al-Latif Muhammad Kabara.* Teacher at the Vocational Training Center in Birnin Kudu (Kano state). A nephew and disciple of N.K. During the Maulid 'Abd al-Qâdir celebrations in Kano he is responsible for the press.
5. *M. Bashiru Naqib Kabara.* A cousin and muqaddam of N.K., died on 28 May 1980. He was leader of the Friday dhikr in the Dâr al-Q. mosque.
6. *M. Basullahi Muhammad Bashir Kabara.* Son of (5) and muqaddam of N.K. Since his father's death he leads the Friday dhikr in the Dâr al-Q. mosque.
7. *M. Dan Yelwa Kabara.* A nephew and muqaddam of N.K. He studied at al-Azhar in Cairo and is employed at BUK as a civil servant.
8. *Shaykh 'Ali Kumasi.* One of the most renowned scholars of the Q. in Kano; imam of the Sanusi Dantata mosque in Unguwar Koki. This mosque was connected with the Ma'had 'ulûm ad-dîn. For his biography see section 2.3.
9. *M. 'Abd ar-Rahman b. 'Ali Kumasi.* A grandson of (8), dis-

ciple of Yusufu Abdullahi Makwarari, and a muqaddam of N.K. By profession he is a civil servant. He studies concurrently in the Department of History at BUK.

10. *M. Yusufu Abdullahi Makwarari.* He is generally regarded as being N.K.'s most important muqaddam in Kano and his local representative: he organizes and leads the activities of the Q. in Kano during N.K.'s absence. In addition he is imam of a mosque of his own in Unguwar Makwarari and one of the most renowned scholars of the Q. in Kano. His emphasis in teaching is on Qur'ân, tafsîr, ḥadîth, and fiqh. He is also the spiritual leader of the extended Makwarari family which belongs to the most important economic pillars of the Q. in Kano. The mosque of Y. A. Makwarari was founded by himself in 1945. It is connected with a school where classes in tafsîr and ḥadîth are offered. These classes are presently attended by about five hundred scholars and students from Kano and the region, who are usually malamai intent on extending their own knowledge. Y. A. Makwarari teaches on all days of the week except Thursdays and Fridays. On Friday afternoon a dhikr is conducted in his mosque.

11. *al-Hajj Ibrahim Isa Abdullahi Makwarari.* One of the most important followers and supporters of N.K., a nephew of (10), managing director of the Bayajidda Amenity Trading Company, and chairman of the managing board of the Q. in Kano. I. I. Abdullahi is personal advisor of N.K. in all organizational and financial affairs (see also section 2.3).

12. *al-Hajj Ibrahim Makwarari.* A muqaddam of N.K. and brother to Y. A. Makwarari. He was the founder of the mosque of the Q. in Unguwar Rijiyar Hudu and continues to be its imam. He is a religious scholar whose specialties are the Qur'ân and fiqh. The Rijiyar Hudu mosque was founded in 1945. It is connected with a school for fiqh, taṣawwuf, tafsîr, and naḥw.

13. *al-Hajj Bala Abdullahi Makwarari.* A half brother to (10), and one of his disciples.

14. *M. A. Baba Makwarari.* A disciple of (10) and founder of the Sheshe mosque of the Q. He is a muqaddam of N.K. The Sheshe mosque was founded in 1964 and is still led by A. Baba Makwarari.
15. *al-Hajj Balaga Masukwani.* Founder and imam of the Balaga mosque in Unguwar Masukwani (1959). A disciple of (10) and muqaddam of N.K. in Kano.
16. *M. Usman Na Balaga.* Founder and imam of the Balaga mosque in Unguwar Kofar Mazugal (1964). A student of (10) and a muqaddam of N.K. His school places special emphasis on taṣawwuf.
17. *M. Hussaini Trader.* Father of (18) and (19), and founder of a mosque of the Q. in Unguwar Bakin Zuwo. He was a disciple of (10) and is a muqaddam of N.K. After his death in 1987 his son M. Yahya Husaini Trader followed him as imam of his mosque.
18. *M. Mai Sahena Trader.* Founder of another mosque of the Q. in Unguwar Bakin Zuwo (1959). A student of (10) and a muqaddam of N.K. After his death M. 'Abd al-Qadir became imam of his mosque and in 1982 was in turn succeeded by M. Baba. In the mosque a regular bandiri-dhikr is conducted.
19. *M. Yahya Husaini Trader.* A student of (10), muqaddam of N.K., and imam of the second mosque of the Q. in Unguwar Bakin Zuwo where a regular bandiri-dhikr takes place.
20. *al-Hajj 'Abd al-Mutallib Shuwaish.* Another disciple of (10).
21. *M. A. Abubakar.* A student of (10), founder of the first mosque of the Q. in Unguwar Limanci (1963), and a muqaddam of N.K.
22. *M. 'Abd al-Qadir Isiaku Makwarai "al-Ustadh."* A disciple of (10) and imam of his own mosque in Unguwar Makwarari.
23. *al-Hajj Sharu Bala.* Muqaddam of N.K. in Kano, a religious scholar and a businessman. Originally he had been

a disciple of (10); later he founded the Malanganari mosque of the Q. In 1975 he moved from there into Unguwar Ayagi and established a new mosque of the Q., which he integrated with a great Qur'ânic school. By 1987 the school had a capacity of about one thousand students. It is also connected with a workshop for the production of wooden slates (allo). M. Sharu Bala leads the solemn recitation of the Qur'ân on the last Friday of each month in the Dâr al-Q. mosque of N.K. He is also one of the most important financial supporters of the Q. in Kano.

24. *Shaykh Gariballa Nasiru.* A muqaddam of N.K. and presently director of the Gwale Islamiyya Primary School in Gwale, as well as imam of the school.
25. *M. Dahiru Khalid.* Together with (24) he is director of the Gwale Islamiyya Primary School.
26. *al-Hajj Sabo Danbatta.* One of the most important supporters of the Q. in Kano. He financed the construction of the Gwale Islamiyya Primary School and of the Goron Dutse Islamiyya Secondary School.
27. *M. Aminu Ahmad.* Another important supporter of the Q. in Kano. He resides in Unguwar Sani Mai Nagge and controlled the trade in perfumes in Kano. His son Sani Ahmad, who is presently managing the company, was the first indigenous trader in Kano to open a pharmacy.
28. *al-Hajj Musa "U.A.C."* An important supporter of the Q. in Kano, residing in Unguwar Gwammaja. He obtained his nickname "U.A.C." because he started working as an agent for that company. Presently he is owner of the company al-Maniam which specialized in the production of windows and doors in Kano.
29. *al-Hajj Sanusi Dantata.* He is without doubt the most important contemporary supporter of the Q. in Kano (see also sections 2.3 and 2.5).
30. *A. A. M. Idris.* The founder and imam of a mosque of his own in Unguwar Yakasai (1954) and a muqaddam of N.K.

31. *M. A. Mazankwarai.* Founder and imam of his own mosque in Unguwar Mazankwarai (1963) and a muqaddam of N.K. in Kano. His mosque is connected with a school which specialized on fiqh and taṣawwuf.
32. *M. Musa b. Sa'd.* Brother of Malam Muhammad Sidi, the former leader of the Shâdhiliyya in Kano. A muqaddam of N.K.
33. *M. Mukhtar Atamma.* Founder and imam of a mosque in Fagge (1950). Leader of the Q. in Fagge and muqaddam of N.K. He works as lecturer in the Department of Arabic at BUK and is especially interested in ḥadîth. His mosque is connected with a school with a population of about six hundred students. The school employs fifteen teachers.
34. *M. Shehu Dan Lagos.* Imam of the Dandali mosque of the Q. in Unguwar Dandalin Turawa and a muqaddam of N.K.
35. *M. 'Abd al-'Azîz.* Captain of the Nigerian army. He is a disciple of N.K.
36. *al-Hajj Kabiru Dan Babban Malami Madabo.* Son of the present Babban Malami Madabo. He is from an old Tijâni family and a disciple of N.K.
37. *M. Yusuf Muhammad Bello.* He was the imam of the Indabawa mosque of the Q. and director of the al-Hassan Dantata Islamiyya School in Koki, a student of N.K. In the Ikhtilâṭ dispute he belonged to the the few supporters of 'Ali Kumasi.
38. *M. Ado Kurawa.* From Unguwar Kofar Dan Agundi, a judge and disciple of N.K.
39. *M. Adamu Na Ma'aji.* A student of Shaykh Sa'd b. Aḥmad, first imam of the Marmara mosque in Unguwar Alfindiki, teacher and patron of N.K., and one of the most important scholars of the Q. in Kano. He died in 1954.
40. *M. Kamal ad-Din Adamu.* Son of (39) and founder of the Jundullahi organization in Kano (see section 5.4). He was

imam of the Marmara mosque of the Q. in Unguwar Alfindiki and a muqaddam of N.K. until his death in 1986.

41. *M. Garba Adamu.* Brother of (40) and son of (39), he is at present imam of the Marmara mosque and a muqaddam of N.K. The mosque is connected with a school with an enrollment of about three hundred students.

42. *M. Sadi.* Founder and imam of a mosque of his own in Unguwar Alfindiki. His mosque is connected with a school which has about two hundred students. Emphasis in teaching is on taṣawwuf, tawḥid, and fiqh. Every Wednesday there is a bandiri-dhikr.

43. *M. Sharif Haddad.* A muqaddam of N.K., imam of the Allah Daya mosque, and before that imam of the Bakin Ruwa mosque of the Q. The Allah Daya mosque is financed by Sanusi Dantata and is connected with a school, where fiqh and taṣawwuf are taught.

44. *M. Abubakar Ramalan (Ramadhan).* One of the most famous scholars of the Q. in Kano, founder of a mosque in Unguwar Tudun Nufawa (1940) and its imam, affiliated with N.K., a friend of 'Ali Kumasi, student of Adamu Na Ma'aji, and member of the Committee of Astronomers in Kano. Apart from Malam Mai Sikeli he is reputed to be one of the most renowned scholars of 'ilm al-falak (astrology) in Kano. His mosque is connected with a school.

45. *M. Abubakar Mai Sikeli.* Student of Adamu Na Ma'aji, founder of the Kofar Mazugal mosque of the Q. (1943), and its imam. He was affiliated with N.K. and a friend of 'Ali Kumasi as well as Abubakar Ramalan. Like the latter he was a particularly renowned astrologer in Kano. His successor as imam of his mosque is Malam Ibrahim.

46. *M. Ibrahim.* Successor of (45) as imam of the Kofar Mazugal mosque of the Q. in Kano.

47. *M. Na Baba.* A muqaddam of N.K. in Unguwar Mandawari in Kano.

48. *M. Khamis Dorawar Bebeji.* Another muqaddam of N.K. in Kano.

49. *M. Sadiq Alfindiki.* A muqaddam of N.K. in Kano. He has a school of his own on the first floor of the Marmara mosque of the Q. in Unguwar Alfindiki, an Islamiyya Primary School consisting of four classes.
50. *M. Sharif Ahmad Na Bade.* Muqaddam of N.K. in Kano, imam of the Rijiyar Hudu mosque of the Q., director of a school of his own.
51. *M. Muhammu Haido.* Apart from Malam Atamma he is one of the most important scholars of the Q. in Fagge. Like Malam Atamma he comes from the Air region in present-day Niger. He is owner of a bookshop, a muqaddam of N.K., imam, and founder (1940) of a mosque in Fage. This mosque is connected with a school which specializes on ḥadîth.
52. *M. Muhammad Bakatsine.* A muqaddam of N.K. and timam of the Falu mosque in Unguwar Gwammaja. After his death Malam Shuaibu followed him as imam of his mosque.
53. *M. Shuaibu.* Successor of (52) as imam of the Falu mosque, a muqaddam of N.K. in Kano.
54. *M. Muhammad Limanci.* A muqaddam of N.K., founder and imam of a mosque in Unguwar Limanci (1964).
55. *al-Hajj Sulaiman Hausawa.* A disciple of N.K.
56. *M. Tanku Tudun Nufawa.* A muqaddam of N.K. in Kano and founder of the second mosque of the Q. in Unguwar Tudun Nufawa. He is now deceased.
57. *M. Qarib Allah.* Son of Tanku Tudun Nufawa and his successor as imam of the Tudun Nufawa mosque of the Q.
58. *M. Muwadda.* Imam of the Sharifai mosque of the Q. and muqaddam of N.K. This mosque in Unguwar Sharifai is said to have been founded by al-Maghili.
59. *M. Umaru b. A. Bahadeji.* Imam of the Dambazau mosque of the Q., which was founded by Abdullahi dan Fodio in 1807. He is a muqaddam of N.K.
60. *M. 'Ali.* Imam of the Unguwar Kabuga mosque of the Q. and a muqaddam of N.K.

61. *M. Musa Muhammad.* Imam of the Bakin Ruwa mosque of the Q., which was founded by (43). He is a teacher at the Advanced Teachers Training College in Gwale, Kano. He is also a muqaddam of N.K.
62. *M. Shehu Bayarabi.* Imam of the Rijiyar Ungoro mosque of the Q. on the Kurmi market in Kano and a muqaddam of N.K.
63. *M. Lawwan.* Imam of the Dala mosque of the Q.-'Arûsiyya in Kano. He is now deceased. The Dala mosque was founded in the late nineteenth century by Malam Ahmad b. 'Ali. The two other mosques affiliated with the Q.-'Arûsiyya are situated in the Unguwoyi Makwarari and Cediyar Hudu.
64. *M. Ibrahim Kyauta.* Imam of the first mosque of the Q. in Unguwar Madabo, a Tijâni-controlled quarter.
65. *M. Shuaibu.* Imam of the second Q. mosque in Unguwar Madabo.
66. *M. Hasan.* Imam of the Gabarai mosque of the Q.
67. *M. Usman Bala.* Imam of the third Q. mosque in Unguwar Makwarari in Kano.
68. *M. Sanusi Abdullahi.* Imam of the fourth mosque of the Q. in Unguwar Makwarari.
69. *M. 'Ali Khalil.* Imam of the second mosque of the Q. in Unguwar Alfindiki, a split-off from the orignal Sharifai mosque.
70. *M. Sidi Karami.* Imam of a mosque of his own in Unguwar Alfindiki.
71. *M. Uba Abdullahi.* Imam of the third Q. mosque in Unguwar Alfindiki.
72. *M. Sidi.* Imam of the Halla-Halla mosque in Unguwar Alfindiki, a mosque which was founded in the early twentieth century by Malam Sa'd b. Ahmad. This mosque was the first zâwiya of the Q. in Kano. A regular bandiri-dhikr is conducted in the mosque.
73. *M. Sidi Muhammad.* Imam of the Shatshari mosque of the Q.

74. *M. Mudi.* Imam of the Sudawa mosque of the Q.
75. *M. Ahmad.* Imam of the Jingau mosque of the Q. in Kano.
76. *M. Na Adamu Jos.* Brother of Malam Garba Tudun Nufawa and muqaddam of N.K. in Jos.
77. *M. Muhammad Bello Abubakar.* A muqaddam of N.K. in Kaura-Namoda (Sokoto), Inspector of Education at the Ministry of Education in Sokoto, a son-in-law of N.K.
78. *al-Hajj Muqaddam Fadl.* Muqaddam of N.K. in Kaura-Namoda.
79. *M. Latif O. Jimoh.* Muqaddam of N.K. in Sokoto, teacher at the Sokoto State College of Education.
80. *M. 'Abd al-Hakam Muntaqa Kumasi.* Muqaddam of N.K. in Zaria.
81. *M. Usman Baba Liman.* Muqaddam of N.K. in Gombe, employee at the Gombe Area Court.
82. *M. Usman Makhmud Bappail.* Muqaddam of N.K. in Gombe.
83. *M. Ahmad Rufa'i Alfa Nda Salati.* He was affiliated with N.K. and one of the most important scholars of the Q. in Ilorin and Yorubaland. He died in 1966.
84. *al-Hajj Abubakar Siddiq Kadara.* Muqaddam of N.K. in Ilorin (acording to Ahmad he is khalîfa of the Q. in Ilorin).
85. *al-Hajj Abd ar-Rashid Ajikanle.* Muqaddam of N.K. in Ibadan and imam of the university mosque of Ibadan.
86. *al-Hajj Ahmad Onaopepo.* Muqaddam of N.K. in Ife.
87. *al-Hajj Abd al-Aziz Olohungbo.* Khalîfa of the Q. in Abeokuta.
88. *M. Umaru Muqaddam.* Muqaddam of N.K. in Ibadan-Sabo.
89. *al-Hajj Ibrahim Daodu Lagungu.* Muqaddam of N.K. in Ede.
90. *al-Hajj Ibrahim Nda Salati.* Khalîfa of the Nda-Salati mosque in Lagos, son of (83), and leader of the Q. in Lagos.

91. *al-Hajj Kamal ad-Din Balogun.* Muqaddam of N.K. and lecturer in the Department of Arabic at the University of Ibadan.
92. *al-Hajj Liadi Agopapa.* Muqaddam of N.K. in Iseyin.
93. *al-Hajj Mudathir Anpopo.* Muqaddam of N.K. in Oyo.
94. *al-Hajj Muhammad Ibrahim an-Nufawi.* Muqaddam of N.K. and khalîfa of the Q. in Ilorin. He died in 1982.
95. *al-Hajj Murtada Raji.* Muqaddam of N.K. in Osogbo.
96. *al.Hajj Najm ad-Din Olorioniwasi.* Muqaddam of N.K. in Ibadan.
97. *M. Junaid Oloso.* Muqaddam of N.K. in Lagun (Lagos).
98. *al.Hajj Yusuf Jimoh.* Muqaddam of N.K. in Lagos.
99. *al-Hajj Abd al-Karim Kobomoje.* Muqaddam of N.K. in Ibadan.
100. *M. Abubakar Abd al-Qadir.* Muqaddam of N.K. in Agadez (Niger).
101. *M. Muhammad Ahmad.* Muqaddam of N.K. in Agadez.
102. *M. Khalifa Isma'il.* Muqaddam of N.K. in Agadez.
103. *M. Ahmad Muhammad Bakai.* Muqaddam of N.K. in Agadez.
104. *M. Bakari.* Muqaddam of N.K. in Gudumaryam (Niger).
105. *M. Muhammadu.* Muqaddam of N.K. in Gure (Niger).
106. *M. Aminu Sisi.* Muqaddam of N.K. in the Republic of Mali.
107. *M. Alfa Muhammad Sisi.* Muqaddam of N.K. in Mali.
108. *M. Shaykh Salihi Annuri.* Muqaddam of N.K. in Chad.
109. *M. Alo Ebni Salihu.* Muqaddam of N.K. in Chad.
110. *al-Hajj Idris.* Muqaddam of N.K. in Ghana.
111. *M. Shehu Tittasa.* Muqaddam of N.K. in Niger.
112. *M. Shehu Alfa Taslimi.* Muqaddam of N.K. in Benin.
113. *M. Shehu Nurani.* Muqaddam of N.K. in Karachi (Pakistan).
114. *M. Abd al-Wujud Tatari.* Muqaddam of N.K. in Moscow.
115. *M. Abd l-Latif Tatari.* Muqaddam of N.K. in Moscow.
116. *M. Riyauddin.* Muqaddam of N.K. in Tashkent (Uzsbekistan).

117. *M. Shehu Abubakar.* Muqaddam of N.K. in London.
118. *M. Shehu Umar.* Muqaddam of N.K. in Zanzibar. (This claim seems more or less to have been made for propaganda: Shehu Umar is not only older than N.K., he is also a descendant of an old sharifian family. He died in 1986/87.)
119. *M. Abu Gala Muhammad.* Muqaddam of N.K. in Amman (Jordan).
120. *M. Shehu Iqbal.* Muqaddam of N.K. in Lahore (Pakistan).

Appendix 2

Communiqué of the Meeting of the Committee of Scholars from 3 February to 5 February 1979

In the name of God the Beneficient and the Merciful; Peace and Blessings of God on the Prophet Muhammed, his Kinsmen and his Companions.

After that, the committee of scholars set up by this council with the responsibility of checking the differences between Muslims met twice at Lagos; the first in the month of October 1978 and the second from 3–5 February 1979.

The scholars met with good intentions in the hope of getting a solution acceptable to all Muslims. It has been felt most convincingly that God has accepted their service.

The scholars wrote their own version in relation to their understanding of what was meant by Islam and mystic sects. The version of each scholar was read and discussed.

The scholars agreed.

1. That all the books written in each field are likely to contain both corect and erratic entries. It was therefore agreed to ignore checking their contents. Each specialized scholar should therefore stick to his field.
2. The scholars agreed that books written on Sufism are actually meant for Sufists; and should not be investigated if their field was not properly known.
3. Any course that would bring about cooperation between Muslims should be emphasized.
4. It is unlawful to remove an error if by removing it a bigger error will be brought about.

5. Anybody who referred to another person as an infidel: one of them is the one.
6. The scholars also agreed that belonging to a sect (Darika) is not compulsory on Muslims; but looking for someone to follow in religion is compulsory, as getting a person to be upright on his own is very rare.
7. The scholars also unanimously agreed that the ḥadîth in which angel Jibril came to the prophet(s) asking for the meanings of Islam, Imân, and Iḥsân has covered three things:
   a. The meaning of Islam
   b. The meaning of Imân
   c. The meaning of Iḥsân

   The field that explains Islam is what is known as fikhu and its furu's (branches). The field that explains Imân is what is known as Ilm at-tawḥid wa-l-kalam. The field that investigates Iḥsân is what is known as taṣawwuf; and all that was attached to it in form of meditations (wuridai) or ecstasies (azkaru) are collected mysticisms.
8. The scholars also unanimously agreed on the meaning of wahyi. In a book entitled "Fara'id al-Jalilah" written by Shehu Abdullahi of Gwandu it has been explained that wahyi (revelation) could be through an angel or by inspiration or by dreams or though an inscription. When revelation reaches prophets in any of these ways its implications are the same.

   Revelation that evil demands action or restrictions in accordance with sharî'ah is only limited to the prophets. But inspiration to saints is an intuitive knowledge from God which does not cover any new directive outside the sharî'ah.
9. The scholars also agreed that claiming to be a prophet is infidel, but claiming to have inspiration is not infidelity.
10. They have agreed that dreams are of three types:
    a. There is a dream direct from God; which never always agrees with the sharî'ah.

b. There is a dream which comes from human illusions.
c. There is a dream that contains nothing and it originates from the devil.

11. The scholars agreed that the prophet(s) has said that "prophethood has seized only mubasharat" (inspiration), that is, for a believer to foresee something good in a dream, or for someone to foresee it on his behalf.
12. The committee also is hereby advising Muslims,
    a. to learn about their religion; to act in accordance with the Qur'ân and ḥadîth on the translations given by the scholars of Sunna.
    b. to stop branding one another as infidels on issues which were differently understood.
    c. to remain as directed by God in the verse: wa-i' taṣimû bi-ḥabl Allahi jamî'an wa-lâ tafâriqû
    d. that the scholars are advising emirs and their helpers on what involves Qur'ânic exegesis that anybody who does not qualify to translate it should not be permitted to do so in public.

    Finally, the scholars pray that may God make us succeed and grant us peaceful coexistence and prosperity in the whole country.

Those who unanimously agreed on the foregoing are

	Witnesses to the accord are:
Alhaji Nasir Kabara	Brigadier Shehu M. Yar'adua
Alhaji Isma'ila Ibrahim	Alhaji M. D. Yusuf
Alhaji Abubakar Mahmoud Gumi	Dr. Shehu Galadanci
Alhaji Sharif Ibrahim Saleh	Dr. Sani Zahradeen

Appendix 3

A Chronology of the Clashes between the 'Yan Izala and the Sufi Brotherhoods 1978–1980

10 March 1978: Clash between 'Yan Izala and members of the Sufi brotherhoods in Tudun Wada (Kaduna).

17 March 1978: During a skirmish in the Barnawa mosque in Kaduna the imam of the mosque, al-Ḥâjj Aliyu Muhammad, is killed.

21 April 1978: Clash between 'Yan Izala and followers of the Tijâniyya in Margu, Pankshin Local Government (LG), Plateau State. The 'Yan Izala attack the local police station in order to liberate imprisoned 'Yan Izala.

28 May 1978: Clashes again in Tudun Wada (Kaduna).

19/20 June 1978: Fights between 'Yan Izala and Tijânis in Gombe, Bauchi State. The car of a Tijâni is burned.

22 June 1978: The 'Yan Izala attack a police station in Gombe; one of the aggressors is killed.

29 June 1978: Clashes between 'Yan Izala and followers of the ṭuruq in Gabasawa.

18 August 1978: Many people wounded in fights between 'Yan Izala and Tijânis in Kurgwi, Shendam LG, Plateau State.

18 September 1978: Incident in Anka LG, Sokoto State, in which nine preachers of the 'Yan Izala, led by Muhammad Rabi, are saved from lynching by the village mob only by the intervention of the elders.

1 October 1978: Clashes between 'Yan Izala and followers of the ṭuruq in Kawo (Kaduna).

29 October 1978: Isma'ila Idris preaches in Jos: members of the

'Yan Izala should no longer marry off their daughters to followers of the ṭuruq since the latter are unbelievers.

13 November 1978: A preacher from Kano, Idris Abdullahi, is almost lynched in Minna when preaching that the followers of the Tijâniyya, the Qâdiriyya, and the other "sects" were unbelievers and mushrikûn (heathen), as they worshipped mortals.

9 March 1979: In Maiduguri a police commissioner is killed by followers of the 'Yan Izala.

13 November 1979: During clashes between 'Yan Izala and followers of the ṭuruq in Danja, Funtua LG, Kaduna State, a mosque is destroyed. Two people die.

5 March 1980: In fights between 'Yan Izala and followers of the ṭuruq in Makurdi, Benue State, some police officers are beaten.

30 March 1980: During clashes between 'Yan Izala and followers of the ṭuruq in Kurgwi, Shendam LG, Plateau State, six people are wounded.

2 April 1980: In Kano two preachers of the 'Yan Izala are killed in new clashes.

27 May 1980: Fights between 'Yan Izala and followers of the Sufi brotherhoods result in a death.

13 July 1980: Despite a ban on preaching, supporters of the 'Yan Izala break into the central mosque of Wukari, Gongola State, to preach.

24 September 1980: Clashes between 'Yan Izala and followers of the ṭuruq in Anchauia, Ikara LG, Kaduna State; many houses are burned down, and eight police officers are wounded.

6 October 1980: Further clashes between 'Yan Izala and members of the Sufi brotherhoods in Gusau (Sokoto State).

21 October 1980: Fights in Gusau.

2 November 1980: During clashes in Yelwa, Shendam LG, Plateau State, a follower of the 'Yan Izala is killed and two police officers are wounded.

16 November 1980: During fights between 'Yan Izala and members of the Fityân al-Islâm in Kaura-Namoda (Sokoto State) a Dan Izala is killed. (For documentation relating to the clashes between the 'Yan Izala and the ṭuruq see Aniagolu Report [Lagos 1981], Quadri 1981 and 1985, Ahmed 1986.)

Some data concerning the above mentioned incidents between the 'Yan Izala and the Sufi brotherhoods should be treated with caution. It is possible that responsibility for some of these riots has been laid at the doorsteps of the 'Yan Izala by the media, as well as by the security forces, in order to discredit the movement as a "dangerous" movement that ought to be fought and banned. The reports on the 'Yan Izala between 1978 and 1980 may easily give the impression that all problems, unrest, and conflicts of that particular time were connected with the activities of the 'Yan Izala. A similar impression is created by the style of reporting on violent clashes since 1980. True or false, responsibility for these riots has commonly been attributed to the Maitatsine movement. It is therefore quite probable that a number of these incidents were the result of local factors and had nothing to do with the conflict between the 'Yan Izala and the ṭuruq. On the other hand, the escalation of violence since 1978 nurtured the tendency to express social tensions with violent means. From this point of view the conflict between the 'Yan Izala and the Sufi brotherhoods may be seen as symptomatic for the overall political climate of the time.

Appendix 4

The Constitution of the Jamâ'at Izâlat al-Bid'a wa-Iqâmat as-Sunna of 8 February 1978

Note: The following text has been translated from Hausa into English by Jibril H. Yola. The original Hausa version is cataloged in the archive of the Department of Islamic Studies at the University of Bayreuth.

Constitution of the organization for revival of Islam and removal of Satanic innovation (Jama'atu Izalatil Bid'a)
Rules and regulations of the Islamic organization for eradication of Satanic innovation (Jama'atu Izalatil Bid'a)

1. Name: The confirmed name of the organization is Jama'at Izalatil Bid'a.
   a. Its meaning: Eradication of Satanic innovation in Islamic religion which others introduced into it later on so as to undermine and weaken its foundation.
   b. Jama'atu Izalatil Bid'a is an Islamic organization which established its headquarters at Jos, Plateau State. The organization is not a Sufi order nor is it a secret organization. It does not approve any innovation or adding of new things which were not brought by the Prophet and which were not in the authentic ḥadîths of the Prophet Muhammad, peace and blessing of Allah be upon him.
   c. Izalatil Bid'a is a purely religious organization which relies entirely on the Qur'ân and the authentic ḥadîths. It has nothing to do with politics nor does it discriminatate on the basis of color, tribe, or race.

2. Aims and Objectives
   a. Our aim is to spread the religion of Allah as it is in the Qur'ân and ḥadîths.
   b. In reality we seek to revive all those thing which Allah has made obligatory on Muslims in their devotion to Him in the hearts of the followers of Islam.
   c. We shall opppose any Muslim who brings anything which is not contained in Islam and but who then claims that it is Allah who reveals it to him after the death of our leader Prophet Muhammad (p.b.h.). We also dismiss any claim to the effect that the Prophet has hidden something which he did not explain at the time when he was alive, but only after many centuries. We furthermore dismiss claims of having received a new message or the idea that the Prophet has given something to another person after his demise.
   d. We believe that the Prophet (p.b.h.) has delivered the message with which Allah has sent him to the whole of humanity; he had not withheld anything from which Allah has commanded him to deliver. And the message as it is presented in the Qur'ân at the time of the Prophet's presentation is the only thing to be relied upon, and we have to work with it.
   e. We shall confirm to good Muslims that anybody who brings any form of worship and claims that he has been maintaining contact with the Prophet or that the Prophet has been visiting him whether in dream or in any other form after his demise is a liar, for his claims do not conform to the Qur'ânic verse which says: "Innaka mayyitun, wa innahum mayyitun [sic]" (Qur'ân 39:31) and the Prophetic ḥadîth which says: "Wa iza matal abdu, ka dâ'at a'mâluhu [sic]". Because of this any Muslim who belies Allah and his Prophet is a kâfir unless he repents.
   f. We shall oppose anything which is invented and added to the rules of Islam which is unknown in Islamic regula-

tions: It is improper for Muslims to accept such things, because it is un-Islamic.

g. We shall devote our time to preaching so as to enlighten the people in various ways such as printing pamphlets, or using the media, or by any other means which can help to extend to people what their obligations are in matters concerning the worship of Allah.
h. We shall try to ensure unity of the Muslims of this country.
i. We shall defend this objective from selfishness or whims at all costs.

3. Representation or membership of the organization

The membership of this organization is open to all Muslims provided that one is ready to accept its rules and regulations as detailed in the following pages.

a. The first condition for belonging to this organization is the acceptance of the five pillars of Islam which every prospective member, male or female, must do. These are: I) unity of God—Tawhîd, II) prayer—Ṣalah, III) Fasting —Ṣaum Ramadhân, IV) Zakât, V) Pilgrimage—Ḥajj for those who have the means. And that one should not belong to any Sufi order.
b. It is necessary for the prospective member, male or female, to reject any form of innovation which is opposed to sharî'a.
c. It is necessary for any prospective member of the Izala to be a Muslim who accepts the leadership of the Prophet Muhammad (p.b.h) and to accept that He is the seal and the last Prophet of Allah and that He delivered the message as Allah has sent it to all humanity.
d. No money should be paid in order to become a member of this organization. However, if one wishes one can make donations or alms or zakât to the organization which can be used to run its day-to-day activities.

4. Friendly relations

It is possible to enter into friendly relations with any organization inside or outside Nigeria.

a. The organization welcomes any other organization wherever it may be in the world to establish friendship with it provided that there are no disagreements on matters of principles or objectives which may be observed in its constitution.
b. Izalatil Bid'a cannot enter into friendly relations with any other organization except on certain conditions, rules and regulations.

5. Councils and Authorities

This organization has five councils that are responsible for running its day-to-day affairs, and that have full executive powers.

a. The councils may be created when the need arises: as a result of a new development or of conditions obliging the organization to adopt a new strategy. The executive council is the only body that can make the decision in this respect.
b. The councils are:
    I. Council of elders
    II. Council of patrons
    III. Executive council
    IV. Working council
    V. Preaching council
c. All appointments in respect to any of these councils will be released in writing from the office of the Secretary General.
d. Explanation of the structure of the councils is detailed below:
    I. Council of elders

    The organization has a very high regard for this council; its leader may be one of the Muslim emirs of this county—Nigeria. All the Muslim emirs of this country may be members of the council in their capacity as patrons of Islamic organizations in Nigeria. Respectable scholars may also be in the council provided that the executive council approves of their membership in accordance with the rules and regulations of the organization.

A) The executive council is the council empowered to elect members of the council of elders annually or as it seems necessary.

B) Anybody who is elected into this council has the right to accept or reject the post for which he is elected. He is not obliged to serve the organization before or after he has been elected.

C) Qualification for membership of the council of elders depends on one's practical engagement and dedication to the organization.

II. Patrons of the organization

Members of the council of patrons will be elected every year or from time to time or as it is deemed necessary.

A) The chairman of the council of patrons will also be an elected member of the council.

B) The members of the council should be well versed in Islamic affairs, they should not belong to any Sufi order, and they may be chosen from any part of this country without regard to tribe, place of birth, age, or lineage, as long as they are good people and well educated in Islamic affairs and they have the zeal with which to promote Islam and to encourage unity among the Muslims.

C) It is necessary for every member of the council to accept the aims and objectives of the Jamatu Izalatil Bid'a from section 2a to g and that he should not belong to any Sufi order.

D) This organization will seek advice from the council of elders from time to time whenever the issues which affect Islam and the Muslims arise.

III. Council of the preachers

This council is comprised of scholars who preach on behalf of the organization. They should be dedicated and offer their services for the sake of Allah. All of them can be confirmed by the learned men of the organization.

A) Apart from the few who are going to be elected by the organization to preach on its behalf, anybody who wishes to preach for the organization is welcomed, but he has to submit his written application.

B) The preachers' council like the other councils in the organization should have its own leader. All the other members are under him, and he presides over all meetings of the council. He may assign responsibilities to others according to their abilities and based on their election to take charge of their responsibilities.

C) Any preacher who has an interest in joining the council must apply to the secretary general of the organization who will present the application at the executive council meeting for consideration.

D) Any prospective member who wishes to join the council, whether he is elected or he has applied on his own, has to accept the conditions as laid down by the executive council of the organization:

(1) That he should be a good Muslim who strictly adheres to the injunctions of Islam, and his conduct should be worthy of emulation.

(2) Before anyone is considered for preaching or elected for it, he has to prove that he has three years experience in preaching.

(3) That he has to adhere strictly to the five

pillars of Islam and he has to accept the objectives and beliefs of the Jamatu Izalatil Bid'a.

(4) That he should not belong to any Sufi order or support or sympathize with a Sufi order, that he should not be a hypocrite, and that he should not accept anything which is added to Islam apart from the purely Islamic teaching which is already known.

(5) That he should be dedicated and devoted to the extent that whenever he is called upon, whether day or night, he is prepared to go where needed in order to promote the religion of Islam.

(6) No preacher has the power to preach according to his own personal views in the name of Jamatu Izalatil Bid'a without presenting to the chairman of the council of preachers the topic or area in which he wants to preach in writing; the chairman must read it and approve it if it merits approval.

e. The President

He shall lead all the activities of the organization. He may attend the important meetings of the organization; he may be well informed of all the activities the organization has carried out or intends to carry out, including the time such activities are to be engaged in.

A) He shall be the chirman of the joint annual meeting.

B) The post may be contested and elections held, whereas the tenure of the office is three years.

C) The president has the power to make modifications in time of need in order to promote the activities of the organization.

D) He has the power to give directives on how to spend the money or how to save it or how it is obtained. He gives directives on when to withdraw money from the bank, although he is not permitted to sign checks nor may he keep hard cash on behalf of the organization.

E) He has the power to approve the opening of a new branch of the organization; he also has the power to accept or reject a prospective entrance into a friendly agreement with another organization.

f. The Assistant President

He assists the president. He is also responsible for running the secretariat of the organization. He chairs the meetings of the organization.

A) He chairs the general or emergency meetings or the meetings of the working committee of the organization.

B) He has the power to execute or advise the executive council on the admittance of a person into the organization or giving a post to another member or to create an adhoc committee to execute a specific assignment in the name of the organization.

g. Secretary General

He is responsible for the general administration of the organization's secretariat, how to run it and the meetings of the union.

A) He always calls for important and emergency meetings or committee meetings and ensures that the meetings are conducted properly.

B) He receives letters on behalf of the organization or any important correspondence, and he replies to these letters on behalf of the organization.

C) He takes charge of organizing and running the

office of the organization and all those working under him.

D) He gives directives to other secretaries under him on the appropriate approach to activities as the need arises or on affairs of running the organization or any other corrective measure, and he spells out what is to be done in areas under his control.

E) With the permission of the executive council, the secretary general together with the treasurer and the financial secretary serve as signataries for bank checks. He may also sign any other important document which has to do with the finances of the organization.

h. Deputy Secretary General

He may assist the secretary general in his functions as stipulated above. He may work on behalf of the secretary general or execute anything to which he is assigned.

i. Assistant Secretaries

They may work on behalf of the secretary general as above mentioned.

j. Treasurer

He is responsible for taking care of the wealth of the organization on trust.

A) He is responsible for receiving and paying out money.

B) He keeps receipt of income and expenditure and sends copies to the executive council and another copy to the secretary general.

C) He may sign a check for payment or withdrawal of money on behalf of the organization.

k. Assistant Treasurer

He assists the treasurer; he may also work on behalf of the treasurer when the treasurer directs him to do so or he may be given specific duties to carry out.

A) He is a member of the finance committtee.

B) He keeps the reports of income and expenditure of the organization.

l. Financial Secretary

He explores ways of generating funds for the organization. He informs the secretary general of his activities and the type of work that he intends to undertake.

A) He chairs the meetings of the finance committee.

B) It is his responsibility to know the financial strength of the organization at all times.

C) It is only with his consent that the money of the organization may be spent.

D) He is responsible for taking care of the wealth of the organization, including any of its assets.

E) He receives reports of the organization's monthly expenditures and works through their contents. He also receives such reports from the treasurer and works through the receipts and submits his reports to the executive council.

m. Assistant Financial Secretary

He assists the financial secretary or acts on his behalf when permitted to do so. He is also a member of the financial commitee. He may also carry out specific duties that may be assigned to him.

n. Auditor General

He has the sole responsibility of auditing the finances of the organization.

A) He is also a member of the finance committee.

B) He collects all documents relating to the finances of the organization.

C) He knows the financial status of the organization at any time.

D) He may institute a committee of enquiry in consultation with the financial secretary to investigate the finances of any of the organization's branches.

o. Assistant Auditor General
He may assist the auditor general. He may also act on behalf of the auditor general when he is directed to do so.

p. Secretary of Information
He is responsible for informing and enlightening the public on the activities of the organization. His duties include the following:
   A) He enlightens the public or offers explanations on behalf of the organization.
   B) He may request a monthly or periodical press conference.
   C) He informs the members and the public when a general meeting is to be held or when a preaching session is to take place.

q. Assistant Information Secretary
He assists the secretary of information. He may also act on the latter's behalf if he is requested to do so.

r. Chief Organizer (planning)
He is subordinate to the secretary general, and the two work jointly in carrying out their duties.
   A) He may arrange for a preaching session to take place provided that the executive council gives directives to that effect.
   B) He arranges for Islamic seminars on behalf of the organization.
   C) He assists the leaders of the scholars in arranging preaching sessions or selecting those who may preach or deliver addresses on certain occasions on behalf of the organization.
   D) He may invite renowned scholars and be hospitable to them during the period of their visit to the organization.
   E) He is the chairman of the planning committee; he may also advise the executive council on where to hold a preaching session.

s. Assistant Chief Organizer
He is deputy to the chief organizer; he may also act on his behalf when requested to do so.

t. Public Relations Secretary
He is responsible for ensuring binding relationships and peace. He may make peaceful settlements among the members. He may also ensure good relationship between the members of the organization and outsiders, namely, nonmembers. His functions include the following:

A) To reconcile members whenever there is a misunderstanding among them or a misunderstanding between the members and the outsiders.
B) To enlighten the members and the rest of the people on the beliefs and good objectives of the organization and peaceful coexistence.
C) He assists in the selection of Qur'ânic verses and sound ḥadîths of the Prophet and advises the chairman of the preaching committee in order that the organization may maintain its good objectives and does not deviate from the teaching of the Qur'ânic verses.
D) He submits the Qur'ânic verses and the ḥadîths to the executive council to approve them before being published for public use.
E) He leads the committee for friendly relations. He may observe and sample public opinion, namely, their approval or disapproval of the activities of the executive council.

u. Assistant Public Relations Secretary
He is the deputy of the secretary; he may represent him and also assist him.

v. Complaints Secretary
He is responsible for taking care of and protecting the constitution of the organization. He should also protect the image of the executive council of the organization.

A) He receives criticism—both constructive and negative—from the public relations secretary relating to the activities of the executive council or any of the members of the organization from the public. His functions involve both internal and external affairs of the organization.

B) He submits the complaints and criticism and the judgments which are then passed on to the disciplinary committee which will subsequently make enquiries and determine the appropriate measures to be taken in such matters.

C) He takes care of external relations so as to maintain adherence to the rules and effectively deal with issues likely to confront the organization.

D) He gives advice on minor changes or overhauling of the executive council.

E) He is the chairman of the disciplinary committee.

w. Deputy Complaint Secretary
He may act on behalf of the secretary; he may also represent him. He may also be given special duties to carry out. He may also assist the secretary.

6. Arrangement of the working committees
Five main committees have been established. These are responsible for the execution of plans and for agreeing on objectives designed to improve the affairs of the organization at all times.

a. Working committees may be increased for a certain period or for a specific time, so as to settle emerging issues as may be required, particularly those regarding the issues which confront the organization.

b. Each committee should have five elected members selected from any section of the organization so as to serve as members of a committee.

c. Each committeee when assigned to do a specific task

should have a chairman who will be from the executive council whose rank will not be less than that of the secretary general or his assistant.

d. Each committee when assigned to do a specific task should liaise with the secretary general since he is he head of service of the various committees. He also receives reports and submits them to the executive council.
e. There are five established working committees for the Jama'at Izalatil Bid'a. They are as follows:
   I. Finance Committee
      It is responsible for taking care of the means of generating funds to the organization.
      A) The important duty of this committee is to explore ways and means which this organization should follow so as to generate enough funds to run its day-to-day activities.
      B) Other duties of the committee include giving advice on how the organization should spend its monies in an economic way. The committee also advises the executive council on financial matters.
      C) The financial secretary is head of the finance committee. He has five or six members subordinate to him who will be elected by the executive council.
   II. Guidance Committee
      It is a permanent committee which arranges sermons or meetings. Its functions are:
      A) Securing places where preaching may always be done.
      B) Enlisting preachers and preparing sermons or enlightenment at the meeting or at the preaching points.
      C) Taking care of invited guests, their meals and accommodation, health care, travel arrange-

ments, and any other necessary things they may require during their stay.

D) Assisting the preachers' council in securing scholars who may assist the organization's regular preachers for some time.

E) The head of the guidance commitee is its secretary, and his assistant is the committee's secretary at its meetings. The committee comprises five members. The membership may be increased when the need arises.

III. Disciplinary Committee

Its duty is to reconcile and discipline members on behalf of the organizations. Its main functons are:

A) To make bylaws for the organization from time to time.

B) To propose a code of conduct and present it to the executive council for incorporation into the organization's constitution.

C) To pass judgment or disciplinary measures against any of the executive council members or any other member who is found guilty of stirring unrest or dissension and breaking the constitutional provisions of the organization.

D) To receive public complaints and forward them to the executive council.

E) The committee is to be lead by its secretary.

IV. Communication Committee

The committee has the responsibility to ensure the well-being of the people; it may further reconciliations to promote peaceful coexistence among the members of the organization as well as with outsiders. Its functions are:

A) To call for a meeting so as to inform the public and the members on the activities of the organization.

B) To prepare texts for publication, sale, or distribution to the public.

C) It arranges short courses, meetings, and sermons for the well-being of society. Its main aim in this respect is to further the spread of Islam and the Jama'at Izalatil Bid'a.

D) This committee will be headed by the communication secretary.

E) The public enlightenment secretary is also to be its secretary. He assists the communication secretary.

V. Central Committee (to cater to the activities of the organization)

This committee is the mother of the organization. It gives commands or directives or investigates and carries out all the activities of the organization. Its functions are:

A) To produce objectives and plans of activities which may be carried out on either a long-term or short-term basis.

B) To explain these objectives further so that none may be left in darkness, this also caters to the questions and enquires which are likely to be made. It has the powers to pass judgment on anything which has to do with how to carry out the functions of the organization and any other issue which is likely to arise.

C) To work toward ensuring unity between all the branches of the organization and its employees.

D) To work for a generally planned strategy which covers all the activities of the organization and all the activities of the secretaries.

E) To institute caretaker committees for the remaining sections of the organizations.

F) The head of this committee is the secretary general.

Appendix 5

Ibrahim Sulaiman: Islam in Nigeria (*New Nigerian*, 27 Mar. 1988)

In this last and final part of our reflection on the state of Islam today, we wish to concentrate our attention on Nigeria. What is the state of Islam in Nigeria? What are the problems, and the prospects. Perhaps the best way to measure the state of affairs in the house of Islam is to take a closer look at the two poles of the Islamic intelligentsia: the ulama and the elite. The Muslim elite, so says the simple truth, is indeed a very powerful class, at least from the political, economic, and, to a very great extent, military point of view. It is no exaggeration to say that they are in a position to run the nation in any way they want. But at the same time—and this is the crux of the matter—the Muslim elite is destined for a tragic fate. Except for a few elements among them, the whole class is afflicted with a fatal disease implanted in them by colonialism. This disease has has two major symptoms: the pathological fear of the cross, and the passionate love for the dross of earthly life.

The cross bestrides the psyche of the Muslim elite like a colossus. They shiver and quake at the very mention of the cross, and to appease this powerful god, everything is being sacrificed. The organic integrated structure of Islam has been sacrificed, and Islam itself is subjected to continous definition to allow secularism to gain a foothold in the domain of Islam, and to accommodate a philosophy and an order of life imposed on us by the Euro-Christian civilization.

Whenever in power, the Muslim elite would constitute themselves in an army to fight Islam, which they see as a threat. And whenever there is a crisis between Islam and the cross, you can see more clearly the level of their capitulation. Strange and disgraceful laws begin to operate, and logic, facts, common sense, and justice lose their value. If you are an arsonist, you shall hang. If you murder a Muslim, you shall go free.

The Muslim elite, in short, has lost the courage to call themselves Muslims. The reward for this pathetic capitulation and for serving as mercenaries for the cross can indeed be fabulous: power, wealth, and castles; and to cap it all, a swarm of elegant girls ready for service. The elite loath to be identified with Islam so they do not lose these privileges. And Allah, in His wise ways, allows them to obtain all they desire, but reserves for them public disgrace and the contempt of men and history.

The ulama on their part are scarcely any better. Every time they meet, they congratulate themselves for being heirs of the prophets, not caring to examine their actions and lifestyles to see if they measure up to the standards of the prophets. "We do not bequeath wealth," Prophet Muhammad said, anxious to dissociate the legacy of the prophets from the wealth-seeking ulama. As personal empire builders many of our ulama spend more time among those in the corridors of power than they spend in promoting the cause of Islam. A few thousand Naira is all that an oppressive government needs to buy off their conscience. And this is how tyranny and misery have befallen Nigeria, and the ulama have remained silent. When they opted for wealth, Allah took away from them the legacy of Muhammad.

Thus the Muslim intelligentsia has, to a considerable extent, betrayed the cause of Islam. This betrayal has had a spillover effect even in the secular pretensions of the elite. Give them a state to manage, they will turn it into a Hollywood. Give them a university to administer, and you will see ineptitude and hedonism in their classical forms. A trail of ruin and destruction follows them wherever they go, and this is only because they have pulled down their own faith and way of life. Similar spillover effects can be seen in the activities of the ulama. Since the truth has been bought from them, what else remains but wranglings and damaging disputes? Thus, in a sense, all is not well with the Muslim community in Nigeria.

Add to this the imperialist factor. Only recently the American ambassador in Nigeria went about from state to state with the sole aim of preventing the launching of the Islamic Endowment Fund by the Council of Ulama. This was only one out of several instances when the ambassador took it upon himself to plot and scheme against Islam and to interfere in the affairs of Muslims. Of course, America is regarded as a superpower, and when you are a superpower your ambassador can afford to behave in weak and dependent nations as an alternative president. The point here is that the invisible hand of imperialism works day and night to pull down the edifice of Islam. France, Germany, Britain, and Israel work closely with their master, the U.S.A., to defeat Islam in West Africa, and most events in this region in which France or Britain or the U.S.A. are involved must be read from this perspective. What is then the prospect for Islam? First of all, in spite of all these difficulties, the overwhelming presence of Islam cannot be denied. It seems very clear that in its onward thrust, Islam will determine the nature and orientation of all other religions and change the destiny of Nigeria. Already, Christianity is slowly and steadily altering its cardinal principles as well as its basic character in order to bear a closer resemblance to Islam. There is now a Christian pilgrimage. Over Radio Kaduna, a Christian program announced that there exists what it called Zakan Krista, or a Christian zakât [zakât is Islam's third pillar]. The future Christians will perhaps be called Ahmad, or Hassan, or Fatima, because Islamic names are an embodiment of dignity and nobility and are unique in their beauty; he will pay "zakât" and go on "hajj" and will do many other duties Islam imposes on Muslims. Christians themselves may not be able to know precisely what they are, Muslims or Christians. Christianity may also rebel against Jesus Christ, who says "My kingdom is not of this world," and cross over to the more attractive and lucrative kingdom of the world. We will find pastors and archbishops sitting comfortably in local government offices as chairmen and councillors. Caesar would have completely overthrown the kingdom of God. All this will happen to Christianity in consequence of its competition with Islam. Opposition to Islam would grow in strength and ferocity, especially from the secular state as well as from America and its satellite states. The Muslim elite who, as a rule, prostrate first to the U.S.A., before prostrating to Allah, would be ordered to hit hard on the Muslim umma, using the machinery of state; and many other pressures would be brought to bear on Islam. Perhaps a time might come when Muslims would be called upon to make the supreme sacrifice by the thousands.

It is in those trying times that Islam would finally lay off its heavy burdens, and absorb those among the elite and ulama who are truly worthy of Islam and cast the rest into the dustbin. Then would begin in earnest the process of transformation. No one is in a position to say exactly how Islam would respond to all these pressures. Islam might go underground, and Nigeria would have an Essence Community to contend with. Or Islam might decide to operate as an open society in broad daylight. Or it might respond in many other ways not known to us at the moment, as Allah may determine. For Allah has placed at the disposal of Islam innumerable forces, the nature and dimension of which are known only to Him alone.

Appendix 6

Communiqué of the Council of 'Ulama' on the Occasion of the Kafancan Riots in March 1987 (*New Nigerian*, 18 June 1987)

In the Name of Allah, the Compassionate, the Merciful

All praise is due to Allah, the Lord of the Power, Who gives power to whom He wills, takes power away from whom He wills: in His hand is all Good, over all things does He exercise absolute power—how excellent is this Lord Supreme, and how excellent this Giver of Succor! May peace and blessings of Allah be upon Muhammad, his family, his companions, and all who follow the Right Guidance.

The Council of 'Ulama, after a careful study of the events of the last few months, especially the unfolding of crisis which started in Kafancan on 6 March 1987, and with sense of duty to Allah, and in view of the responsibilities it shoulders on behalf of the Muslim Umma, hereby addresses the nation as follows:

The Attack on Islam in Kafancan

The Kafancan massacre followed a definite pattern which betrays its premeditated and orchestrated nature. First, there was a vicious attack on the integrity of the Messenger of Allah, Muhammad, peace and blessings of Allah be upon him, by a Christian priest. Muslim students present at the scene predictably protested, because it is the duty of every Muslim to defend the honor of the Messenger of Allah. This was followed by the desecration of the mosques and profaning of the Sacred Qur'ân by burning and vandalism in a manner suggesting extreme and pathological hatred of Islam and its sacred symbols. Then the Christians, to complete their insult and provocation, went ahead, and in a cold-blooded manner, murdered at least fifteen Muslims, the majority of them students who dedicated themselves solely to the study and memorization of the Qur'ân, in addition to indiscriminate destruction of Muslim property. The bodies of most of the murdered Muslims were also set on fire, in utter disregard of human conscience and decency.

All this was done without due regard for the consequences it might bring on the corporate existence of Nigeria, and in defiance of Muslim feelings and sensibilities. The whole of this tragic drama has all the characteristics of an attempt by the caucus of the so-called Northern Christians to set Nigeria on fire and destroy its corporate existence. The keen historian may easily discern in the pattern of this frontal attack on Islam as reminiscent of the Crusades. When the Crusaders captured Jerusalem in 1099, they desecrated the Sacred Mosque, and according to Steven Runciman, "rushed through the streets and into the houses and mosques killing all that they met, men, women, and children alike. When Raymond of Aguilers later that morning went to visit the Temple area, he had to pick his way through corpses and blood that reached up to his knees. . . . The massacre at Jeruslaem profoundly impressed all the world."

Many centuries have passed since the days of the Crusades, yet very little has the Christian attitude toward Muslims changed: in 1903, the Crusaders from England massacred Muslims at Bedeji and set their bodies ablaze. Now the fire of the Crusades has been rekindled; we are witnessing once again Christian intolerance and barbarism.

Reactions in Muslim Towns

Muslims, in many parts of Kaduna State and elsewhere in an understandable sense of outrage over the disgraceful carnage in Kafancan, reacted spontaneously by setting fire to property—mainly buildings associated with vice, corruption, or decadence, such as brothels, hotels, and beer parlors—and to a number of churches. By any standard, Muslims have acted with restraint, avoiding bloodshed almost entirely, especially keeping in mind the circumstances which invited their anger. It must be said that the blame for the rupture in the harmony and peace that have existed for so long must be borne by those Christians who, spurred by extreme fanaticism and intolerance, have adopted opposition to Islam as a way of life, indeed as their religion. Muslim tolerance is otherwise beyond reproach, as evidenced by the large number of non-Muslims who have their homes and have established themselves among Muslims, enjoying the tolerance, fairness, benevolence, and forbearance of Muslims as well as the social peace provided by Islam.

Role of the Army

The Kafancan crisis has helped to expose the otherwise hidden trends that have been going on for many years in the Nigerian army. It may be recalled that the army intervened in the crisis ostensibly to enforce the curfew imposed by the Kaduna State government. But the real purpose for the intervention was to enable the army to wage war on the Muslim umma. Muslims were put under virtual siege, and a reign of terror was unleashed on them. Muslims were arrested in large numbers, tortured, and detained indiscriminately; some had their possession stolen; some were humiliated in the presence of their families; and unspeakable acts of aggression were committed against many others by soldiers, acting in the name of the federal government. Soldiers not only abused and scorned Muslim leaders but Islam itself; they forced one imam in Zaria to drink from sewage water, and another in Kaduna was shot dead in cold blood. There are other acts perpetrated on Muslims that the heart shudders to recount because of their sordid nature and out of fear of exposing Nigeria as a nation devoid of any respect for human dignity, and the Nigerian army as a beastly and uncivilized institution.

It is quite clear that the Nigerian army did not intervene to resolve the crisis but to defend Christianity and persecute Muslims. Throughout its sordid operation, the army abdicated its primary responsibility to defend the nation as a whole, and to treat Nigeria as one integrated entity; instead it allied itself wholly and unreservedly with a narrow, sectarian cause. At the end of the day, the army created the impression that it was not a national institution but a Crusader force, that it is a sworn enemy of Islam and the Muslim umma, that it has no respect for justice and fairness: all this tends to suggest that the internal structures and composition of the army have been deliberately manipulted over the years to promote the cause of Christianity and damage the fundamental interests of Islam. The question to be asked is whether it is wise and safe for an institution which shoulders the ultimate responsibility to defend the nation as a whole to adopt so openly a hostile and aggressive attitude toward the greater section of the people of the nation, without considering the long-term consequences on the survival of the nation. By its ill-considered partiality, the army may have succeeded in undermining Muslim confidence to the extent that it will make Muslims regard every soldier as an enemy to be fought.

Role of Security Organizations

The security and law enforcement agencies were deployed to find out the truth, and nothing but the truth, of the matter. But a different picture emerged at the end of the day: the security agencies, like the Nigerian army, are at war with Islam. The following facts speak for themselves:

- These agencies arrested hundreds of Muslims, many of them children under the age of ten, and most at the insistence of a Christian clique with which they have entered into a conspiracy to undermine the Muslim community. Most of the arrests were made out of malice, and without reliable evidence or authority.
- These agencies, in alliance with the judiciary, effected the escape of the prime mover of the entire crisis: "Reverend" Bako. Since then the police and the Special Investigation Panel have not found it necessary to tell the nation why they let "Reverend" Bako escape the arm of justice, or why they

have not been forthcoming in finding the root cause, and the other prime movers, of the carnage in Kafancan.

- The security agencies have fabricated reports on Islamic organizations—especially the Muslim Students' Society of Nigeria—and Muslim leaders in order to blackmail these organizations and individuals, and damage their credibility. This, of course, is but part of an organized psychological warfare against Islam by Christians who have managed to infiltrate these agencies and are manipulating the machinery of the state to fight Islam. To lie is in itself a great evil, but to lie against highly respectable organizations and Muslim leaders of impeccable record in the name of the state is not only evil but immoral, and it represents the ultimate betrayal of the nation.
- The Special Investigation Panel (SIP)—more than two-thirds of whom are Christians—has, instead of looking for the truth, used all available means to cover up the crimes in Kafancan, to sever the obvious and incontrovertible links between the Kafancan massacre and the events in Kaduna, Zaria, and other places. It appears to Musims, indeed to all fair-minded people, that the Special Investigation Panel and other agencies are not interested in the facts but are on a mission to find faults with Muslims, and inflict harm on them. This is their own way of serving the interest of Nigeria.

Federal Government Tribunal

On the basis of the above facts and in view of the hostile and offensive manner in which the investigations and the arrests of Muslims were carried out, it is only fair for Muslims to cast doubt on the ability of Karibi-Whyte Tribunal to do justice to Muslims. The fact that the tribunal fled from Kaduna to the bush, coupled with the fact that so far only Muslims are brought to face trial, helps to confirm Muslim fears and suspicion, and may indeed suggest that the tribunal was deliberately running away from the consequences of the miscarriage of justice. So much injustice has been done to Muslims already, which need not be aggravated by the tribunal. Moreover, it will be particularly revolting to the conscientious mind to see hundreds of Muslims being prosecuted for reacting to premeditated murder of fellow Muslims while the murderers themselves and those who wanted to set the country on fire are nowhere to be seen. Justice demands that destruction of life must be accorded greater attention and be considered of graver consequences than destruction of property. Muslims, therefore, insist that all those who have murdered Muslims and set their dead bodies on fire, and all those who have participated in the desecration of mosques and the Holy Qur'ân, must be tried first before the Muslims, who are driven to action by a sense of outrage, are put on trial. Muslims will continue until they are answered: Where is "Reverend" Bako and how did he escape? Where are the murderers of Kafancan? Whose interest were the security agencies serving throughout their operation? How many Muslims have the army killed or tortured to death?

The Way to Peace and Harmony

Peace and social harmony are desirable goals to pursue as they are essential for the survival and progress of any nation. But the realization of these goals is being determined by the number of factors which must be addressed as a matter of urgency.

There have been long-standing attitudes of government toward ignoring the fact that Muslims constitute the majority of people in Nigeria; as a result the Muslim presence has often not been reflected in the composition, structure, and policies of the government. The Armed Forces Ruling Council presents a false and unjust picture of Nigeria: there is certainly no justifiable reason for the preponderance of Christians in the highest ruling body of a country with a Muslim majority. Similarly the preponderance of Christian governors, and the imposition of Christian governors over Muslims, as in Bauchi, Lagos, Oyo, and several other states, is certainly not the best way to win the confidence of the Muslims or to have an effective and acceptable administration. It can only be seen as part of a strategy to destablilize the Muslim umma and destroy its cohesion.

The composition of the armed forces, the police, and security agencies is heavily biased against Muslims. Indeed, there have been persistent efforts to edge out Muslims in the recruitment policies, and to fill the forces with the so-called Northern Christians. The admission into the Nigerian Defense Academy which is deliberately designed to exclude Muslims, the frustration and indiscriminate dismissal of Muslim cadets, the hostile posture of the commandant against Islam—all constitute an open scandal, and Muslims are surprised that the government has so far done nothing to rectify the situation. Muslims will not accept a situation where the nation's armed forces, the police, and security organizations are turned into bastions of Christianity which can be marshaled against Islam. The attitude of the Nigerian army in the last crisis has convinced Muslims that the preponderance of Christians in the army has a purpose other than the defense of the country. The need has arisen therefore for a comprehensive reorganization of the armed forces, the police, and security organizations so as to make them truly national where every community is represented on the basis of their number and strength, in all the states of Nigera.

Islam enjoins Muslims to seek an acceptable, enduring means of coexistence with people of other faiths, and this Muslims have endeavored consistently to do. But Christians in this country have all along adopted a culture of hate and opposition to Islam, and have sought, whenever they have the opportunity, to use state apparatus—whether it is the army, civil service, or educational institutions—to damage the interests of Islam. As long as this culture of hate is not abandoned, any move toward peace will be premature and unworkable. Muslims will never sue for peace at all costs. Peace must be established on a framework of honor, reciprocal obligation, and mutual respect—nor indeed will Muslims compromise the fundamental interests of Islam just to obtain peace with others.

In addition, Muslims find government's uncritical and slavish associations with Christians and neocolonial interests, even when those interests are a direct threat to Nigeria distasteful and unacceptable. There are in this country airfields serving the Vatican and other Christian missions as if Nigeria is not an independent country. The Council of 'Ulama hereby demands the immediate closure of all missionary airfields because their presence and operation is a negation of our sovereignty, and because, as recent events have shown, they are detrimental to the overall interests of Islam.

There are indeed fundamental differences between Islam and Christianity in the matter of faith, but these differences are not matters for debate, dialogue, or negotiation. Allah, most Exalted is He, has said the final word about them. He says: "Verily, in the sight of God, the nature of Jesus is as the nature of Adam, whom He created out of dust and said unto him, "Be"—and he is. This is the truth from thy Sustainer; be not, then, among the doubters! And if anyone should argue with thee about this truth after all the knowledge that has come unto thee, say: Come! Let us summon our sons and your sons and our women and your women, and ourselves and yourselves; and let us pray together humbly and ardently, and let us invoke God's curse upon those (of us) who are telling a lie. . . . And if they turn away (from this truth)—behold, God has full knowledge of the spreaders of corruption" (Qur'ân: 3:50–63).

The ongoing crisis, which has been engineered to distract the attention of Muslims from the vital issues in the country, will in no way succeed in its goals. Muslim demand for the full and uninhibited application of the Sharî'a remains not only a priority but a lifetime objective of the Council of 'Ulama, and of every Muslim in the country. So also has the demand for Islamic education, a just and equitable economic system, and an appropriate political dispensation. Muslim total opposition to secularism remains firm and unshakable; the idea of separation of religion and state is universally acknowledged as a Christian concept and is absolutely alien to Islam. Muslims want to live entirely under the guidance of Islam, in obedience to Allah and his messenger and have nothing whatsoever to do with secularism!

Finally, the Muslims all over the country are hereby called upon to do all in their power to defend the cause of Allah and to take all necessary steps to defend themselves as they can no longer rely on the state and its security agencies. For the Muslims have every reason to believe that the army, the police, and state security services are not willing to protect the life, honor, and property of Muslims. The Muslims are also called upon to take it a duty to pray to Allah for Islam to prevail and for the continued strength of the Muslim umma. Allah's message is sufficient an assurance and a consolation: "Turn unto Allah for aid, and have patience in adversity. Verily, all the earth belongs to God: he gives it as a heritage to such as He Wills of His servants; and the future belongs to the God-conscious. . . . It may well be that your Sustainer will destroy your foe and make you inherit the earth: and thereupon He will behold how you act" (Qur'ân: 7:128–29).

Dr. Omar Bello
Secretary General
The Council of 'Ulama'

Appendix 7

Communiqué of the Council of 'Ulama' on the Occasion of the Establishment of a Support Fund for the Council of 'Ulama' in Kano on 15 March 1988 (Pamphlet, Kano, 4 Mar. 1988)*

In the name of Allah the beneficent, the most merciful.
First anniversary of Kafancan massacre.

It is now a year since the wicked massacre of defenseless Muslims in Kafancan. Our hearts are heavy with grief as we mourn the first anniversary of this atrocious act.

We pray to Allah to give our massacred brothers respite, to deal with those vandalistic criminals, and to give us the strength and determination to rout out his enemies wherever they may be.

However, while we continue to mourn our assassinated brethren, the thought of the wicked, high-handed, and myopic manner of the investigations, trial, and subsequent sentence of Muslims arrested during the Kafancan crisis makes our hearts even heavier.

It has been reported that the Karibi-Whyte tribunal has wound up its sitting and that it has disposed of all the cases brought before it; we will deem it pertinent to ask a few questions:

1. Why is it that not a single Christian was jailed while several Muslims have been jailed?
2. Who started the crisis and killed innocent lives?
3. Does it mean that the churches burned by Muslim youths in vengeance for their murdered brothers are more important than the lives of these Muslims who were killed in cold blood?

4. Why is it that Rev. Bako has been allowed to escape and still has not been brought to account?
5. What is the fate of those Muslims who have been jailed? Are they going to languish in prison while those who committed murder are walking about the streets?

Hence, the government or anyone who thinks that there will be peace while innocent Muslims are still in prison is merely deceiving himself and out of touch with reality.

We, the entire Muslim population, will not fold our hands and watch our brothers languish in prison.

With each passing day, our fury increases and we realize more that the government has made itself our archenemy. However, history is a living testimony to the fact that tyranny has its end which in most cases is abrupt and terrible; it seems this is what is about to occur in this country.

We hereby call on all Muslims to be ready to answer the call to defend the noble religion of Islam.

We call for the unconditional release of all jailed Muslims; however, if this does not occur it means that the government is calling for its Waterloo, and Insha-Allah this will soon befall it.

Peace be upon those who follow the guidance

17 Rajab 1408

(4 March 1988)

Maps

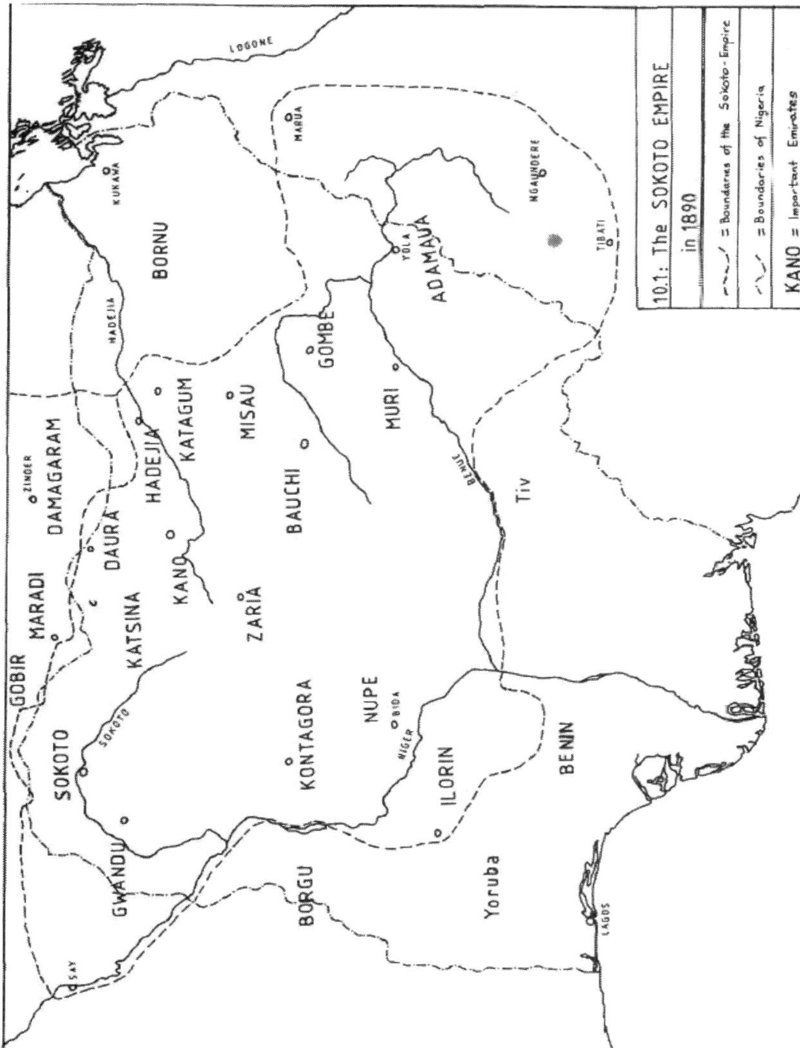

1 The Sokoto Empire in 1890

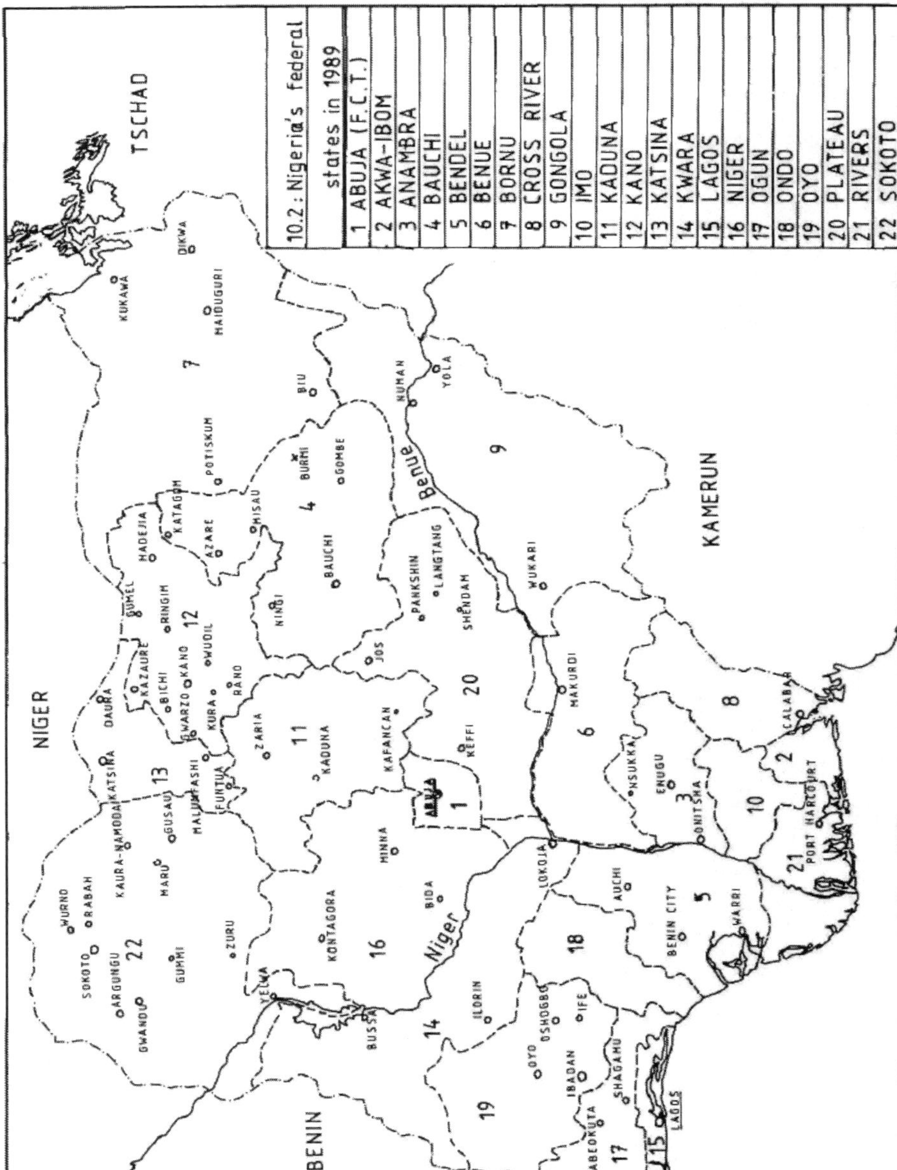

2. Nigeria's Federal States in 1989

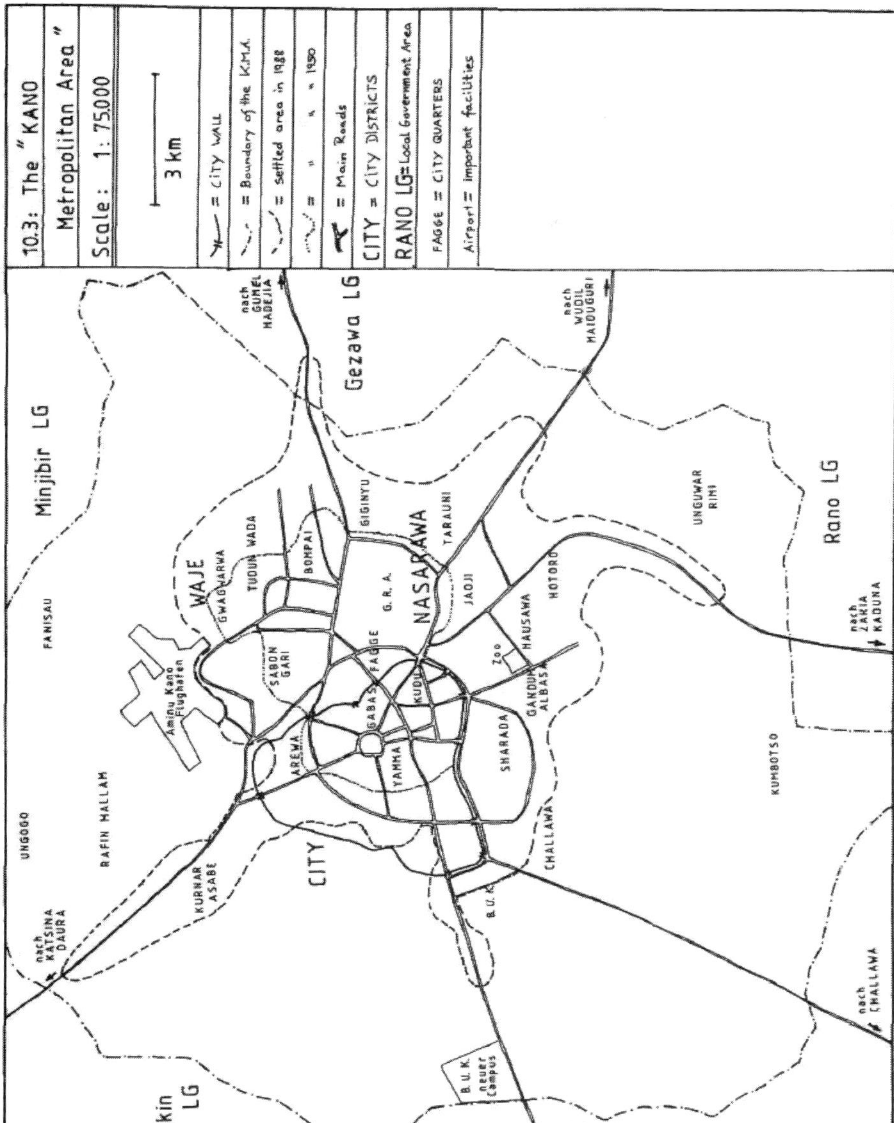

3. The "Kano Metropolitan Area"

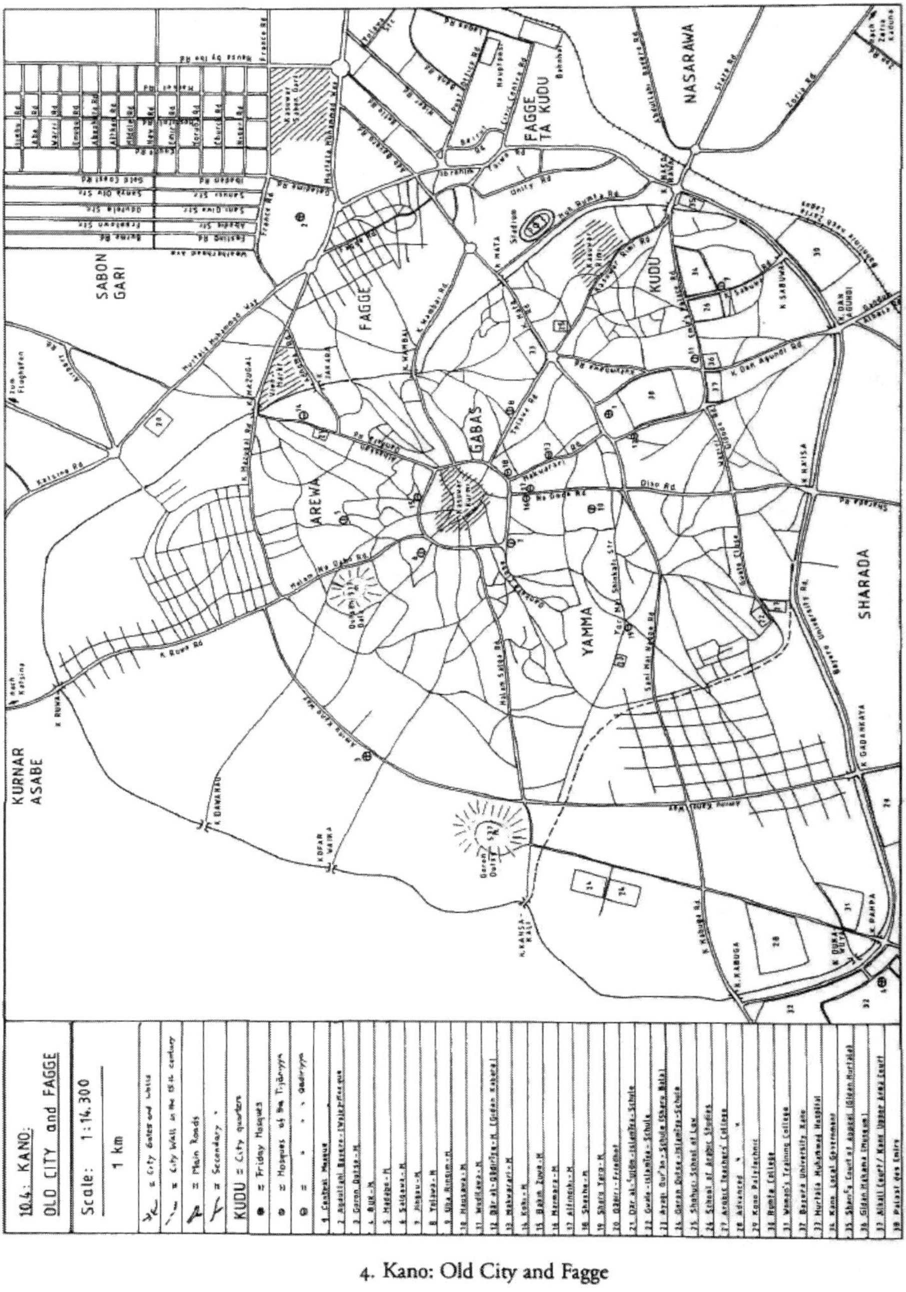

4. Kano: Old City and Fagge

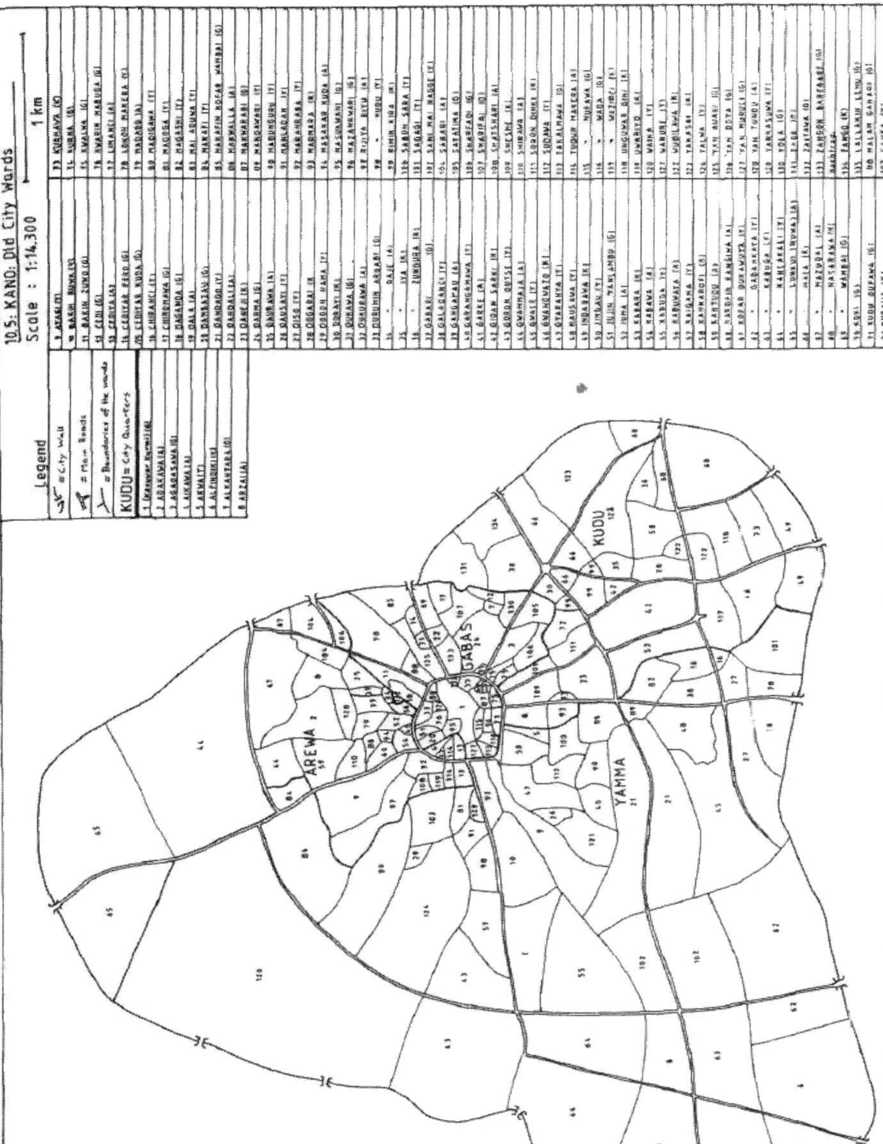

5. Kano: Old City Wards

List of Interlocutors

Note: All data refer to the state of affairs as of May 1988. Subsequent changes have not been considered. Only those individuals are mentioned with whom I had at least one long interview. They all deserve my unrestricted gratitude.

1. 'Abdallah, Muhammad. Lecturer at the Bornu College of Islamic Studies, Maiduguri.
2. Abdullahi, Muhammad. Head of the Department of Library Science, ABU, Zaria.
3. Abdullahi, Ibrahim Isa. Managing Director of the Gidan Bayajidda in Kano, head of the Management Board of the Qâdirîyya in Kano, Unguwar Makwarari, Kano.
4. Abdullahi, Shehu 'Umar. Lecturer in the Department of Islamic Studies, BUK, Kano.
5. Abubakar, Aminu d-Din. Leader of the Daawa Organization in Kano, Sulaiman Crescent, Nasarawa, Kano.
6. Abubakre, 'Abd ar-Razaq. Lecturer in the Department of Religious Studies, former president of the MSS, University of Ilorin, Ilorin.
7. Ahmad, A. E. Lecturer in the Department of Islamic Studies, University of Ibadan, Ibadan.
8. Ahmad, 'Abd al-Muta'al. Lecturer in the Department of Islamic Studies, BUK, Kano.
9. Albasu, Sabo A. Lecturer in the Department of History, University of Sokoto, Sokoto.
10. Alkali, Hamidu. Director of the Center of Transsaharan Studies, University of Maiduguri, Maiduguri.
11. Amir, Aminu. Member of the MSS at BUK, Kano.
12. Anwar, Auwalu. Lecturer in the Department of History, University of Maiduguri, Maiduguri.

13. Atamma, Mukhtar. Lecturer in the Department of Arabic, BUK, Kano, imam of the Atamma Mosque of the Qâdirîyya in Fagge, Kano; Goron Dutse, Kano.
14. Baba, Abdullahi. Employee at the Center of Islamic Legal Studies of ABU, Zaria, member of the Jamâ'at Izâlat al-Bid'a wa-Iqâmat as-Sunna, Zaria.
15. Bako, Sabo. Lecturer in the Department of Political Science, ABU, Zaria.
16. Balogun, S. O. Head of the Department of Islamic Studies, University of Sokoto.
17. Barkindo, Bawuro. Lecturer in the Department of History, BUK, Kano.
18. Biu, Muhammad Kolo. Assistant Secretary General of the Jamâ'at Naṣr al-Islâm, 'Ali Akilu Way, Kaduna.
19. Bugaje, Usman. Member of the Islamic Trust of Nigeria and the Huda-Huda publishing house, Samaru, Zaria.
20. Bugaje, Hauwa Usman. President of FOMWAN in Kano.
21. Dan Asabe, A.U. Head of the Department of History, Advanced Teachers' College, Kano.
22. Dauda, Aliyu. Lecturer at the School of General Studies, BUK, Kano.
23. Daura, Muhammad Bello. Senior Research Fellow at the Center of Islamic Legal Studies, ABU, Zaria.
24. Doi, 'Abd ar-Rahman. Director of the Center of Islamic Legal Studies, ABU, Zaria.
25. Edamivoh, Saidu Abdulazeez. Student at the School of General Studies, BUK, Kano.
26. Galadanci-Starratt, Priscilla. Lecturer at the School of General Studies, BUK, Kano.
27. Garba, Asma'u Saeed. Lecturer at the Department of History, BUK, Kano.
28. Garba, Tijani. Lecturer at the Department of History, BUK, Kano.
29. Gujba, Kaigama. Principal of the Bornu College of Islamic Studies, Maiduguri.

30. Gumbi, Ahmad Muhammad Sanusi. Publisher, Safanu Road, Unguwar Sarkin Musulmi, Kaduna.
31. Gumi, Abubakar Mahmud. Former Grand Kadi of the Northern Region, Kaduna.
32. Gumi, Nuru d-Din Abubakar. Son of (31), student at Kaduna Polytechnic, Kaduna.
33. Hadi, M. S. Librarian at the Center of Islamic Legal Studies, ABU, Zaria.
34. Hunwick, John. Professor at Northwestern University, Evanston, Illinois.
35. Ibrahim, A. S. Student at BUK Kano, chairman of the "Mosque Committee" of the MSS in 1987, Kano.
36. Idris, Isma'ila. President of the Jamâ'at Izâlat al-Bid'a wa-Iqâmat as-Sunna, Jos.
37. Ikara, Bashir. Direktor of the Gidan Arewa, Kaduna.
38. Innuwa, Aminu Musa. Student at Rumfa-College, Kano, member of the MSS, Sani Mai Nagge, Kano.
39. Jami'u, Sulaiman Muhammad. Lecturer in the Department of Islamic Studies, BUK, Kano.
40. Kabara, Nasiru Muhammad. Leader of the Qâdirîyya in Kano, Nigeria, and Africa, Unguwar Kabara, Kano.
41. Kabara, Shehu Usman. Lecturer in the Department of Arabic, BUK, Kano, nephew of Nasiru Kabara, New Campus, Kano.
42. Kabara, Ibrahim Matabuli. Son of Shehu Usman Kabara, student at BUK, Kano.
43. Kabara, Abdul-Lateef Muhammad. Head of the Department of Islamic Studies at the Vocational Training Center, Birnin Kudu, Kano State.
44. al-Kafawi, Sadiq Muhammad. Lecturer in the Center of Islamic Legal Studies of ABU, Zaria, secretary of the Council of 'Ulama', Zaria.
45. Kane, Ousmane. Grandson of Ibrahim Niass, Université Paris VII.
46. Kani, Ahmad Muhammad. Lecturer in the Department of

History, University of Sokoto, previously research fellow at the Northern History Research Scheme at Ahmadu Bello University, Zaria.

47. Karfi, Shehu Danladi. Lecturer in the Center of Islamic Legal Studies, ABU, Zaria.
48. Kaura-Namoda, Ja'far Makau. Lecturer in the Department of Islamic Studies, University of Sokoto, Sokoto.
49. Khalid, Aliyu. Student in the Department of Religious Studies, University of Jos, Jos.
50. Kumasi, 'Abd ar-Rahman b. 'Ali. Grandson of 'Ali Kumasi, civil servant, and student in the Department of Arabic, BUK, Kano.
51. Kurawa, Ibrahim Ado. Student at the School of General Studies, chairman of the Mosque Committee of the MSS, BUK, Kano.
52. Kurawa, Wada Tafida. Librarian of the Aminu Kano School of Islamic Legal Studies of Kano Polytechnic, Kano.
53. Last, Murray. Senior Lecturer at University College, London.
54. Lavers, John. Senior Lecturer in the Department of History, BUK, Kano.
55. Lubeck, Paul. Senior Lecturer at the University of California, Santa Cruz.
56. Maigari, Dahiru. Lecturer in the Department of Islamic Studies, BUK, Kano.
57. Maikarfi, 'Umar. Head of the Department of Mathematics, ABU, Zaria.
58. Malumfashi, 'Umar. Lecturer in the Department of Islamic Studies, BUK, Kano.
59. Minna, Mahmud. Head of the Department of History, BUK, Kano.
60. al-Miskin, Tijani. Lecturer in the Department of Islamic Studies, University of Maiduguri, Maiduguri.
61. Mohammed, Hassan. Student of mathematics and geography, BUK, Kano.

62. Moten, 'Abd ar-Rashid. Lecturer in the Department of Political Science, BUK, Kano.
63. Muhammad, 'Abd as-Samad. Company Secretary of the Dar al-'Arabiya Publishing House (Beirut) for Nigeria, publisher of Abubakar Gumi, Kano.
64. Muhammad, Ibrahim. Librarian of the departmental library of the Department of Islamic Studies, BUK, Kano.
65. Mukhtar, M. F. Lecturer in the School of General Studies, BUK, Kano.
66. Mustapha, Abubakar. Lecturer in the Department of Islamic Studies, BUK, Kano.
67. Naniya, Tijani. Lecturer in the Department of History, BUK, Kano.
68. Nur Alkali, Muhammad. Vice chancellor of the University of Maiduguri, Maiduguri.
69. Rufa'i, Muhammad Ahmad. Lecturer in the Department of History, BUK, Kano.
70. Sada, I. N. National President of the MSS in 1977/78, head of the Department of Islamic Law of the Faculty of Law at the Center of Islamic Legal Studies, ABU, Zaria.
71. Sa'id, Halil b. Director of the library, BUK, Kano.
72. Saleh, Abubakar. Lecturer in the Department of History, ABU, Zaria.
73. Ṣâliḥ, Ibrahim. Religious scholar of the Tijâniyya, Maiduguri.
74. Saminu, Bala. Employee at Aminu Kano Airport in Kano.
75. Shea, Phil. Lecturer in the Department of History, BUK, Kano.
76. Shittu, Hamza. Mechanic and owner of a garage in Tudun Wada, Zaria.
77. Sulaiman, Ibrahim. Lecturer in the Center of Islamic Legal Studies, ABU, Zaria.
78. Tukur, Balarabe. Librarian of the Center of Islamic Studies in Sokoto.
79. Tukur, Tijani. Religious scholar of the Tijâniyya in Sani Mai Nagge, Kano.

80. 'Umar, Muhammad Sani. Lecturer in the Department of Religious Studies, University of Jos, Jos.
81. Ungawa, Tukur B. Lecturer in the School of General Studies, BUK, Kano.
82. Yakubu, Yahaya I. Student of library science, ABU, Zaria.
83. Yola, Jibril Hamani. Lecturer in the Department of Islamic Studies, BUK, Kano.
84. Yusuf, Bilkisu. Editor-in-chief of the *New Nigerian*, previously at the Kano daily *The Triumph*, press chief of FOMWAN, Kaduna.
85. Zahradeen, Muhammad Sani. Head of the Department of Islamic Studies, BUK, Kano.

Bibliography

Archival Material from the Nigerian National Archives Kaduna (NAK)

SNP 16 CC 0015, "History of Islamic Political Propaganda in Nigeria.
SNP 17 K 4448, Vol. II.
SNP 17-11807, Vols. I/II/V, "Pilgrimage to Mecca."
SNP 17-11784, "Pilgrimage to Mecca."
SNP 15-320, "Islamic Fraternities."
SNP 15-328, "Pilgrimage of Muhamman Dikko, Emir of Katsina."
SNP 17-5669, Vol. II, "Mohammadanism."
SNP 17-11807 B, "Pilgrimage Control Scheme."
Kano Provincial Files (KPF), No. 1942, "Pilgrimage."
KPF, No. 1812, "Arabic and Religious Instruction."
KPF, No. 1304, Vol. I, "Engagement of Sudanese Teachers."
KPF, No. 1075/5.1, "Teaching of Arabic."
KPF, No. 3645, "Notes on Pilgrimage."
KPF, No. 5056, "Pilgrims from Hadejia and Gumel."
KPF, No. 7094, "Annual Report Kano Province 1949."
KPF, No. 6560, "Annual Report Northern Region 1946."
KPF, No. 6394, "Annual Report Kano Province 1946."
KPF, No. 6023, "Annual Report Northern Division 1945."
KPF, No. 5996, "Annual Report Northern Provinces."
KPF, No. 5788, "Annual Report Northern Division 1944."
KPF, No. 5512, "Annual Report Northern Division 1943."
KPF, No. 3967.
KPF, No. 3868, "Personal File Shaikh Awad Ahmad."
KPF, No. 3513, "Annual Report Northern Division 1940."
KPF, No. 1336, "Annual Report Northern Division 1934."
KPF, No. 1942.
KPF, No. 1304, Vol. I.
KPF, No. 2131, "Muslim Missionaries."
Bornu Provincial Files (BPF), No. 4350, Vol. I.
BPF, No. 896, "Pilgrimage."
BPF, No. MM 12-4349.
BPF, No. 5409, "Pilgrimage."
BPF, No. 2714, "Pilgrim Instructions."
BPF, No. 2714, Vol. I, "Pilgrim Instructions."

Katsina Provincial Files (KatPF), No. 4222-1241, "Report on the Kano Disturbances."
KatPF, No. 2413.
KatPF, No. 2700-915.
KatPF, No. 1150-511, "Islamic Fraternities."
KatPF, No. 1151, "Annual Report Northern Provinces 1927."
KatPF, No. 3575, "Annual Report Katsina Province 1944."
KatPF, No. 3696/5.1, "Annual Report Katsina Province 1945."
KatPF, No. 3696, "Annual Report Katsina Province 1946."
KatPF, No. 3851, "Annual Report Katsina Province 1947."
KatPF, No. 3967, "Annual Report Katsina Province 1948."
KatPF, No. 4028, "Annual Report Katsina Province 1949."
KatPF, No. 4028, "Annual Report Katsina Province 1950."
Sokoto Provincial Files (SPF), No. 4622-905, "Riot in Sokoto Town."
SPF, No. 6851, "Annual Report Sokoto Province 1947."
SPF, No. 6319, "Annual Report Sokoto Province 1945."
SPF, No. 6982, "Disturbance in Argungu Division."
SPF, No. 7225, "Annual Report Sokoto Province 1948."
SPF, No. 8318, "Annual Report Sokoto Province 1954."
Zaria Provincial Files (ZPF), No. SCH/1, Vol. I, "Training and Employment of Kadis."
ZPF, No. 2386-1315.
ZPF, No. 4398, "Annual Report Zaria Province 1948."
ZPF, No. 4957, "Annual Report Zaria Province 1951."
ZPF, No. 4182, "Annual Report Zaria Province 1946."
ZPF, No. 5404, "Annual Report Zaria Province 1954."
ZPF, No. 5240, "Annual Report Zaria Province 1953."
ZPF, No. 4708, "Annual Report Zaria Province 1949."
ZPF, No. C-4040, "Foreign Office Reports Pilgrimage 1931–1934."
ZPF, No. IMM 8, "Pilgrims to Mecca."
ZPF, No. 4032-I, "Intelligence Reports."
ZPF, No. C.68, "Muslim Movements in Nigeria."
ZPF, No. C.68, Appendix, "A Note on Moslem Religious, Social, and Political Movements in Nigeria."
ZPF, No. SCH I, "Report on the Committee on Higher Muslim Education."
ZPF, No. 4013, "Yantubu Sect of Muslims."

Literature

Abba, Isa Alkali. 1976. *Islam in Adamawa in the 19th and 20th centuries.* M.A. thesis, Zaria.
Abdullahi, Shehu Umar. 1984. *On the search for a viable political culture: Reflections on the political thought of Shaikh Abdullahi dan Fodio.* Kaduna.
Abubakar, Muhammad Awwal. 1985. *Islamic preaching in Plateau state: The role of Mallam Ahmadu Arabi Jos.* B.A. thesis, Jos.
Abubakar, Sa'ad. 1977. *The Lamibe of Fombina.* Zaria.

Bibliography

Abun-Nasr, J. M. 1965. *The Tijaniyya.* London.

———. 1966. The Salafiyya movement in Morocco: The religious bases of the Moroccan nationalist movement. In I. Wallerstein, *Social change in the colonial situation,* 489–501. New York.

———. 1971. *A History of the Maghrib.* Cambridge.

———. 1985. Militant Islam: A historical perspective. In E. Gellner, *Islamic dilemmas,* 73–93. Berlin.

———. 1988. Zur politischen Bedeutung der Berufungsgerichte für die Muslime in Nigeria. *Die Welt des Islams* 28: 38–61.

———. 1993. *Muslime in Nigeria: Religion und Gesellschaft im politischen Wandel seit den 50er Jahren.* Hamburg.

Adams, C. C. 1968. *Islam and modernism in Egypt.* New York.

Adamu, Muhammad Uba. 1968. Some notes on the influence of North African traders in Kano. *Kano Studies* 1 (4): 43–49.

Adekilekun, Abdul-Lateef. 1989. *Selected Islamic organizations in Nigeria (1916–1986).* Ilorin.

Adeleye, R. A. 1971. *Power and diplomacy in Northern Nigeria, 1804–1906.* London.

Ahmed, Asif Folarin. 1986. *The Qadiriyyah and its impact in Nigeria.* Ph.D. thesis, Ibadan.

Ajani, Raji Rasheed. 1982. *The influence of the 'Ishriniyat on Arabic and Islamic culture in Nigeria.* Ph.D. thesis, University of Michigan.

Ajayi, J. F. A., and M. Crowder. 1971. *History of West Africa.* Vol. 1. London.

Alkantara, Umaru Khalil. 1986. *The literary life of Shaikh 'Ali Kumasi.* B.A. thesis, Jos.

Aniagolu Report of Tribunal of Inquiry on Kano Disturbances. 1981. Lagos.

Anwar, Auwalu. 1989. *Struggle for influence and identity: The ulama in Kano, 1937–1987.* M.A. thesis, Maiduguri.

Ba, Amadou-Hampaté. 1962. *L'empire peul du Macina.* Paris.

Bako, Sabo. 1985. *Maitatsine revolts in Nigeria: Another case of class struggle.* Seminar paper, Zaria.

Balogun, I. A. B. 1965. *The life and works of 'Uthman dan Fodio.* Lagos.

———. 1967. *A critical edition of the Ihyâ' as-sunna wa ikhmâd al-bid'a of 'Uthman b. Fudi, popularly known as Usuman dan Fodio.* Ph.D. thesis, London.

———. 1977. *Islam versus Ahmadiyyah in Nigeria.* Lahore.

Barkindo, B. M. 1983. *Studies in the history of Kano.* Kano.

Barth, Heinrich. 1857. *Reisen und Entdeckungen in Nord- und Central-Africa.* Gotha.

Bashir, Ibrahim Lawan. 1983. *The politics of industrialization in Kano: Industries, incentives and indigenous entrepreneurs 1950–1980.* Ph.D. thesis, Boston.

Batran, A. A. 1981. *Sidi al-Mukhtar al-Kunti and the recrudescence of Islam in the Western Sahara and the Middle Niger.* Ph.D. thesis, Birmingham.

Becker, Christoph. 1969. *Kano: Eine afrikanische Großstadt.* Hamburg.

Behrman, Lucy. 1970. *Muslim brotherhoods and politics in Senegal.* Cambridge, Mass.

Bello, Ahmadu. 1962. *My life*. Zaria.

Bergstresser, Heinrich. 1988. Wirtschaft und Politik in Nigeria: Rolle und Funktion der Militärs im Vorfeld der dritten Republik. *Afrika Spectrum* 2: 183–200.

Besmer, Freemont. 1971. *Hausa court music in Kano, Nigeria*. Ph.D. thesis, New York.

Bienen, Henry. 1985. *Political conflict and economic change in Nigeria*. London.

Bivar, A. D. H., and M. Hiskett. 1962. The Arabic literature of Nigeria to 1804. *BSOAS*. 25: 577–96.

Blanckmeister, E. B. 1989. *Din wa Daula: Islam, Politik und Ethnizität im Hausaland und in Adamawa*. Emsdetten.

Blätter des Informationszentrum 3. Welt, Nr. 147 (1988). *Politisierung des Islam*. Freiburg.

Blichfeld, J. O. 1985. *Early Mahdism*. Leiden.

Boissevain, J. 1978. *Friends of friends: Networks, manipulators and coalitions*. Oxford.

Boyd, Jean. 1982. *The contribution of Nana Asma'u Fodio to the Jihadist movement of Shehu dan Fodio from 1820–1865*. M.A. thesis, London.

———. 1989. Sultan Abubakar III. of Sokoto (1903–1988). In J.-L. Triaud, *Islam et sociétés au sud du Sahara*, vol. 3, pp. 119–27.

Brenner, Louis. 1984. *West African Sufi*. London.

———. 1988. Concepts of tariqa in West Africa: the case of the Qadiriya. In D. B. Cruise O'Brien and Christian Coulon, *Charisma and brotherhood in African Islam*, pp. 33–52. Oxford.

Brockelmann, Carl. 1935/1943. *Geschichte der arabischen Literatur*. Leiden.

Cedzich, Renate. 1982. *Die Ideenwelt der Muslimbrüderschaft dargestellt an Werken Sayyid Qutbs*. M.A. thesis, Erlangen.

Chamberlin, J. W. 1975. *The development of Islamic education in Kano city, Nigeria, with emphasis on legal education in the 19th and 20th centuries*. Ph.D. thesis, Columbia University.

Christelow, Allen. 1984. *Religious protest and dissent in Northern Nigeria: From Mahdism to Quaranic integralism*. Seminar paper, Evanston.

———. 1987. *Three Islamic voices in contemporary Nigeria*. In William R. Rott, *Islam and the political economy of meaning*, pp. 226–53. London.

Clarke, Peter B. 1982a. *Integration through conflict? An assessment of the aims of Islamic fundamentalism in contemporary Northern Nigeria*. Seminar paper, London.

———. 1982. *West Africa and Islam*. London.

Clarke, Peter B., and Ian Linden. 1983. *Islam in modern Nigeria*. Mainz.

Cohen, Abner. 1969. *Custom and politics in urban Africa: A study of Hausa migrants in Yoruba towns*. London.

Coleman, James C. 1958. *Nigeria: Background to nationalism*. Berkeley.

Council of 'Ulama'. 1988. Pamphlet. Kano, 4 Mar. 1988.

Cruise O'Brien, D. B. 1971. *The Mourides of Senegal*. Oxford.

Cruise OBrien, D. B., and C. Coulon. 1988. *Charisma and brotherhood in African Islam*. Oxford.

Bibliography

Dan Asabe, Umar Abdulkadir. 1987a. *Comparative biographies of selected leaders of the Kano commercial establishment.* M.A. thesis, Kano.

———. 1987b. *The traders of Kasar Kano in the 19th and 20th centuries: The case of the Agalawa.* Seminar paper, Kano.

Dawakinkudu, Abbati Idris. 1986. *Sufi-order in Kano: A case study of the development and activities of the Tijaniyyah tariqah.* B.A. thesis, Jos.

Doi, 'Abd ar-Rahman. 1984. *Islam in Nigeria.* Zaria.

———. 1989. The impact of English law concepts on the administration of Islamic law in Nigeria. *Bayreuth African Studies Series* 11: 25–56.

Dudley, Billy J. 1968. *Parties and politics in Northern Nigeria.* London.

———. 1982. *An introduction to Nigerian government and politics.* Bloomington.

Duran, Khalid. 1985. *Islam und politischer Extremismus.* Hamburg.

Elayo, Aminat Dauda. 1984. *Jama'atu Nasril Islam: Two decades of activities in Nigeria.* B.A. thesis, Jos.

Encyclopaedia of Islam. 1986. Vol. 1. Leiden.

Ende, W., and U. Steinbach. 1984. *Der Islam in der Gegenwart.* Munich.

Etienne, Bruno. 1977. *L'Algerie: Cultures et revolution.* Paris.

Federation of the Muslim Women's Associations in Nigeria. 1985. *Program of the FOMWAN.* Minna.

———. n.d. *An introduction to the Federation of Muslim Womens' Associations in Nigeria.* Minna.

Feinstein, Alan. 1987. *African revolutionary: The life and times of Nigeria's Aminu Kano.* Boulder.

Fika, Adamu Muhammad. 1978. *The Kano civil war and British over-rule, 1882–1940.* Ibadan.

Fischer-Weltalmanach 1989. 1988. Frankfurt.

Fischer, H. J. 1963. *Ahmadiyyah: A study in contemporary Islam on the West African coast.* Oxford.

Fodio, Usman dan. 1986. *Iḥyâ' as-sunna wa-ikhmâd al-bid'a.* Kano.

Funtua, S. A. 1980. *Jama'atu Isalatil Bidia wa Ikamatis Sunna society in Nigeria.* B.A. thesis, Kano.

Gamâ'at Izâlat al-Bid'a wa-Iqâmat as-Sunna. 1978. *Tsarin Ka'idojin Kungiyar Jama'atu Izalatil Bid'ah wa Ikamatis Sunna.* Jos (Copy in the collection "Islam in Afrika," Lehrstuhl für Islamwissenschaft, Universität Bayreuth).

Garba, Asma'u Saeed. 1983. *The biography of Shaykh Sa'id b. Hayatu.* B.A. thesis, Kano.

Gumbi, Muhammad Ahmad Sanusi. 1987. *Tarihin Shaikh Abubakar Mahmud Gumi.* Kaduna.

Gumi, A. M. 1976. *Al-'Aqîda aṣ-ṣaḥîḥa bi-muwâfaqat ash-sharî'a.* Ankara.

———. 1981. *Musulunci da abin da ke rushe shi.* Zaria.

Gwarzo, Hassan Ibrahim. 1972. *The life and teachings of al-Maghili with particular reference to the Saharan Jewish community.* Ph.D. thesis, London.

Haarmann, Ulrich. 1987. *Geschichte der arabischen Welt.* Munich.

al-Haddad, A. S. 1982. *Aṭ-Ṭarîqa al-qâdirîya wa-iqâma maukiba fi kânû.* B.A. thesis, Kano.

al-Hajj, M. A. 1968. A 17th century chronicle on the origins and missionary activities of the Wangarawa. *Kano Studies* 1 (4): 7–16.

———. 1973. *The Mahdist tradition in Northern Nigeria*. Ph.D. thesis, Zaria.

Hallam, W. K. R. 1969. The Bayajida legend in Hausa folklore. *Journal of African History* 7: 47–60.

al-Hassan, Na Ayuba. 1986. *Yantatsine: An analysis of the Gardawa uprising in Kano, Nigeria, 1980–85*. M.A. thesis, Kano.

Hickey, Raymond. 1984. The Maitatsine uprisings in Nigeria. *African Affairs* 83: 51–56.

Hill, Polly. 1969. Hidden trade in Hausaland. *Man* 4 (3): 393–409.

———. 1972. *Rural Hausa: A village and a setting*. Cambridge.

———. 1977. *Population, prosperity and poverty: Rural Kano 1900 and 1970*. Cambridge.

Hiskett, M. 1960. Kitâb al-farq. *Bulletin of the SOAS* 23: 558–79.

———. 1973. *The sword of truth*. New York.

———. 1980. The "Community of Grace" and its opponents, the "rejecters": A debate about theology and mysticism in Muslim West Africa with special reference to its Hausa expression. *African Language Studies* 17: 99–140.

———. 1984. *The development of Islam in West Africa*. London.

———. 1987. The Maitatsine riots in Kano 1980: An assessment. *Journal of Religions in Africa* 17 (3): 209–23.

Hobsbawm, E. J. 1959. *Primitive rebels*. New York.

Hock, Klaus. 1992. How religious are "Religious riots": A case study from Bauchi-State, Nigeria. *Afrika-Spectrum* 1: 43–58.

Hodgkin, Thomas. 1975. *Nigerian perspectives*. London.

Hodgson, Marshall G. S. 1974. *The venture of Islam*. Chicago.

Hogendorn, Jan S. 1978. *Nigerian groundnut exports*. Zaria.

de Hoghton, B. 1967. *Militant Islam and British attitudes towards Islam in Northern Nigeria, 1896–1923*. M.A. thesis, Birmingham.

Hourani, Albert. 1962. *Arabic thought in the liberal age, 1798–1939*. London.

Hunwick, John O. 1974. *al-Maghili's replies to the questions of Askia al-Hajj Muhammad*. Ph.D. thesis, London.

———. 1981. Songhay, Bornu and Hausaland in the sixteenth century. In J. F. A. Ajayi and M. Crowder, *A History of West Africa*, vol. 1, pp. 264–301. Burnt Mill.

———. 1984. *Neo-Hanbalism in Southern Nigeria: The reformist ideas of al-Hâjj Adam al-Ilûrî of Agege*. Seminar paper, Evanston.

Husseini, Umaru S. 1988. Conditions for military withdrawal from politics: Lessons from Nigeria (1970–79). *Farfaru Journal of Multi-disciplinary Studies* 2 (1): 85–100.

Ibrahim, Jibrin. 1988. Les uniformes des Lycéennes Nigerianes. *Politique Africaine* 29: 101–4.

———. 1989. The politics of religion in Nigeria: The parameters of the 1987 crisis in Kaduna state. *Review of African Political Economy* 45/46: 65–82.

———. 1991. Religion and political turbulence in Nigeria. *Journal of Modern African Studies* 29: 115–36.

Imam, Yunusa Abdulsalami. 1980. Nûr ud-Deen Society of Nigeria, Jos Branch. B.A. thesis, Dept. of Islamic Studies, Bayero University, Kano.

Informationen zur politischen Bildung. 1982. *Der Islam und die Krise des Nahen Ostens.* vol. 194. Bonn.

Ishaku, Aliyu. 1976. *The role of Jam'at Nasr al-Islam in propagation of Islam in Northern Nigeria.* B.A. thesis, Kano.

Isichei, Elizabeth. 1983. *A history of Nigeria.* London.

———. 1987. The Maitatsine risings in Nigeria 1980–85: A revolt of the disinherited. *Journal of African Religions* vol. 17 (3): 194–208.

'Iyâḍ, al-Qâḍî. 1950. *Kitâb ash-shifâ'.* Cairo.

Jabata, 'Ali Abubakar/an-Nufawi, Muhammad Ibrahim. 1978. *Raf' ash-Shubuhât 'ammâ fi l-qâdirîyya wa-t-tijânîyya min ash-shaṭaḥât.* Lagos.

Jah, Umar. 1973. *Sufism and the 19th century Jihad movements in the Western Sudan: A case study of al-Hajj 'Umar al-Futi's philosophy of Jihad and its Sufi basis.* Ph.D. thesis, Montreal.

Jamâ'at Naṣr al-Islâm. 1975. *Constitution.* Kaduna.

Jami'u, Muhammad Sulaiman. 1986. *Socio-economic factors behind the religious disturbances in Nigeria: A case study of Maitatsine syndrome.* M.A. thesis, Kano.

Jansen, J. J. G. 1974. *The interpretation of the Koran in modern Egypt.* Leiden.

Jibia, Abubakar Muhammad. 1982. *Religion as an instrument of mobilization: A critical analysis of the Maitatsine crisis.* B.A. thesis, Kano.

Johnson, M. 1983. Periphery and centre in the 19th century Kano trade. In B. Barkindo, *Studies in the history of Kano,* pp. 127–46. Kano.

Kaba, Lansine. 1974. *The Wahhabiyya Islamic reform and politics in French West Africa.* Evanston.

Kabara, Nasiru Muhammad. 1958. *An-Nafaḥât an-nâṣirîya.* Zaria.

———. 1972. *An-Naṣîḥa aṣ-ṣarîḥa fi l-radd 'alâ al-'aqîda aṣ-ṣaḥîḥa.* Kano.

Kabara, Shehu Usman. 1981. *Shakhṣiyat ash-shaikh muḥammad an-nâṣir kabara wa-adabuhu.* M.A. thesis, Khartoum.

Kafanga, Muhammad Sani. 1972. *Al-Minaḥ al-ḥamîda fi l-radd 'alâ fâsid al-'aqîda.* Beirut.

Kane, Ousmane. 1989a. La confrérie "Tijaniyya-Ibrahimiyya de Kano et ses liens avec la zawiya mère de Kaolack. In J.-L. Triaud, *Islam et sociétés au sud du Sahara,* vol. 3, pp. 27–40.

———. 1989b. *Islamic reform in Senegal and its implications for religious and political life.* Seminar paper, Bayreuth.

———. 1989c. La vie, les idées et les enseignements de Cheikh Ibrahim Niass du Senegal. In J.-L. Triaud, *Islam et sociétés au sud du Sahara,* vol. 3, pp. 294–95.

———. 1990. Les mouvements réligieux et le champ politique au Nigeria septentrional: Le cas du réformisme musulman à Kano. In J.-L. Triaud, *Islam et sociétés au sud du Sahara,* vol. 4, pp. 7–24.

Kani, Ahmad Muhammad. 1981. The rise and influence of scholars in Hausaland before 1804. *Kano Studies,* new series, 2 (2): 129–45.

———. 1986. *The role of intellectuals in the Sokoto caliphate with special reference to 'Abd al-Qadir b. al-Mustafa.* Seminar paper, Zaria.

al-Karsani, Awad al-Sid. 1985. *The Tijaniyya order in Western Sudan: A case study of Khursi, an Nahud and al-Fasher.* Ph.D. thesis, Khartoum.

———. 1988. *The Tijaniyya order doctrine reconsidered.* Seminar paper, Bayreuth.

Kerr, Malcolm H. 1966. *Islamic reform: The political and legal theories of Muhammad 'Abduh and Rashid Rida.* Berkeley.

Khalid, Sulaiman. 1985. *Izala movement and religious reform in Northern Nigeria: A case study of Sokoto.* B.A. thesis, Sokoto.

Kudu, Mohammed Aliyu. 1984. *The role of Jama'atul Nasril Islam as an Islamic organization.* B.A. thesis, Sokoto.

Kusimo, Murtada Abdul Aziz. 1979. *Islamic organizations in Nigeria.* B.A. thesis, Jos.

Lange, Dierk. 1987. The evolution of the Hausa story: from Bawo to Bayajidda. *Afrika und Übersee* 70 (2): 195–209.

Lange, D., and S. Berthoud. 1972. L'interieur de l'Afrique Occidentale d'après Giovanni Lorenzo Anania. *Cahiers d'histoire mondiale,* 14 (2): 299–351.

Laoust, Henri. 1939. *Essai sur les doctrines sociales et politiques de Taki ad-Din Ahmad b. Taimiya.* Cairo.

Last, Murray. 1967. *The Sokoto caliphate.* London.

———. 1979. Some economic aspects of conversion in Hausaland. In N. Levtzion, *Conversion to Islam,* pp. 236–46. New York.

———. 1983. From Sultanate to Caliphate: Kano ca. 1450–1800. In B. Barkindo, *Studies in the history of Kano,* pp. 67–92. Kano.

———. 1988. Charisma and medicine in Northern Nigeria. In D. B. Cruise O'Brien and C. Coulon, *Charisma and brotherhood in African Islam,* pp. 183–204. Oxford.

Lavers, J. 1984. *Popular Islam and unpopular dissent: Religious disturbances in Northern Nigeria.* Seminar paper, Urbana.

———. 1987. *Two Sufi communities in 17th and 18th century Bornu.* Seminar paper, London.

Lawan, Yabawa. 1982. *The causes and issues of Bulumkutu disturbances.* B.A. thesis, Kano.

Lethem, G. J., and G. J. F. Tomlinson. 1927. *History of Islamic political propaganda in Nigeria.* London.

Levtzion, Nehemia. 1973. *Ancient Ghana and Mali.* New York.

———. 1975. Northwest-Africa from the Maghrib to the fringes of the forest. *Cambridge History of Africa,* vol. 4, pp. 142–222. Cambridge.

———. 1977. The western Maghrib and Sudan. *Cambridge History of Africa,* vol. 3, pp. 331–462. Cambridge.

———. 1987. *Eighteenth century renewal and reform in Islam: The role of the Sufi turuq in West Africa.* Seminar paper, London.

Loimeier, Roman. 1988. Das "Nigerian Pilgrimage Scheme": Zum Versuch, den Ḥaǧǧ in Nigeria zu organisieren. *Afrika Spectrum* 2: 701–14.

———. 1991. The writings of Nasiru Kabara (Muhammad an-Nâsir al-Kabarî). In J. Hunwick, *Sudanic Africa,* vol. 2, pp. 165–74. Evanston.

———. 1992. The dynamics of religious unrest in Northern Nigeria. *Afrika Spectrum* 1: 59–80.

———. 1993. Auseinandersetzungen im islamischen Lager. In J. M. Abun-Nasr, *Muslime in Nigeria*, pp. 127–64. Hamburg.

Loimeier, Roman, and Anke Bosaller. 1995. Radical Muslim women and male politics in Nigeria. In M. Reh and G. Ludwar-Ene, *Gender and identity in Africa*, pp. 61–70. Hamburg.

Loimeier, Roman, and Stefan Reichmuth. 1993. Bemühungen der Muslime um Einheit und politische Geltung. In J. M. Abun-Nasr, *Muslime in Nigeria*, pp. 41–82. Hamburg.

Lovejoy, Paul. 1973. *The Hausa Kola trade 1700–1900: A commercial system in the continental exchange of West Africa.* Ph.D. thesis, University of Wisconsin.

———. 1980. *Caravans of Kola: The Hausa Kola trade 1700–1900.* Zaria.

Lubeck, Paul. 1981. Class formation at the periphery: Class consciousness and Islamic nationalism among Nigerian workers. *Research in the Sociology of Work*, 1: 37–70.

———. 1985. Islamic protest under semi-industrial capitalism: Yan Tatsine explained. *Africa* 55 (4): 369–89.

———. 1986a. *Islam and urban labor in Northern Nigeria.* Cambridge.

———. 1986b. Islamic protest and oil-based capitalism: Agriculture, rural linkages and urban popular movements in Northern Nigeria. In M. Watts, *State, oil and agriculture in Nigeria*, pp. 268–90. Berkeley.

Mabogunje, A. L. 1971. *Urbanization in Nigeria.* New York.

Madigawa, Lawan Aliko. 1978. *Schools of Tafsir in Kano.* B.A. thesis, Kano.

Mahadi, Abdullahi. 1982. *The state and the economy: The Sarauta system and its role in shaping the society and economy of Kano with particular reference to the 18th and 19th centuries.* Ph.D. thesis, Zaria.

———. 1985. The Jihad and its role in strengthening the Sarauta (kingship) system in Hausaland in the 19th century: The case of Kano. In J. F. A. Ajayi and B. Ikara, *Evolution of political culture in Nigeria*, pp. 118–28. Lagos.

Maigari, Muhammad at-Tahir. 1981. *Ash-shaikh ibrâhîm an-niass as-sunughâlî.* M.A. thesis, Beirut.

Mai Sa'ida, Lawali. 1987. *Disunity among Muslim Ummah (a case study of Kaura-Namoda town).* B.A. thesis, Sokoto.

Malami, Alhaji Shehu. 1989. *Sir Siddiq Abubakar III.* Ibadan.

Martin, B. G. 1976. *Muslim brotherhoods in 19th century Africa.* Cambridge.

Mattes, Hans-Peter. 1986. *Die innere und äußere islamische Mission Libyens.* Mainz.

Merad, 'Ali. 1967. *Le reformisme musulman en Algerie de 1925 à 1940.* Paris.

Meyer, Bärbel. 1975. *Zur Geschichte und Organisation islamischen Elite-Wissens im Zentralsudan unter besonderer Berücksichtigung des Kalifats von Sokoto.* Hamburg.

Meyer, Thomas. 1989. *Fundamentalismus in der modernen Welt.* Frankfurt.

Ministry of Finance and Economic Planning (Statistical Unit). 1983. *Statistical yearbook.* Kano.

Minna, M. T. M. 1982. *Sultan Muhammad Bello and his intellectual contribution to the Sokoto caliphate.* Ph.D. thesis, London.

———. 1985. Bello and the Tijaniyya: Some light about the conversion controversy. *Kano Studies*, new series 2 (3): 1–18.
al-Misri, F. H. 1963. The life of Shehu Usman dan Fodio before the Jihad. *Journal of the Historical Society of Nigeria*, 2 (4): 435–48.
———. 1968. *A critical edition of Dan Fodio's "Bayân wujûb al-hijra 'alâ 'ibâd."* Ph.D. thesis, Ibadan.
Mitchell, R. P. 1969. *The society of the Muslim brothers*. London.
Muhammad, Abdullahi. 1976. *A Hausa scholar-trader and his library collections: The case study of Umar Falke of Kano, Nigeria*. Ph.D. thesis, Evanston.
Muslim Students' Society. 1984. *The history and the history-makers of the Muslim Students' Society Nigeria*. Ibadan.
Mustafa, Abubakar. 1979. *Islam and modernism*. B.A. thesis, Kano.
———. 1987. *The contribution of Sayfawa 'Ulama' to the study of Islam, c. 1086–1846*. Ph.D. thesis, Kano.
Nadel, S. F. 1942. *A black Byzantium*. London.
an-Naqar, Umar. 1972. *The pilgrimage tradition in West Africa*. Khartoum.
Nasarawa, Muhammad Alhasan. 1981. *Islam in Plateau state, 1800–1980*. M.A. thesis, Ibadan.
Niass, Ibrahim. 1988. *Kâshif al-ilbâs 'an faiḍat al-khatam abî al-'abbâs*. Kaolack.
Nicolas, Guy. 1981. "Guerre sainte" à Kano. *Politique Africaine* vol. 1, pp. 47–70.
Nienhaus, V., and M. A. Choudoury. 1988. Islamische Wirtschaftskooperation: Möglichkeiten undd Auswirkungen in der Weltwirtschaft. In Bayerische Landeszentrale für politische Bildung, *Weltmacht Islam*, pp. 511–28. Munich.
Norris, H. T. 1975. *The Tuareg: Their Islamic legacy and its diffusion in the Sahel.* Warminster.
———. 1982. *The Berbers in Arabic literature*. London.
———. 1987. *The silsila of the Maḥmûdiyya ṭarîqa in the Qudwa of Shaikh (Abûl-'Abbâs) Aḥmad aṣ-Ṣâdiq b. al-Shaikh Uwayis al-Lamtûnî*. Seminar paper, London.
Ogunnika, Z. O. 1982. *Mechanisms of tension management in a plural society: A study of inter-ethnic relations in Kano City, Nigeria*. Ph.D. thesis, New York.
Okediji, Florence A. 1972. *An economic history of Hausa-Fulani emirates of Northern Nigeria 1900–1939*. Ph.D. thesis, Ibadan.
Oloruntimehin, B. O. 1972. *The Segu Tukulor Empire*. London.
Oloso, Kamil Koyejo. 1981. *The contribution of the Muslim Students' Society of Nigeria to the Islamic resurgence in Southern Nigeria (1954–1980)*. M.A. thesis, Ibadan.
———. 1984. *Hajj and its operations in Nigeria (1954–1980)*. Ph.D. thesis, Ibadan.
Operschall, C., and C. Teuber. 1987. *Libyen: Die verkannte Revolution*. Vienna.
Osswald, Rainer. 1986. *Das Sokoto-Kalifat und seine ethnischen Grundlagen*. Beirut.
Osuntokun, A. 1987. *Powerbroker: A biography of Sir Kashim Ibrahim*. Ibadan.
Othman, Shehu. 1984. Classes, crises and coup: The demise of Shagari's regime. *African Affairs* 83: 441–61.
Paden, John N. 1973. *Religion and political culture in Kano*. Berkeley.

———. 1986. *Ahmadu Bello: Sardauna of Sokoto.* Zaria.

Palmer, H. R. 1967. The Kano chronicle. In H. R. Palmer, *Sudanese memoirs.* London.

Patton, Adell. 1987. An Islamic frontier polity: The Ningi mountains of Northern Nigeria, 1846–1902. In I. Kopytoff, *The African frontier,* pp. 193–213. Bloomington.

Peters, Jimi. 1987. Nigeria's intelligence system: An analysis. *Afrika Spectrum* 2: 181–92.

Philips, John E. 1985. The islamization of Kano before the Jihad. *Kano Studies,* new series 2 (3): 32–52.

Pittin, Renée. 1979. *Marriage and alternative strategies: Career patterns of Hausa women in Katsina City,* Ph.D. thesis, London.

Quadri, Yasir Anjola. 1981. *The Tijaniyyah in Nigeria.* Ph.D. thesis, Ibadan.

———. 1985. A study of the Izalah, a contemporary anti-Sufi-organization in Nigeria. In *Orita,* pp. 95–108.

Rahman, Fazlur. 1970. Revival and reform in Islam. *Cambridge History of Islam,* vol. 2B, pp. 632–56. Cambridge.

Rauch, Theo. 1979. Industrielle Wachstumszentren in Nigeria. *Afrika Spektrum* 3: 249–65.

Reissner, Johannes. 1984. Die militant-islamischen Gruppen. In W. Ende and U. Steinbach, *Der Islam in der Gegenwart,* pp. 470–86. Munich.

Robinson, David. 1985. *The holy war of Umar Tal.* Oxford.

Rufa'i, Muhammad Ahmad. 1986. *History of the spread of Islam in the Niger-Benue-confluence area, Igalaland, Ebiraland and Lokoja, ca. 1900–1960.* Ph.D. thesis, Kano.

Saad, Elias N. 1983. *Social history of Timbuktu.* Cambridge.

Sa'id, Halil b. 1978. *Revolution and reaction: The Fulani Jihad in Kano and its aftermath, 1807–1919.* Ph.D. thesis, University of Michigan.

———. 1983a. *Shehu Muhammad Nasiru Kabara: The leader of the Qâdiriyya Sûfi-ṭarîqa in Nigeria.* Seminar paper, Paris.

———. 1983b. Notes on taxation as a political issue in the 19th century Kano. In B. Barkindo, *Studies in the history of Kano,* pp. 117–26. Kano.

Ṣâliḥ Ibrâhîm. 1986. *al-Mughîr 'alâ shubuhât ahl al-ahwâ' wa akâdhîb al-munkir 'alâ kitâb at-takfîr.* Beirut.

Sanusi, Muhammad Shuaib. 1987. *Conflicts and controversies among the Muslim Ummah (a case study of Argungu town).* B.A. thesis, Sokoto.

Sartain, E. M. 1975. *Jalal ad-Din al-Suyuti.* Cambridge.

Schacht, Joseph. 1964. *An introduction to Islamic law.* Oxford.

Schulze, Reinhard. 1990. *Islamischer Internationalismus im 20. Jahrhundert.* Leiden.

Schweitzer, Thomas. 1989. *Netzwerk-Analyse.* Berlin.

Scott, P. H. G. 1953. *A survey of Islam in Northern Nigeria in 1952.* Kaduna.

Shanono, Shehu Muhammad. 1976. *Abubakar Mahmoud Gummi as a Mujaddid in Nigeria in the 20th century.* B.A. thesis, Kano.

Shea, Philip James. 1975. *The development of an export-oriented dyed cloth industry in Kano Emirate in the 19th century.* Ph.D. thesis, University of Wisconsin.

Skinner, Neil. 1977. *Alhaji Mahmudu Koki.* Zaria.

Smith, M. G. 1960. *Government in Zazzau.* London.

———. 1964. The beginnings of Hausa society. In J. Vansina, R. Mauny, and L. V. Thomas, *The historian in tropical Africa,* pp. 339–55. London.

Smith, Abdullahi. 1981. The early states of the central Sudan. In J. F. A. Ajayi and M.-A. Crowder, *A history of West Africa,* vol. 1, pp. 152–95. Burnt Mill.

———. 1983. The Kano chronicle as history. In B. Barkindo, *Studies in the history of Kano,* pp. 31–56. Kano.

Solaja-Alagago, R. O. 1984. *Evolution of Anwarul-Islam movement of Nigeria: The Nigerian solution to the Ahmadiyyah problem.* M.A. thesis, Ibadan.

Stewart, C. C. 1973. *Islam and social order in Mauretania.* Oxford.

Streck, B. 1985. Netzwerk: Der transaktionale Einspruch gegen das Paradigma der struktural-funktionalen Ethnologie. *Anthropos* 80: 569–86.

Sulaiman, Ibrahim. 1978. *Woman and society.* Seminar paper, Bureau for Islamic Education, Kano.

———. 1986. *A revolution in history: The Jihad of Usuman dan Fodio.* London.

———. 1987. *The Islamic state and the challenge of history.* London.

Tahir, Ibrahim. 1975. *Scholars, Sufis, saints and capitalists in Kano, 1904–1974.* Ph.D. thesis, Cambridge.

———. 1981. *The last imam.* London.

Takaya, B. J., and S. G. Tyoden. 1987. *The Kaduna Mafia.* Jos.

Taswirar Jihohin Arewa (Atlas of the North). 1983. London.

Traore, Alioune. 1983. *Cheikh Hamahoullah.* Paris.

Trimingham, J. S. 1949. *Islam in the Sudan.* London.

———. 1959. *Islam in West Africa.* Oxford.

———. 1962. *A history of Islam in West Africa.* Oxford.

———. 1971. *The Sufi orders in Islam.* Oxford.

Tsiga, Ismaila A. 1992. *Sheikh Abubakar Gumi: Where I stand.* Ibadan.

Ubah, C. N. 1979. The Emirates and the central government. In Y. B. Usman, *The Sokoto seminar papers. Studies in the history of the Sokoto Caliphate,* pp. 296–319. Zaria.

———. 1985. Continuity and change in the political administration of the Nigerian emirates: The Kano example 1900–1960. In J. F. A. Ajayi and B. Ikara, *Evolution of political culture in Nigeria,* pp. 129–46. Lagos.

Umar, Muhammad Sani. 1983. *Islamic revivalism today: The case of Jama'atu Izalat al-bid'ah wa iqamat al-sunna.* B.A. thesis, Jos.

———. 1988. *Sufism and anti-Sufism in Nigeria.* M.A. thesis, Kano.

Umaru, Usman. 1976. *The development of Islamiyya schools in Kano metropolitan, Kano State.* Kano.

Usman, Y. B. 1979. *The Sokoto seminar papers: Studies in the history of the Sokoto caliphate.* Zaria.

———. 1981. *The transformation of Katsina, 1400–1883.* Zaria.

———. 1987. *The manipulation of religion in Nigeria, 1977–1987.* Kaduna.

Voll, J. O. 1975. Muhammad Hayyat al-Sindi and Muhammad ibn 'Abd al-Wahhab: An analysis of an intellectual group in eighteenth century Madina. *Bulletin of the SOAS* 38: 32–39.

———. 1980. Ḥadith scholars and ṭariqahs. *Journal of Asian and African Studies* 15: 264–71.
———. 1982. *Islam: Continuity and change in the modern world.* Boulder.
Wali, Yusufu. 1981. Kitâb al-Nasab. *Kano Studies*, new series, 2 (2): 1–10.
Watts, Michael. 1983. *Silent violence: Food, famine and peasantry in Northern Nigeria.* Berkeley.
Weber, Max. 1920. *Gesammelte Aufsätze zur Religionssoziologie, vol. 1, Die protestantische Ethik und der Geist des Kapitalismus.* Tübingen.
———. 1922. *Wirtschaft und Gesellschaft.* Tübingen.
Whitaker, G. S. 1970. *The politics of tradition: Continuity and change in Northern Nigeria, 1946–1966.* Princeton.
Willer, Heidi. 1989. *Hausa und levantinische Unternehmer in Nordnigeria: Ein Vergleich.* Ph.D. thesis, Bayreuth.
Williams, David. 1982. *President and power in Nigeria: The life of Shehu Shagari.* London.
Williams, G., and T. Turner. 1978. Nigeria. In J. Dunn, *West African states: Failure and promise.* Cambridge.
Winder, R. B. 1965. *Saudi Arabia in the nineteenth century.* New York.
Yola, J. H. 1980. *The Sufi orders in Gongola state.* M.A. thesis, Kano.
Yunusa, Salisu Alhaji. 1981. *Izalatul Bid'at wa Ikamatu Sunna: Eradication of Bid'at and the establishment of Sunnah.* B.A. thesis, Kano.
Yusuf, Adamu Tanko. 1983. *The spread of Qadiriya brotherhood in Kano.* B.A. thesis, Kano.
Zahradeen, M. S. 1976. *'Abd Allah ibn Fodio's contribution to the Fulani Jihad in 19th century Hausaland.* Ph.D. thesis, Montreal.
Zebadia, Abdelkader. 1974. *The career and correspondence of Ahmad al-Bakkay of Timbuktu.* Ph.D. thesis, London.
Zillikens, Klaus. 1985. Zum Konflikt zwischen bäuerlichen und feudalen Grundbesitzverhältnissen in Nordnigeria. *Afrika Spectrum* 1: 83–96.

Newspapers and Periodicals

Afkar-Inquiry (Vol. 3, no. 11, Nov. 1986)
Africa Events (Vol. 3, no. 8, Aug. 1987)
Amana (15 Jan. 1988, 15 Mar. 1988)
The Analyst (Vol. 2, no. 5, 1987)
Concord (22 Dec. 1987, 29 Dec. 1987)
The Democrat (10 Dec. 1989, 23 Dec. 1989)
The Guardian (24 Apr. 1988)
al-'Ilm (3 Feb. 1973, 5 Jan. 1974, 4 Feb. 1974, 5 Feb. 1974, 6 Jan. 1975, Jan.-Mar. 1982, Jan.-Mar. 1985)
The Muslim Woman—Magazine of the FOMWAN (Vol. 1, no. 1, 1988) (Minna)
National Concord (10 Nov 1987, 6 Apr. 1988, 18 Nov. 1988)
New African (No. 257, Feb. 1989)
New Nigerian (14 Jan. 1982, 14 Feb 1982, 3 Nov. 1982, 6 Nov. 1982, 13 Nov. 1982, 15 May 1984, 6 June 1984, 28 Jan. 1987, 18 June 1987, 7 Nov. 1987, 24 Nov.

1987, 26 Nov. 1987, 28 Nov. 1987, 29 Dec. 1987, 8 Jan. 1988, 19 Jan. 1988, 25 Jan. 1988, 28 Jan. 1988, 11 Feb. 1988, 5 Mar. 1988, 27 Mar. 1988, 18 Apr. 1988, 27 Sept. 1988, 4 Nov. 1988, 7 Nov. 1988, 14 Nov. 1988, 15 Nov. 1988, 20 Nov. 1988, 22 June 1990)

Newswatch (9 Nov. 1987, 28 Dec. 1987, 14 Mar. 1988, 30 Mar. 1988, 9 Jan. 1989, 23 Jan. 1989, 20 Feb. 1989, 27 Feb. 1989, 6 Mar. 1989, 18 Apr. 1989, 16 Oct. 1989, 7 May 1990)

Nigerian Economist (Vol. 1, no. 6, 1987)

Süddeutsche Zeitung (6 Feb. 1989)

Sunday Times (10 Mar. 1974)

The Pen (Vol. 2, no. 1, 1987, Vol. 2, no. 7, 1987, Vol. 2, no. 9, 1987, Vol. 3, no. 13, 1988, Vol. 4, no. 1, 1989)

The Reporter (7 Nov. 1987, 28 Dec. 1987, 19 Jan. 1988, 12 Apr. 1988, 27 Sept. 1988, 9 Nov. 1989, 1 Dec. 1989, 2 Dec. 1989, 11 June 1990)

This Week (Vol. 6, no. 7, 1987, Vol. 7, no. 4, 1988, Vol. 7, no. 5, 1988, Vol. 7, no. 8, 1988)

Today (3 Dec. 1989)

The Triumph (19 Dec. 1987, 29 Dec. 1987, 22 Feb. 1988, 14 Mar. 1988, 6 Apr. 1988, 16 May 1990, 27 May 1990, 14 June 1990)

West Africa (19 Aug. 1961, 20 Mar. 1978, 1 June 1981, 25 Aug. 1982, 8 Nov. 1982, 15 Nov. 1982, 15 Aug. 1983, 18 May 1987, 22 June 1987, 18 Jan. 1988, 20 Feb. 1989, 3 Apr. 1989, 30 Apr. 1990, 26 May 1991, 8 Sept. 1991, 29 Sept. 1991, 27 Oct. 1991, 3 Nov. 1991, 30 Mar. 1992, 5 Apr. 1992, 7 June 1992, 19 July 1992, 26 July 1992, 27 Sept. 1992, 18 Apr. 1993, 25 June 1993, 4 July 1993, 14 Nov. 1993, 5 Dec. 1993, 12 Dec. 1993, 19 Dec. 1993, 5 May 1996)

Index

Index

Index